Emerging Economies During and After the Great Recession

International Papers in Political Economy Series
Series Editors: **Philip Arestis** and **Malcolm Sawyer**

This is the twelfth volume of the series *International Papers in Political Economy (IPPE)*. This series consists of an annual volume with a single theme. The objective of *IPPE* is the publication of papers dealing with important topics within the broad framework of Political Economy.

The original series of *International Papers in Political Economy* started in 1993, until the new series began in 2005, and was published in the form of three issues a year with each issue containing a single extensive paper. Information on the old series and back copies can be obtained from the editors: Philip Arestis (pa267@cam.ac.uk) and Malcolm Sawyer (e-mail: mcs@lubs.leeds.ac.uk).

Titles include:

Philip Arestis and Malcolm Sawyer (*editors*)

EMERGING ECONOMIES DURING AND AFTER THE GREAT RECESSION

FINANCE AND THE MACROECONOMICS OF ENVIRONMENTAL POLICIES

FISCAL AND DEBT POLICIES FOR THE FUTURE

ECONOMIC POLICIES, GOVERNANCE AND THE NEW ECONOMICS

THE EURO CRISIS

NEW ECONOMICS AS MAINSTREAM ECONOMICS

PATH DEPENDENCY AND MACROECONOMICS

CRITICAL ESSAYS ON THE PRIVATISATION EXPERIENCE

POLITICAL ECONOMY OF LATIN AMERICA
Recent Economic Performance

ALTERNATIVE PERSPECTIVES ON ECONOMIC POLICIES IN THE EUROPEAN UNION

FINANCIAL LIBERALIZATION
Beyond Orthodox Concerns

21st CENTURY KEYNESIAN ECONOMICS

International Papers in Political Economy
Series Standing Order ISBN 978–1–403–99936–8
(*outside North America only*)

You can receive future titles in this series as they are published by placing a standing order. Please contact your bookseller or, in case of difficulty, write to us at the address below with your name and address, the title of the series and the ISBN quoted above.

Customer Services Department, Macmillan Distribution Ltd, Houndmills, Basingstoke, Hampshire RG21 6XS, England

---

Emerging Economies During and After the Great Recession

Edited by

Philip Arestis
Director of Research, Cambridge Centre for Economic and Public Policy, University of Cambridge, UK, and Professor of Economics, University of the Basque Country, Spain

and

Malcolm Sawyer
Emeritus Professor of Economics, University of Leeds, UK

palgrave
macmillan

First published 2016 by
PALGRAVE MACMILLAN

Palgrave Macmillan in the UK is an imprint of Macmillan Publishers Limited, registered in England, company number 785998, of Houndmills, Basingstoke, Hampshire RG21 6XS.

Palgrave Macmillan in the US is a division of St Martin's Press LLC, 175 Fifth Avenue, New York, NY 10010.

Palgrave Macmillan is the global academic imprint of the above companies and has companies and representatives throughout the world.

Palgrave® and Macmillan® are registered trademarks in the United States, the United Kingdom, Europe and other countries.

ISBN 978–1–137–48554–0

This book is printed on paper suitable for recycling and made from fully managed and sustained forest sources. Logging, pulping and manufacturing processes are expected to conform to the environmental regulations of the country of origin.

A catalogue record for this book is available from the British Library.

Library of Congress Cataloging-in-Publication Data
Emerging economies during and after the great recession / Philip Arestis, Malcolm Sawyer.
pages cm—(International papers in political economy; volume 12)
Includes bibliographical references and index.
ISBN 978–1–137–48554–0 (hardback)
1. Developing countries—Economic conditions—21st century.
2. Recessions—Developing countries. 3. Financial crises—Developing countries. 4. Global Financial Crisis, 2008–2009. I. Arestis, Philip, 1941– editor. II. Sawyer, Malcolm C., editor.
HC59.7.E4757 2016
338.5'42—dc23 2015027816

Typeset by MPS Limited, Chennai, India.

Contents

List of Figures

List of Tables

Preface

This is the twelfth volume of the series of *International Papers in Political Economy* (*IPPE*). This series consists of an annual volume with a single theme. The objective of *IPPE* is the publication of papers dealing with important topics within the broad framework of Political Economy.

The original series of *International Papers in Political Economy* started in 1993 until the new series began in 2005 and was published in the form of three issues a year with each issue containing a single extensive paper. Information on the old series and back copies can be obtained from the editors: Philip Arestis (e-mail: pa267@cam.ac.uk) and Malcolm Sawyer (e-mail: mcs@lubs.leeds.ac.uk).

The theme of this twelfth volume of eight papers is 'Emerging Economies During and After the Great Recession'. The papers were initially presented at a one-day conference held at St Catharine's College, Cambridge, UK, 26 March 2015, organised by the Department of Land Economy, University of Cambridge, under the aegis (and with the financial support) of the Cambridge Trust for New Thinking in Economics. The papers were subsequently presented at the 12th International Conference, titled 'Developments in Economic Theory and Policy', held at the University of the Basque Country UPV/EHU, Bilbao, Spain, 25–26 June 2015, which fully supported and funded the special sessions at which the papers included in this volume were presented. We are grateful to the organisers of the Bilbao conference and to the Cambridge Trust for all the help and funding provided.

Notes on the Contributors

Nigel F.B. Allington is a member of the Centre for Economic and Public Policy, Department of Land Economy, University of Cambridge; Fellow and Director of Studies in Economics, Downing College, University of Cambridge, and Fellow Research Professor of Applied Macroeconomics, Grenoble Ecole de Management. He has published widely in academic journals and books. His most recent publication is *From Hubris to Disgrace: The Philosophy, Politics and Economics of Finance in the 21st Century* (2015).

Philip Arestis is Professor and University Director of Research, Cambridge Centre for Economic and Public Policy, Department of Land Economy, University of Cambridge, UK; Professor of Economics, Department of Applied Economics V, Universidad del País Vasco, Spain; Distinguished Adjunct Professor of Economics, Department of Economics, University of Utah, US; Research Associate, Levy Economics Institute, New York, US; Visiting Professor, Leeds Business School, University of Leeds, UK; Professorial Research Associate, Department of Finance and Management Studies, School of Oriental and African Studies (SOAS), University of London, UK. He was awarded the British Hispanic Foundation 'Queen Victoria Eugenia' award (2009–10); also awarded the 'homage' prize for his contribution to the spread of Keynesian Economics in Brazil by the Brazilian Keynesian Association (AKB), 15 August 2013. He served as Chief Academic Adviser to the UK Government Economic Service (GES) on Professional Developments in Economics (2005–13). He is a holder of the FAcSS (Fellow of the Academy of Social Sciences) award of the Academy of Social Sciences for contributions to Social Sciences. He has published widely in academic journals, and he is, and has been, on the editorial boards of a number of economics journals.

Luiz Fernando de Paula is Professor of Economics at the University of the State of Rio de Janeiro, and Researcher of the National Council for Scientific and Technological Development (CNPq), both in Brazil. He was the Chairman of the Brazilian Keynesian Association (AKB) in 2009–13. He has been Visiting Research Fellow at St Antony's College (2000–01) and the Centre for Brazilian Studies (2006), both at the University of Oxford, and at Desigualdades/Freie Universitat Berlin (2014). His papers have been published in the *Cambridge Journal of Economics, Journal of Post Keynesian*

Economics, ECLAC Review, International Review of Applied Economics, and *Brazilian Journal of Political Economy,* among others. He has co-edited (with Professor Philip Arestis), *Monetary Union in South America* (2003) and *Financial Liberalization and Economic Performance in Emerging Countries* (Palgrave Macmillan, 2008). He is also the author of *Financial Liberalization and Economic Performance: Brazil at the Crossroads* (2011). His research interests are in the areas of macroeconomic policy, monetary economics, banking, development economics and Post Keynesian economics.

Fernando Ferrari-Filho is Professor of Economics at the Federal University of Rio Grande do Sul and Research Fellow in Economics at CNPq, Brazil. Former Visiting Scholar, Department of Economics/ University of Illinois, Fleming Visiting Fellow in Economics, Centre for Brazilian Studies/University of Oxford, and Glynn Visiting International Scholar, The Williams School of Commerce, Economics, and Politics/ Washington and Lee University. His research interests are in the areas of macroeconomics, post-Keynesian theory, financial and currency crises, international monetary system, and stabilization and growth. He is the author, editor, co-author and co-editor of a number of books. His articles have appeared in the *Journal of Post Keynesian Economics, Journal of Economic Issues, Investigación Económica, International Review of Applied Economics, Cepal Review,* and *Review of Political Economy,* among others.

Yiannis Kitromilides is an Associate Member of the Cambridge Centre of Economic and Public Policy, Department of Land Economy, University of Cambridge. He has previously taught at the University of Greenwich, University of Westminster, University of Middlesex and the School of Oriental and African Studies, University of London. He has published in refereed journals and contributed chapters in books in the areas of public sector economics, the political economy of public policymaking, nationalization of banking, economics of austerity, the euro area crisis and the economics of climate change.

Dic Lo is Reader in Economics at the School of Oriental and African Studies (SOAS), University of London, UK. His areas of interest are China and globalization, Soviet-type economic systems and their transformation, East Asian economic institutions and development, and comparative political economy. He is the author of many journal articles and three books, *Alternatives to Neoliberal Globalization: Studies in the Political Economy of Institutions and Late Development* (Palgrave Macmillan, 2012); *China's Transformational Growth: A Structural-Institutional Analysis* (in Chinese, Economic Science Press, 2001); and *Market and Institutional Regulation in*

Chinese Industrialisation, 1978–1994 (Macmillan, 1997). He is a member of the editorial board of the *Journal of Post Keynesian Economics*, and is associate editor of the Chinese quarterly journal *China Review of Political Economy*.

John S.L. McCombie is Professor and Director of the Cambridge Centre for Economic and Public Policy, Department of Land Economy, University of Cambridge and Fellow in Economics, Downing College Cambridge. He is currently an editor of *Spatial Economic Analysis* and a former editor of *Regional Studies*. His research interests include the study of national and regional growth disparities, EU regional policy, economic growth and the balance-of-payments constraint, and criticisms of the aggregate production function and conventional measures of the rate of technical progress. In 2007/8, he was a specialist advisor to the House of Lords European Union Sub-committee on Economic and Financial Affairs and International Trade, which examined EU regional policy. He has been an economic consultant to the World Bank and the Asian Development Bank. His most recent co-edited books are *Issues in Finance and Monetary Policy* (Palgrave Macmillan, 2007), *The European Union: Current Problems and Prospects* (Palgrave Macmillan, 2007), and *Economic Growth: New Directions in Theory and Policy* (2007).

Özlem Onaran is Professor of Workforce and Economic Development Policy at the University of Greenwich. She has done extensive research on issues of inequality, employment, globalization, crisis, and wage-led growth. She has directed research projects for the International Labour Organization, the Vienna Chamber of Labour, the Austrian Science Foundation, and is currently working on a project funded by the Institute for New Economic Thinking. She is a member of the Scientific Advisory Board of the Hans Boeckler Foundation, the Coordinating Committee of the Research Network Macroeconomics and Macroeconomic Policies and the Policy Advisory Group of the Women's Budget Group, and a research associate at the Political Economy Research Institute of the University of Massachusetts, Amherst. She has authored more than sixty articles in books and peer reviewed journals such as the *Cambridge Journal of Economics, World Development, Environment and Planning A, Public Choice, Economic Inquiry,* the *European Journal of Industrial Relations,* the *International Review of Applied Economics, Structural Change and Economic Dynamics, Eastern European Economics,* and the *Review of Political Economy.*

Cem Oyvat is a lecturer at the University of Greenwich in the Department of International Business and Economics. He received his

PhD in Economics from the University of Massachusetts, Amherst, in 2014 with a dissertation titled 'Essays on the Evolution of Inequality'. His dissertation examines the impact of agrarian structures on income inequality over the long run and also the validity of the Kuznets hypothesis. His research interests include income distribution in the developing world, agrarian structures and land inequality, urbanization, informal sector, gender economics, wage-led growth and the effects of globalization on growth and distribution. His articles have appeared in the *Cambridge Journal of Regions, Economy and Society,* and *Structural Change and Economic Dynamics*. He has also taught courses at Boğaziçi University, Turkey, as a visiting lecturer.

Malcolm Sawyer is Emeritus Professor of Economics, Leeds University Business School, University of Leeds, UK. He is the principal investigator for the European Union funded research project Financialisation, Economy, Society and Sustainable Development (FESSUD: www.fessud.eu). He is managing editor of the *International Review of Applied Economics,* on the editorial board of a range of journals and editor of the series New Directions in Modern Economics. He has published widely in the areas of post Keynesian and Kaleckian economics, industrial economics and the UK and European economies. He has authored 11 books and edited 24, has published over 100 papers in refereed journals and contributed chapters to over 100 books.

Ahmad Seyf is currently teaching at the Department of Management and Human Resources at Regent's University, London. He has also taught at Staffordshire University, and University of Boston, London. His main research interests are international business economics, globalisation and the economic and social history of the Middle East. He is a bilingual writer, having written extensively on Iran, his country of birth. Recent publications include 'Population and Agricultural Development in Iran, 1800–1906' in *Middle Eastern Studies,* 2009, and 'Iran and the Great Famine, 1870–72' in *Middle Eastern Studies,* 2010. His books include *Iran's Contemporary Political Economy* (2012), *The Economy of Iran under Ahmadinejad* (2012) and *Crisis in Despotism in Iran* (2014).

Howard Stein is Professor of African Studies at the University of Michigan and also teaches in the Department of Epidemiology. He is a development economist educated in Canada, the USA and the UK. He is the editor or author of more than a dozen books and edited collections and more than 100 journal articles, book chapters and reviews. He has published papers on foreign aid, finance and development, structural adjustment and neoliberalism, health and development, institutional transformation and development, industrial policy, Export Processing Zones, agricultural policy, poverty and rural property right transformation. Publications include *Beyond the World Bank Agenda: An Institutional Approach to Development* (2008), *Good Growth and Governance in Africa: Rethinking Development Strategies* (2012, co-edited with Joseph Stiglitz, Akbar Noman, and Kwesi Botchway) and *Gendered Insecurities, Health, and Development in Africa* (2012, co-edited with Amal Fadlalla). He was also the principal co-author of the United Nations Economic Commission for Africa's *Economic Report for Africa 2014: Dynamic Industrialization in Africa*. His most recent title, *Institutions and Industrial Policy in Africa: Toward Structural Transformation and Inclusion,* is forthcoming (2016).

1
Main and Contributory Causes of the Recent Financial Crisis and Economic Policy Implications

Philip Arestis
University of Cambridge, UK, and University of the Basque Country, Spain

Abstract: We locate the main causes of the recent financial crisis on three factors. The first two of these were financial liberalization and its associated distributional effects (redistribution from wage earners to the financial sector) in the US and elsewhere. Both of these factors gave substantial impetus to the development and extension of new forms of securitization and the use of derivatives. This financial engineering practice, the third main factor, led to the growth of the instruments labelled as collateralized debt obligations (CDOs), particularly in the form of collateralized mortgages. There were also three contributory factors, which exacerbated the process of the main causes: the international imbalances, mainly as a result of the growth of China; the monetary policy pursued by countries over the period leading to the crisis; and the role played by the credit rating agencies. We discuss the economic policy implications of the financial crisis before we summarize and conclude.

Keywords: Financial Crisis, Main and Contributory Causes, Economic Policy Implications, Coordination of Economic Policies

JEL Classification: D30, E44, E58, E60

1.1 Introduction[1]

We discuss the origins of the recent financial crisis, which began in the US in the autumn of 2007 and spread to 2008 and 2009, and subsequently led to the 'Great Recession'. In doing so, we distinguish between main factors and contributory factors. The main factors contain three key features: distributional effects, financial liberalization and financial innovation. The contributory factors also contain three features: international imbalances, monetary policy, and the role of the credit rating agencies. In discussing the origins of the current crisis we are very much aware of the limitations of current macroeconomics. Indeed, we agree with Minsky (1982), who argued about three decades ago that "from the perspective of the standard economic theory of Keynes's day and the presently dominant neoclassical theory, both financial crises and serious fluctuations of output and employment are anomalies: the theory offers no explanation of these phenomena" (p. 60; see, also, Arestis, 2009; and Palley, 2012).

The recent financial crisis and the 'Great Recession' that ensued were caused by US financial liberalization, which helped significant income redistribution effects from wages to the profits of the financial sector in the US; both features enabled and promoted the financial innovations that followed them. An interesting statistic on this score is reported in Philippon and Reshef (2009) with regard to the US. This is the pronounced above-average rise in the salaries of those employed in finance. Relative wages, the ratio of the wage bill in the financial sector to its full-time-equivalent employment share, enjoy a steep increase over the period mid-1980s to 2006. What explains this development is the policy of deregulation, followed by the rapid expansion in financial innovation. The deregulation impact, according to the authors, accounted for 83 per cent of the change in wages. Indeed, wages in the financial sector are higher than in other sectors, even after controlling for education.

The three contributory factors are suggested as features that promoted, rather than caused, the 'financial crisis'. We take the view that although these factors were important, they were not its main causes. Rather, they were accentuating the process of the main causes rather than being part of the main factors of the crisis. We also discuss the economic policy implications of the financial crisis and the 'Great Recession' before we finally summarize and conclude. It should be noted at this early stage that the focus of this contribution is on the US economy and experience.

1.2 Main factors

We begin with the distributional effects as one of the main causes.

1.2.1 Distributional effects

The steady but sharp rise in inequality from around the 1980s (see, for example, Atkinson, 2015) is an important feature of this period.[2] Galbraith (2012a) suggests that "inequality was the heart of the financial crisis. The crisis was about the terms of credit between the wealthy and everyone else, as mediated by mortgage companies, banks, ratings agencies, investment banks, government sponsored enterprises, and the derivatives markets" (p. 4). In the US "The top 1 per cent of households accounted for only 8.9 percent of income in 1976, but this share grew to 23.5 percent of the total income generated in the United States by 2007" (Rajan, 2010, p. 8). Also, "The richest 1 percent of American households owned about 35 percent of national wealth in 2006–2007 ... a far greater share than in most other developed countries" (Wade, 2012, p. 12). Further evidence by Piketty (2014) shows that between the outbreak of World War I in 1914 and the 1970s, both levels of income inequality and the stock of wealth in the US fell dramatically. Since the 1970s, however, both income inequality and the stock of wealth have returned to the pre-1914 levels. Indeed, and as Piketty (op. cit.) suggests, in the past 30 years or so in the US nearly 75 per cent of the aggregate income growth has gone to the top of the distribution. Still further evidence by Atkinson et al. (2011) shows that the share of US total income going to the top income groups had risen dramatically prior to 2007. The top pre-tax decile income share reached almost 50 per cent by 2007, the highest level on record. The share of an even wealthier group – the top 0.1 per cent – more than quadrupled from 2.6 per cent to 12.3 per cent over the period 1976 to 2007. Real wages had fallen even behind productivity well before the onset of the 'Great Recession' (we may note that in the US wages constitute the most important component of incomes). The share of the top 5 per cent total income of households increased from 22 per cent in 1983 to 34 per cent in 2007; and household debt to GDP ratio over the period 1983–2008 almost doubled (Kumhof and Rencière, 2010a; see also 2010b). Indeed, and as Piketty (2014) shows, the income share of the top 1 per cent in English-speaking countries (especially in the US) has risen since 1980; the same 1 per cent appropriated 60 per cent of the increase in US national income between 1977 and 2007. The declining wage and rising profits share were compounded by the increasing concentration of earnings at the top, especially in the financial sector.[3]

The IMF managing director and the governor of the Bank of England have clearly stated at a conference in London ('Inclusive Capitalism', 27 May 2014) that rising inequality is a threat to economic growth and financial stability. The IMF managing director (Lagarde, 2014) made the point that "One of the leading economic stories of our time is rising income inequality, and the dark shadow it casts across the global economy" (p. 11). The IMF managing director went on to suggest that "The facts are familiar. Since 1980, the richest 1 percent increased their share of income in 24 out of 26 countries for which we have data. In the US, the share of income taken home by the top one percent more than doubled since the 1980s, returning to where it was on the eve of the Great Depression. In the UK, France, and Germany, the share of private capital in national income is now back to levels last seen almost a century ago" (p. 11). The Governor of the Bank of England (Carney, 2014) clearly stated in his speech that "Bankers made enormous sums in the run-up to the crisis and were well compensated after it hit. In turn, taxpayers picked up the tab for their failure. That unjust sharing of risk and reward contributed directly to inequality but – more importantly – has had a corrosive effect on social fabric of which finance is part and on which it relies" (p. 36).

Turning to the share of profits in relation to income in the case of the US, the following comments are very relevant. We note that profitability at the end of 2001 fell to an all-time low. This may have been the result of shifting production abroad, due to the increasing challenge of the US from other industrialized countries, such as Japan, Europe and especially China. It all gathered pace in the era of globalization. However, the picture of profits is not shared by financial companies. The share of the financial sector to GDP almost doubled in size between 1981 and 2007, and more recently accounted for 8 per cent of US GDP (Philippon, 2008). Between 1981 and 2007 the US financial sector, as measured by the ratio of private credit to GDP, grew from 90 per cent to 210 per cent. In addition, a sharp, nearly sixfold increase occurred, in their profitability since 1982. Indeed, and over the same period, as we have stated earlier wages in the financial sector were higher than in other sectors, even after controlling for education (Philippon and Reshef, 2009). Financial sector relative wages, and the ratio of the wage bill in the financial sector to its full-time-equivalent employment share, enjoyed a steep increase over the period mid-1980s to 2006.[4]

The redistribution feature was helped greatly by attempts at financial liberalization in many countries around the world. Of particular importance for our purposes was the financial liberalization framework in the US, especially following the repeal of the 1933 Glass–Steagall Act in 1999. Both the redistribution and the financial liberalization policies led to a period of financial engineering in the US, which spread worldwide to produce subsequently the 'Great Recession'. We turn our attention next to the subject of financial liberalization.

1.2.2 Financial liberalization

The US experienced financial liberalization from around the mid-1970s. In 1977 the authorities introduced the deregulation of commissions for stock trading, and subsequently investment banks were allowed to introduce unsecured current accounts. This was followed in the 1980s by the removal of Regulation Q, that is, the removal of ceilings on retail-deposit interest rates. The repeal of the key regulation Glass–Steagall Act of 1933[5] in 1999 (promoted by the US financial sector, who used as their main argument the experience of the so-called Big Bang of 1986 in the UK) was the most important aspect of the US financial liberalization for the purposes of the question in hand.[6] The final step in the process was another major and relevant legislative phase, which was the repeal of the Shed–Johnson jurisdictional accord of 1982, which banned regulation of over-the-counter derivatives. That repeal was enacted through the Commodity Features Modernisation Act (CFMA) of December 2000; it is also the case that "In the 2000s deregulation was followed by desupervision, as US regulatory authorities made calculated decisions not to investigate financial-sector practices" (Galbraith, 2012b, p. 4).

However, the repeal of the 1933 Glass–Steagall Act that took place in 1999 was the apotheosis of the financial liberalization in the US. The 1933 Glass–Steagall Act had been designed to avoid the experience of the 1920s in terms of the conflict of interest between the commercial and the investment arms of large financial conglomerates (whereby the investment branch took high levels of risk tolerance). The ultimate aim of the 1933 Glass–Steagall Act had been to separate the activities of commercial banks and the risk-taking 'investment or merchant' banks along with strict regulation of the financial services industry. In effect, the Glass–Steagall Act of 1933 broke up the most powerful banks. The goal was to avoid a repetition of the speculative, leveraged excesses of the 1920s/1930s. The repeal of the Act in 1999 enabled investment banks to branch into new activities, and allowed commercial banks to encroach on the investment banks' other traditional preserves. Not just commercial banks but also insurance and other companies, like the American International Group (AIG), were also involved in the encroaching.[7]

All these financial liberalization attempts were important in promoting financial innovations in the US financial markets. In our analysis we discuss their importance before turning our attention to the financial engineering that emerged directly from them and led to the financial crisis.

When fixed commissions were in place, investment banks would book stock trades for their customers; deregulation meant greater competition, entry by low-cost brokers and thinner margins. Then, in the late 1970s, investment banks were allowed to invade the commercial bank territory, through the creation of 'money market' accounts (current accounts that were unsecured). Removing Regulation Q allowed fluctuations in interest rates, thereby forcing commercial banks to compete for deposits on price, which led them to pursue new lines of business. Such new business was in response to the investment banks' needs for short-term funding. It created, however, a financial crisis in the 1970s and 1980s when savings banks and loans could not fund themselves as a result of the narrowing of the margins of lending and borrowing rates. Investment banks moved into originating and distributing complex derivative securities, such as collateralized bond obligations (normal investment bonds backed by pools of junk bonds). However, that was not a great success and the move collapsed in the second half of the 1980s, and that occurred in view of the wide fluctuations in the backed bond prices.[8]

However, that originate-and-distribute failure was followed by a new initiative of asset-backed and mortgage-backed securities, which gained a clientele in the 1990s. That was enabled in part by the relaxing of the 1933 Glass–Steagall Act in 1987, when the Federal Reserve Bank (the Fed) allowed 5 per cent of bank deposits to be used for investment banking, and then further promoted in 1996 when 25 per cent of deposits were allowed for the same purpose. In further developments 1997 saw the introduction of the Broad Index Secured Trust Offering (BISTRO), a bundle of credit derivatives based on pools of corporate bonds, and later there was also the launch of other types of financial derivatives, Collateralized Mortgage Obligations (CMOs), based on pools of subprime mortgages, and Collateralized Debt Obligations (CDOs) based on other debt.[9] BISTRO was not a great success in view of the corporate sector's booms and recessions at that time. However, CMOs and CDOs, which were based on mortgages and other assets, were received favourably due to the steady growth of the housing and other relevant markets. This was to prove one of the main causes of the financial crisis: the originate-and-distribute model of securitization and the extensive use of leverage.

1.2.3 Financial innovation

The repeal of the 1933 Glass–Steagall Act in 1999 enabled investment banks to branch out into new activities, and it allowed commercial banks to encroach on the investment banks' other traditional preserves. It was not just commercial banks that were involved in this encroaching. Insurance companies, such as the American International Group (AIG), and hedge funds were also heavily involved. Haldane (2010, Chart 2) shows clearly that the 1933 Act was effective from the 1930s to the late 1980s[10] when, as mentioned above, the US authorities began to relax it at the same time as the redistribution effects and the attempts at financial liberalization. In fact, concentration in the US banking sector remained flat over that period. The revoke of the restrictions of the 1933 Glass–Steagall Act in 1999 with the Gramm–Leach–Bliley Act, thereby allowing the co-mingling of commercial and investment banking, and finally the repeal of the 1933 Act in 1999, which allowed commercial and investment banks to mingle together, had the dramatic effect of increasing the share of the top three largest US banks from 10 per cent to 40 per cent between 1990 and 2007 (Haldane, 2010, p. 9). Interestingly enough, that dramatic increase in the size of the US banking is not mirrored by similar effects in other industries. Haldane (op. cit.) shows that "The largest banking firms are far larger, and have grown faster, than the largest firms in other industries", so that "the too-big-to-fail problem has not just returned but flourished" (p. 9). Furthermore, Haldane (op. cit.) argues that "A similar trend is discernible internationally: the share of the top five largest banks in the assets of the largest 1000 banks has risen from around 8 percent in 1998 to double that in 2009" (p. 9).

Another interesting and relevant observation is that the non-bank less regulated and supervised mortgage lenders contributed disproportionately to the boom in mortgages. Dagher and Fu (2011) demonstrate this proposition and show that while in 2003 the non-bank mortgage lenders accounted for only around one-third of mortgage lending, they contributed more than 60 per cent to the increase in mortgage lending between 2003 and 2005. The same authors have suggested, therefore, that the exercise of more stringent regulation could have averted some of the volatility in the housing market.

The repeal of the Glass–Steagall Act in 1999 allowed the merging of commercial with investment banking, thereby enabling financial institutions to separate loan origination from loan portfolio, and promoting the emergence of the originate-and-distribute model. Indeed, financial institutions were able to use risk management in their attempts to dispose of their loan portfolio. House prices continued to rise over the period 1999 to late 2006, which enabled households to borrow against equity they had built up in their properties. In addition, risk aversion fell sharply, thereby producing the mispricing of risk that led to the credit crisis in 2007–8. This underpricing of risk came about by low risk spreads whereby the differentials between risky assets and safe assets declined substantially. It came about, in particular, over the long period 2001–5 of unusually low nominal, and very low real interest rates. But even over the longer period of the late 1980s/early 1990s to 2007, macroeconomic risks were thought to have been reduced substantially in view of the 'great moderation' or 'great stability' or even 'Non-Inflationary Consistently Expansionary (NICE)' era of low and stable inflation and steady growth.

As a result, financial institutions could provide *risky* loans without applying the three Cs: Collateral, Credit history and Character (meaning that the person or institution would be able to pay the loan off, even in hard times). This fostered a new activity that relied on interlinked securities mainly emerging from, and closely related to, the subprime mortgage market. (The subprime mortgage is a financial innovation designed to extend home ownership to risky borrowers; the term 'subprime' refers to borrowers who are perceived to be riskier than the average borrower because of their poor credit history). Rising home prices encouraged remortgaging, thereby leading to a substantial expansion in the subprime mortgage market. As a percentage of total mortgages we observed the following phenomenal increase over this period: 1994: 5 per cent; 1996: 9 per cent; 1999: 13 per cent; 2006: 20 per cent; 2007: 47 per cent. Those developments, as mentioned above, led to an important financial innovation, namely securitization. Financial institutions engineered this new activity, which relied on interlinked securities, the CMOs and CDOs. The sale of CMOs and CDOs to international investors turned the US housing bubble into a global problem and provided the transmission mechanism for the contagion to the rest of the world. The world of CMOs and CDOs exploded at a stunning pace between around 2004 and 2007, yielding substantial profits for the relevant financial institutions. Goda and Lysandrou (2014) show that "The market for these products had remained fairly small until about 2002, but between that time and early 2007 it had grown 12-fold in size, from US$0.25 trillion to approximately US$3 trillion, i.e. to a size sufficient to spread panic in the money and interbank markets when it totally collapsed in August that year" (p. 301). It should also be noted that between 1998 and 2007 mortgage debt, as a percentage of disposable income, increased by more than 50 per cent from 61 per cent to 101 per cent.

Banks proceeded to set up trusts or limited liability companies with small capital bases, that is, separate legal entities, known as Structural Investment Vehicles (SIVs). Parallel banking, or what has been termed the shadow banking system, was thereby created outside the control and the regulatory umbrella of the authorities.[11] The operation of these SIVs was financed by borrowing from the short end of the capital markets at a rate linked to the interbank interest rate (Libor). The short-term capital thereby raised was used by the SIVs to buy the risky segment of the loan portfolio of the mother company, mainly risky mortgages. The risky loan portfolio was then repackaged in the form of CMOs and CDOs and sold to other banks and the personal sector, both to domestic and foreign investors; in terms of the latter it was mainly to Europeans. So long as the short-term rate of interest was lower than the long-term rate, and, in combination with the high commissions charged, big profits were secured, and the housing market turned into a bubble. It is true that after the internet bubble collapsed in March 2000 there was considerable fear, especially in the US, that price deflation might ensue. That fear, especially on the part of monetary policy makers, along with the apparent world glut of savings (Bernanke, 2005), led to a period of low nominal policy interest rates.

When the yield curve was inverted – that is, long-term interest rates became lower than short-term rates – the subprime mortgage market simply collapsed. It occurred following a period of a policy of rising interest rates (mid-2004 to mid-August 2007) after a prolonged period of abnormally low interest rates (initially from 1997 to 1998 but more aggressively after the internet bubble of March 2000 and even more so after November 2001, until central banks began to raise interest rates in 2004). The subprime mortgage market began its downward direction soon after; this occurred by late 2005 when the housing market peaked with that process accelerating, and more dramatically so, by the end of 2006. The collapse of the subprime mortgage market also helped to bring about the end of the housing boom and the burst of the housing bubble. Defaults on mortgages spread to investment banks and commercial banks in the US and across the world via the elaborate network of CMOs and CDOs.[12] Furthermore, the collapse of the subprime market spilled over into the real economy through the credit crunch and the collapse in equity markets; and all of that led to the freezing of the interbank lending market after August 2007. A significant recession emerged after the end of 2008: the 'Great Recession'. And as Haldane (2010) shows, the social costs of the crisis were significant worldwide; they were of the magnitude of several trillion dollars. Indeed, the social costs of the same financial crisis far out weighted the direct monetary costs of the related bailouts.

A pertinent question is why regulators appeared to have been ignorant of such reliance of the financial system on the parallel banking sector in 2007 and before, when clearly they should not have been. It surely must be the case that the regulation regime, such as it was at the time, must have been totally indifferent and ineffective. Even after the eruption of the August 2007 financial crisis and the ensuing 'Great Recession', the parallel banking sector has continued to thrive. The shrink of big western banks' balance sheets and their retreat from lending[13] has enabled the shadow banking since then to fill the gap and thereby to expand even more substantially than before the crisis.[14] Regulators do not seem to be concerned about these developments, however. The reason may very well be that they see the shrinking of banks and, in particular, the transfer of risky assets to other parts of the financial system as a desirable development in that it makes the financial system appear safer; shadow banking thereby disseminates risk beyond banks. Also, since shadow banks do not take deposits, sudden and destabilizing withdrawals could not take place. These developments should still be regulated closely, however, so that the relevant pre-August 2007 experience with regard to the shadow banking, as explained above in this sub-section, is not repeated.

1.3 Contributory factors

We begin with the international imbalances as one of the three contributory factors.

1.3.1 International imbalances

The process described so far was accentuated by the international imbalances, which were built up over a decade or more. The rise of China, in combination with the decline of investment in many parts of Asia following the 1997 crisis in that region, created a great deal of savings. Those savings were channeled mainly into the US, helping to put downward pressure on US interest rates, which along with the Fed low interest rate policy pursued at the same time, enabled households there to live well beyond their means. Low interest rates simultaneously helped to push up asset prices, especially house prices, thereby allowing the financial sector to grow rapidly. The explosion of the banking sector enabled lending to households and businesses to expand substantially, along with lending to other banks. All these imbalances created a more buoyant market for financial institutions, thereby helping to promote substantial innovation in the area of financial engineering (see Arestis and Karakitsos, 2010, for further details). They also helped to bring about the inversion of the yield curve referred to above. The increase in liquidity helped the subsequent increase in the demand for long-term assets, thereby lowering the long-term rate of interest and increasing the short-term rate.

The 'privilege' enjoyed by the US dollar as the world's currency encouraged and enabled savings to be channeled mainly into the US, helping to put downward pressure on US interest rates. In addition, the increasing allocation of manufacturing jobs to the relatively low-wage areas of Asia, and China in particular, where there was a well-educated low-cost workforce, combined with developed world technology, helped to keep down wages and hence lower inflationary pressures in the US and elsewhere. This, along with the channeling of savings into the US, also enabled the low-to-mid-income households there to rely increasingly on credit as a means of survival.

One important implication of this analysis, and to avoid the 'privilege' of the dollar mentioned above, is the possibility of regulating the international monetary system. Global imbalances contributed to previous crises, and were an important item on the agenda at the Bretton Woods conference held in 1944. Indeed, Keynes (1980) recognized the asymmetry of the obligations imposed on the countries involved with the problem of adjusting international imbalances. Keynes (op. cit.) argues, "To begin with, the social strain of an adjustment downwards is much greater than that of an adjustment upwards" but also "the process of adjustment is *compulsory* for the debtor and *voluntary* for the creditor. If the creditor does not choose to make, or allow, his share of the adjustment, he suffers no inconvenience. For whilst a country's reserve cannot fall below zero, there is no ceiling which sets an upper limit. The same is true for international loans if they are to be the means of adjustment. The debtor *must* borrow; the creditor is under no such compulsion" (p. 6). In terms of the current international imbalances they have been allowed to continue for a long period in view of the privileged position of the US as the issuer of the world's reserve currency. The August 2007 financial crisis experience clearly implies that designing an international monetary system to avoid the problems alluded to by Keynes (op. cit.) is long overdue.

1.3.2 Monetary policy

This aspect springs from the focus of monetary policy on price stability as the main objective of economic policy, which implies the use of frequent interest rate changes as a vehicle to controlling inflation. The impact of this policy has been the creation of enormous liquidity and household debt in the major economies, which reached unsustainable magnitudes and helped to promote the current crisis. This was particularly the case after the burst of the IT bubble in March 2000 when central banks, led by the Fed, pursued highly accommodative monetary policies to avoid a deep recession. Looking at debt statistics (see, BIS, 2008, p. 29), the following developments are evident. Outstanding household debt between 1998 and 2002 in the US averaged 76.7 per cent of GDP; between 2003 and 2007 the average shot to 97.6 per cent of GDP; over the same periods, outstanding household debt, including mortgage debt, jumped from 72.0 per cent to GDP to 94.3 per cent of GDP in the case of the UK. In the Euro Area it rose from 48.5 per cent to 56.6 per cent, respectively. This suggests that while monetary policy did not play a major role in causing the crisis it was, nonetheless, largely responsible for promoting it. Furthermore, and over the period 1997 to 2007, the ratio of US financial sector debt to GDP rose by 52 per cent; over the same period the total US private debt to GDP rose by 101 per cent. Similar numbers apply in the case of other developed countries, notably UK, Ireland, and Spain. Another interesting set of US statistics is the following. In 1989 the debt to income ratio was around 60 per cent for the top 10 per cent of household incomes and around 80 per cent for all other groups; in 2007, the respective ratios were around 80 per cent for the top 10 per cent, 250 per cent for the bottom quintile, and between 150 and 180 per cent for the middle groups.

It should be clear that the dominant argument that increased liquidity is always beneficial may not be so wide-ranging. Diminishing marginal utility and associated increased financial activity relative to real economic activity along with speculation create increasing dangers of destabilizing herd. This implies that an 'optimal level' of liquidity is evident. However, there is a serious complication in that although "an optimal level of liquidity, with increased liquidity and speculation valuable up to a point but not beyond that point" there is nonetheless "the complication for practical policy makers that the point of optimal benefit is impossible to define with any precision, that it varies by market, and that we have highly imperfect instruments through which to gain the benefits without the disadvantages" (Turner, 2010, p. 28). The enormous liquidity created over the period in view of the monetary policy pursued at the time, must have surpassed the 'optimal level' to which we have just referred.

It is also important to note that the credit part of liquidity was particularly important in promoting the 'Great Recession', as Schularick and Taylor (2009) show. It is the case, though, that policymakers and proponents of the current macroeconomic paradigm, the 'New Consensus Macroeconomics' theoretical framework, do not take credit and money seriously; they have no role to play in monetary policy. Indeed, the proponents firmly believe that macroeconomic outcomes are independent of any financial factors. They ignore that "financial factors can have a strong, distinct, and sometimes even dominant impact on the economy" (Schularick and Taylor, op. cit., p. 1; see, also, Arestis, 2009). The credit system, though, could potentially have a role in producing financial instability, closely related to the proposition that 'financial crises are credit booms gone wrong', an argument that is often attributed to Minsky (1986). Interestingly enough, Schularick and Taylor (2009) produce evidence that supports this view. Utilizing a linear probability model, along with a probit model, conclude "that a credit boom over the previous five years is indicative of a heightened risk of a financial crisis" (p. 20). Schularick and Taylor (op. cit.) also suggest that "the use of credit aggregates, rather than monetary aggregates, is of crucial importance", a result that leads to the further conclusion that "credit is a superior predictor, because it better captures important, time-varying features of bank balance sheets such as leverage and non-monetary liabilities" (p. 22). An important implication of these results for monetary policy purposes is that to the extent financial stability is the focus of monetary policy then a better target to focus on is credit aggregates in view of its superior power to predict incipient crises. Even policymakers recognise the importance of the 'credit view' of financial crises. For example the ex-Chairman of the UK's Financial Services Authority has expressed a firm interest in this view along with the suggestion of the importance to regulate credit (Turner, 2010).

As a result of these developments, the transmission mechanism of monetary policy has changed: the buildup of household debt and asset holdings has made household expenditure more sensitive to short-term interest rate changes. Furthermore, the current high debt levels, combined with the difficulties in the 'real' sector, imply that lenders and equity holders stay away from the market place; not forgetting the presence and magnitude of toxic assets, which pose real problems that still need to be sorted out. The dangers with this type of conduct of monetary policy are clear. Frequent changes in interest rates can have serious effects: low interest rates cause bubbles; high interest rates work through applying economic pressures on vulnerable social groups. Regulatory and prudential controls thereby become relevant and necessary.

1.3.3 Role of credit rating agencies

Credit rating agencies (CRAs) have played an important role both in the global credit crisis and in the subsequent sovereign debt crisis, which assumed enormous proportions in the Economic and Monetary Union

(EMU), and they have attracted considerable criticism for both. The increasing power of CRAs started in the US where they were granted the official designation of 'Nationally Recognized Statistical Rating Organisations'. Their role in the economy is to forecast the probability of default on the repayment period of the issuer of a debt liability. While CRAs provide information on the audit quality, namely on the probability of default of financial products, they say nothing about the potential for systemic risk. The latter is the danger of a chain reaction that emanates from a number of financial institutions faced with serious difficulties. It follows that while it may be rational for firms and investors to be guided by ratings in their investment decisions, they can destabilize the financial markets at a systemic level in the process.

This is not the only criticism that has been levelled on CRAs. They have also been accused as bestowing AAA credit rating to toxic assets, which were thereby treated as completely safe.[15] It is true that the complex structure of the CMO and CDO markets complicated the task of credit rating institutions, which erroneously assigned AAA-status to many worthless papers. In fact, some 80 per cent of the total value of CMOs and CDOs were given AAA credit rating, thereby treated as completely safe (Goodhart, 2009).[16] The overstated credit ratings contributed to the growth of the CMO and CDO markets in the upswing, but also to their downfall in the downswing. In the aftermath of the subprime crisis in the US, CRAs were blamed for their high initial ratings of structured finance securities in that they did not reflect the true risks inherent in those securities. This unfortunate episode emerged in view of the CRAs that rated only the credit default risk and not market or liquidity risk. For example, government debt with a rating of AAA had a different and superior overall quality as compared with the AAA of CMOs and CDOs. Many lenders who bought CMOs and CDOs were under the impression that all three types of risks were included in the rating of these tranches. They were, thus, confusing the AAA rating of government bonds and CMOs/CDOs and others. This criticism has been summarized more bluntly by Greenspan (2010): "The venerated credit rating agencies bestowed ratings that implied AAA smooth-sailing for many a highly toxic derivative product" (p. 13); and that "despite their decades of experience, the analysts of the credit rating agencies proved no more adept at anticipating the onset of the crisis than the investment community at large" (p. 12).

A further problem is the role of CRAs in the economy. This is to forecast the probability of default on the repayment period of the issuer of a debt liability. Their job is, therefore, relevant forecasting. The accuracy of their forecasts is clearly an important issue, which should be susceptible to ex post accountability. On this score there is no check on their forecasts since it is left to the CRAs themselves what precisely to publish. This is, then, another serious criticism of CRAs, which stems from their role in the economy, which is not undertaken and executed properly.

Also conflict of interest is another important feature of the CRAs, in view of the fact that they are paid by the issuers, not by investors. In fact, the larger CRAs receive most of their revenues from the issuers they rate. These fees were enhancing their revenues and profits substantially during the boom; thereby creating potentially a serious conflict-of-interest case. This could very well have distorted upwards their ratings. They have actually been accused on this score in terms of their over optimism of their ratings of CMOs and CDOs and other securitized assets. Although reputation and competition might protect this upward bias, the super-normal profits earned and the fact that issuers seek out that CRAs that provide the highest rating, "indicate(s) a prime facie case for bias" (Goodhart, 2009, p. 121). He et al. (2011) test and confirm the conflict of interest hypothesis. They conclude that "the conflict of interest problem of rating agencies likely played a significant role in the evolution of the MBS markets" (p. 135; where MBS stands for Mortgage-Backed Securities). The CRAs have, thus, been heavily accused for lacking independence from the institutions they rate, who pay for the assessments.

It may very well be the case, though, that CRAs got this assessment of the credit default wrong. Although there is no evidence of this proposition, it may very well be the case that insufficient competition amongst the CRAs means that they are not beyond reproach (Goodhart, 2009, chapter 2). In terms of the US monetary policy makers, Greenspan (2010) admits, "We at the Federal Reserve were aware as early as 2000 of incidents of some highly irregular subprime mortgage underwriting practices. But regrettably we viewed it as a localized problem subject to standard prudential oversight, not the precursor of the securitized subprime mortgage bubble that was to arise several years later" (p. 7, footnote 13).

It follows from this discussion that there is sufficient consensus that CRAs contributed to the August 2007 financial crisis. This is mainly in view of the CRAs erroneously assigned AAA-status to many worthless papers, which did not reflect the true risks inherent in those securities. This unfortunate episode emerged in view of the problems discussed above. The IMF (2010a) report suggests that CRAs had exposed 'some flaws in the system' including overreliance on ratings, which led Kiff

(2010) to conclude that "ratings have inadvertently contributed to financial instability – in financial markets during the recent global crisis and, more recently, with regard to sovereign debt" (p. 1). Furthermore, and in the case of sovereign debt, the IMF (2010b) report argues that credit rating agencies should shoulder some of the blame for 'the sell-offs of securities' when they are downgraded (the so-called 'cliff effect'). Kiff (2010) proceeds to suggest that credit rating agencies "may pay insufficient attention to sovereign debt composition and contingent liabilities, though in some cases they do not have access to all the information they need" (p. 1). The same report encourages the provision of more information and timely data by the countries on their sovereign debt, including disclosure of contingent liabilities.

The inevitable question that arises from the above analysis is whether had CRAs assigned lower credit ratings, would investors have reacted in a way that would have muted the supply of subprime mortgages? The relationship between initial credit ratings and prices of CMOs/CDOs is examined in the study conducted by Ashcraft et al. (2011). Their sample utilized includes 56,764 relevant securities from 3,069 subprime deals issued from 2001 to 2007. The sample covers around 90 per cent of subprimes issued over the period (see Ashcraft et al., 2010, for more details on the data utilized). Controlling for a set of security and loan characteristics, Ashcraft et al. (2011) conclude that there is a positive relationship between initial credit ratings and prices of CMOs/CDOs; more specifically, "A one-notch improvement in the credit rating is associated with a decline in yield spreads of about 20 basis points" (p. 217). Relevant asset prices are therefore very sensitive to credit ratings. The implication of these results is clearly that they strongly reinforce "the view that decisions about regulation of the credit rating industry are important and should be weighed carefully by policy-makers" (Ashcraft et al., 2011, p. 118). It clearly is the case, then, that reforming CRAs is long overdue.

1.4 Policy implications

A number of economic policy implications follow from our analysis. Monetary policy that manipulates the rate of interest solely to achieve price stability should be abandoned. The coordination of monetary, fiscal and financial stability policies becomes paramount. Distributional effects should also be accounted in the conduct of economic policies. There is also the question of CRAs, which should be properly regulated. These are the main policy implications, which we discuss and elaborate upon in what follows. We begin by considering the importance of distributional effects in economic policies.

1.4.1 Importance of distributional effects in economic policy

Clearly, recent experience, as our analysis above has shown, demonstrates that the distribution of income and wealth, if not tackled, can lead to crisis, as the case was with the recent financial crisis. Distribution of income from wages to profits, especially at the top end of the financial sector, was one of the main causes of the financial crisis. We have argued, in Arestis and Sawyer (2011), for the importance of accounting 'distributional effects' in both economic theory and policy, which have been fatally ignored. This is an important finding in view of the fact that "Until the crisis, it is difficult to identify a period in the past 50 years when inequality was close to the top of the public policy or academic agenda" (Haldane, 2014; see, also, Stiglitz, 2012). Still there is no general tendency towards greater economic equality, as others have also demonstrated (see, for a recent contribution, Piketty, 2014); on the contrary, unequal distribution continues unabated. Distributional effects should be a major objective of policy as this is also clear from our analysis. And to quote a relevant conclusion from an IMF study (Kumhof and Rencière, 2010b), "Restoring equality by redistributing income from the rich to the poor would not only please the Robin Hoods of the world, but could also save the global economy from another major crisis" (p. 31; see, also, Bordo and Meissner, 2012, and Stiglitz, 2012).

These propositions are supported by empirical evidence, as, for example, the findings of Onaran and Galanis (2012) show: "Our empirical estimations ... examining the effect of income distribution on growth in sixteen large developed and developing countries offer three important findings to understand this adverse development. First, domestic private demand (i.e. the sum of consumption and investment) is wage-led in all countries ... Second, foreign trade forms only a small part of aggregate demand in large countries ... Similarly, if countries, which have strong trade relations with each other ... are considered as an aggregate economic area, the private demand regime is wage-led. Finally, the most novel finding of this paper is that even if there are some countries, which are profit-led, the global economy is wage led. Thus, a simultaneous wage cut in a highly integrated global economy leaves most countries with only the negative domestic demand effects, and the global economy contracts. Furthermore some profit-led countries contract when they decrease their wage-share, if a similar strategy is implemented by their trading partners" (p. 28). It clearly is the case then that pro-labour distributional policies that promote wage policies, strengthening the welfare state, the status of labour unions by changing union legislation to foster collective bargaining, and financial regulation are important and relevant policies (see, also, Stockhammer, 2013). These arguments are further strengthened in view of the causes of the unequal distribution discussed in this contribution. Kristal and Cohen (2013) provide empirical evidence, based on 43 US private non-agricultural industries between 1969 and 2007, which suggests that "the erosion of pay-setting institutions, mainly unionization and the real minimum wage, explains about 50 percent of rising wage inequality in U.S. private industries between 1969 and 2007, while the spread of computer technology explains 12–14 percent between 1969 and 1997 and 21–24 percent between 1988 and 2007" (p. 37). It is also the case that "similar results showing a larger effect of de-unionization (vs. computerization) on inequality were found in Germany (King, 2013), as well as in a study on 22 developed countries (OECD, 2011)" (Kristal and Cohen, 2013, p. 37). Furthermore, Furceri and Loungani (2013) suggest two further contributors to increased inequality. "The first is the opening up of capital markets to foreign entry and competition, referred to as capital account liberalization. The second source is policy actions by governments to lower their budget deficits. Such actions are referred to as fiscal consolidation in economists' jargon and, by their critics, as 'austerity' policies" (p. 25). Furceri and Loungani (2013) refer to 58 episodes of large-scale capital account reforms in 17 advanced economies to conclude that "on average, capital account liberalization is followed by a significant and persistent increase in inequality. The Gini coefficient increases by about 1 percent a year after liberalization and by 2 percent after five years" (p. 26). It is also argued by Furceri and Loungani (op. cit.) that "Over the past 30 years, there were 173 episodes of fiscal consolidation in our sample of 17 advanced economies. On average across these episodes, policy actions reduced the budget deficit by about 1 percent of GDP. There is clear evidence that the decline in budget deficits was followed by increases in inequality. The Gini coefficient increased by 0.2 percentage point two years following the fiscal consolidation and by nearly 1 percentage point after eight years" (pp. 26–7).

The Economist (2014a) supports the argument that redistributing income does help to increase aggregate demand. Ostry et al. (2014) provide evidence on the relationship between inequality, redistribution and growth to conclude that "First, inequality continues to be a robust and powerful determinant both of the pace of medium-term growth and of the duration of growth spells, even controlling for the size of redistributive transfers... And second, there is surprisingly little evidence for the growth-destroying effects of fiscal redistribution at a macroeconomic level" (pp. 25–6). Such a strategy should be complemented by fiscal and moneatry policies, along with proper co-ordination of them, as we argue below. The objective should be full employment. Fiscal policy in particular is an important dimension in this regard. The study by Muinelo-Gallo and Roca-Sagalés (2011) employs an endogenous growth model that incorporates fiscal policy and economic growth along with their effects on income inequality. Pooled-panel estimations are undertaken for 43 upper-middle- and high-income countries for the period 1972–2006 to conclude that increases in public investment expenditure reduce inequality without harming output, regardless of whether they are financed through direct or indirect taxes. Reforming taxes to make them fairer is another important aspect of fiscal policy. Indeed, Berg and Ostry (2011) show that a redistributive tax system is associated with higher and durable economic growth. Korinek and Kreamer (2013) advocate redistributive policies "such as higher taxes on financial sector profits that are used to strengthen the social safety net of the economy would constitute such a mechanism" (p. 6). Raising the minimum wage and indexing it to inflation is another important tool to fight inequality (see, for example, *The Economist*, 2014a). A further example, and priority, is the removal of subsidies for the 'too-big-to-fail' financial insitutions for such a policy initiative would help to remove, to a large extent, one of the main contributory factors to the surge in wealth at the top of income distribution – and to the financial sector in particular. A recovery led by domestic demand and increase in the wage share in the global economy would help to reverse the major factor of inequality behind the global crisis. Gains in competitiveness can and should be achieved through productivity increases rather than wage reductions and weak labour conditions. In this sense, strong trade unions, collective bargaining and high minimum wages are all beneficial.

Indeed, the immense accumulation of wealth in the financial sector, as shown above, should not be accompanied by austerity measures. It should, instead, be tackled by raising taxes on upper-income holders and cutting war expenditure (Crotty, 2011, for example). The IMF (2014) study summarizes the argument and concludes that there is growing evidence that high income inequality has increased in recent decades in both developed and developing countries (as well as emerging), and has been detrimental to macroeconomic stability and growth. It is thereby of paramount importance for governments to employ fiscal policy to influence income distribution. This should be undertaken through both tax and spending policies. As for specific guidance on the use of fiscal policy for redistribution, this, it is suggested, is a country-specific problem. Piketty (2014) argues that with such substantial redistribution effects, a global progressive tax on individual net worth would offer the best option for keeping inequality under control. Those with low incomes would pay little, while those who have billions would pay a lot. Such tax would require international cooperation, of course. Although implementing such a tax would be a serious challenge politically, Piketty (op. cit.) suggests that if the EU and the US supported such a tax, it would be a great beginning. An additional measure is the implementation of a financial transaction tax (see, for example, Arestis and Sawyer, 2013) designed to curb speculation and raise funds for public investment. We would also suggest that raising the minimum wage, capping high pay, strengthening trade unions, and education policies, are further examples that can help redistributive effects. At the end of the day, though, tackling unequal distribution is an area where very little progress, if any, has been undertaken.

1.4.2 Financial stability

In terms of financial stability we may begin by agreeing with the conclusion of the IMF (2009) study that "the instruments used to pursue financial stability are in need of sharpening and refining" (p. 5; see, also, Blanchard et al., 2010). IMF (2010b) goes a step further to suggest that financial stability in the form of macro prudential policies is the way forward. Indeed, the same publication suggests that if the current low interest rates were to produce excessive risk-taking or bubbles, these should be addressed through macro-prudential policies and not through the interest rate policy measure. IMF (2010d) suggests a macro-prudential approach to contain systemic effects of 'too-important-to-fail' institutions, including non-bank institutions. Bean et al. (2010) conclude that macroprudential policy is a better policy to prevent asset and credit bubbles than merely monetary policy. In addition, Yellen (2014) asserts that "a macroprudential approach to supervision and regulation" should play the main role in financial stability instead of monetary policy, which "faces significant limitations as a tool to promote financial stability". Still, Yellen (op. cit.) argues, it is important to note that "the pursuit of financial stability is complementary to the goals of price stability and full employment".

It is true that only microprudential policies had been the basis of the regulatory framework prior to the 'Great Recession'. A number of writers have argued that the regulatory framework was problematic because of that deficiency (see Hansen et al., 2011, and a number of additional references therein). A macroprudential approach is thereby of enormous importance. Hansen et al. (op. cit.) summarize the argument very well: "A microprudential approach is one in which regulation is partial equilibrium in its conception and aimed at preventing the costly failure of individual financial institutions. By contrast, a 'macroprudential' approach recognizes the importance of general equilibrium effects, and seeks to safeguard the financial system as a whole. In the aftermath of the crisis there seems to be agreement among both academics and policymakers that financial regulation needs to move in a macroprudential direction" (p. 3). The difficulty with only a microprudential framework is that since it attempts to tackle problems with individual institutions, the overall result could very well be a serious damage to the economy as a whole. It is, thus, paramount for a macroprudential to co-exist with a microprudential one.

Furthermore, macroprudential policy acts more directly at the source of the problem. It is a 'system-wide oversight' approach, and as such it "would broaden the mandate of regulators and supervisors to encompass consideration of potential systemic risks and weaknesses as well" (Bernanke, 2005). In terms of the macroprudential tools, Hansen et al. (2011) discuss six sets of such tools: time-varying capital requirements; higher-quality capital; corrective action targeted at capital as opposed to capital ratios; contingent capital; regulation of debt maturity; and regulating the shadow banking system. They offer empirical evidence to conclude that macroprudential regulation is of paramount importance. The danger is that "given the intensity of competition in financial services, they will also drive a larger share of intermediation into the shadow banking realm" (Hansen et al., p. 25). Regulating this system, long overdue in our view, along with the rest of the financial system is the obvious conclusion, although this is "a complex task, and one that will require a variety of specific tools" (Hansen et al., p. 25). Still such regulation is of vital importance, however complex such a task might be. It is not the case that such attempts have not been initiated. Kashyap et al. (2014) suggest that "Bank regulations involving capital requirements have been substantially refined". However, "Other changes to rules regarding liquidity, or to give regulators other powers over, say dividends or loan-to-value (LTV) standards have been delayed. Indeed, it is fair to say that there is still no unified framework that organises thinking about how to proceed" (p. 2).

At the same time, however, there should be a coordination of monetary and macroprudential policies, and also those aiming to achieve more general financial stability. Financial stability policy measures should "include capital requirements and buffers, forward-looking loss provisioning, liquidity ratios, and prudent collateral valuation" (IMF, 2010c, p. 3). Still, and along these lines, price stability "should remain the primary objective of monetary policy" (p. 3); interestingly enough, though, the argument is not for price stability to be the single objective of economic policy. It is also suggested that "changes to central bank liquidity operations and broad crisis management frameworks are needed to address moral hazard. Changes to enhance the flexibility of central bank operational frameworks will improve the resilience of the system. Institutions and markets that are potential recipients of liquidity support, in times of stress should be monitored and regulated" (p. 3). So the focus here seems to be primarily on systemic financial stability. All these changes, IMF (op. cit.) argues, "should be done in a way that preserves central bank independence" (p. 4). As argued below, though, central bank independence would not be suitable under conditions of coordinated policies.

Another important and obvious policy implication that follows from our analysis is that the focus of monetary policy to meet the single objective of inflation should be abandoned. King (2009) suggests that "price stability does not guarantee stability of the economy as a whole" and that "Inflation targeting is a necessary but not sufficient condition for stability in the economy as a whole" (p. 5). Bean et al. (2010) are also clear on this issue when they argue that monetary policy "seems too weak an instrument reliably to moderate a credit/asset price boom without inflicting unacceptable collateral damage on activity" (p. 32). IMF (2009) is also very clear on this score:, "We must learn lessons from the events of the past two years. They cannot be final conclusions because the present crisis has some way to run. But one stands out. Price stability does not guarantee stability of the economy as a whole."

It follows from this discussion that financial stability and monetary policy should be the responsibilities of the central bank. This means, of course, that central banks would have an added objective – that of financial stability. Financial stability has not been addressed properly, and as such it requires further investigation. The focus of financial stability should be on the proper control of the financial sector so that it becomes socially and economically useful to the economy as a whole, as well as to the productive economy in particular. Banks should serve the needs of their customers rather than providing short-term gains for shareholders and huge profits for themselves. Such an additional objective, however, raises the issue of how to incorporate financial stability in the loss function of the central bank in view of the fact that it is impossible to measure such a variable. Blinder (2010) raises the issue and wonders "whether the right loss function is actually lexicographic, with financial stability logically prior to the other goals" (p. 4). This is a serious challenge for those central banks that use the 'New Consensus Macroeconomics' modelling framework (see, for example, Arestis, 2009, 2011).

1.4.3 Coordination of economic policies

We may begin this subsection by quoting the ex-IMF Managing Director, who asked the question: "What about fiscal policy? Under the old paradigm, fiscal policy was definitely the *neglected child* of the policy family. Its role was limited to automatic stabilizers – letting budget deficits move up and down with the cycle – and discretionary policy was regarded with deep suspicion. But fiscal policy had a *Sleeping Beauty* moment during the crisis – with monetary policy running out of steam, and with the financial system on its knees, the forgotten tool arrived to prop up aggregate demand and save the world from an economic freefall. We need to rethink fiscal policy" (Strauss-Kahn, 2011, p. 3). Indeed, we have to rethink fiscal policy seriously and suggest that the time has come to assign a strong macroeconomic role to it, along with coordination with other relevant economic policies (Arestis, 2012).

Clearly, monetary and financial stability policies should be coordinated. But we go further and argue that it is vital for full coordination of both policies with fiscal policy, along with discretion in applying them (Arestis, 2015). Fiscal policy should be used both in the short term and in the long term to address demand issues. In this respect, relatively frequent adjustments to fiscal stances in the light of macroeconomic developments are necessary. Regional and industrial policies should be employed to create the required capacity. The perception of how one reaches such a conclusion relies heavily on the belief that the objectives of macroeconomic policy are sustainable (environmental and otherwise), along with equitable economic development and growth. Within this general focus, the main objective of macroeconomic policy is the achievement of full employment of the available labour force. Achieving such an objective would require, inter alia, the maintenance of a high level of aggregate demand consistent with the full employment of labour. In addition, it is necessary to provide sufficient productive capacity to enable the achievement of full employment, where sufficient is to be interpreted in terms of quantity, quality and geographical distribution. In this sense, industrial and regional policies are required to enhance supply. Public expenditure, particularly investment, can also be structured to ease supply constraints.

The coordination of economic policies is therefore paramount. There is also ample empirical evidence that is very supportive of the theoretical propositions just proposed (see Arestis, 2012, for a comprehensive review and summary of the relevant empirical evidence). An interesting example is the study by Eggertsson (2006) who concludes that under fiscal and monetary policy coordination, fiscal multipliers are higher than when no policy coordination prevails; they are, indeed, bigger than those found in the traditional Keynesian literature. The fiscal policy multiplier under coordination is 3.4 in the case of the real spending multiplier, and 3.8 under the deficit spending multiplier. When no policy coordination is present, that is, when the central bank is 'goal independent', the real spending multiplier is unchanged, while the deficit spending multiplier is zero. Fiscal policy, though, is most effective when monetary policy is accommodative; and to quote Coenen and Straub (2005) "With no monetary accommodation, the inflation pressures lead to an upward movement in real interest rates and thereby offset, in part, the effects of the fiscal stimulus on GDP. In contrast, with monetary accommodation and nominal interest rates held constant, the increases in inflation give rise to decreases in real interest rates. As a result accommodative monetary policy complements the fiscal policy stimulus and intensifies its effects on real GDP" (p. 51). It is also important to note that under such coordination central bank independence cannot be sustained; and it should be abandoned. In any case, and as argued in Angeriz et al. (2008), the experience with central bank independence, in a number of countries around the world, has not been such a success once all different relevant angles are considered. Namely, the characteristics that are important for independent central banks to achieve, namely inflation level, persistence in inflation and inflation volatility, seem to have very little to do with central bank independence.

It follows from the above analysis that the main operation of any central bank should be directed towards financial stability. The events leading to the 'Great Recession' testify to this important requirement. With the objective of financial stability, the central bank would become more like a Central Financial Agency (CFA). It would be responsible for policies, which seek to influence the credit and lending policies of the full range of financial institutions.

1.4.4 Reforming credit rating agencies

In any type of reform, the role of credit rating agencies (CRAs) should be seriously revised. A number of suggestions on this score are worthy of consideration. Abolishing them in view of their unacceptable performance in over-rating might be one way forward; changing the manner of their remuneration is another. In this sense, looking carefully into the conflict of interest that arises from their fees paid by the issuers, rather than by the investors, thereby introducing a strong incentive to boost ratings, is long overdue. Indeed, it would be better to get investors who buy the rated bonds to pay the CRAs rather than the issuers of them (Cole and Cooley, 2014). Credit ratings should be more transparent; they should publish their methodologies and include more details about their work, so that investors can easily check their credibility. The Dodd–Frank Act of 2010 provided a way forward in an attempt to tackle this issue – the introduction of a new Office of Credit Ratings to supervise closely the work of credit rating agencies. However, although this was an important aspect of the Act, it has not yet been implemented. The President of the European Commission has suggested the placing of credit rating agencies under the direct supervision of a 'European Securities and Markets Authority'; this proposal is still in its infancy. The Chancellor of Germany and the President of France proposed 'a clampdown on credit rate agencies'. The Bank of England, and to a lesser extent the ECB, signal a clear break away from credit rating agencies. Despite this critique the CRAs business model, with its Nationally Recognised Ratings Organisation in the US, remains in place and underpins it. Indeed, the three big CRAs were continuing to record high profits well after the financial crisis of August 2007, as reported in the *Financial Times* ('Big Credit Rating Agencies under Fire', 5 May 2014).

A further interesting result that relates to the August 2007 financial crisis is from a Bertelsmann Foundation study (Fuchs and Gehring, 2013), which suggests that there is 'home bias' in sovereign ratings. Fuchs and Gehring (op. cit.) define 'home country' "as the country where the agency's headquarters is located or, alternatively, as the country of origin of its major shareholders. Accordingly, we refer to a 'home bias' in sovereign ratings if a rating agency gives preferential treatment to its home country and to countries with close economic, political and cultural ties to it. Thus, in our definition a home bias is a deviation of the actual rating level from what would be predicted solely by the sovereign's economic and political fundamentals" (p. 3). The study utilizes monthly dyadic panel data on sovereign ratings – the logic of which is that the sovereigns employed are non-independent – issued by nine CRAs[17] based in six countries from January 1990 to June 2013, and covers 143 sovereigns. Its purpose is to investigate empirically the extent to which there is systematic evidence for home bias in sovereign debt ratings. The study focuses on the extent to which "credit rating agencies assign better ratings to their home country as well as to countries that are geopolitically and economically aligned with, or culturally similar to it" (p. 4). Fuchs and Gehring (2013) conclude that there is convincing empirical support for the existence of home bias in sovereign debt ratings. The evidence is even stronger after the onset of the August 2007 financial crisis. It is also the case that "The extent to and the areas in which agencies are prone to a home bias differ across agencies. Specifically, we find that four agencies provide significantly better ratings to their home country than what would be justified by their assessments of the economic and political fundamentals of other sovereigns. Moreover, five agencies assign significantly better ratings to those countries to which home country banks have a higher relative risk exposure, and six agencies are to some degree affected by cultural distance as measured by linguistic differences and common language. Overall, the home bias in sovereign ratings appears to be driven by economic and cultural ties, not geopolitics" (p. 4).

An alternative to the CRA model has been proposed. This is the proposal by the Bertelsmann Foundation (2012a, 2012b) which suggests the establishment of an international non-profit CRA, labelled as INCRA, which should be funded as a sustainable endowment. It would, thereby, "provide a new legal framework that is based on an endowment solution to guarantee sustainability and security for its long-term existence" (Bertelsmann Foundation, 2012a, p. 4). It is also suggested under this framework that "The G20 would be the best forum to evaluate the political will for giving a new institution a chance – an institution that would be embedded in the markets but also in the society overall" (Bertelsmann Foundation, 2012a, p. 5). In order to fund this suggestion it is argued that an initial injection of $400m should be accumulated from a broad range of donors. The latter would include governments, international bodies (such as the IMF and the World Bank), foundations and non-government organizations and the financial services industry. The governance structure of the INCRA would comprise the following committees: the funders; the management body; the stakeholder committee, which would appoint and oversee the management body and would ensure independence of the analytical function of INCRA from the funders; and the credit policy committee, which would ensure the quality of the ratings. The clear intention for the INCRA "is that it would be able to better signal coming crises before they happen, with investors and issuers knowing that INCRA has no other agenda but to provide independent, conflict-free opinions" (p. 27). In terms of what would INCRA rate, it is straightforward for it would "rate only national government securities, and then supranationals after the first year of its existence" (p. 28).

Gkionakis et al. (2014) is another study that is critical of the CRAs and proposals to reform them are suggested. In this view, CRAs have caused problems with the proposition that the most recent and "The biggest casualty was the Eurozone periphery, which was downgraded far too heavily during the 2009–11 sovereign debt crisis as the rating committees repeatedly overruled the signals coming from fundamentals and to an unprecedented extent" (p. 1). Gkionakis et al. (op. cit.) propose an alternative that is based on estimating the 'objective' component of ratings, namely the component of ratings that depends on measurable 'fundamentals' of creditworthiness, while the 'subjective component', that is, the assessment by the rating committees that modify the signals, should be used as a residual. So the alternative used for estimation purposes employs a relationship derived from a single regression based on the objective component variables and treating the subjective element as part of the stochastic-error term of the regression. The main objective component variables are: nominal GDP, GDP per capita, GDP growth, public debt, current-account-to-GDP ratio, external debt-to-GDP ratio, indicator variables on whether the relevant country has defaulted previously, whether the country is an advanced or otherwise country, government effectiveness, and rule of law.

Their main empirical findings show that "the Eurozone's periphery is on average rated almost five notches below what their fundamentals signal, while the Fragile Five[18] are on average rated almost two notches above their fundamental (or objective) signals" (p. 1). More specifically, "Spain, Portugal, and Ireland are all five notches below where they should be, while Italy is underrated by four notches. For Portugal this is the difference between its current junk status and investment grade. At the other end of the scale, Brazil, Indonesia and Turkey are overrated" (p. 17). It is thereby concluded "that the self-appointed credit committees have caused more damage than good as their over rulings of macro fundamentals have been somewhat random in both directions, and with serious distortions in recent years" (p. 18). These findings and conclusion lead the study to the suggestion that "the CRAs be stripped of their regulatory powers for sovereign ratings. Anything with a regulatory role should be carried out by agents of the state, or in this case all states. Therefore, to replace them in this role, we suggest that an international body be mandated with the development of a set of macro indicators (along the lines of what we have shown here to be the CRAs' objective signal), and that these indicators replace the role in regulatory and other policy matters presently played by the CRAs" (p. 18). Failing in terms of this suggestion, the alternative for the ratings agencies is that they "should be forced to substantially increase transparency, including publishing a separate breakdown of the objective and subjective components of ratings, the minutes of the rating committees, and the voting records" (p. 18).

All the suggestions discussed in this subsection are relevant and important, and, unfortunately, long overdue.

1.5 Summary and conclusions

We have highlighted the origins of the August 2007/2008 financial crisis and of the subsequent Great Recession. We have emphasized the main causes of them, namely distributional effects, financial liberalization and financial architecture, along with the contributory ones: international imbalances, monetary policy and the role of the credit rating agencies. More intervention on the policy front is needed, along with the proper coordination of fiscal with monetary/financial stability policies. Distributional effects and financial stability should be major parts of the economic policy objectives. A properly regulated and functioning banking system is paramount to allow economic activity to expand. A further and related recommendation is that reforming the credit rating agencies is urgent and paramount.

It is the case, however, that when it comes to the question of the implementation of the policy initiatives the news is disappointing. In fact, five years since the Dodd–Frank Act of July 2010 and the banking reform remains a work in progress across the world. The IMF Managing Director was right to argue at a conference in London ('Inclusive Capitalism', 27 May 2014) that the finance industry is responsible for the lack of meaningful banking sector reforms in view of their 'fierce industry fightback'. Indeed, the absence of action on this score has meant that 'non-banks colonise former bank territory' (*Financial Times*, 2 June 2014), which is vacated by traditional banks in view of 'increased' regulation. Such territory comprises of private debt, property debt and trade finance, where banks used to lend money. In view of the new regulations that banks have to hold more capital against such debt, they no longer participate in these activities; or when participating they only do so as originators with selling on the debt to other such as non-bank asset entities.

The unregulated shadow banking sector is thereby increasing substantially in size. In the case of the US, this development could very well be due to the fact that the Dodd–Frank Act of July 2010 has failed so far to fix properly the US regulatory system. The reason could be that the Fed is not responsible for monitoring systemic risk. It is instead the Financial Stability Oversight Council, which sits under the umbrella of the Treasury. Be that as it may, it is the case that it is not just in the US that such inactivity is in place, but elsewhere too. For it is true that worldwide progress on financial reform is extremely slow; and worrying poverty of action is in place. The IMF Managing Director (Lagarde, 2014) suggests that "the behaviour of the financial sector has not changed fundamentally in a number of dimensions since the financial crisis"; and proceeds to complain that "The bad news is that progress is still too slow, and the finish line is still too far".

Notes

1. The author is grateful to Malcolm Sawyer for helpful comments. The usual disclaimer applies.
2. It should be noted that rising inequality preceding the August 2007 financial crisis is not the only one in the history of financial crises. The same pattern had preceded the financial crash of 1929. And as Haldane (2014) suggests, "Between 1920 and 1928, the income share of the top 5% rose from little more than a quarter to more than a third. Household debt relative to GDP doubled. Inequalities widened and balance sheets fattened. And the upshot was the same: a huge economic contraction when the credit bubble popped" (p. 5; see, also, Kumhof and Rencière, 2010a, 2010b).
3. See, also, the study by Arestis and Karakitsos (2013), where it is shown that the unfavourable trends in the US real wage rate prior to 2007 were partly reflected in the wages and salaries of private and government employees. Ever since the beginning of the 1970s to the end of 2009, the share of wages and salaries to GDP had fallen by an astonishing 9 per cent to 44.5 per cent.
4. Korinek and Kreamer (2013) examine the redistribution effects of financial deregulation to conclude that they lead to "a higher incidence of credit crunches and more severe externalities on workers in bad times" (p. 5).
5. The Glass–Steagall Act of 1933 is actually part of the Banking Act of 1933. It is subsections 16, 20, 21 and 32 that are widely referred to as the 'Glass–Steagall Act of 1933' (see Russell, 2014, footnote 2). Russell (op. cit.) suggests that "The Banking Act of 1933 emphasized the deterrence of speculation as a requisite of bank stability, and its Glass-Steagall provisions were largely viewed as protecting the banking system from contamination by the speculative pressures that may emerge when depository banks involve themselves in security markets" (p. 108).
6. It should be noted that prior to the financial liberalization period, from around the late 1930s and the early 1970s, there had been direct controls on bank lending and exchange controls on international flows, which may very well have contained innovation and efficiency in the banking sector. It was also the case, and as Bordo et al. (2001) demonstrate, that the period late 1930s-early 1970s was free from serious banking crises.

7. It is interesting to note that as from 1933 and for decades the US financial regulatory framework "encouraged the relative financial stability and low interest rates characteristic of the 'golden age' of Keynesian economics in the United States. As the deregulatory impulses of a resurgent neoliberalism gathered steam, several provisions of the New Deal Financial reforms were either undermined or repealed in the 1980s and 1990s, culminating in the repeal of the Glass-Steagall provisions in 1999" (Russell, 2014, p. 114).
8. This raises the issue of the difference between originate-and-distribute and originate-and-hold models. In the originate-and-hold model bank loans are held in the banks' own portfolios. In the originate-and-distribute (or originate-to-securitize) model bank loans are re-packaged and sold to other banks, foreign banks and the domestic and foreign personal sector. The latter model transfers the loan risk from the bank to whoever buys the Asset Backed Securities (ABS). Then the Commodity Futures Modernization Act (CFMA) of December 2000 emerged. This Act deregulated single-stock futures trading, and provided certainty that products offered by banking institutions would not be regulated as futures contracts. CFMA enabled and legitimized credit-default swaps (CDSs, which are credit derivative contracts between two parties, whereby there is guarantee in case of default), thereby creating a potentially massive vector for the transmission of financial risk throughout the global system.
9. CDOs were originally developed for the corporate debt markets, but over time they encompassed the mortgage and mortgage-backed security markets.
10. Haldane (2010) concludes that the Glass–Stegall Act of 1933 regime satisfied 'robust' regulatory criteria "And so it proved, lasting well over half a century without a significant systemic event in the US" (p. 14). See, also, Russell (2014).
11. An interesting comparison in terms of the size of the shadow banking sector in the US and the Euro Area is provided by the ECB (2012): "In the United States the size of the shadow banking system, measured as the total amount of its assets, was comparable to the size of the banking system in the second quarter of 2011, while in the euro area it represented less than half of the total assets of the banking sector. However, the size of assets held by financial intermediaries that are not regulated as banks is still important in the euro area, especially in some countries" (p. 5). In terms of individual countries in the Euro Area, the big players in terms of their shadow banking sectors are Ireland, Luxemburg and the Netherlands alike (ECB, 2012, p. 23).
12. Coval et al. (2009) argue that by "offering AAA-ratings along with attractive yields during a period of relatively low interest rates, these products were eagerly bought up by investors around the world" (p. 4).
13. It is reported in the Economist (2014b) that the retreat of banks from bank lending to business in the main Western countries since the eruption of the financial crisis in August 2007 has been significant. In the US it is 6 per cent below its high at that time; in the UK it has been reduced by 30 per cent and in the euro area the decline has been 11 per cent. The reduction of bank lending to consumers is reported to have been less. The Financial Stability Board (FSB) estimates that shadow bank lending, in the 20 big economies it deals with, rose from $26 trillion in 2002 to $71 trillion in 2012 (figures as reported in the Economist, op. cit.). Interestingly enough, in China shadow banking grew by 42 per cent in 2012, and is still growing. It is also interesting

to note that the asset-backed securities innovation is back in vogue and seen as a cheap source of funding (see Bank of England and European Central Bank, 2014).

14. ECB (2012) warns that "the forthcoming implementation of Basel III, with the introduction of more stringent capital and liquidity requirements for credit institutions, and the provisions to be applied to insurers may provide further incentives for banks to shift part of their activities outside of the regulated environment and therefore increase shadow banking activities" (p. 5).
15. A relevant case is the decision of the US Department of Justice, which sued in February 2014 the Standard & Poor's (S&P) credit rating agency for $5 billion in that it knowingly issued overgenerous ratings.
16. In the study by Ashcraft et al. (2011) it is reported that on a value-weighted basis 80 to 90 per cent of CMOs and CDOs received the AAA credit rating.
17. The nine CRAs referred to in the text are: Capital Intelligence, Dagong Global, Dominion Bond Rating Services, Feri EuroRating Services, Fitch Ratings, Japan Credit Rating Agency, Moody's Investor Services, Rating and Investment Information, and Standard & Poor's (Fuchs and Gehring, 2013, p. 5).
18. The so-called 'Fragile Five' are: Brazil, India, Indonesia, South Africa and Turkey.

References

Angeriz, A., Arestis, P. and McCombie, J. (2008) 'Does Central Bank Independence Affect Inflation Persistence and Volatility?', CCEPP Working Paper, Cambridge Centre for Economic and Public Policy, Department of Land Economy, University of Cambridge.

Arestis, P. (2009) 'New Consensus Macroeconomics and Keynesian Critique', in E. Hein, T. Niechoj, and E. Stockhammer (eds), *Macroeconomic Policies on Shaky Foundations – Whither Mainstream Economics?*, Marburg, Germany: Metropolis Verlag.

Arestis, P. (2011) 'Keynesian Economics and the New Consensus in Macroeconomics', in E. Hein and E. Stockhammer (eds), *A Modern Guide to Keynesian Macroeconomics and Economic Policies*, Cheltenham: Edward Elgar Publishing Limited.

Arestis, P. (2012) 'Fiscal Policy: A Strong Macroeconomic Role', *Review of Keynesian Economics*, 1(1), pp. 93–108.

Arestis, P. (2015) 'Coordination of Fiscal with Monetary and Financial Stability Policies Can Better Cure Unemployment', *Review of Keynesian Economics*, 3(2), pp. 233–47.

Arestis, P. and Karakitsos, E. (2010) 'Subprime Mortgage Market and Current Financial Crisis', in P. Arestis, P. Mooslechner and K. Wagner (eds), *Housing Market Challenges in Europe and the United States*, Basingstoke: Palgrave Macmillan.

Arestis, P. and Karakitsos, E. (2013) *Financial Stability in the Aftermath of the 'Great Recession'*, Basingstoke: Palgrave Macmillan.

Arestis, P. and Sawyer, M. (2011) 'Economic Theory and Policies: New Directions after Neoliberalism', in P. Arestis and M. Sawyer (eds), *New Economics as Mainstream Economics*, Annual Edition of International Papers in Political Economy, Basingstoke: Palgrave Macmillan.

Arestis, P. and Sawyer, M. (2013) 'The Potential of Financial Transactions Taxes', in P. Arestis and M. Sawyer (eds), *Economic Policies, Governance and the New Economics*, Annual Edition of International Papers in Political Economy, Basingstoke: Palgrave Macmillan.

Ashcraft, A., Goldsmith-Pinkham, P. and Vickery, J. (2010) 'MBS Ratings and the Mortgage Credit Boom', Federal Reserve Bank of New York Staff Report 449, New York: Federal Reserve Bank of New York.

Ashcraft, A., Goldsmith-Pinkham, P. Hull, P. and Vickery, J. (2011) 'Credit Ratings and Security Prices in the Subprime MBS Market', *American Economic Review: Papers & Proceedings*, 101(3), pp. 115–19.

Atkinson, A.B. (2015) *Inequality: What Can be Done?*, Cambridge, MA: Harvard University Press.

Atkinson, A.B., Piketty, T. and Saez, E. (2011) 'Top Incomes in the Long Run of History', *Journal of Economic Literature*, 49(1), pp. 3–71.

Bank of England and European Central Bank (2014) 'The Case for a Better Functioning Securitisation in the European Union', *A Discussion Paper*, Prepared by Bank of England and European Central Bank Staff, May. Available at http://www.bankofengland.co.uk/publications/Documents/news/2014/paper300514.pdf.

Bank of International Settlements (BIS) (2008) *Annual Report*, June, Basel, Switzerland: Bank for International Settlements.

Bean, C., Panstian, M., Penalver, A. and Taylor, T. (2010) 'Monetary Policy After the Fall', *Federal Reserve Bank of Kansas City Annual Conference*, Jackson Hole, Wyoming, 28 August.

Berg, A.G. and Ostry, J.D. (2011) 'Inequality and Unsustainable Growth: Two Sides of the Same Coin?', IMF Staff Discussion Note 11/08, Washington, DC: International Monetary Fund. Available at http://www.imf.org/external/pubs/ft/sdn/2011/sdn1108.pdf.

Bernanke, B.S. (2005) 'The Global Saving Glut and the US Current Account Deficit', Sandridge Lecture, Richmond, Virginia: Virginia Association of Economics, 10 March.

Blanchard, O., Dell'Ariccia, G. and Mauro, P. (2010) 'Rethinking Macroeconomic Policy', IMF Staff Position Note, SPN/10/03, Washington, DC: International Monetary Fund.

Blinder, A.S. (2010) 'Commentary: Rethinking Monetary Policy in Light of the Crisis', Federal Reserve Bank of Kansas City Annual Economic Symposium, 28 August, Jackson Hole: Wyoming.

Bertelsmann Foundation (2012a) *Blueprint for An International Non-profit Credit Rating Agency (INCRA)*, April, New York: Bertelsmann Stiftung.

Bertelsmann Foundation (2012b) *Country Ratings Report: An International Non-profit Credit Rating Agency (INCRA)*, October, New York: Bertelsmann Stiftung.

Bordo, M.D., Eichengreen, B., Klingebiel, D. and Martinez-Perio, M.S. (2001) 'Is the Crisis Problem Going More Severe?', *Economic Policy*, 32, pp. 51–82.

Bordo, M.D. and Meissner, C.M. (2012) 'Does Inequality Lead to a Financial Crisis?', *Journal of International Money and Finance*, 31(8), pp. 2147–61.

Carney, M. (2014) 'Inclusive Capitalism', speech given at the conference on 'Inclusive Capitalism', London, 27 May. Available at http://www.inc-cap.com/IC_ESSAY_Book_Introduction_Keynotes.pdf.

Coenen, G. and Straub, R. (2005) 'Does Government Spending Crowd in Private Consumption? Theory and Empirical Evidence for the Euro Area', IMF Working Paper 05/159, Washington, DC: International Monetary Fund.

Cole, H. and Cooley, T. (2014) 'Rating Agencies', NBER Working Paper 19972, March, Washington, DC: National Bureau of Economics Research.

Coval, J., Jurek, J. and Stafford, E. (2009) 'The Economics of Structured Finance', *Journal of Economic Perspectives*, 23(1), pp. 3–25.

Crotty, J. (2011) *The Great Austerity War: What Caused the US Deficit Crisis and Who Should Pay to Fix It?*, Amherst: University of Massachusetts.

Dagher, J.C. and Fu, N. (2011) 'What Fuels the Boom Drives the Bust: Regulation and the Mortgage Crisis', IMF Working Paper WP/11/25, Washington, DC: International Monetary Fund.

Eggertsson, G.B. (2006) 'Fiscal Multipliers and Policy Coordination', Federal Reserve Bank of New York Staff Reports, No. 241, New York: Federal Reserve Bank of New York.

European Central Bank (ECB) (2012) 'Shadow Banking in the Euro Area: An Overview', Occasional Paper Series, No. 133, April, Frankfurt: European Central Bank.

Furceri, D. and Loungani, P. (2013) 'Who Let the Gini Out?', *Finance & Development*, 50(4), pp. 25–7.

Fuchs, A. and Gehring, K. (2013) 'The Home Bias in Sovereign Ratings', Discussion Paper Series No. 552, Department of Economics, University of Heidelberg.

Galbraith, J.K. (2012a) *Inequality and Instability*, Oxford: Oxford University Press.

Galbraith, J.K. (2012b) 'New Thinking and a Strategic Policy Agenda', *OECD Forum*, Paris, 21–3 May.

Gkionakis, V., Nielsen, E. And Vernazza, D. (2014) 'The Damaging Bias of Sovereign Ratings', *UniCredit Global Themes Series*, no. 21, March, Milan: UniCredit Bank.

Goda, T. And Lysandrou, P. (2014) 'The Contribution of Wealth Concentration to the Subprime Crisis: A Quantitative Estimation', *Cambridge Journal of Economics*, 38(2), pp. 301–27.

Goodhart, C.A.E. (2009) *The Regulatory Response to the Financial Crisis*, Cheltenham: Edward Elgar Publishing Limited.

Greenspan, A. (2010) 'The Crisis'. Brookings Papers on Economic Activity, Spring. Available at http://www.brookings.edu/~/media/Files/Programs/ES/BPEA/2010_spring_bpea_papers/spring2010_greenspan.pdf.

Haldane, A.G. (2010) 'The $100 Billion Question', speech at the Institute of Regulation & Risk, North Asia (IRRNA), Hong Kong, 30 March 2010. Available at http://www.bankofengland.co.uk/archive/Documents/historicpubs/speeches/2010/speech433.pdf.

Haldane, A.G. (2014) 'Unfair Shares', speech at the Bristol Festival of Ideas Event, 21 May. Available at http://www.bankofengland.co.uk/publications/Documents/speeches/2014/speech732.pdf.

Hansen, S.G., Kashyap, A.K. and Stein, J.C. (2011) 'A Macroprudential Approach to Financial Regulation', *Journal of Economic Perspectives*, 25(1), pp. 3–28.

He, J., Qian, J. and Strahan, P.E. (2011) 'Credit Ratings and the Evolution of the Mortgage-Backed Securities Market', *American Economic Review: Papers & Proceedings*, 101(3), pp. 131–5.

IMF (2009) *World Economic Outlook – Sustaining Recovery*, October 2009, Washington, DC: International Monetary Fund. Available at http://www.imf.org/external/pubs/ft/weo/2009/02/index.htm.

IMF (2010a) *World Economic Outlook – Recovery, Risk, and Rebalancing*, October 2010, Washington, DC: International Monetary Fund. Available at http://www.imf.org/external/pubs/ft/weo/2010/02/index.htm.

IMF (2010b) 'Central Banking Lessons from the Crisis', *Monetary and Capital Markets Department*, 27 May 2010, Washington, DC: International Monetary Fund. Available at https://www.imf.org/external/np/pp/eng/2010/052710.pdf.

IMF (2010c) 'Shaping the New Financial System', *IMF Staff Position Note, SPN/10/15*, Monetary and Capital Markets Department, 3 October, Washington, DC: International Monetary Fund. Available at http://www.imf.org/external/pubs/ft/spn/2010/spn1015.pdf.

IMF (2010d) *Global Financial Stability Report: Sovereigns, Funding, and Systemic Liquidity*, October 2010, Washington, DC: International Monetary Fund. Available at http://www.imf.org/external/pubs/ft/gfsr/2010/02/index.htm.

IMF (2014) 'Fiscal Policy and Income Inequality', IMF Policy Paper, 23 January, Washington, DC: International Monetary Fund. Available at http://www.imf.org/external/np/pp/eng/2014/012314.pdf.

Kashyap, A.K., Tsomocos, D.E.P. and Vardoulakis, A. (2014) 'Principles for Macroprudential Regulation', Booth Working Paper No. 14–19, Chicago Booth, 30 June. Available at http://ssrn.com/abstract=2460937.

Keynes, J.M. (1980) 'Activities, 1940–1946: Shaping the Post-War World: The Clearing Union', *Collected Writings, vol. 25*, London: Macmillan.

Kiff, J. (2010) 'Reducing Role of Credit Ratings Would Aid Markets', *IMF Survey Magazine: IMF Research*, 29 September, Washington, DC: International Monetary Fund. Available at http://www.imf.org/external/pubs/ft/survey/so/2010/res092910.htm.

King, J. (2013) 'Technological Change, Union Decline, and the Rise in German Wage Inequality, 1979–2012', paper presented at the RC28 Spring Meeting in Trento, May.

King, M. (2009) *Speech at the Mayor's Banquet for Bankers and Merchants of the City of London*, The Mansion House, 17 June 2009. Available at_http://www.bankofengland.co.uk/publications/speeches/2009/speech394.pdf.

Kristal, T. and Cohen, Y. (2013) 'The Causes of Rising Wage Inequality: What Do Computerization and Fading Pay-Setting Institutions Do?', Working Paper, 19 June. Available at http://ssrn.com/abstract=2424144 or http://dx.doi.org/10.2139/ssrn.2424144.

Korinek, A. and Kreamer, A. (2013) 'The Redistributive Effects of Financial Deregulation', NBER Working Paper 19572, October, Washington, DC: National Bureau of Economic Research.

Kumhof, M. and Rencière, R. (2010a) 'Inequality, Leverage and Crises', IMF Working Paper 10/268, Washington, DC: International Monetary Fund.

Kumhof, M. and Rencière, R. (2010b) 'Leveraging Inequality', *Finance and Development*, 47(4) (December), pp. 28–31.

Lagarde, C. (2014) 'Economic Inclusion and Financial Integrity', speech given at the Conference on *Inclusive Capitalism*, London, 27 May. Available at http://www.inc-cap.com/IC_ESSAY_Book_Introduction_Keynotes.pdf.

Minsky, H.P. (1982) *Can 'It' Happen Again: Essays on Instability and Finance*, Armonk, NY: M.E. Sharpe.
Minsky, H.P. (1986) *Stabilizing an Unstable Economy*, New Haven, CT: Yale University Press.
Muinelo-Gallo, L. and Roca-Sagalés, O. (2011) 'Economic Growth and Inequality: The Role of Fiscal Policies', *Australian Economic Papers*, 50(2–3), pp. 74–97.
OECD (2011) 'Divided We Stand: Why Inequality Keeps Rising', Paris: OECD Publishing.
Onaran, O. and Galanis, G. (2012) 'Is Aggregate Demand Wage-led or Profit-led? National and Global Effects', International Labour Organization (ILO) Working Papers, No. 478623.
Ostry, J.D., Berg, A. and Tsangarides, C.G. (2014) 'Redistribution, Inequality, and Growth', IMF Staff Discussion Note, February. Available at http://www.imf.org/external/pubs/ft/sdn/2014/sdn1402.pdf.
Palley, T.I. (2012) *From Financial Crisis to Stagnation: The Destruction of Shared Prosperity and the Role of Economics*, Cambridge: Cambridge University Press.
Philippon, T. (2008) 'The Evolution of the US Financial Industry from 1860 to 2007', Working Paper, November, New York University.
Philippon, T. and Reshef, A. (2009) 'Wages and Human Capital in the US Financial Industry: 1909–2006', NBER Working Paper no. 14644, January, Washington, DC: National Bureau of Economic Research.
Piketty, T. (2014) *Capital in the Twenty-First Century*, Cambridge, MA: Harvard University Press (translated by A. Goldhammer).
Rajan, R.G. (2010) *Fault Lines: How Hidden Fractures Still Threaten the World Economy*, Princeton, NJ: Princeton University Press.
Russell, E.D. (2014) 'Lessons from the Glass–Steagall Act', in G.A. Epstein, T. Schlesinger and M. Vernengo (eds), *Banking, Monetary Policy and Political Economy of Financial Regulation: Essays in the Tradition of Jane D'Arista*, Cheltenham: Edward Elgar Publishing Limited.
Schularick, M. and Taylor, A.M. (2009) 'Credit Booms Gone Bust: Monetary Policy, Leverage Cycles and Financial Crises, 1870–2008', NBER Working Paper No. 15512, Cambridge, MA: National Bureau of Economic Research.
Stiglitz, J. (2012) *The Price of Inequality: The Avoidable Causes and Invisible Costs of Inequality*, New York: W.W. Norton and Company.
Stockhammer, E. (2013) 'Why Have Wage Shares Fallen? A Panel Analysis of the Determinants of Functional Income Distribution', International Labour Organization (ILO), Conditions of Work and Employment Series No. 35.
Strauss-Kahn, D. (2011) 'Global Challenges, Global Solutions', An Address at George Washington University, Washington: International Monetary Fund, 4 April. Available at http://www.imf.org/external/np/speeches/2011/040411.htm.
The Economist (2014a) 'Social Mobility: A Memo to Obama', and 'Inequality v Growth', 1 March.
The Economist (2014b) 'Shadow and Substance', *Special Report: International Banking*, 10 May.
Turner, A. (2010) 'What Do Banks Do? What Should They Do and What Public Policies are Needed to Ensure Best Results for the Real Economy?', speech given at the CASS Business School, 17 March. Available at http://www.fsa.gov.uk/pubs/speeches/at_17mar10.pdf.

Wade, R. (2012) 'Why Has Income Inequality Remained on the Sidelines of Public Policy for so Long?', *The Challenge Magazine*, 56(3) (May/June), pp. 21–50.
Yellen, J.L. (2014) 'Monetary Policy and Financial Stability', The 2014 Michel Camdessus Central Banking Lecture, International Monetary Fund, Washington, DC, 2 July. Available at http://www.federalreserve.gov/newsevents/speech/yellen20140702a.htm.

2
The Emerging Economies and the Great Recession

Ahmad Seyf
Regent's University, London

Abstract: This chapter examines the impact of the recent global crisis on emerging economies and draws a number of policy conclusions. It shows that the impact of the crisis was more pronounced in countries that had initial weaker fundamentals and greater openness to global financial and trade links. It is also revealed that while emerging economies had exhibited some resilience through the early stages of the financial turmoil, they have been hit hard since the mid-2008. While this is partly explained by the collapse in world trade and the sharp drop in commodity prices, this will not tell the full story. Misguided policies in the major economies of the world, especially the USA, produced a dangerous situation in some of the emerging economies, leading to the creation of bubbles. This chapter investigates the transmission mechanisms that seem to be in operation in this regard; and will conclude by offering policy recommendations to the emerging economies to reduce their exposure to external vulnerabilities.

Keywords: Global crisis, Emerging markets, Bubbles, Neoliberalism, Accumulation

JEL Classifications: E12, E24, E44, F02, F33, F42

2.1 Introduction[1]

This chapter examines the impact of the recent global crisis on emerging economies and draws a number of policy conclusions. A distinction must be made between the initial impact and what has been happening ever since the 2008 crisis in these economies. Two issues should be explored further here. First, it is not clear whether the real causes of the crisis have been properly understood by official policy makers and hence policy measures taken at best turned out to be ineffective. Second, related to the first point and in contrast to Baker (2009) who believes that "the story of these financial bubbles is a tale of major institutional failures" (p.3), a lot more than that is in order. It is an inevitable outcome of an economic philosophy – Neoliberalism – that had been dominant and created an environment in which crisis occurred. Given its dominant position in policy-making circles it seems that, denying or not understanding the real causes of the crisis, it is only capable of producing bubbles, thereby, replacing one set of bubbles by another. So the bubbles thus generated expand and burst, leaving at times trillions of dollars of devastation in their wake, and yet the policy makers refuse to appreciate the essential similarity between the first one and the second one and, undoubtedly the third one. The other two pillars of the dominant economic philosophy in the last 40 years are:

- Concurrent with neoliberalism, globalization was encouraged the main function of which was to prepare the ground for the implementation of these policies.
- Lastly, financialization of capitalism intensified. That is to say that the centre of gravity has moved from the production of value in the real sector into speculative transactions in the financial markets and to the generation of rent.

What we faced in 2008, was the collapse of this tripartite economic and business model. Furthermore, the responses to the Great Recession was so far by and large in the same wane.

The bubbles this time – in the post-2008 period – have been generated mainly in the emerging economies. This assertion would be discussed at length in subsequent pages of this chapter. Keynes is right that the 'job is ill-done'.

> ... Speculators may do no harm as bubbles on a steady stream of enterprise. But the position is serious when enterprise becomes the bubble on a whirlpool of speculation. When the capital development of a country becomes a by-product of the activities of a casino, the job is likely to be ill-done... (Keynes, 1936, p. 142)

It is argued in the rest of this chapter that in many countries, 'capital development' has become the 'by-product' of not one but many 'casinos'.

2.2 Phase one: the immediate impact of the financial crisis on emerging economies

Before going any further we need to clarify a number of issues. First, while emerging economies have some common characteristics, it is important to avoid overgeneralization. In other words, country-specific features of these emerging economies should be highlighted for a better understanding of how they might have been affected by the crisis or by post-crisis policies. A few examples may be useful here. China, for instance, has never been in favour of the Washington Consensus and has not followed the neoliberal model. In the post-crisis period, however, this seems to have changed. China has gradually turned itself into the world's largest manufacturing powerhouse. By contrast, from the early 1990s India has promoted a series of liberalization reforms, focusing on services, especially information technologies. This said, however, both followed an export-led growth model. Brazil – as well as other Latin American economies – on the other hand suffered from the so-called 'lost' decade of the 1980s. Brazil, in particular, seems to have worked hard during the presidency of Lula to reverse some of the earlier reforms and while Brazil has become a respectable manufacturing exporter, allocated substantial resources for the growth and development of its agricultural sector. As indicated earlier, two phases should be distinguished.

- February 2007 up to the collapse of Lehman Brothers in September 2008. In this period there is a financial crisis.
- Post-Lehman Brothers collapse, when the financial crisis intensifies to become a fully developed economic crisis, the Great Recession.

Prior to that period, however, rising delinquencies and defaults on subprime mortgages had started to cause some concerns in December 2006. Among others, the New Century Financial Corporation, the second largest subprime mortgage lender, informed investors that it had suffered losses in the final quarter of 2006 and it subsequently declared itself bankrupt in April 2007. However, the Fed, in contrast to market expectation, did not raise its interest rate and very soon the markets appeared to have recovered – indeed, they reached a new high in the spring of 2007. In June 2007 several European banks and investment vehicles became implicated in losses and experienced financing problem as a result (the financial institutions affected included IKB in Germany, and, BNP Paribas in France). The financial turmoil in BNP

Paribas, France's largest bank, sent shock waves of panic in European money markets. By August 2007, it was clear that there was a serious financial crisis at the core of the global financial system. There were three notable developments:

- Central banks interventions began.
- Interest rates started to increase.
- Money markets seized up.

At this stage it appeared unlikely that emerging economies would be affected seriously. Dooley and Hutchinson (2009) have argued in favour of a 'decoupling, recoupling hypothesis', that is, financial markets in the emerging economies were decoupled from the US, not initially affected by it, but " the linkages dramatically re-emerged [recoupled] by late summer or early fall 2008" (p. 14). Llaudes et.al. (2010) offer a more complex set of relationships between the two. At first, they argue for a 'decoupling phase', that is to say emerging economies were no longer dependent on the demand from advanced economies to sustain a robust rate of growth. The next phase they labelled 'recoupling' and this follows the collapse of Lehman Brothers. This collapse triggers panic in the global economic landscape and almost all emerging economies have been seriously affected. The final stage in their analysis is 'a re-decoupling stage' and by this stage they refer to a gap that appeared between the high-vulnerability economies and others. Economies with low to medium vulnerability have almost recovered fully and it is only highly vulnerable emerging economies that remain depressed.

The initial impact of the financial crisis on emerging economies was rather weak, because the structure of financial sectors in these economies, not only in the late summer or early autumn of 2008 but also in the period leading to the financial meltdown, was different from financial sectors in the advanced capitalist economies. These are some of the differences:

- The financial sectors' balance sheets were not exposed to toxic assets in the same way.
- Derivatives were used much less frequently.
- Credit default swaps and collateralized debt obligations were not used as extensively as in the advanced economies. (Boorman, 2009)

When set against this background, from the viewpoint of emerging economies, the global financial crisis has been different in three major ways. First, unlike in any of the previous experiences, the source of the sharp reduction in capital inflows on this occasion has been a severe liquidity squeeze in the financial markets of the developed economies. Indeed, the slowdown in financial flows to the emerging economies followed from the virtual standstill in the credit markets in the USA and the UK, spreading to other major financial markets soon, only to be eased a little while later by quantitative easing and ultra-easy monetary policy. Second, international credit markets seized up. This has had a very serious impact on countries with big current account deficits that relied heavily on international debt to manage the situation. Third, emerging market countries have also witnessed a substantial fall in their exports as the financial crisis turned into an economic crisis hitting consumer spending in the developed world. Hence, given the strong downturn in the global economy, countries have been unable to export their way out of the crisis, even though a large number of countries experienced substantial devaluations of their currencies. It is in this context that easy money – combined with historically low interest rates, central banks allowed cash flows to build up within the banking systems – come to the rescue, but, as we shall see, made the situation even worse.

Emerging economies that had a weak fundamental and enjoyed greater trade and financial linkages were, in general, affected more seriously by these events. The growth of the global economy fell in 2009 by 6 percentage points from its pre-crisis peak and between the 3rd quarter of 2008 and the 1st quarter of 2009, on average the output in emerging economies fell by 4 percentage points. In some emerging economies, especially those in Europe, the real output contracted by 11 per cent between the 3rd quarter of 2008 and the 1st quarter of 2009 (Llaudes et al. 2010, p. 3). Emerging economies that were more open and integrated with the rest of the world were more affected by the ensuing crisis and by contrast, those that had improved policy fundamentals could manage the situation much better and suffered less contraction. In the case of economies, such as China and India which had a much lower growth rate but did not actually shrink and it is here that a decoupling hypothesis has been offered, that is, these economies were no longer dependent on demand from developed economies to sustain robust rate of growth. The IMF, in its initial responses to the Great Recession, advocated the hypothesis of decoupling of the emerging economies from developed economies and referred to emerging economies as the 'new engine of growth' for the world economy (IMF, 2007 and 2010). Ghosh (2013) re-asserted this point and suggested that BRICS have the potential of being a positive force in world affairs – in view of the sluggish growth in the developed economies, this viewpoint was especially significant. This assertion is primarily based on the following factors:

- The potential market size in these economies. This claim needs further clarification as it seems to be mainly based on the size of the population at the expense of ignoring income distribution in these countries. Using the example of India, it is true that, by 2007, forty wealthy Indians were worth a total of over $350 billion, or nearly $9 billion a piece, but at the same time, we also know that "more than three-quarters of the population lives on less than $2 per day" (McNally, 2011a, p. 135). Mexico is a good example too. The country was promised great gains from integration within the NAFTA treaty but "the minimum wage has fallen by 40 percent, the best paid workers have suffered an 18 percent cut in income, hundreds of thousands have been forced off the land; and 80 million people now live below the poverty line" (McNally, 2011a, p. 129). In short, this pattern of income distribution will not create sufficient domestic demand for a healthy growth of the economy.
- Their recent growth rates and greater integration in the globalization process. It is further to be noted that China is the main global exporter of manufacturing goods. India is a significant exporter of services and Brazil and Russia are major producers/exporters of raw materials. This viewpoint, however, seems to ignore the fragility of this model. If the growth in the major economies is not revitalized, hence, an export-led growth model would face serious difficulties in practice as it did happen in 2008. We now know "In the uncertain times in the aftermath of Lehman's bankruptcy global industrial production declined over 20 percent and exports plummeted by over 40 percent causing a 'recoupling' of emerging market countries with advanced economies" (IMF, 2009, p. 5). Bibow (2010, p.4) has shown how the world economy suffered following the financial meltdown in 2009 as compared with the crisis in 2001 or during the Asian crisis of the late 1990s. In all these cases, there was a contraction, but the one occurred in 2008 was by far the most serious. This sharp decline in GDP growth was reflected in global trade causing similar contraction.

ILO (2015, p. 3) shows the relationship between the developed and emerging economies much better. It is true that emerging economies faced a lower growth rate, but did not face a negative growth, whereas in the developed economies, the rate of economic growth turned into negative. My final point here concerns the impact of China. If we exclude China from the emerging economies, the immediate impact of the financial meltdown changes, that is, while the contraction in the emerging markets was by no means as serious as the contraction in the advanced economies, excluding China, these economies suffered negative growth too (UN, 2015, p. 24).

One common feature of the studies by ILO (2015) and UN (2015) is highly relevant. While both studies confirm that there was a recovery in 2010, not only in the emerging economies but also in the developed economies, the growth trend afterwards is downward in both, that is, the average rate of growth not only declined for the developed economy but also for the emerging economies, with or without China.

Let us look at a number of emerging economies and see how seriously they have been impacted during this phase. This section is mainly based on Bibow (2010, pp. 11–25) see also IMF (2010, pp. 25–30).

Let us start with Russia. Following the 1998 crisis, the boom in oil prices helped to increase the Russian current account surplus until 2008; however, when the financial crisis began and the oil price plummeted, there was a sharp decline in surplus. Following the fall in the price of oil, net FDI into the country went negative and there was a fall in foreign reserve as the government tried to protect the value of rubbles which was declining.

In the case of South Africa, ever since 2003, the current account deficits have grown significantly, but large capital inflows helped to finance the deficits. Following the crisis, trade declined and with it there was a fall in the deficits too but capital inflow stopped in the second half of 2008 as well. The rand depreciated very sharply and the authority decided not to intervene to help the national currency.

In Poland, however, trade deficits increased after 2006, but, following the crisis, as Polish imports fell more sharply than exports, trade was in balance by Q1 of 2009. In addition, from mid-2007 capital inflows increased but in the second half of 2008, there was a sharp decline. FDI into Poland declined too. The zloty depreciated very sharply as a result.

In the case of Argentina, there was a positive balance in its trade with the rest of the world in the post-2001 crisis, but as both imports and exports declined in Q4 of 2008, the balance more or less stayed the same. Argentina's financial balance was positive during 2005 to 2007, but in 2008 there was a sharp turn and it became negative. The peso depreciated greatly and the central bank had to utilize some of its reserve in its defence. Up to Q2 of 2009, FDI into Argentina was not affected by the international crisis.

Another Latin American economy that was affected in similar manner was Brazil. Following the 2002 crisis, Brazil developed a healthy positive balance of trade. The decline began in 2007 and turned negative in 2008 primarily because the real had sharply appreciated. Capital inflows into Brazil were maintained at a relatively high rate until the autumn of 2008. Towards the end of 2008, FDI into Brazil held up but portfolio investment stopped almost completely. It may have been for this stoppage that the real started to lose value and some foreign reserves were used to minimize the rate of decline.

For many years, China maintained a pegging arrangement with the dollar, and enjoyed an increasing trade surplus. In the space of six years, China's trade surplus increased from $35 billion in 2002 to more than $426 billion in 2008. When the global crisis began China's exports were seriously affected and declined by about one-third, from $764 billion for the second half of 2008 to $521 billion in the first half of 2009.

India's situation was different and hence it was affected differently by the international crisis. Despite liberalization and economic reforms, India suffered a persistent current account deficit in the 1990s. The current account had a surplus during 2000–04 but went into deficit soon thereafter. As a result of the commodity price boom that happened in 2008, India's current account deficit turned into a small surplus in Q1 of 2009. Portfolio investment sharply declined in Q1 of 2008 and the same pattern was repeated by other forms of investment by non – bank institutions in Q2 of 2008. Decline in capital inflows of different descriptions was translated into a decline in the value of the rupee, requiring intervention by the central bank to stop the rot.

By contrast, Indonesia enjoyed current account surpluses since 1998 and as both its imports and exports were hit by the crisis, the balance did not change much. On the contrary, the financial account of the country had a deficit from 1998 up to 2005. The pre-crisis boom was reflected into a small surplus in these accounts for 2006–07. Currency was pegged with the dollar and its value started to fluctuate in the final quarter of 2008, foreign reserves were used to stabilize the market.

The situation in South Korea was slightly different. Following the earlier crisis in the late 1990s, South Korea enjoyed a current account surplus from 1998 onward which turned into a deficit during the first three quarters of 2008. Towards the end of 2008, as imports declined more than the exports, the current account went into surplus again. Portfolio investment of different descriptions followed a different pattern altogether and by the end of 2008 it suffered a sharp decline. As a result, the won came under severe pressure and sizeable deployment of foreign reserves was not effective to contain the won's sharp depreciation during 2008.

In the case of Malaysia, for the whole period between 1998 and mid-2008, the country enjoyed current account surpluses together with financial account deficits. These deficits worsened sharply after the crisis. By the second half of 2008, most financial inflows into Malaysia declined, causing a sharp depreciation of the ringgit. The central bank had to intervene using foreign reserves to help the currency.

Mexico seemed to have suffered the same fate. Current account deficits, together with financial account surpluses overall – except for the 1995 crisis – resulting in reserve accumulation, characterized Mexico's balance of payments until late-2008. The depreciation of the peso began in the third quarter of 2008 and financial account deficits started to rise in the first half of 2009. Despite the fact that the current account improved in 2009, the pressure on the currency absorbed a sizeable part of the foreign currency reserves of the country.

The Philippines, on the other hand, enjoyed surpluses on current and financial accounts enabling a sizeable foreign currency reserves to be accumulated. However, financial inflows started to decline in the final quarter of 2007 and continued during the second quarter of 2008, turning into deficit in the final quarter of 2008. Like other emerging economies, the national currency, peso, depreciated sharply requiring intervention by the central bank of Philippines.

The pattern in Turkey was similar to that in many other emerging economies. Persistent current account deficits from 2003 onwards were more than offset by capital inflow allowing the country to accumulate a modest level of foreign reserves. Following the financial crisis, Turkish trade declined, imports fell by more than exports, hence current account deficits improved slightly. In the fourth quarter of 2008 financial account worsened sharply as financial inflows almost stopped and the lira depreciated. From 2009 onwards, the FDI into Turkey also started to decline.

The overall picture emerging from these findings as above confirms that emerging markets experienced the repercussions of the crisis at the core of global finance largely as a common event, a sudden stop or reversal in private capital flows that was hitting countries in a quite indiscriminate manner, even countries that had appeared to be in a 'sound and safe' position due to reduced external vulnerabilities. As to the composition of capital flows, the current crisis has also confirmed that foreign direct investment as compared with portfolio investment of different descriptions is relatively more stable and less volatile.

All countries experienced sudden stops or reversals in portfolio inflows at some point, but portfolio outflows naturally only played a role in cases that had liberalized this category.

2.3 Phase two: the emerging economies and the Great Recession

In addition to the crisis itself, how have the emerging economies been affected by policies and developments in the epicentres of the financial crisis, namely, the USA and the rest of the main capitalist economies in Europe?

By contrast to previous crises affecting these countries, the Great Recession is distinctly different. In most cases in the last fifty years, the financial crisis began in these economies, whether the East Asian crisis of the late 1990s or the collapse of Argentina in 2001. There were, of course, many cases in which the crises began in the developed economies, such as the saving and loans crisis in the USA in the early 1980s and dot.com bubble burst of 2001, but, on this occasion, the Great Recession is exogenous to the emerging market and other developing economies. Hence it is important to study the transmission mechanism. As we shall see later, different researchers seem to suggest different transmission mechanisms.

First, let me give some indications of the scale of the recession. McNally (2011b) asserts that "the Great Recession was the deepest and longest decline experienced by global capitalism since the catastrophic collapse of 1929–33. The 30 large economies of the Organization for Economic Cooperation and Development (OECD) underwent a 6 per cent contraction in Gross Domestic Product (GDP) with jobless rates jumping two-thirds higher on average. World industrial output fell 13 per cent, international trade dropped by 20 per cent; global stock market plunged 50 percent" (p. 37).

Other sources give different picture of the situation. WTO (2009) stated that global trade declined by 9 per cent in 2009.[2] Asmundson et al. (2011) seems to give a higher rate of decline of global trade as does Bibow (2010, p. 5).

For some countries the fall in exports in 2009 was greater than 40 per cent (ibid., p. 5). It is true that in the previous two decades prior to the crisis of 2007, these economies had faced either currency or financial crisis. The crisis in the East Asian economies in the late 1990s or Argentina in 2001 are just two examples of this. While the impact on affected economies may have been different, the timetables of the crises appeared to be very similar. A sudden stop of capital flows was usually followed by a sharp contraction in economic activities. However as their currencies faced serious devaluation in the process, it created further limitation by enlarging the burden of debt in foreign currencies. Yet this also helped them to recover from the crisis. In previous cases, these countries were able to increase their net exports to compensate for the contractionary impact of foreign currency liabilities following serious devaluations. The current situation is different in at least two major ways. Firstly, the reason for the sharp reduction in capital inflows has been the emergence of a credit crunch in the financial markets of major capitalist economies and this situation was not present in previous crises. This channel was particularly influential in countries that ran up dangerously large current account deficits and took on substantial international debt. Secondly the contraction in the major capitalist economies, the USA and the main European economies meant that the emerging economies exports to these markets faced severe decline. To put it differently, despite depreciation, the emerging economies were unable to enhance exports as a mechanism to get out of the crisis.

So far the above argument illustrates two main transmission mechanisms of the crisis to emerging economies; one being the trade channel and the other the financial channel. Other transmission channels have been at work too. One was the withdrawal of funds by some of the major financial institutions from their subsidiaries located in the emerging markets. These institutions needed to rebuild their capital base and this has constrained the available funds for other purposes. Another equally powerful channel was the impact of the crisis on economic activity, namely in the USA and Europe which manifested itself in a sharp contraction in exports from emerging economies. Initially the fall was seen mainly in manufacturing exports but it soon affected the inter-emerging economies trading too. Emerging economies providing raw and intermediate goods for Chinese industries, for instance, have been negatively affected too as Chinese exports began to be affected by the contraction in the USA and Europe.

Another channel worth remembering is remittances, which is an important source of income (and especially foreign exchange) in many emerging economies. In addition, the return of workers from abroad could put extra pressure on these regions as these workers would seek employment in already depressed economies.

The crisis began in the USA and spread quickly to Europe and the rest of the world, affecting both financial systems and other economic activities. Up to mid-2008 the decoupling hypothesis had currency as the main argument among many commentators and market players alike. The IMF, among others (2007, 2010), was a major advocate of this hypothesis.

It is generally agreed (Ocampo, 2009) that for most of the emerging economies, the period of 2003–07 represented a period of significant improvement in their external balance sheet. Furthermore, these improvements in practice led to relatively weaker financial links. Hence, the decoupling hypothesis is supposed to be supported by evidence (IMF, 2010; Naude, 2009; Fidrmuc and Korhonen, 2009; Dooley and Hutchison, 2009). The improvement in the external balance was caused primarily by:

- High commodity prices.
- Booming international trade.
- Exceptional financing conditions.
- High levels of remittances.

All these turned negative before the crisis in September 2008 and the rate of deterioration accelerated substantially after the crisis. This trend was so strong that Ocampo (2009) went as far as to suggest that "decoupling proved, in the end, to be a mirage" (p. 705). Khor (2009) also pointed that out for many Asian economies, "there has been a sudden and steep fall in manufacturing exports, the fall being 30 to 50% in many Asian countries" (p. 1). Then there was the fall in demand, prices and export earnings for commodities too. On average, immediately after the crisis the price of food declined by 29 per cent and non-food agricultural products by 44 per cent compared to a year earlier. The largest decline was witnessed in the average price of metals, which declined by 56 per cent (ibid., p. 1). Remittances remain a major source of funds for many developing and emerging countries. They exceed official development assistance and, even with the exception of China, foreign direct investment. They are much less volatile than other sources of funding, such as private debt or even portfolio capital flows. Given the size and the fact that remittances are more stable than other types of capital flows, they can enhance the recipient country's sovereign credit rating which can, in turn, have beneficial impact by lowering borrowing costs. However, the available data[3] seem to show that out of 175 countries about which we have data, the remittances declined in 2009 in 112 countries compared with 2008. To examine this issue further, a sample of 17 emerging countries is utilized and it is only in Mexico and Brazil and Poland that we witness a declining trend in remittances. Whatever the immediate impact of the crisis on remittances, this source of funding has recovered and continued to grow for most of these emerging countries in the subsequent five years.

Using the same sample, the impact on FDI into these economies is examined. With the exception of Philippines, the immediate impact of the crisis in 2008 was a fall in the flow of FDI in all. Even by 2013, India, Pakistan and Turkey had not reached the levels of FDI inflows that they had achieved in 2008. In most of these countries, the situation improved in 2010. China and Brazil, however, continued to attract larger amounts of foreign direct investment; FDI in China almost doubled between 2008 and 2013. However, the immediate impact of the financial crisis was the inflows of FDI declined in all these countries, as can be seen from Figure 2.1. The exception is Philippines, which, attracted slightly more in 2009 than in 2008.

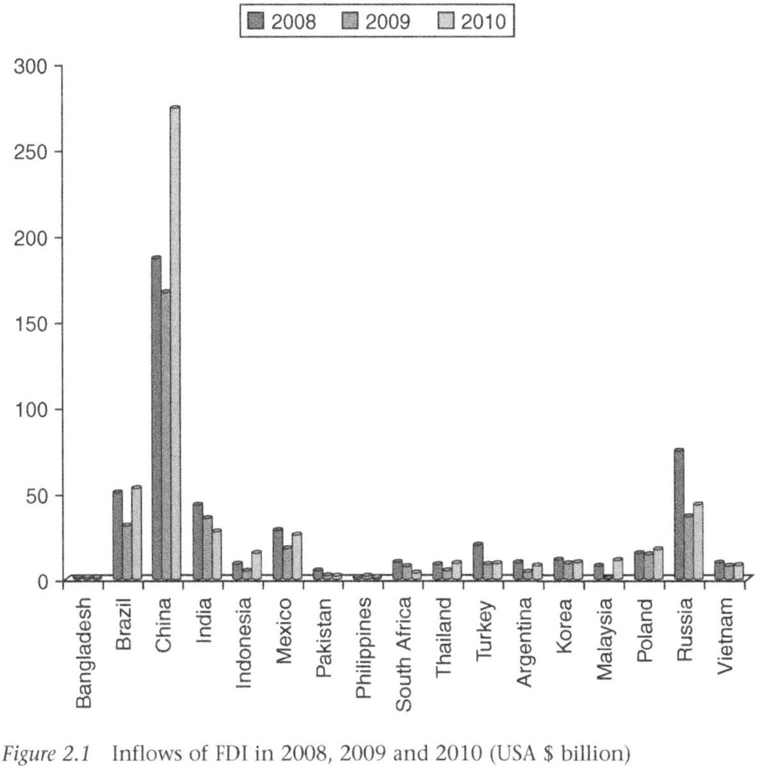

Figure 2.1 Inflows of FDI in 2008, 2009 and 2010 (USA $ billion)
Source: World Bank; available at: http://data.worldbank.org/indicator/BX.TRF.PWKR.CD.DT.

The situation regarding portfolio investment is totally different and inflows are much more volatile. The situation in four of the five BRICS countries is interesting. Brazil, India, Russia and South Africa suffered from a negative net inflow in 2008, but the following year the situation in these countries changed dramatically. Brazil attracted more than $37 billion while India's net inflows approached nearly $25 billion and South Africa also enjoyed net inflows of nearly $9.5 billion. The inflows of portfolio equity to China have also increased sharply in 2009.[4] The changes in current account balances in these countries are revealing too. To see the immediate impact of the financial crisis on these countries' external balance, Figure 2.2 shows how the net current account balance has changed in 2009 and 2010.

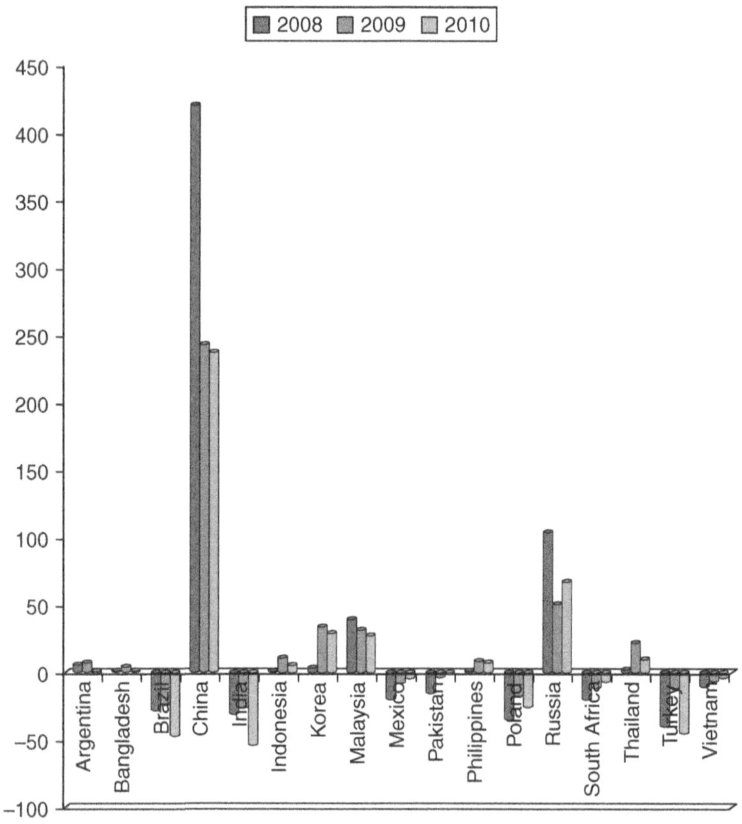

Figure 2.2 Changes in net current account balances in 2008, 2009 and 2010
Source: World Bank; available at: http://data.worldbank.org/indicator/BX.TRF.PWKR.CD.DT.

Two issues are interesting here. One, China's massive trade surplus declines sharply and two, for deficits countries; it seems that an overall decline in global trade in 2009 reduced their deficits too but for most of them, the deficits increased for 2010. However, looking at the percentage changes in the export of good and services, we can see from Figure 2.3 that China's exports seemed to have declined by more than 10 per cent in 2009 as a direct result of global financial crisis.

As can be seen from Figure 2.3, Argentina, Brazil, Malaysia, Mexico, South Africa, Russia, and Thailand all suffered larger falls than China in their exports in 2009. But for 2010, judging by these changes, the growth of exports resumed.

For the first year after the crisis, there was a general consensus among western leaders as to what should be done. It appeared as if there was a change in the direction of economic policy making and almost all these economies turned to utilize a Keynesian-style policy, that is, the debt financing of expansionary fiscal policies. For reasons discussed later, soon there was a U turn and most of these countries went for austerity and utilized effectively deflationary monetary policies. First in Europe and then in the USA a move towards austerity started. It may

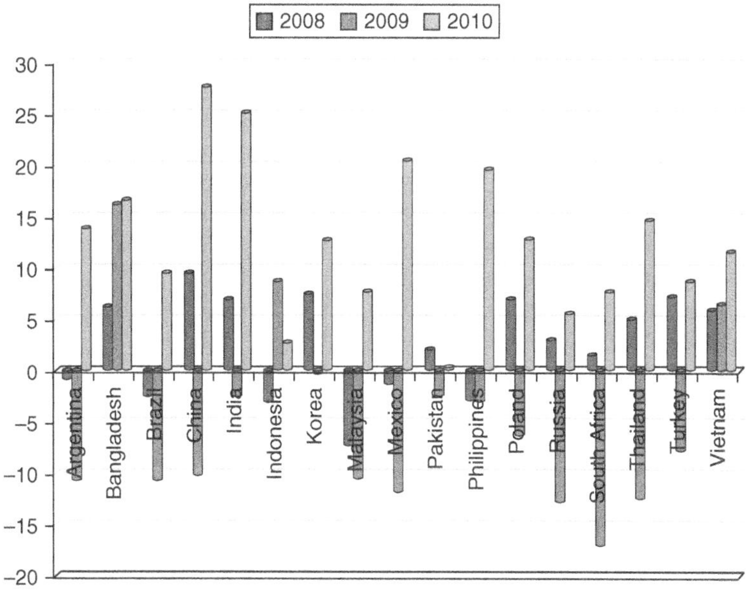

Figure 2.3 Percentage change in export of goods and services
Source: IMF (2015).

not look that way, but it seems as if these measures were tougher in the USA than elsewhere. As a matter of fact, the USA had tightened its structural budget position by 4.9 per cent of GDP between 2010 and 2013. By contrast, the UK tightened its fiscal policy by 3.7 per cent of GDP over the three years, and Italy and Spain tightened by 2.8 per cent and 4.2 per cent of GDP respectively (Bishop, 2013 see also McNally, 2011b, p. 47; Hersh, 2013). Hersh (op. cit.) believes that 2010 midterm elections paved the way for a change in the direction of fiscal policy in the USA. The 2009 American Recovery and Reinvestment Act have been practically replaced by a path of spending cuts and fiscal contraction. Furthermore, McNally (2011b) points out that on top of the proposed cuts in federal spending, tens of billions more are being chopped at state levels, where spending dropped by 7.3 per cent in the 2010 fiscal year. He went on to add that "California has cut health insurance for 900,000 poor children, and the state of Michigan has ordered Detroit to close half its schools" (p. 47). The outcome of this change of direction was slow growth, which turned into negative economic growth in most of these countries. While some researchers blame this change of direction as the main cause of the prolonged recession Akyüz (2014) suggested a different linkage. He argued that debt overhang should have been removed but nothing along this suggestion has been undertaken. In his view, at least part of the debt should have been written down to avoid deflation. Krugman (1988, p. 2) defined debt overhang as the presence of an existing, 'inherited' debt sufficiently large that creditors do not expect with confidence to be fully repaid. Generally speaking, debt overhang refers to a situation where there is a very high level of debts and this could be the case for individuals, corporations and even states. In the case of corporations, their market value could be affected and it is also possible that they may not have enough incentives to expand their activities as the potential benefits of expansion is likely to go to the creditors rather than the shareholders. It is also likely that financial markets may assess this situation rather negatively and be unwilling to lend more. However, as indicated earlier most governments decided to bail out creditor banks, and at the same time enforce austerity on the economy at large. Morris (2008) makes the same point but in a different way. In his view the bailouts perpetuated a standard misconception that prevailed about the credit bubble. It was treated as if this was a 'liquidity' problem whereas many of these bailed out institutions suffered from a 'solvency' problem – that is, they went bankrupt and should have been restructured but instead mostly were injected with more liquidity to play with. There is little evidence showing that this mistaken view has been set aside and a more constructive approach has been utilized. In the post-2008 years, the United States, Japan, and Britain have been injecting trillions of dollars' worth of liquidity into their economies to try to boost recovery and growth. The theoretical argument goes as follows: asset purchases, also known as 'Quantitative Easing', will boost banks' balance sheets, increase liquidity and encourage more lending. This will, in turn, boost spending, growth and create jobs. We also know that in order to encourage this chain of events, all these countries have implemented a loose monetary policy of ultralow interest rates. In contrast to expectations, this policy resulted in an outflow of hot money, chasing better returns around the globe, especially in some emerging economies, which causes asset price bubbles and distorts exchange rates; in some cases, as in South Korea and Malaysia it led to the appreciation of their currencies with inevitable negative consequences for their exports.

On the other hand other researchers offered alternative views on assessing the impact. In this version, the recession ended by the end of 2009 and the situation in the emerging markets was particularly encouraging. IMF (2014) believes "emerging economies are transitioning to more sustainable growth in the financial sector, while addressing macroeconomic vulnerabilities amid a less favourable external financial environment" (p. ix). This sense of optimism that prevails in relation to emerging economies is not right. As discussed above, none of the structural shortcomings of global capitalism has been addressed and hence, instead of creating a bubble at the centre, many bubbles have been generated in many of the peripheries, China included. Whitehouse (2014) writing for Bloomberg pointed out "At a time when consumers and governments in the U.S. and Europe have been trying – with limited success – to pare down or at least stabilize their debt burdens, China has been doing the opposite. Over the past five years, it has pumped more than $13 trillion of credit into its economy, in an effort to keep its growth rate up amid a weak global recovery." This point will be discussed further later, but it suffices to say that the growth of debt in China in the last five years has been truly exceptional. As Buttiglione et al. (2014) have shown, since 2008, Chinese total debt (excluding financial institutions' debt) has increased by a stunning 72 per cent of GDP, or 14 per cent per year, a shift almost double that experienced by the US and UK in the six years that preceded the beginning of their financial crisis in 2008 (p. 68).

As a consequence, China is facing a poisonous combination of high, fast growing leverage and slowing nominal GDP growth. This suggests, in turn, that in future growing difficulties in servicing and repaying debt in a number of sectors are likely. These difficulties might be exacerbated by the fact that market rates are likely to increase as a consequence of ongoing financial reforms.

In contrast to the views expressed by many researchers, many of the structural causes of the financial meltdown have not been addressed. Hence, what is witnessed in many emerging economies, especially as a response to the Great Recession, is a repeat of what we had witnessed in the immediate years before the last crisis. Instead of addressing these structural issues to ensure that we would enter into a steady and, sustainable growth path, one set of bubbles is being replaced by another. It is only a matter of time that these new bubbles would burst and another round of contractions and sharp decline will ensue.

We offer three reasons for this:

1. Systemic financial instability has not been dealt with.
2. Growing inequality and unsustainable balance of payments positions are maintained.
3. Misguided policies pursued in response to the crisis in the USA and Europe.

Instead of removing the debt overhang and restructuring the financial sector, creditor banks have been bailed out at enormous costs to the tax payers. To give an idea about the size of open and hidden 'bail out', the Fed in particular provided more than $16 trillion loans to various financial institutions, not only in the USA but in the world at large. Table 2.1 gives details of these loans.

Despite all these financial facilities, in most countries – affected by the crisis – austerity has been imposed. The fact that Quantitative Easing is still being used by central bankers in the main developed economies – the latest a the time of writing this piece, was the announcement by the ECB for 1.1 trillion Euros programme – confirms my view that a serious problem of insolvency is being mixed up with problem of liquidity. At the same time in many economies that suffer from recession public expenditure cuts have been imposed, which, among other things, widened deflationary gaps in these economies. To the best of my knowledge, nothing serious has been undertaken to reduce the growing income and wealth inequalities in these economies. For instance, in the USA between 2009 and 2011 while the income of the bottom 99 per cent shrunk by 0.4 per cent; the income of the the top 1 per cent grew by 11.2 per cent. The households in the middle now have lower

Table 2.1 Institutions with largest total transaction amounts (not term-adjusted) across broad-based emergency programmes (borrowing aggregated by parent company and includes sponsored ABCP* conduits), 1 December 2007 to 21 July 2010

Borrowing parent company	**US$ billion Total loans**
Citigroup Inc.	2513
Morgan Stanley	2041
Merrill Lynch & Co.	1949
Bank of America Corporation	1344
Barclays PLC (UK)	868
Bear Stearns Companies, Inc.	853
Goldman Sachs Group Inc.	814
Royal Bank Of Scotland Group PLC (UK)	541
Deutsche Bank AG (Germany)	354
UBS AG (Switzerland)	287
JP Morgan Chase & Co.	391
Credit Suisse Group AG (Switzerland)	262
Lehman Brothers Holdings Inc.	183
Bank of Scotland PLC (UK)	181
BNP Paribas SA (France)	175
Wells Fargo & Co.	159
Dexia SA (Belgium)	159
Wachovia Corporation	142
Dresdner Bank AG (Germany)	135
Societe Generale SA (France)	124
All other borrowers	2639
Total	16115

Note: *ABCP refers to commercial paper issued by a special purpose vehicle, or conduit created to purchase asset-backed securities, such as mortgage-backed securities or securities backed by other types of receivables.
Source: Table 8, United States Government Accountability Office (2011, p. 131).

real incomes than they did in 1996 and this is slowing the recovery by holding back aggregate spending (Akyüz, 2014). An initial policy of reflation soon was replaced by fiscal austerity and deflation in many countries to be supplemented by an unconventional monetary policy, zero-bound interest rates policy and quantitative easing later.

This combination of policies has not been effective in easing the debt overhang and has failed to stimulate spending. In places, namely in the emerging economies, which, may have extra spending, this has been mainly debt-financed, that is, this situation reflects an explosion of debt of a different description. The end result is that it has increased the level of financial fragility everywhere. It is true that the USA, as the main initiator of this policy, appears to perform slightly better than the main European economies, but it is not safe either. Two points should be made here. First, there is no doubt that this policy cannot continue indefinitely. Second, it is not clear what the Fed's exit strategy is and how it could be implemented without causing too much disruption in the financial markets. We now know what happened to the currencies of emerging economies, with one or two exceptions, when in May 2013 the Fed signalled its intention to unwind its unconventional monetary policy and reduce the monthly injection of $85 billion by $10 billion-tapering. This led to the emergence of serious problems in many emerging economies, including greater external vulnerability. It is clear the monthly asset purchase of $85 billion did not create growth in the USA, but there is ample evidence that this might have contributed significantly to create financial bubbles in the emerging economies. It is estimated that since the beginning of the policy of quantitative easing in 2009, the Fed has pumped nearly $7 trillion of foreign funds into emerging economies – mostly in the shape of "hot" money into speculative activities. The inflows tended to appreciate local currencies and when the flight began and outflow intensified, local currencies suffered severe depreciation. Following the announcement by the Fed, in Brazil, Turkey, Indonesia and India, currencies lost between 8 and 20 per cent of their value in a very short space of time. In Brazil, the government spent $60 billion to stop the rot in the value of the Real and others have taken similar measures to control the situation (Grey, 2013).

In both cases, there have been unfavourable economic consequences. Inflationary pressure and asset bubbles are two known impacts that would be explored later. One side effect of this was that it demolished the hypothesis that emerging markets have decoupled from the developed economies and have become a new engine for global economic growth. The growth surge in the emerging markets before the crisis was driven mainly by exceptional but unsustainable global economic conditions closely linked with – and fuelled by – credit- and debt-led consumption bubbles in the main economies of the West. Likewise, their supposed recovery after 2009 was by and large driven by bubbles too, but this time in emerging economies. With minor exceptions, the medium and long-term prospects look bleak primarily because the USA and Europe failed to establish conditions for robust and stable growth. My earlier comment about the declining global economic trend is, in fact, a proof that this package is not working.

As for the emerging economies, before this is too late, they must embark upon policies to reduce their unhealthy dependence on foreign markets and foreign capital, especially speculative hot money. After the bounce-back in 2010, growth has started faltering almost everywhere (see ILO (2015), UN (2015) for the post-2010 trend). The measures taken by policy makers in the epicentres of the financial crisis may have prevented a banking collapse hence ending the financial crisis but not the economic crisis and the Great Recession. The economic crisis is alive and kicking. China's policy response to the crisis through massive investment in infrastructure and property to offset the decline of its exports to advanced economies provided a major boost to commodity exporters. As indicated above, China's exports declined by more than 10 per cent in 2009 and the trade surplus plummeted by 42 per cent – from $421 billion in 2008 to $243 billion a year later. For the subsequent five years this level of trade surplus has not been achieved. The main driver for the massive stimulus plan seems to have been concerns about the sluggishness in foreign markets. However, there is a serious concern that it could have been implemented more wisely avoiding unnecessary risks. But first, why we should be concerned about the health of the Chinese economy? Barnett's (2014) chart showing the contributions of various economies to world's GDP is interesting and revealing. On the face of it from 2001 – with one exception – China has been making a bigger contribution to global growth than the USA and this situation is unlikely to change over the course of the next few years. Given this evidence, it seems safe to suggest that if China does not 'feel well' it could potentially contribute to lower growth for the rest of the world.

Having this point in mind, it is worth remembering that China could not continue to fill its demand gap with investment. The increasing inequality in income distribution and wealth must be addressed too. The share of labour in relation to the GDP continues to fall, reaching 37 per cent in 2005, declining from 50 per cent of GDP in 1990 (McNally, 2011a, p. 57). Hilary (2013, p. 19), confirming the trend, gives slightly different figures; in his account it fell from 53 per cent to 41.4 per cent in the years between 1998 and 2005. Too much investment would inevitably lead to excess capacity and further, as a large portion of these investments are debt financed, in view of sluggish external demand, over indebtedness could backfire before long. One important factor that fuels debt-led consumption and mercantilist growth models is that this declining trend of labour share in the national income has been globalized. In Latin America and the Caribbean, for instance, the share of income going to wage decreased by 13 percentage points in just ten years, while similar declines were also experienced in Asia (10 per cent), and the industrialized North (9 per cent). The Euro Area countries experienced a 10 per cent decline between 1980 and 2000. In the case of Mexico the decline was from an average of 38.5 per cent in 1980–85 to just 29.9 per cent in 2004–07 (Hilary, 2013, pp. 17–18). My main conclusion so far is rather simple and straightforward. A sustainable post-crisis growth model can neither rely on the 'debt-led consumption boom' nor on the 'export-led mercantilist' models of the past. Tackling the global distribution problem is thus fundamental if the Great Recession is to be effectively tackled.

2.4 Bubbles, bubbles, and more bubbles

This section offers, a brief analysis of the bubbles that have been created in a number of emerging economies. As with all bubbles, the issue is not whether these bubbles would burst- but, rather, when we would face another phase of a serious global crisis, especially as China seems to be suffering from these bubbles too. Indeed, let me turn first to consider the case of China.

2.4.1 Bubbles in China

This particular economic bubble began in the emerging economies in 2009. Its main driver was China's aggressive credit-driven infrastructure-based growth strategy to boost its economy during the financial crisis. The implementation of this policy led to a global raw material boom that generated, in turn, a windfall for commodities exporting countries, mainly emerging markets and Australia. This boom began to attract the attention of global investors who were keen to diversify away from the depressed markets in the advanced capitalist economies that were at the epicentre of the ongoing financial crisis. Two further factors contributed to the growth of the bubble:

- Rock-bottom interest rates in the USA, Europe and Japan.
- According to the IMF (2014) "ultra-loose monetary policy" and" unconventional monetary policy" (p. 4) are being used. But, the impact of this policy is revealing. Colombo (2014b) has pointed out that "Extremely low interest rates in the West and Japan, combined with the U.S. Federal Reserve's multi-trillion dollar quantitative easing or QE programs resulted in a $4 trillion torrent of speculative "hot money" that flowed into emerging market investments from 2009 to 2013".

The mechanism was simple. Borrow at low interest rates from the USA and Japan markets and 'invest' in high-yielding emerging market assets.

Demand for emerging markets assets soared leading to bigger bond bubbles, and cheap borrowing encouraged debt-driven infrastructure booms. What we witness in many emerging countries is an alarming credit growth combined with an equally dangerous property price bubble. In the case of China, in the past five years the total assets of Chinese bank have exploded by an unprecedented $15.4 trillion – some two and a half times the GDP of the country – whereas the total assets of the Big 4 Central Banks combined - Fed, ECB, BOJ, and BOE – stood at only $9.8 trillion![5]

It is worrying that China's total debt – government, non-financial corporate, household, and financial sectors – has quadrupled from $7.4 trillion in 2007 to $28.2 trillion in mid-2014, with this latter figure representing 282 per cent of GDP. The Chinese economy has added $20.8 trillion of new debt since 2007, which represents more than one-third of global growth in debt. The largest driver of this growth has been borrowing by non-financial corporations, including property developers. What is worrying about China's debt, in addition to a sharp rise in the overall level of debt, is the spectacular growth of corporate debt in China, which as a percentage of the GDP – 125 per cent – is one of the highest in the world. The debt of financial institutions, which stood at just 7 per cent of GDP in 2000, jumped to 65 per cent of GDP in 2014. Government's debt, which stood at 23 per cent of GDP in 2000, has almost tripled by 2014, reaching 66 per cent of GDP (McKinsey Global Institute, 2015, p. 75). Regarding the emergence and development of the financial bubble in China, there are at least three areas of concern:

- More than half of the entire new loan is linked with the real estate market.
- Unregulated and rapidly growing shadow banking accounts for 30 per cent of new lending.
- Rapid growth in lending to local government financial vehicles, many of which may struggle to repay the loans.

One writer on China, Curran (2015) pointed out the following issues, " – among the risks, bad loans, overpriced stock and a frothy property market are flashing danger from China's economy and putting pressure on a fragile financial system – similar to conditions that triggered Japan's fall". While the debt-driven programme has certainly helped the economy, it is quite likely that it has increased the fragility of the financial system. Overall, there is a real concern about the health of China's economy. For instance, a poll of global investors in 2011, reported by Bloomberg, produced worrying results. 45 per cent say they expect a financial crisis within the next five years and an additional 40 per cent anticipate a Chinese crisis after 2016. Lynch (2011) claimed that there is 'a speculative credit-driven bubble that cannot be sustained' and this view in supported by 53 per cent but China's neighbours seem more concerned and 60 per cent of Asia-based respondents agree with this proposition. The suggestion that China may be suffering from a financial bubble is nothing new. Hung (2011) pointed out that the Chinese Academy of Social Science had warned in 2007 that "China was witnessing an unsustainable expansion of an asset bubble reminiscent of what Japan experienced in the 1980s" (p. 217). In the same year the Chinese Premier admitted that development path in China was "unstable, unbalanced, uncoordinated and unsustainable" (ibid., p. 217). As a response to this unsavoury situation intensified by global financial crisis and the collapse of Chinese exports, the government implemented one of the largest stimulus programmes in the world, $586 billion over two years or around 15 per cent of the GDP (World Bank, 2010; Naughton, 2008, p. 2; Moyo, 2012, p. 7).[6]

While this stimulus programme may have prevented a financial collapse, it, nevertheless, failed to address the fundamental and structural problems of the economy. But what are these structural problems? Hung (2011) asserted that in 2006, more than 75 per cent of China's industries were plagued by overcapacity and the case for there being overinvestment was already strong in 2005 (p. 219). Weak intersectoral and geographical mobility exacerbated this problem. State-owned banks contributed to this problem too by lax lending practices. These banks offered easy credit to "insolvent or profligate state-owned industrial enterprises, of which roughly 40 per cent incurred losses in 2006" (ibid., p. 219). Private enterprises were not treated in the same way. One possible reason why state-owned banks used lax lending practices was to maintain social and political stability by delaying massive layoffs. Related to my earlier point about the maladjusted economic structure in the emerging markets, let me take this issue a little further by looking closer at China. Actually, China suffers from two serious structural problems.

- Industrial overcapacity and overinvestment (Roberts, 2013; EUCCC, 2009; Qinglian, 2015).
- Underconsumption (Freeman, 2013; Fung, 2015)

Other East Asian economies at a similar stage of development, while not allowing the emergence of independent labour unions, used widespread pre-emptive redistribution policies, such as:

- Land reform.
- Provision of free education.

As a result, there was less unequal income distribution. This applies to pre-1997 crisis as in the post-crisis years, inequality has increased in these economies (Singh and Singh, 2014; Feng, 2011; Zhuang et al., 2014; Page, 1994).

These measures:

- Helped create sizeable domestic markets (Jomo, 2006, Page 1994).
- Buffered them against the vagaries of the world market.

China has not done anything of this kind. Class, urban - rural and regional inequalities expanded hand in hand with the economic miracle. Poverty in the rural area increased[7] and there was extensive unemployment. Export-oriented capital created jobs, but, jobs disappeared faster from battered state-owned factories, hence, high rural unemployment resulted. The growth of wages in China was much slower than other economies in Asia. While the Gini coefficient declined significantly in Taiwan, for instance – from nearly 0.6 during 1950s to 0.3–0.4 in the 1970s – it went up in China from 0.33 in 1980 to 0.45 in 2007 (Hung, 2011, p. 221). Yu Xie (2012) has given astonishing estimates of Gini coefficients in China, 0.675 for the rural China and 0.655 for the urban population (p. 72). Whatever the actual magnitude of the Gini coefficients in China, the rising trend is not debatable. However, this led, in turn, to a decline in share of consumption in the GDP, being less than 40 per cent and dropping since 2004. At the same time, the share of investment, which was around 40 per cent, went up to 45 per cent in 2009 (Hung, 2011, p. 221). The combination of overinvestment and underconsumption has increased China's dependence on foreign demand. Any prolonged recession in the rest of the world is bound to depress China's growth prospect further. The vulnerability of this structure stems from the fact that a big chunk of this investment is debt financed. Further, the combination of underconsumption and overinvestment and overcapacity tend to lower the rate of profit and potentially lead to economic crisis. In the case of China, the crisis has not yet happened. How can we explain this paradox? Two possible explanations are offered:

- Bubble-driven investment in the real estates.
- China tried to maintain its global competitiveness by not allowing much of their gains to improve the living standards, and the consumption power of the working class.

More profits in China led to more corporate savings instead of wage increases for their employees, but excess industrial capacity, gluts and sluggish consumption growth is almost certain to lead to falling prices, which would, in turn, narrow down the profit margins. Up to 2008, debt-financed consumption in the USA and a few other economies helped to maintain this vulnerable model. But the situation has changed now and it seems as if emerging economies, like China, must perform this function too as global demand is not large enough to sustain it. Higher revenue for the state enabled it to bail out the state banks and state enterprises. Large foreign reserves eased credit expansion in the banking sector leading to more debt-financed investment which, ended up, in turn, building more excess production capacity. So long as debt – led consumption was practiced in the advanced capitalist economies – with the exception of Germany – exports from China surged, surging investment. Germany, however, like China by supressing domestic wage growth employed a mercantilist model with its Euro Area neighbours (Lapavitsas et. al. 2012). On the eve of the Great Recession, China's economy may be described as high and ever-increasing dependence on export and debt-financed investment on the one hand, and low domestic consumption on the other. An equally important structural problem in China was its heavy dependence on the USA, to the extent that more than 30 per cent of China's exports used to go to the USA. The serious shortcoming of the China's development model is its hyper-growth of exports at the expense of the sluggishness of its domestic consumption. The use of foreign reserves to buy US debt is not for its high returns, but is mainly due to a deliberate policy by Asian central banks to finance USA's escalating current account deficit to secure the continuous increase in USA demand for their exports. In short, if anything was to happen in the USA, this engine would halt and this is precisely what happened in 2008. To put it differently, China is, in fact, in a 'dollar trap', that is, it has no choice but purchasing US debts and other dollar assets, hence – perpetuating the hegemonic role of the dollar with all the problems that it entails for the global economy. In post-2008, in addition to a fall in export, yuan appreciated too, hence profitability of China's export sector – by far the most important sector of the economy – was negatively affected. In late 2008 and in 2009, exports declined further. In response to this situation in November 2008, a $570 billion stimulus package was launched. The hope was it would be mainly on social spending, medical insurance and social security, but only 20 per cent was earmarked for these sectors (Hung, 2011, p. 225) and most of it went into investment in capital assets in sectors already suffering from excess capacity. Yu (2010) estimated the size of the stimulus at $580 billion and added that there was an expansionary monetary policy too. Furthermore, local governments across the country also implemented expansionary packages and, according to Yu, the total value was 18 trillion yuan, about $2610 billion or 63 per cent of the GDP (p. 12). This massive stimulus plan, while preventing a collapse of the economy, failed to rebalance the structure and promote domestic consumption. This plan turned out to be a massive state-led investment to expand productive capacity further, while waiting for export markets to pick up. In the short term, the plan seemed useful but the difficulty is more than 90 per cent of GDP growth in 2009 was solely driven by fixed asset investment which was by and large financed by loan explosion and government spending. Data for 2010 shows the same trend, as fixed investment growth exceeded 23 per cent while overall GDP grew only 10.3 per cent (Hung, 2011, p. 227). Most of these investments are of low quality with dubious profitability. While domestic consumption and export's shares in GDP declined there was an upsurge in the share of fixed asset investment. The last time that China enjoyed a double-digit growth was in 2010, but since then there has been a declining trend in growth. It could have been a lot worse had there not been the massive stimulus programme. That may be true, but the way it is being conducted could prove to be a disaster for China and also for the world economy at large. It is quite possible that the growth rate would fall further as fiscal deficits and non-performing loans start to bite. The problem could be exacerbated by extra overcapacity created by the stimulus package. As part of the monetary expansion, the Central Bank – the People's Bank – of China cut the interest rate and relaxed bank reserve requirements to make more credit available. Financial deleveraging – deliberate policy to reduce the growth of debt – has been set aside and put on hold. In addition to the factors just mentioned, over the next few years, China's growth rate is likely to deteriorate further by:

- Lack of a new engine of growth.
- Bubble in the real estate sector.

While in the USA a declining manufacturing sector works at 80 per cent of capacity, China is currently operating at 70 per cent (Minxin, 2015). What this means is Chinese manufacturing firms will not return to financial health unless the demand for Chinese goods increases sufficiently to fill and then go beyond this 10 per cent gap. This is unlikely to happen as Chinese export markets, are in poor shape, with the European Union deeply in crisis and the USA not as proactive as it had been in the pre-crisis period. At present, the internal demand is insufficient to replace foreign demand. In 2013 investment accounted for 54 per cent of the GDP growth and represented about 50 per cent of the national economy. In line with overcapacity, the rise in investment continued and as shown by Yu (2010, p. 22), in 2008, it was slightly less than 50 per cent of GDP. This is particularly troublesome as Chinese export markets are not expanding. Hence, sooner or later, this rising excess capacity would have to be reduced which could turn into a serious crisis.

Yu (2010) has also shown that the share of investment which was about 25 per cent of GDP in 2001 increased to nearly 50 per cent over the course of just seven years (p. 22). Household consumption, on the other hand, makes about 40 per cent and any attempt to move towards a consumption-led economy will require years of deliberate policies to increase the wage share in the national economy – of which there is currently no sign. If anything this trend is declining and, consequently, there is a serious problem of underconsumption in China.

The situation in China is almost the opposite of what happened in other Asian economies to the extent that even a study by the World Bank (Jianwu and Kuijs, 2007) pointed out that "the declining role of wages and household income in the economy are the key driver behind the declining share of consumption in GDP" (pp. 11–12). McNally (2011a) suggests that "So mammoth is China's working class, today at 750 million, that it is one and a half times larger than the labour force of all the thirty countries of OECD combined". He adds, however, that "the country's surplus labour force alone is three times larger than the entire manufacturing workforce of the OECD countries. This is a key reason why after thirty years of market-driven growth, wages in China's manufacturing industries are only around 5 percent of the USA level" (p. 52). Kavoussi (2012) confirms McNally's view by giving a figure of $23.32 an hour as the cost of employing a factory worker for the USA and $1.36 for China. Not only is wage growth very slow, but there have not been any redistributive measures either. Under China's household registration system, rural migrants lack the legal right to reside permanently in the cities. On the other hand, despite the fact that they fill nearly three-quarters of all manufacturing jobs, China's migrant workers are deprived of access to social services, and their children do not have the right to attend public schools.

All in all, domestic demand is not increasing sufficiently to reduce China's increasing dependence on foreign markets. While this is an important consideration, an equally important problem – is to be found in the real estate sector. Including all the upstream and downstream industries, this sector accounts for 25 to 30 per cent of China's GDP. Hence it is essential that the health of this sector should be re-established but the main question is how. It is estimated that there are 64.5 million empty flats and apartments across China and the only way to bring any life into this sector is to liquidate this excess inventory (Moreno and Blanco, 2014, p. 212). Either income distribution should change seriously or the price should fall substantially. There is no suggestion that the first option may even be contemplated let alone being tried. A substantial fall in prices may be an effective option to correct the situation. But this could bring a whole host of other risks into play. Colombo (2013a) has shown the house prices are in fact rising.

If prices fall too much that would hurt those who have poured their fortune into investment properties and even more significantly it will also trigger defaults by overleveraged real estate developers who can no longer service or repay their bank loans. It is true that the Chinese state will take the necessary measures, given its massive foreign currency reserve, to avoid a financial meltdown, but addressing some of the existing problems of the real estate sector would undoubtedly depress short term growth of the economy. From 2000 to 2007 total debt of China grew only slightly faster than GDP but since then, debt had risen rapidly, increasing from 158 per cent of GDP in 2007 by middle of 2014 the total debt reached 282 per cent. In relation to local governments' debt in China, it was reported in 2014 that 20 per cent of all new loans were used to pay old debts and 40 per cent of all repayment and debt servicing were financed by land sale (McKinsey Global Institute, 2015, p. 76). The point is that land sale cannot go for ever. It is estimated that 45 per cent of total debt (excluding financial sector debt) nearly $9 trillion is directly or indirectly related to real estate bubbles in the country. China's government debt, 55 per cent of GDP, remains low by international standards, but more than half is owed by local governments. It is important to note that accompanying China's 15 per cent fiscal stimulus was an equally massive monetary injection as well. Part of the money injection came from China's central bank and its state owned banks, which loaned significant sums to state owned enterprises and other businesses starting 2009–10. But part also came from opening China in late 2009 to shadow banking, which freed up liquidity both from within China and resulted in massive capital inflows from foreign investors.

A good deal of private debt explosion in China has also taken the form of dangerous short-term debt that requires frequent 'roll over' and refinancing. By 2014 a third of all new debt created in China was 'roll over' refinancing of prior debt. That means that should interest rates rise too far or too fast, many businesses heavily indebted to shadow banks will not be able to roll over that debt, and will have to default. (Rasmus, 2015). While shadow banking is booming in Western banking capital, it is growing at phenomenal rates in China. Shadow banking refers to the supply of credit outside traditional banks, such as from private equity investors, money market funds, repurchase agreements and securities lending.

By the 2nd quarter of 2014 these institutions provided $6.5 trillion or 30 per cent of total debt in China. There is a tendency to under-assess the risk that seems to exist in China. The main reason given is China's enormous foreign currency reserves, about $4 trillion as of mid-2014. The point usually not taken on board is what is likely to happen to the value of yuan if this reserve is used to avoid a financial collapse. Selling foreign assets and converting them back into yuan, would cause significant appreciation of the national currency and would seriously harm export industries which by all account are the main drivers of China's economy in recent years.

Before the crisis, the Chinese were rather cautious in using the facilities offered by shadow banking but this approach has changed in post-crisis years. It was revealed in 2012 that this sector in China grew from only several hundred billions of dollars in 2008 to more than $6 trillion by the end of 2012. In terms of annual growth, the assets under shadow banking management increased by 125 per cent in the second half of 2009, followed by another 75 per cent rise in 2010. In the next two years, 2011 and 2012, the annual growth is slightly down, 35 and 33 per cent respectively but by 2013 the total assets managed by shadow banking in China went up to $8 trillion. In 2014, another trillion dollars was added, hence the total stood at $9 trillion by the end of 2014 (Rasmus, 2015).

About a quarter of credit provided by shadow banking was to local governments, in order to finance infrastructural development. We also know that since 2010 local government debt in China has increased by more than 70 per cent. It seems the motive to allow shadow banking greater role in China is linked with China's aggressive fiscal and monetary stimulus programme initiated in 2009 which helped the economy to recover quickly form the 2009–10 global crash. In contrast to major economies that relied heavily on monetary instruments – with insignificant fiscal stimulus, such as the USA – China has introduced a major twin stimulus programme. In 2009, the stimulus package in China was about 15 per cent of GDP and there was an equally massive monetary injection too. It is with monetary expansion that shadow banking plays its role and credit and debt offered by this sector accelerated to more than $9 trillion, according to McKinsey Institute (McKinsey Global Institute, 2015, p. 75). One worrying sign here is that this sharp growth is more or less almost exclusively private sector debt and much of this debt is provided by the shadow banking sector. The second worrying aspect of this development is most of the private sector debt is short term in nature, which requires frequent 'roll over' and refinancing. By 2014, more than a third of all new debt in China was 'roll-over', namely refinancing debt that had already been incurred. This type of debt structure is highly risky as this means that if interest rates rise too much or too quickly, many of the borrowers who borrowed in the shadow banking sector may be unable to roll over and may have to default. Defaults would surely lead to panic sell-offs of financial securities, which could potentially lead to credit crunch and a further slowing down of growth in the real sector. What would happen to bubbles in the real estate sector or the unsustainable debt of local governments are two of the further concerns of policy makers in China. In short, over the course of just four years, the growth of shadow banking seems to have created an environment, which has created all the preconditions for a serious financial crisis. Some of these possibilities are not simply theoretical – for example, there are already some signs showing that the situation is risky. This began in spring 2013 when China tried to slow the asset price bubbles by making loans more expensive. The authorities' actions quickly led to a credit crunch and the economy slowed down. Those borrowers, especially the local governments who were unable to borrow from the traditional banking sector moved to the shadow banking sector and as a result the bubble increased in size. In June 2013, China responded and reduced the rate of interest and also added a mini-stimulus package. Cutting interest rates, however, meant that the levels of debt increased and the shadow banking sector has also provided more loans. The real sector started to slow down and this continued throughout 2013. By 2014, the rate had risen again and another mini-stimulus package was introduced. A number of developments are observable here:

- The growth rate remains low by China's standard.
- The yuan began to gain value. Between 2007 and 2014, the yuan appreciated by about 20 per cent against the dollar – its value changed from 7.61 yuan to a dollar in 2007 to 6.158 in 2014.[8]
- The housing price bubble has recently shown some sign of deflation (Bird, 2015; Fung, 2015). It was reported the prices of new homes in big Chinese cities fell 4.3 per cent in December (2014) from a year earlier, the largest drop since the current data series began in 2011 (Fung, 2015). Bird (2015) pointed out that "prices tumbled 5.7 percent in the year to February (2015), falling across 66 of China's 70 biggest cities".

From then on the main concern was how to prevent a sharp decline in the value of yuan or in the prices of houses. Furthermore, a mild credit crunch caused growing defaults among the industrial and commercial firms with some having to be bailed out by the state. Some 'hot money' owners moved their money into the Hong Kong stock market, and the activities of local governments slowed down as credit has become more difficult and expensive to come by. The slowing of growth continued. It is in this context that China's growth for 2014 is about 7 per cent down from the average rates of 10–12 per cent a decade ago (Rasmus, 2015).

2.4.2 Bubbles in Turkey

The evidence of a bubble in an emerging market economy is not limited to China. Turkey offers another case in point. On the back of an epic boom in consumption and construction, the Turkish economy had enjoyed impressive growth in recent years. It seems that the economic boom developed into a dangerous bubble, which is very similar to the one that caused the meltdown in 2008. In Turkey, familiar factors contributed to the creation of the bubble:

- Foreign 'hot money' inflows.
- Ultra-low interest rates.
- Rapid credit growth.
- Soaring asset prices.

Loans to Turkey's private sector have increased more than five times between 2008 and 2014, even though the country's GDP only increased by less than 8 per cent during this period (Keles, 2015). The emergence and further growth of a bond bubble enabled a corporate borrowing spree that caused Turkey's external debt, debt owed to foreign creditors, surged to a record high of $397 billion or nearly 50 per cent of GDP by 2014 (World Bank, 2015). One worrying aspect of this development is that 90 per cent of Turkish corporate debt is denominated in foreign currencies. We also know that between May 2013 and September 2014 Turkish lira lost about 26 per cent of its value (Sonmez, 2014), adding to the debt burden. A further concern is that over a third of this debt – $129.1 billion – is short-term debt, with an original maturity of one year or less. Turkish short-term debt has more than tripled since 2005, from $38.9 billion to more than $129 billion in 2014. Consumer spending has been the primary engine of economic growth in the last decade, but much of this consumption is financed by debt and, hence, unsustainable. Personal loans grew at a scorching 61 per cent annual rate from 2005 to 2008 and continued to increase after the crisis. Loans to households were increasing at an average annual rate of 28 per cent in 2013. Zalewski (2014) has pointed out that household debt has continued to rise in the last few years and from a figure of only 7.5 per cent of disposable income in 2003 had jumped to 55.2 per cent by 2013.

Similarly, credit card debt increased by 77 per cent from 2010 to mid-2013 (Colombo, 2014). There is $45 billion outstanding credit card debt, nearly a third of which is considered to be underperforming. Pooler's (2014) data seem to show that the scale of non-performing debt may be a lot less than what is given by Colombo (2014). What is worrying, however, is the fact that a declining trend in non-performing loans that started in 2010 and continued during 2011, has been reversed and increased in the subsequent two years, as shown by Pooler (2014).

Let us not also forget that there is serious asset price inflation in Turkey too. House prices in Turkey have increased by 53 per cent between 2009 and 2014. The outstanding mortgage debt increased five-fold between 2005 and 2012 (EMF, 2013, p. 85).

In a recent report, Kynge (2014) draw attention to a serious risk that exists in Turkey. He argued while Russia has enough foreign reserves to meet its external financing requirement for nearly 15 years, Turkey's reserves would run out in less than four months.

2.4.3 Bubbles in Thailand

Another case of a dangerous bubble economy that has appeared in recent years in an emerging market is in Thailand. The inflow of international 'hot money' was so extensive that ten - year government bond yields fell from their previous value of 4 to 6.5 per cent to just over 3 per cent. Foreign 'hot money' went also into the Thai stock market and since 2008 the value of the stock market has quadrupled. Traditionally, exporting played a significant role in the macro-management of the economy but in recent years debt-funded domestic demand is replacing the country's exports. Household debt grew at 13.6 per cent per year since 2008 and the country's household debt to GDP ratio, which stood at 45 per cent a decade ago, is now more than 77 per cent. During 2010–12 the household debt grew at 17 per cent per year, while household credit provided by credit card, leasing and personal loan companies rose at a blistering 27 per cent annual rate. In addition to household debt, the government of Thailand has also increased its spending by 40 per cent since 2008. The structure of external debt of the country has changed too. The short-term debt to total external debt ratio has almost doubled in the last decade too which means that Thailand is more vulnerable to short-term interest rate changes (Colombo, 2013).

2.4.4 Bubbles in South Africa

South Africa is another case showing signs of a bubble economy. In the last decade, South Africa's GDP grew by 38 per cent but during the same period, private sector debt has skyrocketed by 225 per cent. Since 2008, the economy grew by 12.7 per cent whereas private sector debt went up by 45 per cent. There has been a dangerous growth of money supply too. It went up by more than 400 per cent in the past ten years. Since the global financial crisis of 2008, money supply registered 50 per cent growth. While external debt is not very high by international standards, South Africa's external debt increased by 250 per cent in the last ten years, reaching £136.6 billion in 2014. While the sub-prime mortgage market was collapsing in the USA, South Africa introduced a more dangerous version of this loan in the country in 2007. The banking sector started to introduce unsecured loans, which have been growing at an average annual rate of 30 per cent since its introduction. This type of loan is very attractive to lenders as they charge up to 31 per cent annual interest for them and, like the subprime loans in the USA, the main target market is among the working-class borrowers who may have doubtful creditworthiness and are usually not very knowledgeable about the complexities of financial markets. Total personal loans in 2013 were estimated at more than $140 billion, which represents more than 36 per cent of the country's GDP (Colombo, 2014a).

2.5 Summary and conclusions

In this chapter my main argument is that with minor exceptions, in relation to the emerging economies it is a process of bubble creation, which is being repeated and maintained in these economies. Financialization, given its basic assumptions and principles, is not capable of producing anything but ficticious money and wealth, that is, bubbles of different description. It is further asserted that it is not so much a question if there would be a next round of global financial crisis, but rather when we have to deal with this new round. The only way that this 'crisis trap' could be broken is by taking effective measures to reduce these activities and to slow down the process. Something like the Glass–Steagall Act should be reinvigerated to separate the commercial credit institutions from financial market institutions. Similarly something akin to a Tobin Tax would have to be introduced and there should be serious attempts to reduce market concentration in financial markets. One way to reduce the damage would be to put a Tobin tax on this socially and economically destructive behaviour. In all capitalist economies, cigarettes and alcohol are heavily taxed because of the damage they cause. In many parts of the capitalist world, gambling activities are taxed as a controlling mechanism. The use of VAT taxes or similar sale taxes is being promoted for similar reasons. There should also be a sales tax on the speculative buying and selling of stocks and other financial products in the market.

Most important of all, a very serious redistribution of income and wealth in favour of the working people must be undertaken as a means of reducing the fragility of perpetual international imbalance.

Wall Street and the City lobbyists will try to scare the public into thinking that taxing speculation will somehow kill 'investment' and jobs. Because unemployment is still high, anything that reduces employment growth will be seen as negative. This tax will not reduce job creation, however. In fact, it is financial speculation that does that.

Notes

1. This chapter has greatly benefited from comments provided by Professors Philip Arestis and Malcolm Sawyer. I thank them both. The usual disclaimers apply.
2. https://www.wto.org/english/news_e/pres09_e/pr554_e.htm.
3. http://data.worldbank.org/indicator/BX.TRF.PWKR.CD.DT?page=1.
4. http://data.worldbank.org/indicator/BX.TRF.PWKR.CD.DT?page=1.

5. http://www.globalresearch.ca/china-is-crashing-unsurmontable-credit-bubble-financial-and-industrial-bankruptcies-debt-and-bond-busts/5372573.
6. The size of this package is the same in all these sources, but Moya gives it at 15 per cent of GDP, for the World Bank it is 13.4 per cent and Naughton suggests 12.5 per cent of the GDP.
7. Measuring poverty in general, and in China in particular, is highly controversial. The World Bank in its more recent estimations uses $1.25 per day as the poverty line. However, this approach has been criticized by Reddy (2005) among others. The Chinese authorities, however, use different poverty line definitions, hence, different estimates are available. Using $1 a day, Laccino (2014) suggested a figure of 82 million people living below the poverty line. If international standards of poverty were applied – $1.25 per day – the number would rise to more than 200 million.The Asian Development Bank believes these estimates are too low, and suggests 30 per cent or about 400 million people living under poverty line in China.
8. http://www.ukforex.co.uk/forex-tools/historical-rate-tools/yearly-average-rates.

References

Akyüz, Y. (2013) *Waving or Drowning: Developing Countries After the Financial Crisis*, South Centre, Research Paper 48.

Akyüz, Y. (2014) *Crisis Mismanagement in the United States and Europe: Impact on Developing Countries and Longer-term Consequences*, South Centre, Research Paper 50.

Akyüz, Y. (2015) *Internationalization of Finance and Changing Vulnerabilities in Emerging and Developing Economies*, South Centre, Research Paper 60.

Albo, G. (2012) 'The Crisis and Economic Alternatives', in L. Panitch, G. Albo and V. Chibber (eds), *The Question of Strategy, Socialist Register*, London: Merlin Press.

Asmundson, I., Dorsey, T., Khachatryan, K., Niculcea, I., and Saito, M. (2011) *Trade and Trade Finance in the 2008–2009 Financial Crisis*, IMF Working Paper WP/11/16.

Baker, D. (2009) *Plunder and Blunder: the Rise and Fall of the Bubble Economy*, San Francisco: PoliPoint Press.

Barnett, S. (2014) 'China: Slower Growth, but Bigger Economy'. Available at http://www.huffingtonpost.com/steven-barnett/china-economy-growth_b_5105990.html.

Bibow, J. (2010) *Global Imbalances, the US Dollar, and How the Crisis at the Core of Global Finance Spread to 'Self-insuring' Emerging Economies*, Levy Institute, Working paper no. 591.

Bird, M. (2015) 'China's House Price Crisis is Creating a Perverse Bailout Bubble for Property Companies'. Available at http://uk.businessinsider.com/chinas-house-price-crisis-creating-a-bailout-bubble-for-property-companies-2015-3.

Bishop, K. (2013) 'What Cuts? US Austerity "Tougher Than in Europe"'. Available at http://www.cnbc.com/id/101201622.

Boorman, J. (2009) 'The Impact of the Financial Crisis on Emerging Economies, the Transmission Mechanism, Policy Responses and Lessons', Emerging

Markets Forum. Available at http://osservatoriocrisi.progetti.informest.it/docs/archivio/altri/OERARC76.pdf.

Buttiglione, L., Lane, P.R., Reichlin, L. and Reinhart, V. (2014) *Deleveraging? What Deleveraging?*, Geneva: International Center for Monetary and Banking Studies.

Colombo, J. (2013) 'Thailand's Bubble Economy is Heading for a 1997-style Crash'. Available at http://www.forbes.com/sites/jessecolombo/2013/11/04/thailands-bubble-economy-is-heading-for-a-1997-style-crash/.

Colombo, J. (2013a) 'The Emerging Markets Bubble'. Available at http://www.thebubblebubble.com/emerging-markets-bubble/.

Colombo, J. (2014) 'Why the Worst is Still Ahead for Turkey's Bubble Economy'. Available at http://www.forbes.com/sites/jessecolombo/2014/03/05/why-the-worst-is-still-ahead-for-turkeys-bubble-economy/.

Colombo, J. (2014a) 'A Guide to South Africa's Economic Bubble and Coming Crisis'. Available at http://www.forbes.com/sites/jessecolombo/2014/03/19/a-guide-to-south-africas-economic-bubble-and-coming-crisis/.

Colombo, J. (2014b) 'Why Singapore's Economy is Heading for an Iceland Style Meltdown'. Available at http://www.forbes.com/sites/jessecolombo/2014/01/13/why-singapores-economy-is-heading-for-an-iceland-style-meltdown/.

Curran, E. (2015) 'China to be Superpower That Wasn't, Sage of Japan Slide Say'. Available at http://www.bloomberg.com/news/articles/2015-03-02/china-will-be-superpower-that-wasn-t-sage-of-japan-demis.

Dooley, M. and Hutchinson, M. (2009) 'Transmission of the US Subprime Crisis to Emerging Markets. Evidence on the Decoupling–Recoupling Hypotheses'. Available at http://www.econstor.eu/handle/10419/64057.

European Union Chamber of Commerce in China (EUCCC) (2009) 'Overcapacity in China: Causes, Impacts and Recommendations'. Available at http://www.europeanchamber.com.cn/en/overcapacity-in-china.

European Mortgage Federation (EMF) (2013) 'A Review of European Mortgage and Housing Markets'. Available at http://hb.betterregulation.com/external/Hypostat%202013%20-%20A%20review%20of%20Europes%20mortgage%20and%20housing%20markets.pdf.

Feng, W. (2011) 'The End of "Growth With Equity"? Economic Growth and Income Inequality in East Asia', *AsiaPacific Issues*, June. Analysis from the East–West Center, no. 101.

Fidrmuc, J. and Korhonen, L (2009) 'The Impact of the Global Financial Crisis on Business Cycles in Asian Emerging Economies'. Available at http://hdl.handle.net/10419/30422.

Freeman, D. (2013) 'China's Consumption to the Rescue?' Available at http://www.understandingchina.eu/Chinaideascommunity/LatestresearchonChina/tabid/887/PostID/2754/Default.aspx.

Fung, E. (2015) 'China Month-on-month December Housing Prices Fall at Slower Pace'. Available at http://www.wsj.com/articles/china-month-on-month-december-housing-prices-fall-at-slower-pace-1421548940.

Ghosh, J. (2013) 'The Global Economic Chessboard and the Role of the BRICS: Brazil, Russia, India, China, South Africa'. Available at http://www.global-research.ca/the-global-economic-chessboard-and-the-role-of-the-brics-brazil-russia-india-china-south-africa/5357502.

Grey, B. (2013) 'Turmoil in Emerging Economies: A Symptom of a Global Crisis'. Available at http://www.globalresearch.ca/turmoil-in-emerging-economies-a-symptom-of-global-crisis/5347057.

Hersh, A. (2013) 'Fiscal Austerity Is Undermining Long-Term US Economic Prospects'. Available at https://www.americanprogress.org/issues/economy/news/2013/06/06/64608/fiscal-austerity-is-undermining-long-term-u-s-economic-prospects/.

Hilary, J. (2013) *The Poverty of Capitalism: Economic Meltdown and the Struggle for What Comes Next*, London: Pluto Press.

Hung, H.-F. (2009) 'America's Head Servant? The PRC's Dilemma in the Global Crisis', *New Left Review*, 60 (November–December).

Hung, H.-F. (2011) 'Sinomania: Global Crisis, China's Crisis', in L. Panitch, G. Albo and V. Chibber (eds), *The Crisis and the Left, Socialist Register 2012*, London: The Merlin Press.

Hung, H.-F. (2013) 'China's Rise Stalled?', *New Left Review*, 81 (May–June).

IMF (2007) *World Economic Outlook, Globalization and Inequality*, October. Available at https://www.imf.org/external/pubs/ft/weo/2007/02/pdf/text.pdf.

IMF (2009) *Review of Recent Crisis Programs*. Available at https://www.imf.org/external/np/pp/eng/2009/091409.pdf.

IMF (2010) *How did Emerging Markets Cope in the Crisis?* Available at https://www.imf.org/external/np/pp/eng/2010/061510.pdf.

IMF (2014) *Global Financial Stability Report, Moving from Liquidity- to Growth-Driven Markets*, April. Available at http://www.imf.org/external/pubs/FT/GFSR/2014/01/pdf/text.pdf.

IMF (2015) *World Economic Outlook Database*, April. Available at http://www.imf.org/external/ns/cs.aspx?id=28.

International Labour Organisation (ILO) (2015) *Global Wage Report 2014/15: Wages and Income Inequality*, Geneva. Available at http://www.ilo.org/global/publications/books/WCMS_324678/lang--en/index.htm.

Jianwu, H. and Kuijs, L. (2007) *Rebalancing China's Economy – Modelling a Policy Package*, World Bank China Research Paper no. 7.

Jomo, K.S. (2006) *Growth with Equity in East Asia*, DESA Working Papers no. 33.

Kavoussi, B. (2012) 'Average Cost of a Factory Worker in the US, China and Germany'. Available at http://www.huffingtonpost.com/2012/03/08/average-cost-factory-worker_n_1327413.html.

Keles, O. (2015) 'An Assessment of Turkish External Debt'. Available at http://www.turkishweekly.net/op-ed/3283/an-assessment-of-turkish-external-debt.html.

Keynes, J.M (1936) *The General Theory of Employment, Interest, and Money*, London: Macmillan.

Khor, M. (2009) 'Statement by the South Centre'. Available at http://www.un.org/ga/president/63/interactive/financialcrisis/southcentre.pdf.

Krugman, P. (1988) *Financing vs. Forgiving a Debt Overhang*, NBER Working Paper, No. 2486.

Kynge, J. (2014) 'Emerging Markets, Fears of Contagion'. Available at http://www.ft.com/cms/s/0/b201ae8e-89a5-11e3-8829-00144feab7de.html#slide0.

Laccino, L. (2014) 'China: More than 82 Million People Live Below Poverty Line'. Available at http://www.ibtimes.co.uk/china-more-82-million-people-live-below-poverty-line-1470313.

Lapavitsas, C. et al. (2012) *Crisis in the Euro Zone*, London: Verso.

Llaudes, R., Salman, F. and Chivakul, M. (2010) *The Impact of the Great Recession on Emerging Markets*, IMF Working Paper, WP/10/237.

Lynch, D. (2011) 'China Will Face Crisis Within 5 Years Investors Say'. Available at http://www.bloomberg.com/news/articles/2011-01-26/china-will-face-crisis-within-5-years-45-of-investors-in-global-poll-say.

McKinsey Global Institute (2015) 'Debt and (Not Much) Deleveraging'. Available at http://www.mckinsey.com/insights/economic_studies/debt_and_not_much_deleveraging.

McNally, D. (2011) *Global Slump: The Economics and Politics of Crisis and Resistance*, Oakland, CA: PM Press.

McNally, D. (2011b) 'Slump, Austerity and Resistance', in L. Panitch, G. Albo and V. Chibber (eds), *The Crisis and the Left, Socialist Register 2012*, London: The Merlin Press.

Minxin, P. (2015) 'China's Slowing Economy: the Worst Yet to Come'. Available at http://fortune.com/2015/01/21/china-economy-growth-slowdown/.

Mishra, P., Moriyama, K., N'Diaye, P., and Nguyen, L. (2014) *Impact of Fed Tapering Announcements on Emerging Markets*, IMF Working Paper, WP/14/109.

Moreno, E.L. and Blanco, Z.G. (2014) 'Ghost Cities and Empty Houses: Wasted Prosperity', *American International Journal of Social Science*, 3(2), pp. 207–16.

Morris, C.R. (2008) *The Two Trillion Dollar Meltdown: Easy Money, High Rollers and the Great Credit Crash*, New York: PublicAffairs.

Moyo, D. (2012) *Winner Take All: China's Race for Resources and What it Means for Us*, London: Penguin Books.

Naude, W. (2009) 'The Financial Crisis of 2008 and the Developing Countries'. Available at http://hdl.handle.net/10419/84665.

Naughton, B. (2008) 'Understanding the Chinese Stimulus Package'. Available at http://www.hoover.org/sites/default/files/uploads/documents/CLM28BN.pdf.

Ocampo, J.A. (2009) 'Latin America and the Global Financial Crisis', *Cambridge Journal of Economics*, 33, pp. 703–24.

Page, J. (1994) *The East Asian Miracle: Four Lessons for Development Policy*, Washington, DC: World Bank.

Piketty, T. (2014) *Capital in the Twenty-First Century*, Cambridge, MA: Belknap Press.

Pooler, M. (2014) 'Tackling Turkish Debt: Will it Work?' Available at http://blogs.ft.com/beyond-brics/2014/05/15/tackling-turkish-debt-will-it-work/.

Qinglian, H. (2015) 'China's "Marshall Plan" Will Not Solve Overcapacity in China's Economy'. Available at http://www.theepochtimes.com/n3/1248064-chinas-marshall-plan-will-not-solve-overcapacity-in-chinas-economy/.

Rasmus, J. (2015) 'China and the Shadow Bankers'. Available at http://www.counterpunch.org/2015/01/09/china-and-the-shadow-bankers/.

Reddy, S.G. (2005) 'Counting the Poor: the Truth About World Poverty Statistics', in L. Panitch and C. Leys (eds), *Telling the Truth, Socialist Register, 2006*, London: The Merlin Press.

Roberts, D. (2013) 'Overcapacity Threatens China Growth'. Available at http://www.bloomberg.com/bw/articles/2013-12-11/overcapacity-threatens-china-growth.

Singh, A. and Singh, G. (2014) *Almost Steady East Asian Rise: Implications for Labour Markets and Income Distribution*, Working Paper no. 456.

Sonmez, M. (2014) 'Lira Leads the Way in Emerging Currency Devaluation'. Available at http://www.hurriyetdailynews.com/lira-leads-the-way-in-emerging-currency-devaluation-.aspx?PageID=238&NID=72573&NewsCatID=344.

Stiglitz, J.E. (2013) *The Price of Inequality: How Today's Divided Society Endangers Our Future*, London: Penguin Books.

United Nations (UN) (2015) *World Economic Situation and Prospects*. Available at http://www.un.org/en/development/desa/policy/wesp/wesp_archive/2015wesp_full_en.pdf.

United States Government Accountability Office (2011) 'Federal Reserve System: Opportunities Exist to Strengthen Policies and Processes for Managing Emergency Assistance', July.

Whitehouse, M (2014) 'Is China's Bubble the Next Financial Crisis?' Available at http://www.bloombergview.com/articles/2014-10-09/is-china-s-bubble-the-next-financial-crisis.

World Bank (2010) 'INFRA Update'. Available at http://siteresources.worldbank.org/INTSDNET/Resources/5944695-1247775731647/INFRA_China_Newsletter.pdf.

World Bank (2015) *International Debt Statistics* Available at http://data.worldbank.org/sites/default/files/ids2015.pdf.

Yu, Y. (2010) *The Impact of the Global Financial Crisis on the Chinese Economy and China's Policy Responses*, Penang: Third World Network.

Yu, X. (2012) *China Family Panel Studies*. Available at http://www.isss.edu.cn/cfps/d/file/EN/Documentation/js/2014-09-18/bedee4470e0469260939e40eac2415c9.pdf.

Zalewski, P. (2014) 'How Debt Threatens Turkey's Economy'. Available at http://www.ft.com/cms/s/0/0b9b66bc-cc98-11e3-ab99-00144feabdc0.html#axzz3a4DRdoQA.

Zhuang, J., Kanbur, R. and Rhee, C. (2014) *Rising Inequality in Asia and Policy Implications*, Tokyo: Asian Development Bank Institute.

3
Africa and the Great Recession: The Dynamics of Growth Sustainability

Howard Stein
University of Michigan, USA

Abstract: Sub-Saharan Africa (SSA) as a whole did remarkably well during the Great Recession. On average, over the 2008–13 period, SSA (excluding South Africa) grew at a rate that was 2.9 per cent higher than that achieved by the world as a whole. The paper explores the reason for this performance. First, a number of African countries in recent years have built up significant reserves and tapped new sources of finance. Like many Latin American and Asian countries, they were able to avoid IMF loans and create policy space for the adoption of anti-cyclical fiscal and monetary policies. Second, SSA countries reoriented their economies away from traditional export markets and sources of FDI toward Asian and other emerging countries which had been less badly affected than their traditional western partners by the recession. Third, both before and during the Great Recession SSA countries continued to rely heavily on commodity production, which allowed them to ride the boom in commodity prices. However, in the long run this reliance generates structural weaknesses that are a threat to the sustainability of growth in SSA.

Keywords: Great Recession, Sub-Saharan Africa, Monetary and Fiscal Policy, IMF, Commodity Boom, FDI, Structural Weaknesses, International Reserves

JEL Classification: E32, E35, 019, 023

3.1 Introduction[1]

The Great Recession was punishing in terms of its severity, ubiquity and prolongation. In the United States, the recession lasted 18 months through June, 2009 and was the longest downturn since the Depression of the 1930s

(NBER, 2015). Unemployment (seasonally adjusted) rose from 4.4 per cent in 2007 to 10 per cent in October 2009; it remained above 6 per cent through September 2014 (BLS, 2015). However, it has been far worse and far more protracted in other regions of the world. Southern Euro Area countries, for example, have now been subjected to years of ill-conceived pro-cyclical policies in return for ongoing debt relief. As of February 2015, the average level of unemployment in the Euro zone was 11.3 per cent compared to 7.5 per cent in 2007, but it was far higher in some countries. Greece has experienced negative growth between 2007 and 2013. Unemployment has gone from 7.8 per cent in 2008 to 27.8 per cent in 2013 with GDP falling nearly 25 per cent (OECD, 2015a; UNCTAD, 2015).

In contrast, Sub-Saharan Africa[2] as a whole did remarkably well during the Great Recession, exceeding global growth by 4.7 per cent in 2008 – and a whopping 6.2 per cent in 2009. Over the period 2008–13 the average annual growth was 2.9 per cent higher as a whole than the global level. The growth level on the continent was a very robust 5.1 per cent, ranking it as thesecond-highest region in the world. This is even more remarkable give how far SSA has lagged behind the rest of the world in recent decades. However, not all countries or subregions fared equally well, with some countries doing much better than others. For instance, both East and West Africa grew by over 4 per cent more than Southern Africa over the period 2008–13 (UNCTAD, 2015). This paper will explore the reasons for the overall performance compared to other regions, the differences within the continent, and the issues associated with the sources of growth, its sustainability and its relationship to the structure of economic activity.

3.2 Economic growth trends in SSA

SSA growth was below global growth in the 1980s and 1990s and was indeed well below that recorded in other developing areas. During those decades, SSA was a focal point of the neoliberal agenda or Structural Adjustment Programs (SAPs) of the World Bank. Between 1980 and 1990, SSA countries were in receipt of 31 structural adjustment loans (SALs), accounting for about 50 per cent of all loans in this category allocated by the Bank globally during those years. By the mid-1990s 37 countries had been in receipt of structural or sectoral adjustment loans (Stein, 2008). With the full-scale introduction of neoliberal policies through the conditionality of the international financial institutions (IFIs) and bilateral donors, SSA growth plummeted in the 1980s to just one-third of the global level. As a result of this, many commentators consider the 1980s to be a lost decade. No region of SSA did well, with Western Africa actually experiencing negative growth during this period. Given population growth rates at 2.5–3 per cent per annum, all subregions experienced negative growth per capita with the overall rate declining by 1.5 per cent per annum.

The 1990s were only slightly better with growth in the subregions ranging below growth in other developing countries. Average growth was also below the 1970s though better than the 1980s; but it was not sufficient to compensate for the declines of the 1980s. By 2000, real per capita income was only slightly above $300 per capita in East Africa. The overall level for SSA was still nearly 20 per cent below the level of the 1980s (UNCTAD, 2015). By 1999, poverty levels had increased to almost 60 per cent of the population (from around 53 per cent in 1981) with 170 million more people living on less than $1.25 per day, the global measure of extreme poverty (Chen and Ravaillion, 2008).

This situation began to change after 2000. Excluding South Africa, growth averaged an impressive 6.7–6.8 per cent between 2000–05 and 2005–08, figures only surpassed by the numbers achieved in Asia, but more than double the rate of growth of the overall global economy. The numbers held up remarkably well during the Great Recession. Only Southern Africa experienced significantly lower growth in 2008 and negative growth in 2009, largely due to the substantial impact of the Great Recession on South Africa, whose economy was more closely tied to western economies than the other countries in SSA. Excluding South Africa, growth in 2008 was still 6.2 per cent close to the trends of the 2000s and above all other regions of the world. In 2009 SSA also did remarkably well, being only slightly lower than the levels of growth in Asia. Overall, growth in SSA (excluding South Africa) did very well during and following the Great Recession, averaging more than 5.6 per cent in the period 2008–11, which is nearly double the growth rate of the previous global recession and its aftermath of 3.2 per cent (1997–2000). How was this achieved? What has changed over the past decade? What are the sources of growth? Are these changes sustainable? How does it relate to the structure of these economies? These questions will frame the focus of the remainder of the paper. We will begin by examining the Great Recession in the context of business cycle theories.

3.3 Africa, business cycles and other drivers of recessions in Africa

Achieving an understanding of the theory of the causes and consequences of economic downturns would seem to be important in terms of placing the Great Recession and its impact on Africa in the context of other recessions. The classic work by the institutionalist Mitchell (1927) and the later neoclassical economic real business cycle theory of people such as Lucas (1981) all focused on the behavior of developed economies. There has to date been relatively little literature on the subject of Africa and the developing countries and what was published has tended to be influenced by theories and assumptions about the nature and length of business cycles generated from the developed country literature (Rand and Tarp, 2002). Many have simply applied stochastic general equilibrium models using real business cycle theory with its absurd assumptions such as perfectly operating markets which have little relevance even to the developed world.[3] One exception to this general trend is Rand and Tarp (2002), who compare the character of business cycles in 15 developing countries (including five in Africa) relative to conditions elsewhere over the period 1980–99. They determine that SSA downturns tend to be longer in duration than other regions in their sample, being prolonged by initial events like oil shocks and the subsequent recessions in developed countries. Both FDI and foreign aid are highly volatile while investment and consumption were strongly pro-cyclical. In spite of a strong need for counter-cyclical policies, these were not implemented. For the group as a whole consumption was much more volatile than growth, something which is not the case in developed countries. In addition, monetary expansion and fiscal spending were strongly pro-cyclical. Though not stated, this is not very surprising given the typical austerity packages of IMF loans to these countries in times of crisis, over the period that was being studied (Stein, 2010). As we will see below, SSA was able to shift its dependency on developed country markets while building reserves and hence it was able to reduce the impact of the second round of shocks from the Great Recession. This allowed many more countries either to avoid the intervention of the IMF or to diminish the duration of IMF loans, thereby cutting down on pro-cyclical conditionality and creating greater policy space for counter-cyclical interventions.

3.3.1 Explanations for the performance

As is frequently the case the IMF was eager to seize the moment generated by the crisis in order to assert that 'good policies', defined according to the usual Fund-style orthodoxy, were responsible for the resilient performance of Africa and other developing areas in the face of the severe downturn following the Great Recession:

> Many emerging market and developing economies have done well over the past decade and through the global financial crisis. These economies

> did so well during the past decade that for the first time, emerging market and developing economies spent more time in expansion and had smaller downturns than advanced economies. Their improved performance is explained by both good policies[4] and a lower incidence of external and domestic shocks: better policies account for about three-fifths of their improved performance, and less-frequent shocks account for the rest. (IMF, 2012, 129)

However, in their zeal to pat themselves on the back, the IMF overlooked the key driving force in places such as Africa, which was more about avoiding IMF policies than implementing them along with the 'positive' shocks associated with the boom in commodity production and its associated foreign investment inflows (Akyüz, 2013). Greater policy space permitted fiscal expansion during the crisis. This was created by the deliberate building up of reserves, which inoculated them from the austerity of the IMF.

One of the approaches has been to look increasingly East for sources of capital inflows and for export markets. Due to the expansion of linkages to the East, SSA was not hit as badly by the downturn which was far worse in some European countries partly because of greater reliance on IMF loans and the implementation of associated austerity measures. In addition, independence from the vagaries and conditionality of foreign aid and international loans from the IFIs has been created by gaining access to new sources of international finance, including remittances and sovereign bond markets. Furthermore, commodity prices held up remarkably well over this period, largely because they have been driven by the continued optimism of hedge funds and other speculators. However, as sentiment has begun to turn against commodities such as oil and the dollar has risen in value, prices have begun to plummet, endangering growth in a number of SSA countries.

As we will see in the next few sections of the paper, there is substantial evidence in support of these propositions.

3.3.2 SSA reserves and their relationship to economic growth

There had been a dramatic increase in reserves in numerical terms and also in the reserve to import ratios in SSA countries prior to the crisis. Between 1997 and 2001, SSA countries had roughly 3.7 months of reserves relative to annual imports. In absolute terms, the quantity of reserves quadrupled between 2004 and 2008, with reserves increasing to more than five months. By 2008 as the crisis hit, SSA countries' reserves had expanded almost sevenfold, reaching an almost unprecedented seven months of reserves. While the numbers were clearly driven by the accumulation of reserves in oil-producing countries resulting from the rise in oil prices, the rise was fairly widespread, with 80 per cent of the countries having at least three months of reserves (IMF, 2014a). The literature on the relationship between reserves and their impact on economic growth has been growing.

The early literature was mixed. Blanchard et al. (2010) and Rose and Spiegel (2009) find that reserves did not protect economies from the Great Recession while Llaudes et al. (2010) find that it had a strong impact with countries with low reserves hit much harder by the Great Recession. One problem was the sample size. Blanchard et al. (2010) only use a sample of 29 countries and only look at emerging economies. Bussière et al. (2015), in contrast, look at a much larger sample of 112 countries which includes both emerging and developing countries. Most sub-Saharan African countries are included in the sample. Using a variety of measures of reserves they test to see if they help protect economies from the impact of the crisis. They find the ratio of reserves to short debt has a large and significant impact in reducing the negative effect of the recession on growth.[5] They also find that the presence of capital controls enhances the impact of reserves as well as acting independently to diminish the impact of the Great Recession. Bussière et al. (2015) see reserves in two different ways. Reserves can act as gunpowder where governments finance imports to keep them at more sustainable levels or intervene to stabilize foreign exchange markets or debt markets. They might also act as a deterrent much like a nuclear device. The mere presence of sufficient reserves builds confidence that the country can intervene in markets if needed thereby deterring overreactions in private markets. The author's evidence is mixed and indicates both purposes. Countries with very large and very little reserves did not use their reserves. Those in the middle range saw significant declines in their reserves. Using reserve ratios from IMF (2014a) and IMF (2005) and aggregate import levels from UNCTAD (2005), we can calculate the nominal reserve levels over time. Between 1997–2001 and 2008 there was a huge jump in the level of reserves which rose from $33.7 billion on average per annum to $229.7 billion. However, there was a significant overall decline in SSA reserves in 2009 and 2010. Reserves fell to only $148.6 billion in 2009 and $139.6 billion in 2011 indicating more usage in the gun powder role. Still there could be some evidence of Bussière et al.'s (2015) deterrent effect in SSA with a number of countries at the upper and lower end exhibiting stable or rising reserve ratios in 2009 and 2010 (IMF, 2014a). SSA governments quickly rebuilt reserves which recovered by 2012 to $226.3 billion or near the peak levels of 2008. The 2013 reserves fell only slightly to $219.4 billion (IMF, 2014a; IMF, 2005; UNCTAD, 2005).

3.3.3 Challenging aid dependence: debt reduction, personal remittances, ODA, sovereign debt markets and FDI in SSA

For many decades SSA countries have had a very high dependence on bilateral and multilateral aid, something which dramatically limited the range of policy choice. Governments were obliged to follow the development strategies embedded in the conditionality tied to donor assistance and the leader in generating donor fashions was the World Bank. While there were some changes to structural adjustment in the 1980s and 1990s, the major shift occurred under the Wolfensohn presidency in the late 1990s with the re-emphasis on poverty reduction – something that had hitherto been largely ignored by the donor community for nearly two decades. The Bank replaced SALs with the introduction of poverty support credits (PSCs) for the low-income countries and development policy loans (DPLs) for middle-income counties. They assisted in debt relief for the least developed countries through the HIPC (highly indebted poor country) initiative. The effort included 'home-grown' country poverty reduction support papers (PRSPs) which outlined the usage of the funds released from debt servicing. In most cases, it allowed for the expansion of spending on education and health – areas which had been badly neglected under SAPs. Yet standard neoliberal policies continued to be embedded in the PRSPs (Stewart and Wang, 2003). They also introduced the comprehensive development framework (CDF). The CDF generated a more human-centered strategy along with the typical neoliberal agenda, and focused on macroeconomic and financial policies. Despite some broadening, however, new neoliberal types of strategies were introduced, including the "Doing Business" project with focused on deregulatory-style indicators and the formalizing of private property rights in urban and rural areas (see Bazbauers, 2014; Stein et al., 2015).

The movement of SSA countries away from aid dependence, with its sometimes punishing conditionality, has been a high priority for many SSA countries. The data in Table 3.1 show two important alternatives to aid, FDI and remittances, which do not carry the baggage of conditionality. The statistics for SSA are quite dramatic. The ratio of remittances and FDI to ODA went from 0.19 to 0.88 in the 1990s due largely to the fall in ODA from donor fatigue with some moderate increases in remittances and FDI. After 2000, largely following the introduction of

Table 3.1 Personal remittances, ODA and FDI in SSA ($ million)

Year	1990	2000	2005	2007	2008	2009	2010	2011	2012	2013
Remit	1638	4301	19613	24958	27500	26173	27858	29722	29814	30853
FDI	1660	6763	21018	29773	38724	39635	33352	42206	41044	44839
ODA	17811	12552	32416	34720	39627	42466	43700	45643	44619	45198
Remitances and FDI/ODA	.19	.88	1.25	1.57	1.67	1.55	1.40	1.58	1.59	1.67
Top Three Oil Exporter Share FDI[1]	.59	.40	.50	.40	.42	.40	.37	.37	.33	.26

Note: [1]Oil exporter list taken from IMF (2014a) and includes seven countries – Angola, Cameroon, Chad, Congo, Equatorial Guinea, Gabon, and Nigeria. The total does not include South Africa.
Sources: OECD (2015); UNCTAD (2015).

the Millennium Development Goals (MDGs), ODA reversed its downward trajectory, expanding almost threefold between 2000 and 2005. However, this was more than compensated by the nearly fivefold increase in remittances and a threefold increase in FDI. Consequently, in 2005 FDI and remittances for the first time exceeded ODA – rising to 1.25 of ODA. Over the next few years growth in all three continued, with FDI and remittances exceeding the expansion of ODA, leading to a ratio to 1.67 just prior to the crisis. All three sources of financing held up remarkably well during the recession, which undoubtedly helped to sustain the levels of economic growth. Remittances declined only in one year (2009) and then by a relatively modest 5 per cent. FDI fell in 2010 by 16 per cent but thereafter continued to climb, with the exception of a slight decline in 2012. Remittances steadily rose during and after the Great Recession, with the earlier peak ratio of 1.67 being attained once again in 2013, reasserting the growing independence from ODA. Overall, by this time financial flows from these three sources were 35 per cent higher than the pre-crisis year of 2007.

Over the past few years, a dramatic new source of international finance became available to sub-Saharan African countries which helped to support the expanded policy space during the Great Recession. National governments in Sub-Saharan Africa have historically borrowed extensively from abroad, but, with the notable exception of South Africa, until recently none have been able to access sovereign bonds denominated in foreign currency.[6] African governments seeking hard currency loans had relied primarily on multilateral and bilateral concessional lending – with all the conditionality baggage – and secondarily on commercial lending from private banks.[7]

While concessional lending, by definition,[8] has terms more favorable to the borrower than those of commercial lending in a narrowly financial sense, multilateral concessional lending comes with strings attached. The conditionalities for which the loans of Bretton Woods institutions are so well known have required governments to adopt and adhere to policies which have had wide-ranging detrimental effects on the economy in general, and the poor in particular, not just in sub-Saharan Africa alone but across the developing world.[9]

For example, the policy of requiring patients at public-sector clinics and hospitals to pay user fees was widely imposed through such conditionalities and may have resulted in three million additional African child deaths in the period 1988–2008.[10] The Bank and the Fund have mandated such policies not only on the extension of new loans but also as a condition of the relief of old and defaulted debt during the heavily indebted poor countries (HIPC) initiative. Similarly, in order to qualify for debt relief, the government of Tanzania had been required to privatize the public water system of Dar es Salaam (Jones, 2012, p. 6), selling it in 2003 to a British company which mismanaged the system so badly that the government renationalized the utility just two years later, eventually winning a judgement against the company in a British court for £3.5 million in cost and damages (Seager, 2008). If a sovereign country can be compelled to adopt destructive policies once to receive disbursement of loan funds and then again in the event of a need for debt relief, a certain wariness of multilateral, concessional, conditional lending on the part of African finance ministers becomes entirely understandable.

The quantity of debt reduction was quite significant, however. External debt in SSA more than tripled between 1980 and 1998 – to a substantial figure of $205 billion. Debt/GDP and debt to exports went from 0.33 to 1.08 and from 1.1 to a completely unsustainable 3.6, respectively. Between 1996 and 2010, $104 billion bilateral and multilateral debt was written off through the HIPC and the Multilateral Debt Relief Initiative covering 30 countries in SSA. By 2006 aggregate external debt fell to $138 billion with ratios declining to very manageable 0.3 for debt/GDP and and 0.6 for debt to exports. Private debt fell below the 1980 level (IDA and IMF, 2010; Stein, 2013).[11] This was a very important factor in reorienting spending from debt servicing toward more productive government expenditures. At the same time it set up the possibility of taking on new forms of private debt.

Although bonds denominated in local currencies are issued routinely by 32 sub-Saharan countries,[12] no sub-Saharan African country had issued a Eurobond for many years until the Seychelles sold a $200 million Eurodollar bond in September 2006.[13] The following year, Ghana became the first HIPC nation to issue sovereign bonds on international markets. Tanzania and Zambia have also been able to float new bond issues on international markets, often with very heavy oversubscription. In the case of Zambia, some $12 billion was offered for a $750 million bond issue. This general pattern of oversubscription continued through 2014. In early December, 2014, Ethiopia became the poorest country to ever tap the global sovereign bond market with a ten-year $1 billion issue, yet was able to attract $2.6 billion in bids with a yield of 6.625 per cent (Platt, 2015).

Olabisi and Stein (2014), Tyson (2015) and Platt (2015) provide the details on the recent history of sovereign bonds. In total, 15 SSA countries participated in these markets over the seven-year period, with multiple issues from countries such as Senegal and Ghana. In 2007, just prior to the start of the Great Recession, three SSA countries were able to issue bonds for a total of $2.2 billion. However, in line with general bond issues worldwide activity was hit by the Great Recession in 2008 and 2009, with only one small issue in 2009 (to Senegal for $200 million). The ability to float sovereign bond issues recovered to pre-recession levels in 2010–12 with seven countries (Côte D'Ivoire, Seychelles, Namibia, Nigeria, Senegal, Zambia and Angola) participating in the markets with aggregate issues of $2.5 billion in 2010, $1.5 billion in 2011 and $1.75 billion in 2012. In 2013 and 2014, the activity increased substantially with a near tripling of the value of the face value of bonds in 2013 to $5.1 billion. In 2014 bond issues rose further, to a historical record of $7 billion. Five of the dozen bond issues in 2013 and 2014 were from first-time entries into the market (Ethiopia, Kenya, Rwanda, Tanzania and Mozambique). By 2014, a total of 15 countries had issued $20.5 billion worth of bonds a not insignificant amount, accounting for roughly 12 per cent of the total reserves of SSA (excluding South Africa).[14]

The funds have been used for a variety of different purposes, including increasing the bargaining power of countries with the IMF. For example, in September, 2014, Ghana issued $1 billion in the face of growing deficits and dwindling reserves just a few days before the scheduled arrival of an IMF mission. Sources indicated that this timing was no coincidence, but was in fact aimed at intentionally increasing their bargaining power with the IMF (Bigg and Kopodo, 2014). Others have been used to deal with outstanding debt. In 1985, for example, Congo defaulted on its foreign debt. By 2004 principal, interest and penalties exceeded 200 per cent of GDP.[15] Countries participating in the HIPC programme of debt relief have an incentive to make at least token payments to creditors as they attempt to achieve the relief of old debts.[16] Congo, however, had an additional reason to pursue a consensual, negotiated resolution with its creditors. As an oil exporter, Congo receives revenues denominated in foreign currencies and deposits them into foreign bank accounts. These overseas assets are vulnerable to writs of attachment issued by foreign courts in response to lawsuits. Over the years many of Congo's creditors had filed and won writs over the country's two decades of default, which, in the absence of a negotiated debt restructuring, they could use to seize funds from any Congolese government bank account they could locate. Thus, in order to safeguard its continued possession of its own oil revenues, Congo decided against a unilateral exchange offer and opted instead to issue a sovereign bond on terms negotiated with its creditors, whose expenses it paid during the negotiation process. Judging by the eventual participation rate of 92 per cent in this debt exchange deal, Congo's creditors deemed these terms an acceptable exit strategy from twenty years of default (Richards, 2010).

Some governments were quite explicit in their usage of funds either to expand their reserves or to engage in fiscal expansion. Seychelles, for instance, used its 2007 $30 million Eurobond to increase its foreign currency reserves (Olabisi and Stein, 2015). In Namibia, funding from the bond issue financed the Targeted Intervention on Employment and Economic Growth, which was a three-year, N$14.7-billion fiscal stimulus programme intended to reduce the country's high unemployment rate by creating 104,000 new jobs (Brown, 2011; Heita, 2011). However, in the majority of cases funds have been used for infrastructural projects which are, by their very nature, expansionary and implicitly counter-cyclical when undertaken during a period of slow economic growth. In Tanzania, funds were used to construct a gas pipeline; in Zambia proceeds were used for a hydroelectric project and for railroad infrastructural rehabilitation; in Rwanda the focus was on electrical projects and to build a convention center; in Nigeria the funds were invested in power generation; finally, in Ethiopia the funds are being used for hydropower and rail projects and to modernize sugar plantations (Olabisi and Stein, 2015; Platt, 2015). Overall, there is little doubt that new sovereign debt expanded the policy space for state-sponsored projects aimed at sustaining higher economic growth both during the recession and afterward. Diversifying the sources of FDI and trade away from the West toward the developing and emerging countries of the East has also helped sustain economic growth during the Great Recession.

3.3.4 Diversifying sources of FDI and export targets

One key element in sustaining economic growth was in looking toward Asia for new sources of FDI. We can see in Table 3.1 that, with the exception of 2010, FDI steadily grew after 2007. The growth was quite remarkable in the face of the global decline in FDI. In 2009, global FDI was 39 per cent below the 2007 level, but up by 33 per cent in SSA. In 2013, global FDI had not yet recovered from the Great Recession and was still 28 per cent below 2007's numbers. In contrast, SSA FDI was 51 per cent above the 2007 level (UNCTAD, 2015).

The data in Table 3.2 illustrate the ability of SSA to move away from a reliance on flows from Western developed countries toward sourcing investment from Asia.

The table captures the two largest recipients of FDI in the four different regions of SSA and compares the yearly averages of FDI stock from 2002–04 to 2010–12. Figures for countries such as the Congo, Nigeria and Zimbabwe are quite dramatic, with a huge increase in flows from Asia leading to a significant rise in the stock of FDI. Overall, the increase in the stock of flows over the decade was from 3.6 per cent from Asian countries to 20.8 per cent of the total. Table 3.2 illustrates that the diversification of FDI toward Asian countries has done little to alter the heavy focus of FDI on oil-producing countries. Data are provided for the FDI share of the top three oil-producing countries in SSA, excluding South Africa. In 1990, nearly 60 per cent of all FDI flows went to the biggest three oil producers; by 2005 the share was still 50 per cent. It is more than a third for every year except 2013, perhaps reflecting the recent dip in oil prices. We will see from the statistics on trade that export growth has been dominated by oil producers. There is little doubt FDI flows have contributed to the expansion of this sector and helped to drive the growing dependence of African countries

Table 3.2 Developing country Asian FDI stock as a percentage of total FDI stock in the largest SSA recipient countries in different subregions, 2002–2012[17]

Country	2002–2004 (%)	2010–2012
Nigeria	2.3	22.6
Côte D'Ivoire	4.3	2.8
Eq Guinea	0.2	9.2
Congo, DRC	8	75.6
Uganda	3	3.4
Kenya	1.8	12.2
South Africa	4.0	5.6
Zimbabwe	5.2	34.4
Average	**3.6**	**20.8**

Source: Calculated from UNCTAD (2014).

on energy exports. This has permitted greater resilience during the Great Recession. Oil-producing countries, for example, grew by an average of 9.9 per cent in the period 2004–08. Growth was still as high as 7.4 per cent and 9.0 per cent in 2009 and 2010, respectively (IMF, 2014a). However, as we will discuss below, this dependence has the potential of exacerbating structural weaknesses that can leave many SSA countries badly exposed to any downturn in energy demand and prices.

Table 3.3 provides data on the direction of trade exports. The figures are quite striking. We saw above that the Great Recession had a much larger impact on the developed world, led by the EU, which experienced average annual negative growth of 0.13 per cent between 2008 and 2013. One key element in sustaining growth was the ability of SSA to diversify its export markets away from the advanced economies. Between 1995 and 2008 the share of exports to the emerging and developing countries increased from 22.7 per cent of the total to 36.7 per cent. This has continued in the aftermath of the Great Recession with the share nearly rising to a half of exports in 2013.

As a result, in 2009, excluding South Africa, SSA exports of goods and services were only 4.6 per cent below the 2007 level, compared with a global decline of 11.8 per cent. By 2013, African exports were 55 per cent above the 2007 level, compared to 34 per cent at the world level (UNCTAD, 2015).

OECD (2011) provides country- and region-specific data on the direction of African exports between 1992 and 2009.[18] Exports to OECD countries from Africa fell from 82 per cent of the total of exports to 62.7 per cent. The most significant drop is in exports to OECD Europe, which had absorbed 57.3 per cent of exports in 1992 but only 35.3 per cent by 2009. The drop is pretty much across the board in Europe both with former colonial powers like France and the UK (from 16.7 per cent of the total to 11.7 per cent) and others. China (including Hong Kong) and

Table 3.3 SSA direction of trade exports, 1995–2013 (percentages of world)

Year	1995	2000	2005	2008	2010	2012	2013
Advanced Economies	76.0	62.8	67.1	61.7	55.1	51.1	47.4
Emerging and Developing Countries	22.7	26.2	28.8	36.7	43.5	45.1	49.2

Source: Calculated from IMF (2015a).

India experienced the most dramatic increase in their share of African exports, rising from 3.3 per cent of the total to 18.8 per cent over the same period. OECD (op. cit.) also provides data on the import side of African trade over the same period of 1992 to 2009. The source illustrates a similar pattern on the import side. Imports from OECD countries fell from 81.5 per cent of the total to 58.4 per cent with the OECD European share falling from 55.1 to 38.5 per cent. Imports from China and India also increased significantly and rose from a tiny 2.7 per cent in 1992 to 17.9 per cent in 2009. There was some notable increase in the gap between the export and imported percentages in some countries and regions. In 1992, the difference in the percentage of exports over imports with OECD Europe was 2.2, but the figure was –3.3 points in 2009, likely indicating rising deficits in trade – even as the share was falling. Trade with China followed a similar pattern with the percentage of exports over imports rising from –0.1 per cent to –1.1 per cent by 2009. In contrast, the pattern went the opposite way with the gap between the percentage share of exports over imports to India rising from 0.7 per cent to 2 per cent.

3.3.5 Disengagement from the IMF

The literature on the impact of IMF policies on economic growth is long and protracted. Critics like Joe Stiglitz (2002) have long complained about the theoretical and ideological narrowness of the IMF with its almost pathological focus on the state as the source of all economic crises. During the Great Recession, a publicity-focused IMF factsheet argued that 'the domestic sources' of economic crises arise from 'excessive monetary creation, unsustainable fiscal deficits, an overvalued domestic currency, political instability, and natural disasters' (IMF, 2008a, p. 1). Later versions of the factsheet have been renamed 'IMF Crisis Lending' and have added 'weak financial systems' to the list, without specifying which part of the financial system (state or private) or its causes.[19] The September 2014 factsheet divides the sources into domestic and external shocks and is slightly vaguer in the language. For example, they now talk of 'inappropriate fiscal and monetary policy which can lead to large economic imbalances' (IMF, 2014b, p. 1). There is no mention of the role of domestic private actors. Still the emphasis is on 'sound policies' which are almost invariably pro-cyclical in nature during crises due to the assumed relationship between government spending and monetary policy and balances.[20] After the start of the crisis, the Fund argued they would shift from their normal position and support an increase in fiscal expenditures to deal with the collapse. This is quite explicit in a now widely quoted IMF paper by Antonio Spilimbergo et al. (2008).[21] However, reviews of the actual programs introduced in the wake of the Great Recession have shown strong evidence of the continuity with past program interventions with their emphasis on pro-cyclical polices (see, among others, Stein, 2010; Van Waeyenberge et al., 2010; Grabel, 2011; Weisbrod et al., 2009; Weisbrod and Ray, 2010). Moreover, the IMF has demonstrated its continued commitment to pro-cyclical policies in Europe over the past five years including the four year 2012 extended facility to Greece. The impact of these policies on economic growth is now widely documented in many articles and books covering many regions and time periods including studies by mainstream economists like Barro and Lee (2002).[22]

A key element in the sustaining of growth was the ability to completely avoid, diminish the frequency or decrease the duration of IMF loans. After the interventions following the Asian crisis, there was widespread anti-IMF sentiment in Asia and Latin America.

The position of Asian governments at the start of the crisis was nicely summed up by Wing Thye Woo of the Brookings Institute:

> Asian countries, especially those in East Asia, have a deep distrust for the Fund, given its 'poor track record' during the 1997 Asian financial crisis and 'no proof' that it has improved its competence over the years... at the moment no Malaysian, Indonesian and South Korean government could go to the IMF and expect to survive. (*China Daily*, Dec. 3, 2008)

In Latin America the online newspaper *Mercotor* reported in October 2008:

> The IMF became the target of popular contempt across the region for conditioning billions of dollars in much-needed loans on a so-called Washington consensus of policy dictates, including privatization, deregulation and balanced budgets. Many Latin American leaders blame those requirements for worsening economic hardships in the 1980s and 1990s rather than easing them, and pan what they consider the IMF continued heavy-handedness. 'The fund is not giving the world what it needs,' Argentine Economy Minister Carlos Fernandez said on behalf of six South American countries at an annual IMF meeting this month. 'Its financial assistance fails to provide the services members seek, as it continues to send immediate negative signals (and) comes with too many conditions.' Raw memories of their

experiences with the IMF tight lending terms make it unlikely that Latin Americans will run for IMF help again. (*Mercotor*, 2008, p. 1)

The data in Table 3.4 capture the economic activity of the IMF since the Asian crisis from the late 1990s through the end of 2014. Overall lending from the IMF following the Asian crisis remained high from 1998 through 2004, before declining rapidly as the global economy recovered. Outstanding General Resource Account (GRA) credit to largely middle-level-income countries fell by an unprecedented 91 per cent by 2007 (from SDR 65 billion to a mere SDR 6 billion), a level not seen since the 1970s (IMF, 2008b). This extraordinary fall did not happen immediately. It began in 2005, when Brazil and Argentina denounced the neo-liberal agenda of the Fund and repaid nearly $25 billion in loans. The battle between Argentina and the IMF was particularly vocal and vitriolic. The *Financial Times* quoted then Argentinian President, Néstor Kirchner, as saying the IMF had 'acted towards our country as a promoter and a vehicle of policies that caused poverty and pain among the Argentine people' (Thomson and Balls, 2005, p. 1). The payment back to the Fund came after two years of extremely poor relations between Argentina and the IMF following the three-year agreement signed in September, 2003. The third quarterly review led to the suspension of payments by the IMF in July, 2004 because Argentina had not complied with sufficient structural reforms. The response to previous reviews was for Argentina to threaten default on the $15 billion owed to the fund. However, this time they simply paid the $1.5 owed and unilaterally suspended the agreement with the IMF until January, 2005 (Cibelis, 2004). Argentina's successful debt swap and rise of reserves in 2005 allowed them to exit from the IMF.

This was followed by repayments from other large debtors, including Indonesia, Philippines, Serbia and Turkey. Even African countries followed suit and did their best to exit the Fund. As indicated in Table 3.4, only 13 SSA countries had programmes with the IMF in 2007 which was 15 fewer than the 1999 level. These repayments, with their subsequent decline in the payment of interests and fees to the IMF, forced the Fund to begin an unprecedented process of restructuring and retrenchment. We can see from Table 3.4, the operating income of the Fund declined, falling by nearly 80 per cent in 2007 compared to 2005 which in itself was well below the average of the previous seven years. In order to better understand the IMF's urgency to engage in such a process, one has to understand that the interests and fees paid only by Argentina between 1995 and 2005 reached an extraordinary sum of $3 billion. If we take

Table 3.4 IMF resources, disbursements, repayments, income and outstanding credit billions SDRs, 1998–2014

	General Resource Account				Out[1] Crd	PRGF-ESF (PRGT-ECF-SBC)-[2]				Out Cr	
Time	Useable Res.	Disburs.	Repay.	Out. Crd	SSA (No.)	Useable Res.	Disb	Repay	Out Crd.	SSA (No.)	Income
1998	53.6	20.6	6.7	60.5	 (4)	9.5	0.9	0.6	6.3	 (22)	2.52
1999	94.9	10.0	19.4	51.1	.334 (4)	10.3	0.7	0.6	6.4	3.7 (28)	2.61
2000	109.7	7.2	15.2	43.0	.088 (2)	11.4	0.5	0.6	6.3	3.2 (23)	2.41
2001	102.5	23.8	13.3	53.5	.060 (1)	14.5	0.9	0.8	6.4	3.0 (25)	2.20
2002	100.2	25.2	15.1	63.6	(0)	15.8	1.3	0.9	6.9	3.4 (24)	2.29
2003	100.7	20.3	18.9	65.0	(0)	15.8	0.8	0.8	6.9	2.8 (22)	2.40
2004	111.4	4.2	13.8	55.4	.064 (1)	15.8	0.8	0.9	6.8	2.9 (18)	2.34
2005	145.2	2.3	29.2	28.4	(0)	15.8	0.4	0.9	6.3	2.6 (18)	2.23
2006	161.2	2.4	21.0	9.8	(0)	15.8	0.5	2.9	3.8	.372 (18)	1.14
2007	165.4	1.0	4.7	6.0	(0)	15.8	0.3	0.4	3.8	1.1 (13)	.48

(*continued*)

Table 3.4 Continued

	General Resource Account				Out[1] Crd	PRGF-ESF (PRGT-ECF-SBC)-[2]				Out Cr	
Time	Useable Res.	Disburs.	Repay.	Out. Crd	SSA (No.)	Useable Res.	Disb	Repay	Out Crd.	SSA (No.)	Income
2008	152.4	13.4	1.9	17.5	.006 (2)	15.8	0.6	0.5	4.0	.745 (18)	.62
2009	290.2	20.5	0.7	37.2	.241 (3)	16.8	1.6	0.5	5.1	2.2 (22)	.53
2010	304.8	20.3	1.9	55.6	.593 (2)	23.5	0.9	1.1	4.8	1.6 (20)	.91
2011	396.9	33.6	2.0	87.3	.797 (2)	25.8	0.9	0.4	5.3	2.1 (17)	1.6
2012	373.1	15.0	12.2	90.0	.027 (1)	26.2	0.9	0.5	5.8	2.0 (19)	2.1
2013	404.5	13.5	19.7	47.5	(0)	26.2	0.8	0.4	6.2	1.6 (13)	2.3
2014	381.5	10.6	25.5	43.7	.029 (1)	26.2	0.5	0.4	6.3	1.6 (12)	2.4

Notes: [1] All figures correspond to SSA countries with outstanding loans with number in brackets relating to no. of countries with active loans during that year. All years except for 1999 and 1998 are taken from IMF (various years) and correspond to information in last report in December of each year using the recorded outstanding credit amount. No. of countries with loan activity are taken from Annual Reports of the IMF (IMF, 1998, 1999). Outstanding Credit for 1999 is taken from IMF, 2000.

[2] In 2010 the Poverty Reduction Growth Fund was renamed the Extended Credit Facility under the Poverty Reduction Growth Trust. Under the PRGT in 2010 loans were allocated for the Extended Shock Facility and for shorter term standby credit facilities.

Sources: IMF (various years; 2008b, 2009; 2015b).

into account the fact that during the same time the administrative costs of the Fund reached a total of $4.85 billion, it is obvious that the repayment of debts by Argentina had a tremendous impact on the IMF's work (Brenta, 2008). In effect, and in light of the wave of repayments during that period, the former IMF's Managing Director, Rodrigo de Rato, announced on May 2006 "the appointment of a committee of eminent persons to provide the Fund with an independent view of the available options for ensuring that it has a sustainable and durable income base with which to finance its running costs over the long term" (IMF, 2006, p. 1). The unprecedented decline in the use of IMF resources through the GRA, the major source of income for the Fund, led to the threat of large losses and the announcement of $100 million dollar cost reduction plan at the Fund in April 2008.[23]

However, with the Great Recession the fortunes of the IMF quickly reversed with 2014 income returning to the level of the early 2000s. However, much of the new income was from loans not to the old customers in Latin America, Asia and Africa but due to large disbursements to countries in Eastern, Central and Southern Europe. There were significant loans to Hungary, Ukraine Iceland and Latvia in 2008. In 2009 Romania, Serbia, Bosnia and Belarus borrowed heavily from the GRA. In 2010, Greece and Ireland joined in with a 26.4 billion SDR standby agreement and 19.5 billion SDR extended agreement respectively along with a large second loan to Ukraine. These loans in combination with lending to other European loans dwarfed all other loans. In December 2010, 83 per cent of all standby and extended loans were to European countries. The historically large users like middle income countries in South America did not participate in a single loan. For example, in December, 2000, six South American countries had loans in this category and constituting 50 per cent of the face value of all agreements. The domination was even greater with a large new facility to Portugal in 2011, and new loans to Serbia and Romania. Lending to Europe hit 91 per cent of the total. The pattern has continued to the present moment with Europe holding 95 per cent of the loans in December, 2012, 87 per cent in December, 2013 and 83 per cent in December, 2014 (calculated from IMF, various years).

What of sub-Saharan Africa? Most countries participate in the concessionary low-income facilities of the IMF, the Poverty Reduction Growth Facility/Trust and the Extended Shock Facility (until 2009), Extended Credit Facility and Standby Credits (from 2010) during the Great Recessions. Like other developing areas, the number of countries taking loans dropped compared to the previous global crisis of the late 1990s and early 2000s. For instance, only 22 countries had outstanding loans in the peak crisis year of 2009, compared to 28 in 1999. Two full years later (2001), the number of countries with programs was still quite high – 25 compared to only 17 in 2011. By 2013, there were only about half the number compared to the same four-five-year period following the Asian crisis (that is, 13 vs 25).

There is little doubt that the comparative absence of IMF programs had a substantial impact on the policy space in SSA during the Great Recession, permitting fiscal and monetary expansion rather than the typical contractionary policies.

3.4 Pro-cyclical and counter-cyclical policy in Africa

As argued above, the changing structure and nature of trade, aid and capital flows seems to have converged to permit the policy space for a greater counter-cyclical intervention.[24] The effort was fairly widespread and undertaken in the early stages of the Great Recession. In South Africa, the government increased public investment amounting to R 787 billion (around USD 100 billion) during 2010–12. The measures were aimed at generating growth with job creation.

In Kenya, government expenditures over 2009–10 increased by roughly 25 per cent from the year before, with financing coming from local infrastructure bonds and foreign aid. The government also undertook a number of other measures to expand the economy, such as the removal of duties on maize and maize products, a decrease in the rate of VAT on electricity, and increasing spending on public works. The focus of the packages was to increase domestic demand to compensate for the decline in exports, to generate employment, to use infrastructure and other tools to improve competitiveness and to expand programmes for the subsidization of food.

In their 2009–10 budget the Tanzanian government increased spending by around 30 per cent on infrastructural projects such as roads and energy projects. Partly as a result of IMF pressure they also raised equivalent revenue, although the overall effect was expansionary for the two-year fiscal periods of 2008–09 and 2009–10.

The Mauritius government also undertook counter-cyclical fiscal policy in May 2008 for the fiscal year 2008–09. The stimulus amounted to 3.4 per cent of GDP and focused on infrastructure, education and raising the competitiveness of domestically focused industries and SMEs. Similarly, in their 2009–10 budget the Ugandan government increased fiscal spending by 29 per cent compared with the previous fiscal year, with a focus on infrastructural and agricultural spending (Kasekende et al., 2010).

Leibfritz and Rottman (2013) illustrate the trend quite clearly. During the previous global downturn in 1997, the pattern was pro-cyclical – with rising revenues, declining expenditures and an overall lowering of deficits relative to GDP. In contrast, there was an opposite trend of counter-cyclical intervention, with expenditures rising, revenue falling and a large increase in the deficits after 2009.

Table 3.5 shows this very clearly, with the swing from a surplus in 2004–08 of 2 per cent of GDP to a deficit of 5.2 per cent in 2009, due to a rise in both expenditures relative to GDP and a fall in revenue. Following the fiscal year 2009, governments continued the high level of fiscal expansion relative to GDP, but the deficit declined because of the rise in revenue which lowered the deficit to 2.8 per cent of GDP. It also differentiates the changes for both African oil exporters and importers. As one can see, the pattern of a rapid rise in deficits in 2009 is even greater in the oil exporters, followed by a decline in 2010–13. The oil importers also show evidence of counter-cyclical fiscal policy with significant increases in government spending relative to GDP. Revenues were fairly stable in 2009, however, leading to less of a rise in the deficit. Unlike oil producers, expenditures continued to increase through 2013 and the deficit continued at an average of 4.5 per cent of GDP.

Governments also undertook counter-cyclical monetary policy through the expansion of the money supply and the lowering of interest rates. Table 3.6 provides data on lending rates for a selection of countries in SSA for which data are available. We can see that the vast majority of countries had lower lending rates in both 2008 and 2009 – or in at least one of the years. The only countries with higher rates in 2008 and 2009 compared with 2007 were Kenya, the Seychelles, Uganda and Zambia. In 2008, the Seychelles and Zambia both signed agreements with the

Table 3.5 African fiscal policy, 2004–2013 (percentage of GDP)

Region		2004–2008	2009	2010–2013
Africa	Revenue	29.5	26.9	28.2
	Expenditure	27.5	32	31.0
	Fiscal Balance	2.0	–5.2	–2.8
Oil Exporters	Revenue	34.0	28.6	30.4
	Expenditure	28.9	34.3	31.7
	Fiscal Balance	5.1	–5.7	–1.3
Oil Importers	Revenue	24.7	24.8	25.6
	Expenditure	25.9	29.3	30.0
	Fiscal Balance	–1.1	–4.5	–4.5

Source: Leibfritz and Rottman (2013).

Table 3.6 Lending rates during the Great Recession, 2007–2011

Country	2007	2008	2009	2010	2011
Angola	17.7	12.5	15.7	22.5	18.8
Botswana	16.2	16.5	13.8	11.5	11.0
Burundi	16.8	16.5	14.1	12.4	13.2
Cape Verde	10.6	10.0	11.0	11.0	9.8
Comoros	10.5	10.5	7.0	7.0	7.3
Congo, Dem. Rep.	47.0	43.2	65.4	56.5	43.8
Djibouti	11.2	11.6	11.1	10.3	10.6
Gambia, The	27.9	27.0	27.0	27.0	28.0
Kenya	13.3	14.0	14.8	14.4	15.0
Lesotho	14.1	16.2	13.0	11.2	10.4
Liberia	15.0	14.4	14.2	14.2	13.8
Madagascar	45.0	45.0	45.0	49.0	52.5
Malawi	27.7	25.3	25.3	24.6	23.8
Mauritania	23.5	20.3	19.5	17.0	17.0
Mauritius	21.9	11.5	9.3	8.9	8.9
Mozambique	19.5	18.3	15.7	16.3	19.1
Namibia	12.9	13.7	11.1	9.7	8.7
Nigeria	16.9	15.5	18.4	17.6	16.0
Rwanda	16.1	16.5	16.1	16.7	–
São Tomé and Príncipe	32.4	32.4	31.1	28.9	27.0
Seychelles	10.9	11.8	15.3	12.7	11.2
Sierra Leone	25.0	24.5	22.2	21.3	21.0
South Africa	13.2	15.1	11.7	9.8	9.0
Swaziland	13.2	14.8	11.4	9.8	9.0
Tanzania	16.1	15.0	15.0	14.5	15.0
Uganda	19.1	20.5	21.0	20.2	21.8
Zambia	18.9	19.1	22.1	20.9	18.8

Source: World Bank (2015a).

IMF. One can also note some countries that lowered rates in 2008 and raised them in 2009. (In some cases, this was due to new agreements with the IMF in 2009.) This includes Angola, DRC, and Tanzania.

Many of the falls in interest rates were the deliberate product of counter-cyclical policy where policy space was available. At the end of 2008, for example, the South African Reserve Bank relaxed monetary policy through October 2009, with a cumulative 500 basis point reduction in its policy rate. The Bank of Mauritius reduced its policy rate by 400 basis points between January 2008 and March 2009.

In Botswana, the Central Bank also reduced its rate on a number of occasions, leading to a significant decline in its lending rate between 2008 and 2011. Tanzania's Central Bank also increased the money supply growth by several percentage points, before the IMF demanded a cut in credit by 10 per cent after 2009 (Stein, 2010; Kasekende et al., 2010).

3.5 Structure of trade and the sustainability of growth in Africa

One disturbing trend in Africa is the continued dependence on the production and export of unprocessed raw materials, with a heavy and growing reliance on petroleum and gas exports. Table 3.7 provides details on the structure of the GDP in Sub-Saharan African countries. There are a number of striking features. First we can see that neoliberalism of the 1980s and 1990s dramatically pushed down government spending relative to GDP to a very low 13–14 per cent after 1990. Second, the biggest structural change is the collapse of manufacturing and the growth of mining. Mining (with some utilities) were roughly 13–14 per cent of GDP in the 1970s and 1980s, rising to 16 per cent in the 1990s.

Table 3.7 GDP components of SSA excluding South Africa, 1970–2012

Average percentage shares of GDP	1970–9	1980–9	1990–9	2000–6	2008	2012
2009						
Consumption	68%	73%	74%	69%	66%	64%
Government expenditure	20%	19%	14%	13%	13%	14%
Investment	17%	13%	16%	17%	18%	20%
Exports	33%	30%	33%	34%	40%	41%
Imports	38%	36%	37%	32%	36%	39%
Agriculture, hunting, forestry, fishing	30%	28%	31%	29%	27%	26%
Industry	40%	40%	32%	35%	36%	37%
Mining, Manufacturing, Utilities	34%	36%	28%	31%	33%	32%
Manufacturing	21%	22%	12%	9%	7%	7%
Construction	6%	4%	4%	4%	4%	5%
Services	30%	32%	38%	36%	37%	37%
Wholesale, retail trade, restaurants and hotels	12%	12%	14%	13%	14%	15%
Transport, storage and communications	5%	5%	5%	6%	6%	6%
Other Activities	14%	15%	18%	17%	16%	16%

Source: Jomo and Von Arnim (2012); UNCTAD (2015).

However, it jumped to 24 per cent after 2000 and in doubled to the range of 25–6 per cent of GDP after the start of the Great Recession compared to the pre-structural adjustment period. This has corresponded to a massive decline in the manufacturing share of GDP from around 20 per cent to 9 per cent in the 1990s to a mere 7 per cent after 2008. The trends reflect the impact of neoliberalism which both dismantled the state organizations and policies that supported manufacturing while pushing SSA to specialize in unprocessed raw material in line with its static comparative advantage. This deindustrializing tendency was built into the underlying economic logic and policies associated with structural adjustment in Africa.

In the world of adjustment, devaluation and import liberalization, the reduction of protectionism and monetary policy that produces positive real interest rates would reward efficient companies while punishing inefficient industries. Companies would have incentives to become more export-oriented, and more labor-intensive and to use more local inputs, allowing the country to exploit its comparative advantage. The result would be a prosperous sector, which would greatly enhance exports while diminishing the use of imports. The poor performance of manufacturing is not surprising. Policies such as interest and exchange rate liberalization and government expenditure cuts, layoffs and austerity were debilitating to local manufacturing companies resulting in depressed markets and bankruptcies. As seen in Table 3.7, by the drop in government spending from around 20 per cent of GDP in the 1970s to 13–14 per cent after 1990, governments were unable to invest in the infrastructure and human capital needed to support competitive manufacturing. Adjustment induced import deregulation and the associated removal of tariffs after the 1980s leading to the flooding of markets that undercut local production (Stein, 1992, 2008; Lall, 1992; 1995; Mkandawire, 1988).

Governments were under great pressure to divest in industry under adjustment. Few companies survived and many companies were deliberately liquidated. Between 1986 and 1998, Tanzania divested 183 parastatals, but only 83 were privatizations (Gibbon, 1999). By 2005, Zambia privatized 261 out of 282 companies in many sectors, including manufacturing. From 1985 through 2005, the number of textile factories fell from 140 to around 50, with an associated collapse of employment by nearly two-thirds. Few of the remaining privatized or restructured factories could produce internationally competitive products for exports (Pitcher, 2007). As some writers have argued, if states had rescued and rehabilitated failing enterprises instead of allowing them to be liquidated or privatized, often leading to bankruptcy, it is likely that SSA's manufacturing sectors would have been able to build on the previous twenty years of accumulated learning and experience. Instead, structural adjustment has largely returned Africa to its colonial-style extractive economy with its emphasis on unprocessed raw materials and cash crop exports (Lawrence, 2005).[25] We can see this clearly in the structure of exports.

UNCTAD (2015) provides a breakdown of exports from SSA by Standard International Trade Classification (SITC) for the period 1995 to 2013 and allows one to differentiate exports into primary commodity exports (SITC 0 + 1 + 2 + 3 + 4 + 68 + 667+ 971), fuel exports and manufacturing exports. There has been a dramatic growth in aggregate exports in recent years. Between 1995 and 2008, the total increased from $48.6 billion to $268.8 billion – a jump of nearly 600 per cent. The biggest source of growth was in fuels, which increased by more than 1,000 per cent over that period. By 2008, they amounted to a whopping 72.1 per cent of the total – up from 39.8 per cent in 1995. Overall, roughly 80 per cent of the increase was from fuels. Due largely to a rise in the value of oil and other key minerals and metals, primary commodity exports rose from an already very high 87.6 per cent of the total in 1995 to an overwhelming 93 per cent. Figures show that little has changed over the course of the Great Recession and its aftermath, with primary commodities constituting 92.5 per cent of exports in 2013. Meanwhile the manufacturing export share dropped by nearly a half – from 11.8 per cent in 1995 to a mere 6.5 per cent in 2008. The heavy reliance on the export of primary commodities has allowed SSA to ride the commodity boom of the past decade, but also leaves the continent susceptible to any downturn. Table 3.8 illustrates the rise in the terms of trade after 2000, increasing by 36 per cent through 2005, and, with the exception of the downturn in 2009, continuing to rise following the Great Recession. By 2012 the terms of trade had nearly double compared to just 12 years before.

These numbers are quite impressive from a historical perspective, but also reveal the clear dangers of relying on commodities whose prices

Table 3.8 Trade indicators, 2000–2013 SSA, excluding South Africa

Year	2000	2005	2008	2009	2010	2011	2012	2013
Terms of trade Index	100.00	136.89	177.80	146.33	168.34	189.91	190.32	187.65
Purchasing Power Index of Exports	100.00	184.43	257.88	204.68	254.86	284.08	288.62	286.95

Source: UNCTAD (2015).

are notoriously volatile. Between 1980 and 1997 the net barter terms of trade fell by 47 per cent (Stein, 2014). Table 3.9 provides information on the price of key commodities exported by SSA countries. It covers the period from 1970 to 2013. Prior to 2000, the last commodity boom in the post-independence period had occurred in the 1970s with an extraordinary rise in a wide variety of commodities, including at least a tripling or more in the price of most agricultural products and a rapid rise in the price of petroleum. The twenty-year period from 1980 to 2000 was not good for the products produced by SSA, with a decline in most commodity prices. The fall was particularly acute in some goods. The price of robusta coffee, for example, plummeted by two-thirds but was not alone in the tropical beverage category – which declined, on average, by 50 per cent. Cotton prices were also 40 per cent below their 1980 levels. The turnaround in prices is also striking, with the tripling of the price of minerals and metals led by the extraordinary rise in the price of petroleum and copper between 2000 and 2008. While more moderate, most agriculturally produced raw materials increased in price, with the price of food more than doubling. We can see that the Great Recession led to an across-the-board decline, which recovered thereafter with most prices matching or even exceeding the pre-Great Recession level by 2011.

It is quite clear that the commodity boom of the past decade created the policy space and opportunity for SSA to adjust their policies and reorient their economies toward greater South–South ties (Salazaar-Xirinachs, Nubler and Kozul-Wright, 2014). This is not unlike the experience of the last commodity boom, which was used to build import-substituting industrialization in Africa (Fransman, 1982). However, the reorientation toward the South has done little to alter the basic structure of these economies. The concern now is that the commodity boom is now completed and we could see a downward cycle on prices with implications to the sustainability of growth in Africa, along with a potential loss of policy space. Table 3.9 also includes data on the movement in commodity prices between the peak month in 2014 and January 2015. The signs for 2014–15 are rather worrisome, with declines of 56 per cent in petroleum, 31.6 per cent in metals and nearly 20 per cent in food and beverages. The simple average from the table generates more than a 20 per cent decline across the board. These trends have continued in 2015. Between January and August metals fell by an additional 15.05 per cent, petroleum by 4 per cent and food and beverages by 8 per cent (Index Mundi, 2015).

A second concern associated with the structure of African economies is the quality of growth in terms of the ability both to reduce poverty

Table 3.9 Commodity Price Indices, 1970–2015 (2000=100)

Year	1970	1980	1990	2000	2005	2008	2009	2010	2011	2012	2013	% change peak '14-Jan, 15[1]
Food	54	183	125	100	127	234	220	230	265	270	255	–17.1
Tropical Beverages	65	212	108	100	126	178	181	213	270	212	174	–6.5
Vegetable Oils and Oils	75	166	107	100	141	298	213	262	333	307	269	–19.1
Agricultural Raw Materials	40	131	128	100	129	198	163	226	289	223	206	–10.0
Minerals, Ores and Metals	54	116	127	100	173	332	232	327	375	322	306	–31.6
Crude Petroleum	8	126	78	100	189	344	219	280	368	372	369	–56.2
Coffee Arabica	70	261	104	100	127	153	139	182	305	215	148	–15.9
Coffee Robusta	98	349	131	100	127	252	183	200	275	263	239	–8.6
Copper	49	78	125	100	169	307	271	406	458	418	391	–20.0
Cotton	46	140	112	100	88	116	105	127	291	138	128	–30.5

[1] Not all categories under this column fully match. This figure for metals, ores etc is only for metals and does not include energy products. The change for tropical beverages also use the general beverage index from Index mundi. The index on vegetable oil, oilseeds and oils etc. combines sunflower and palm oil.

Sources: UNCTAD (2015); Index Mundi (2015).

levels and to generate employment, two important dimensions of the creation of middle classes and the kinds of expenditure flows that can help sustain long-term growth. The elasticities of growth to poverty and employment are very low in SSA. A one percentage growth in GDP leads to a decline in poverty of only 0.95 per cent, which is very anemic by global standards. SSA has the lowest income elasticity of poverty among the six developing areas of the world (Page and Shimeles, 2014).

A key element in poverty reduction is the movement of the labor force from low- to higher-productivity activities which have the potential to pay out higher wages. Industry, and particularly manufacturing, tends to have higher productivity than the service and agricultural sectors. On average, in lower-income Africa, the productivity of labor in manufacturing compared to agriculture is roughly 3.8 to 1. Structurally changing economies from agriculture to industry can have a significant impact on poverty reduction. Page and Shimeles (2014) regress headcount poverty rates on multiple variables, including per capita income, Gini coefficients for income distribution, and the share of employment in agriculture, services and industry. They use a generalized method of moments (GMM) approach and a two-period lag to avoid endogeneity problems. Based on a sample of all developing countries and controlling for the growth of income and the distribution of income, they estimated that the poverty headcount will fall by .8 per cent for each one per cent increase in industrial employment.

Moreover, there is a strong negative relationship between the rate of growth and employment generation with the fastest-growing African countries having the lowest elasticity of employment (Page, 2012). Studies of the direction of the elasticity of growth to employment are also disturbing. Kapsos (2005) analyzes the trends covering the period 1993 to 2003 in SSA and other parts of the world. In the case of SSA, elasticity declined by nearly 30 per cent between 1991 and 1995 and 1999 and 2003.

One particularly important issue is the population structure of African countries which has huge implications for youth employment. Africa has the youngest age structure in the world – in 2011 the ten countries with the youngest average population were in Africa. Projections indicate that Africa could have the largest labor force by 2040, a development that will pose extraordinary challenges. At present, while youth make up 40 per cent of the working-age population they comprise 60 per cent of the unemployed. In some individual countries, the ratio is much higher. In Nigeria, for example, the rate is five to one when comparing youth to general unemployment rates (Page, 2012). Worse still is the effect of the rising levels of migration of young people to urban areas, driven in part by landlessness in villages and the absence of land set aside for youth in some countries that are generating land use plans as part of formalization exercises. In Tanzania, a study of 30 villages in three regions documented a landlessness rate of 11 per cent, with some villages exceeding 30 per cent of the population. For the most part, there was no land set aside in the villages with land use plans.[26] The problem is that in some African countries the youth unemployment rate can be as much as six times higher in urban areas than it is in rural areas.

Worse, most are employed in the informal sector where income is low and uncertain and the working conditions are difficult. An estimated 81.5 per cent of all working people are classified as working poor, well above the global average of 39 per cent. In addition, most new jobs generated tend to be in the informal economy. The problem again is tied to the structure of these economies discussed above. Page (2012) compares SSA to a benchmark of countries that have managed to cross the lower-middle income and achieve both sustained growth and employment generation. Using a selection of low-income African countries, he illustrates that the structural change is far below the benchmark level with the manufacturing share of value added labor employment roughly half of the benchmark. In addition the manufacturing sector that does exist has performed poorly with labor productivity below the levels found in the benchmark.

Despite the high levels of GDP growth labor productivity growth has been anemic with the structural tendencies of SSA countries feeding into this dynamic. Table 3.10 provides data on the trends in output per worker in the four subregions of SSA covering the period from 1980 to 2010.

We can see that the output per worker has been stagnant in East Africa, negative in West Africa and Central Africa in the 1980s and 1990s with a small positive direction after 2000 and a general upward trend in Southern Africa. A quick glance would indicate an upward trend in

Table 3.10 SSA output per worker by subregion, 1980–2010

Region of SSA	1980s	1990s	2000s
East	0.003	0.004	0.03
Central	–0.003	–0.034	0.004
South	0.006	0.007	0.017
West	–0.011	–0.017	0.009

Source: UNECA (2014).

the movement of productivity in line with economic growth which would seem to indicate that the trend away from manufacturing has not hurt productivity. However, McMillan and Rodrik (2011) take the analysis a step further. They argue that that labor productivity can grow due to expansion within a sector or the movement of labor from low- to higher-productivity sectors or what they refer to as structurally transforming productivity growth. They decompose the growth in labor productivity in a sample of 11 African countries and indicate that internal sectoral growth increased by 2.1 per cent while structural transforming labor productivity growth led to a decline of –1.3 per cent. In essence, SSA's deindustrialization has led to the perverse tendency for labor to move from high- to low-productivity occupations over the period 1990–2005, a development which is not a recipe for growth sustainability with shared prosperity.

3.6 Summary and conclusions

The paper has examined the impact of the Great Recession on Sub-Saharan Africa. Sub-Saharan Africa as a whole did quite well during the Great Recession both compared to other regions and also relative to global growth. There were a number of factors responsible for this outcome. An important element was the reorientation of the economies toward Southern trading partners and to sources of alternative FDI inflows. By moving away from their traditional Western partners, who were hit much harder by the Great Recession, they were able to diminish the effect of the downturn. In addition, less reliance on aid from the West which has often been replete with problematic conditionality has permitted greater policy space enhanced by the rise of reserves from new sources of finance and the resource commodity boom of the past decade.

Unlike so many previous downturns, a key element was the ability to avoid IMF programs and to pursue anti-cyclical fiscal and monetary policy during the Great Recession. New financing sources have also permitted historically larger levels of infrastructural spending during the Great Recession, acting effectively as anti-recessionary public work projects The latter section of the paper raises questions on the sources of growth, the structure of economies in Africa, and the sustainability of growth, particularly in the service of broadly shared prosperity for the populations of African countries.

The latter point challenges the wisdom in some circles that the key to changing the problematic way that SSA countries have integrated into the global economy is by enhancing South–South cooperation through greater financial and trade linkages. While this shift was clearly important in diminishing the effect of the global downturn, it has done little to alter the character of trade or the structure of the economy with an overreliance on unprocessed agricultural commodities and minerals. This does not bode well for the sustainability of growth with shared prosperity.

Notes

1. An earlier version of this paper was presented at 'Emerging Economies During and After the Great Recession', sponsored by the Cambridge Trust for New Thinking in Economics, St Catherine's College, Cambridge University, 26 March 2015. Also presented as a plenary session at the International Conference, Developments in Economic Theory and Policy sponsored by the Department of Applied Economics V, Faculty of Economics and Business, University of the Basque Country, Bilbao, Spain, 25–6 June, 2015. Author thanks Sam Cunningham, Philip Arestis and Malcolm Sawyer for their helpful comments.
2. This statistic does not include South Africa.
3. See, for example, Mendoza (1995), Kydland and Zarazaga, (1997) and Pallage and Robe (2001). Later literature like Aguiar and Gopinath (2007) use similar real business cycle models to argue that shocks to trend growth are due to productivity changes rather than short-term fluctuations around a stable trend and caused the higher volatility in emerging economies. This is used to explain things like the higher variations in consumption relative to income, and greater volatility in net exports and income in emerging markets compared to developed countries. The model hinges on an absurd set of assumptions including the notion that agents are aware of the degree of persistence of shocks and adjust their behaviour accordingly in an optimal manner. Hence one can use aggregates like consumption, investment and net exports to identify underlying trends in productivity. For this to occur one must be in the fantasy world (see below) of the permanent income hypothesis. Hence if consumption is lowered more in emerging markets during a downturn it is because it is perceived as a permanent change in the trend line, e.g., if it was transitory there would be less adjusting given the knowledge that the people would soon return to the natural trend of their permanent incomes. Naoussi and Tripier (2010) use the model to explain the higher variations in consumption in SSA, e.g., trend shocks in productivity are even higher in African countries. Rand and Tarp (2002) examine data on variations in income and private and public consumption and find no evidence of behavior associated with the Permanent Income Hypothesis. Of course, the idea that millions of African subsistence farmers and informal sector workers which constitute the majority of the working population fully understand how quotidian shocks affect their transitory vs permanent income is nothing short of absurd to anyone other than a neoclassical economist.
4. They define good policies as the usual suspects including low inflation and inflation targeting, good fiscal and external balances, exchange rate flexibility, trade openness, and so on.

5. Blanchard et al. (2010) also find a positive effect using the ratio of reserves to short term debt which could be from the numerator or denominator. They disaggregate the two possible sources and discover that the change in short-term debt leads to these econometric results not an alteration in reserves. Bussière et al. (2015) reject this argument since it is the ratio itself that is important, e.g., sending the message that debt is easily covered by reserves. Moreover even when they ran regressions using different combinations of reserves to GDP and short term debt to GDP they got ambiguous results. Their working paper version, (Bussière et al.,2014) provides much more information on this than the published version, including the list of countries used.
6. As of June 2013, South Africa had about $10 billion of sovereign bonds outstanding, and, even after all the sovereign bond issues by other countries in sub-Saharan Africa, was still greater at that point than the combined total for all other sub-Saharan sovereigns (BMI June 11, 2013).
7. For example, according to OECD statistics, of the $164 billion in external debt that the governments of sub-Saharan Africa collectively owed at the end of 1990, only 17 per cent was owed to foreign banks, with the remaining 83 per cent owed to OECD governments and international financial institutions, principally the World Bank and the International Monetary Fund (George, 1992). More recently, all private lenders combined accounted for barely 5 per cent of total foreign loans to governments of low-income countries from 2006-2010, compared to 20 per cent from bilateral loans, 11 per cent from the IMF, 34 per cent from the World Bank (2015b) and 29 per cent from other multilateral lenders such as regional development banks (calculated from Jones, 2012, p. 26). Though not specific to sub-Saharan Africa, these figures do give an overall sense of the sources of developing country sovereign borrowing.
8. The International Development Association is the branch of the World Bank which lends to low-income countries, currently defined as countries which had a 2012 GNI per capita of less than $1,205. The Bank defines concessional lending as follows: "The IDA lends money on concessional terms. This means that IDA charges little or no interest and repayments are stretched over 25 to 40 years, including a 5- to 10-year grace period" (World Bank, 2012). On these terms, the grant element of IDA loans exceeds 60 per cent of the total sum lent (IMF and World Bank, 2012, p. 10).
9. There is an extensive literature examining the consequences of IMF loans and associated conditionality on social, political and economic indicators. There seems to be considerable evidence that reforms increase unemployment and poverty rates, exacerbate income equality, lowers economic growth and reduce social services. See Stein, 2010 for a review of some of this literature.
10. Yates (2009, p. 2079). Yates' analysis is a simple back-of-the-envelope extension across two decades using the figure of 153,000 excess child deaths per year, which was the lower bound of the relevant confidence interval resulting from the simulation of the effect of user fees in 20 (unspecified) African countries published in James et al. (2005).
11. Figures do not include South Africa.
12. The sub-Saharan governments which regularly issue bonds in their local currencies are Angola, Benin, Botswana, Burkina Faso, Burundi, Cameroon,

Côte d'Ivoire, the Democratic Republic of Congo, Gambia, Ghana, Guinea, Guinea-Bissau, Kenya, Madagascar, Malawi, Mali, Mauritania, Morocco, Mozambique, Namibia, Niger, Nigeria, Rwanda, Senegal, the Seychelles, Sierra Leone, South Africa, Swaziland, Tanzania, Togo, Uganda and Zambia. The eight member states of the Western African Economic and Monetary Union, or WAEMU, issue bonds denominated in CFA francs. (OECD 2012, p. 29). Interestingly, Gabon and Congo-Brazzaville have issued dollar-denominated Eurobonds but do not regularly issue bonds in their own currencies, although Gabon issued a $180 million CFA franc-denominated bond simultaneously with its Eurobond issue in 2007 (Birch et al., 2012, p. 86).

13. Multiple sources incorrectly list the $750 million Ghanaian Eurobond issue of September, 2007 as the first sub-Saharan Eurobond issue outside of South Africa (see, for example, Sulaiman, 2012).
14. If we take the figure above on reserves for 2013 subtract the $45 billion reserves in South Africa taken from World Bank, 2015a the total falls to around $174 billion. The figure of $20.5 divided by $174 billion is roughly 12 per cent. South Africa dwarfed any individual player in other parts of Africa issuing an estimated $10.9 B of bonds over the 2006–14 period or nearly 25 per cent of reserves (Hakim, 2014).
15. Unless otherwise explicitly indicated, the following discussion of Congolese debt restructuring is based on Richards (2010), an article published in a legal journal and written by a practicing attorney who is partner at a firm that is involved with Congo's creditors in the debt restructuring negotiations.
16. For example, Myanmar, Somalia, Sudan and Zimbabwe have all thus far declined to participate in the HIPC initiative. This may be because they are already making no payments on the old debt that might eventually be canceled, and yet they would need to resume some level of payments during the HIPC debt relief process, which can take years. Thus one could view applying for HIPC debt relief as irrational for these governments unless they strongly desire to regain the ability to borrow new funds in international capital markets (Jones 2012, p. 13).
17. Countries listed are two largest with data available in four sub-regions of SSA East, West, Central and Southern Africa.
18. Figures in this report are from all regions of Africa not just sub-Saharan Africa.
19. As many have argued the IMF, itself, has contributed to the weakening of financial systems by encouraging developing countries to deregulate their financial systems. See Stiglitz (2002).
20. The linkage between government expenditure reductions and monetary contraction is embedded in the Polak financial program model which has provided the rationale for austerity during recessions in the IMF since the 1950s. For a discussion of the problematic nature and assumptions of the model, see Stein (2010).
21. They argue that the economic downturn was driven both by a financial crisis and the collapse in aggregate demand. They indicated the usual option for addressing aggregate demand through devaluations, which is to stimulate exports through monetary policy, was not available. The former because it is a global phenomenon and will only lead to competitive devaluations and the latter because it has already been fully utilized in many countries or

because the financial sectors have become too dysfunctional for it to work. They argued "in these circumstances, the Managing Director of the IMF has called for a sizable fiscal response at the global level..." (Spilimbergo et al., 2008, p. 3).
22. Some examples of studies demonstrating the link between IMF conditionality and economic growth include Dreher (2006); Przeworski and Vreeland (2003); and Vreeland 2003. See Boyer (2012) and Alexiou and Nellis (2013) for the impact of IMF austerity in the context of Europe.
23. This section draws on Stein and Kedar (2010).
24. Of course we assume that counter-cyclical policy is growth enhancing and eases the burden of downturns on populations in Africa countries. We therefore reject arguments such as the crowding out effect of deficits which make little sense in general and even less so in many African countries where banks have large excess liquid reserves. Between 1990 and 2009, the median bank liquid reserves to asset ratio varied in a sample of 18 SSA countries in between 11 per cent to very lofty 19 per cent. In 2009, the level was 19 per cent which was also reached in 2005 and 1993. In contrast, the ratio in the OECD countries and in most of the years in that period was in the 3 to 4 per cent range. See Nana and Samson (2014) for the data and for a study of the causes and consequences of the high liquid reserve ratios.
25. An additional disturbing indicator is the rise in the export concentration index from .24 to .43 from 1995 to 2011 (Harsmar, 2014).
26. The study is part of an ongoing effort to examine the impact of formalization on poverty in Tanzania undertaken by Howard Stein, Faustin Maganga, Kelly Askew and Rie Odgaard between 2009 and 2015 in four regions Dodoma, Kigoma, Manyara and Mbeya. The first stage of the project was financed by the National Science Foundation, between 2009 and 2013 and focused on the regions of Manyara and Mbeya. The current project is supported by a generous grant from the Royal Danish embassy in Tanzania and covers the period 2014 to 2016. The project has already surveyed villages in Dodoma and the region of Kigoma.

References

Aguiar, M. and Gopinath, G. (2007) 'Emerging Market Business Cycles: The Cycle Is the Trend', *Journal of Political Economy*, 115(1), 69–102.

Alexiou, C. and Nellis, J.G. (2013) 'Challenging the Raison d'être of Internal Devaluation in the Context of the Greek Economy', *Panoeconomicus*, 60(6), 813–36.

Akyüz, Yılmaz (2013) 'Waving or Drowning: Developing Countries After the Financial Crisis', South Centre, Research Paper 48, June.

Barro, Robert and Jong-wha Lee (2002) 'IMF Lending: Who Is Chosen and What Are the Effects?', NBER Working Papers Series, no. 8951.

Bazbauers, Adrian Robert (2014) 'The Wolfensohn, Wolfowitz, and Zoellick Presidencies: Revitalizing the Neoliberal Agenda of the World Bank', *Forum for Development Studies*, 14(1), 91–114.

Bigg, M and Kopodo, K. (2014) 'Ghana Sells $1 B. Eurobond at Less Than Expected Rate of 8.125 Pct.", uk.reuters.com/article/2014/09/11/ghana-eurobonds-idUKL5N0RC5HH20140911.

Birch, Cailin, Maxime Longangue, Nathaniel Lowbeer-Lewis and Souhir Mzali (2012) *The Report: Gabon 2012*, London: Oxford Business Group. http://books.google.com/books/about/The_Report_Gabon_2012.html?id=DWrPO8aE7XkC.

Blanchard, O.J., Das, M. and Faruqee, H. (2010) 'The Initial Impact of the Crisis on Emerging Market Countries', *Brookings Papers in Economic Activity*, 41(1) (Spring), 263–323.

Boyer, Robert (2012) 'The Four Fallacies of Contemporary Austerity Policies: The Lost Keynesian Legacy', *Cambridge Journal of Economics*, 36(1), 283–312.

Brenta, N. (2008) *Argentina Atrapada. Historia de Las Relaciones Con el FMI, 1956–2006*, Buenos Aires: Ediciones Cooperativas, 122–5.

Brown, Rowland (2011) 'The Eurobond and other Sticky Subjects', *Namibia*, Issue 005, November: Capricorn Investment Holdings. Available at: http://www.cih.com.na/economics/Documents/Namibia%20and%20the%20Eurobond.pdf.

Bureau of Labor Statistics (BLS) (2015) 'Seasonally Adjusted Unemployment Rate 2005–2015', http://data.bls.gov/timeseries/LNS14000000.

Bussière, M., Cheng, G., Chinn, M.D. and Lisack, N. (2014) 'For a Few Dollars More: Reserves and Growth in Times of Crises', NBER Working Paper, no. 19791.

Bussière, M., Cheng, G., Chinn, M. D. and Lisack, N. (2015) 'For a Few Dollars More: Reserves and Growth in Times of Crises', *Journal of International Money and Finance*, (52), 127–45.

BMI (2013) 'Market Strategy – Regional Asset Class Strategy', 5 June.

Chen, Shaohua and Martin Ravaillion (2008) 'The Developing World is Poorer Than We Thought But No Less Successful in the Fight Against Poverty', World Bank Policy Research Paper, no. 4703, August.

China Daily (2008) 'Bitter IMF Pills Difficult for Asia to Swallow', 3 December.

Cibelis, Alan (2004) 'Argentina and the IFIs: Better off Without Them?', Center for Economic Policy Research, October.

Dreher, Alex (2006) 'IMF and Economic Growth: The Effects of Programs, Loans, and Compliance with Conditionality', *World Development*, 34(50), 769–88.

Fransman, M. (ed.) (1982) *Industry and Accumulation in Africa*, vol. 11, London and Exeter, NH: Heinemann.

George, Susan (1992) 'Uses and Abuses of African Debt', *Dissent*, Summer.

Gibbon, Peter (1999) 'Privatisation and Foreign Direct Investment in Mainland Tanzania, 1992–98', CDR Working Paper Subseries v.99.1.

Grabel, I. (2011) 'Not Your Grandfather's IMF: Global Crisis, "Productive Incoherence" and Developmental Policy Space', *Cambridge Journal of Economics*, 35(5), 805–30.

Hakim, Danny (2014) 'Investors are Eager for African Sovereign Debt, Despite Plenty of Risk', *Dealbook*, 23 October. http://dealbook.nytimes.com/2014/10/23/investors-are-eager-for-african-sovereign-debt-despite-plenty-of-risks/?_r=0.

Harsmar, Mats (2014) 'Structural Improvements in Sub-Saharan Africa', *Southern African Journal of International Affairs*, 21(1), 69–88.

Heita, Desie (2011) 'Namibia: Eurobond Issue Wets [sic] International Appetite', *New Era: Newspaper for a New Namibia*, 2 November. http://allafrica.com/stories/201111020323.html.

International Development Association (IDA) and IMF (2010) 'Heavily Indebted Poor Countries (HIPC) Initiative and Multilateral Debt Relief Initiative (MDRI) – Status of Implementation', Sept. http://www.imf.org/external/np/pp/eng/2010/091410.pdf.

IMF (1998) 'Annual Report, 1998'. http://www.imf.org/external/pubs/ft/ar/1999/.

IMF (2000) 'Financial Statements, Quarterly Report, January 31'. http://www.imf.org/external/pubs/ft/quart/2000fy/013100.pdf.

IMF (2005) 'Regional Economic Outlook, Sub-Saharan Africa, October'. https://www.imf.org/external/pubs/ft/afr/reo/2005/eng/02/pdf/ssareo.pdf.

IMF (2006) 'IMF Managing Director de Rato Appoints Committee of Eminent Persons to Study Sustainable Long-Term Financing of IMF Running Costs'. https://www.imf.org/external/np/sec/pr/2006/pr06100.htm.

IMF (2008a) 'Fact Sheet: Crisis and the IMF Lending'. http://www.imf.org/external/np/exr/facts/crislend.htm.

IMF (2008b) *Annual Report, 2008*, Washington, DC: IMF.

IMF (2009) *Annual Report, 2009*, Washington, DC: IMF.

IMF (2012) 'World Economic Outlook', October. http://www.imf.org/external/pubs/ft/weo/2012/02/pdf/text.pdf.

IMF (2014a) 'Regional Economic Outlook, Sub-Saharan Africa', October. https://www.imf.org/external/pubs/ft/reo/2014/afr/eng/sreo1014.pdf.

IMF (2014b) 'IMF Crisis Lending", September. http://www.imf.org/external/np/exr/facts/crislend.htm.

IMF (2015a) 'Direction of Trade Statistics – Online'. http://elibrary-data.imf.org/QueryBuilder.aspx?key=19784661&s=322.

IMF (2015b) 'Past IMF Disbursements and Repayments from All Members from May 1, 1984 to Dec. 31, 2014'. http://www.imf.org/external/np/fin/tad/extrep1.aspx.

IMF (various years) 'IMF Financial Activities – Update'.

International Monetary Fund and the World Bank. (2012) 'Revisiting the Debt Sustainability Framework for Low-Income Countries'. http://www.imf.org/external/np/pp/eng/2012/011212.pdf.

Index Mundi (2015) 'Commodity Prices'. http://www.indexmundi.com/commodities/.

Jomo, K.S. and Rudiger von Arnim (2012) 'Economic Liberalization and Constraints to Development in Sub-Saharan Africa', in Akbar Noman, Kwesi Botchwey, Howard Stein and Joseph Stiglitz (eds), *Good Growth and Governance in Africa: Rethinking Development Strategies*, Oxford: Oxford University Press.

James, Chris, Saul S Morris, Regina Keith, Anna Taylor (2005) 'Impact on Child Mortality of Removing User Fees: Simulation Model', *British Medical Journal*, 331, 747–9.

Jones, Tim (2012) *The State of Debt: Putting an End to 30 Years of Crisis*, London: Jubilee Debt Campaign, May.

Kapsos, Steve (2005) 'The Employment Intensity of Growth: Trends and Macroeconomic Determinants', International Labor Organization, Employment Strategy Papers, No. 2005/12.

Kasekende, Louis, Brixova, Zuzana and Ndikumana, Leonce (2010) 'Africa: Africa's Counter-Cyclical Policy Responses to the Crisis', *Journal of Globalization and Development*, 1(1), Art. 16.

Kydland, F.E. and Zarazaga, C.E.J.M. (1997) 'Is the Business Cycle of Argentina Different?', *Economic Review-Federal Reserve Bank of Dallas*, 21–36.

Lall, S (1992) 'Structural Problems of African Industry', in F. Stewart, S. Lall and S. Wangwe (eds), *Alternative Development Strategies in Sub-Saharan Africa*, London: Macmillan, 103–44.

Lall, S (1995) 'Structural Adjustment and African Industry', *World Development*, 23(12), 2019–31.
Lawrence, Peter (2005) 'Explaining Sub-saharan Africa's Manufacturing Performance', *Development and Change*, 36(6), 1121–41.
Leibfritz, W. and Rottman, H. (2013) 'Fiscal Policy During Business Cycles in Developing Countries: The Case of Africa', OTH im Dialog: Weidener Diskussionspapiere, no. 36, November. http://econstor.eu/bitstream/10419/88593/1/774482745.pdf.
Llaudes, Ricardo, Ferhan Salman and Mali Chivakul (2010) 'The Impact of the Great Recession on Emerging Markets', IMF Working Papers 10/237, International Monetary Fund, October.
Lucas, R.E. (1981) *Studies in Business Cycle Theory*, Cambridge, MA: MIT.
McMillan, Margaret and Dani Rodrik (2011) 'Globalization, Structural Change and Productivity Growth', in Marco Bacchetta and Marion Jansen (eds), *Making Globalization Socially Sustainable*, Geneva: International Labor Organization, 49–84.
Mendoza, E.G. (1995) 'The Terms of Trade, the Real Exchange Rate, and Economic Fluctuations', *International Economic Review*, 36, 101–37.
Mercotor (2008) 'In Spite of Global Crisis Latin American Countries Avoid IMF', October, 21. en.mercopress.com/2008/10/21/in-spite-of-global-crisis-latam-countries-avoid-imf.
Mitchell, W. C. (1927) *Business Cycles: the Problem and its Settings*, Cambridge, MA: NBER.
Mkandawire, T. (1988) 'The Road to Crisis, Adjustment and Deindustrialisation: The African Case', *Africa Development*, 13 (1), 5–31.
Naoussi, C.F., and Tripier, F. (2010) 'Trend Shocks and Business Cycles in Sub Saharan Africa', Working Paper, LEMNA, EA4272.
Nana, P.N. and Samson, L. (2014) 'Why are Banks in Africa Hoarding Reserves? An Empirical Investigation of the Precautionary Motive', *Review of Development Finance*, 4(1), 29–37.
NBER (2015) 'US Business Cycle Expansions and Contractions'. http://www.nber.org/cycles.html.
Organization for Economic Cooperation and Development OECD (2011) *OECD Factbook 2011–2012: Economic, Environmental and Social Statistics*, Geneva: OECD.
Organization for Economic Cooperation and Development (OECD) (2012) *African Central Government Debt Statistical Yearbook 2003–2010*, Paris: OECD.
Organization for Economic Cooperation and Development OECD (2015a) 'Short Term Labor Market Statistics: Harmonized Unemployment Rate'. http://stats.oecd.org.
Organization for Economic Cooperation and Development OECD (2015b) 'Aid Disbursement to Countries and Regions'. http://stats.oecd.org.
Olabisi, Michael and Stein, Howard (2014) 'Global Finance, Africa, and Sovereign Debt', paper presented at the ASSA Annual Meeting, January.
Olabisi, Michael and Stein, Howard (2015) 'Sovereign Bond Issues: Do African Countries Pay More to Borrow?', *Journal of African Trade*, forthcoming.
Page, John (2012) 'Youth, Jobs, and Structural Change: Confronting Africa's "Employment Problem"', African Development Bank, Working Paper Series, no. 155, October.
Page, John and Abebe Shimeles (2014) 'Aid, Employment, and Poverty Reduction in Africa', WIDER Working Paper 2014/043.

Pallage, S. and Robe, M. A. (2001) 'Foreign Aid and the Business Cycle', *Review of International Economics*, 9(4), 641–72.
Pitcher, Anne (2007) 'What Has Happened to Organized Labor in Southern Africa?', *International Labor and Working Class History*, 72, Fall.
Platt, Gordon (2015) 'Sovereign Debt: African Borrowers Active Ahead of Fed Rate Moves', *Global Finance* January, 15. https://www.gfmag.com/magazine/january-2015/SOVEREIGN-DEBT-african-borrowers-active-ahead-fed-rate-moves.
Przeworski, Adam and James Raymond Vreeland (2000) 'The Effect of IMF Program on Economic Growth', *Journal of Development Economics*, 62, 385–421.
Rand, J. and Tarp, F. (2002) 'Business Cycles in Developing Countries: Are They Different?', *World Development*, 30(12), 2071–88.
Richards, Mark B. (2010) 'The Republic of Congo's Debt Restructuring: Are Sovereign Creditors Getting Their Voice Back?', *Law and Contemporary Problems*, 73(4), 273–99.
Rose, Andrew K., and Mark M. Spiegel (2009) 'Cross-country Causes and Consequences of the 2008 Crisis: Early Warning', CEPR Discussion Papers 7354, CEPR Discussion Papers, July.
Salazaar-Xirinachs, J., I. Nubler and R. Kozul-Wright (2014) 'Introduction, Industrial Policy, Productive Transformation and Jobs: Theory, History and Practice', in J. Salazaar-Xirinachs, J., I. Nubler and R. Kozul-Wright (eds), *Transforming Economies: Making Industrial Policy Work for Growth, Jobs and Development*, Geneva: UNCTAD AND ILO.
Seager, Ashley (2008) 'Tanzania Wins £3m Damages from Biwater Subsidiary', *The Guardian* 11 January.
Spilimbergo, Antonio, Symansky, Steve, Blanchard, Oliver and Cottarelli, Carlo (2008) 'IMF Staff Position Note: Fiscal Policy for the Crisis', SPN/08/01, December.
Stein, H. (1992) 'Deindustrialization, Adjustment, the World Bank and the IMF in Africa', *World Development*, 20(1), 83–95.
Stein, H (2008), *Beyond the World Bank Agenda: An Institutional Approach to Development*, Chicago: University of Chicago Press.
Stein, H. (2010) 'Crises and the Bretton Woods Institutions and the Crises of the Bretton Woods Institutions', in Philip Arestis, Rogerio Sobreira and Jose Luis Oreiro (eds), *An Assessment of the Global Impact of the Financial Crisis*, Basingstoke: Pakgrave Macmillan.
Stein, H (2013) 'Africa and the Perversities of International Capital Flows', *International Papers in Political Economy, 2013*, Basingstoke: Palgrave Macmillan.
Stein, H. (2014) 'Rethinking Industrial Policy in Africa: Toward an Institutional Framework', in Theresa Moyo (ed.), *Trade And Industrial Development In Africa: Rethinking Strategy and Policy*, Dakar, Senegal: Codesria.
Stein, H and Kedar, C. (2010) 'The Economic Crises and the Re-empowerment of the IMF and the World Bank: Lessons from Africa and Latin America', mimeo.
Stein, H., R. Odgaard, F. Maganga, and K. Askew (2015) 'The World Bank and Rural Land Titling in Africa: The Case of Tanzania', Department of Afroamerican and African Studies, University of Michigan, January.
Stewart, Frances, and Wang, Michael (2003) 'Do PRSPs Empower Countries and Disempower the World Bank or is it the Other Way Around?', QEH Working Paper Series, No. 108 (October). http://www3.qeh.ox.ac.uk/pdf/qehwp/qehwps108.pdf.

Stiglitz, J.E. (2002) *Globalization and its Discontents*, New York: W.W. Norton.
Sulaiman, Tosin (2012) 'Zambia Euro Bond Could be African Tipping Point', *The Globe and Mail,* October 5. http://www.theglobeandmail.com/report-on-business/international-business/african-and-mideast-business/zambia-euro-bond-could-be-african-tipping-point/article4592068/.
Thomson, Adam and Balls, Andrew (2005) 'Argentina to Pay Off Loans from IMF', *Financial Times*, 16 December.
Tyson, Judith (2015) 'Sub-Saharan Africa International Sovereign Bonds', Part I and II, ODI, January. http://www.odi.org/publications/9205-sub-saharan-africa-international-sovereign-bonds#downloads.
UNCTAD (2014) 'Bilateral FDI Statistics for 2014'. http://unctad.org/en/Pages/DIAE/FDI%20Statistics/FDI-Statistics-Bilateral.aspx.
UNCTAD (2015) 'On-Line Statistics'. http://unctadstat.unctad.org/EN/.
UNECA (2014) *Annual Economic Report, 2014: Dynamic Industrial Policy in Africa*, Addis Ababa: UNCECA.
Van Waeyenberge, Elsa, Bargawi, Hannah and McKinley, Terry (2010) 'Standing in the Way of Development: A Critical Survey of the IMF's Crisis Response to Low-Income Countries', Eurodad and Third World Network Report, April.
Weisbrot, Mark, Rebecca Ray, Jake Johnston, Jose Antonio Cordero and Juan Antonio Montecino (2009) 'IMF Macroeconomic Policies and the World Recession: A Look at Forty-One Borrowing Countries', Center for Economic Policy Research, October.
Weisbrot, Mark and Rebecca Ray (2010) 'Latvia's Recession: The Cost of Adjustment with an "Internal Devaluation"', Center for Economic Policy Research, February.
Vreeland, James Vernon (2003) *The IMF and Economic Development*, Cambridge: Cambridge University Press.
World Bank (2012) 'What Is IDA?' Available at http://www.worldbank.org/ida/what-is-ida.html.
World Bank (2015a) 'African Development Indicators'. http://data.worldbank.org/data-catalog/africa-development-indicators.
World Bank (2015b) *International Debt Statistics*. http://data.worldbank.org/sites/default/files/ids2015.pdf.
Yates, Rob. (2009) 'Universal Health Care and the Removal of User Fees', *The Lancet* 373, 2078–81.

4
Arab Countries in Transition in the Aftermath of the Great Recession: The Policy Options

Yiannis Kitromilides[1]

Abstract: There are a number of significant 'challenges' currently facing Arab Countries in Transition (ACT). This paper, following a brief examination of the causes and consequences of the 'Arab Spring' revolutions and a review of the current economic outlook for ACTs, presents an account and a critical evaluation of the dominant policy agenda that ACTs are expected to adopt. Although in the aftermath of the global economic crisis of 2007 and the Great Recession of 2008 the dissenting voices in economics re-emerged, they do not appear to have had a significant impact on either the academic or the policy-making orthodoxy. This contribution examines the case for an alternative narrative concerning the policy options of ACT. The IMF claims that there have been some significant shifts in the policy narrative: on 'expansionary austerity', on inequality and redistribution and on the political economy aspects of the reform process in ACTs. The chapter concludes that these shifts are merely cosmetic changes.

Keywords: Transition Economies, Washington Consensus, Neoliberal Economics, Macroeconomic Stabilization, Fiscal Consolidation, Structural Reforms

JEL Classification: O53, H60, F59, P16, P45

4.1 Introduction

The major economic problems faced by many emerging economies can be discussed under three different but interconnected categories: The *unemployment* problem, the *indebtedness* problem and the problem of *structural reforms*. Since most of these problems can be mutually reinforcing, they need to be addressed simultaneously in order to avoid a vicious circle of economic stagnation. High levels of public indebtedness may negatively affect growth, which may cause a rise in unemployment, which may, in turn, create more indebtedness, lower growth, higher unemployment, and so on. There is also an equally familiar set of policy prescriptions for countries seeking assistance from the IMF to tackle these problems. The IMF claims that there have been some significant shifts in the policy narrative: on 'expansionary austerity', on inequality and redistribution and on the political economy aspects of the reform process in 'Arab Countries in Transition'. The paper concludes that these shifts are merely cosmetic changes and do not represent a significant departure from the IMF/World Bank policy paradigm, which still remains, in terms of policy options, for the ACTs the only game in town.[2]

A number of countries have been grouped together and labelled as 'Arab Countries in Transition' (ACT): Egypt, Jordan, Libya, Morocco, Tunisia and Yemen. These are the six countries that, following the 'Arab Spring' revolutions of 2011, are supported by the Deauville Partnership initiated by the G8 countries (now G7, following the suspension of collaboration with Russia) and announced under the French Presidency in May 2011. With the exception of Egypt, the ACTs have some form of engagement with the IMF. In contrast to Eastern Europe, where countries have undergone transition from a centrally planned economy to a market economy, the Arab transition countries were already market economies and their transition was initially a political transition from dictatorship to democracy.[3] In four of these countries – Tunisia, Egypt, Libya and Yemen – regime changes have taken place. In Jordan and Morocco, by contrast, although they remain monarchies, the need for change has been accepted by the political system in both countries and they are now engaging in the transition process under existing regimes.

There is international support for the six transition countries, provided by institutions like the IMF, the World Bank, the African Development Bank, the G8 countries (through the so-called 'Deauville Partnership') and other oil-producing Arab countries, notably the countries of the Gulf Cooperation Council (GCC). Political transition can also lead to economic transformation, which requires, in turn, policy initiatives. The aim of this paper is to evaluate the policy options for ACTs in the post-Great Recession era. Although the Great Recession of 2008 exacerbated the conditions that led to the somewhat prematurely termed 'Arab Spring' popular uprisings in 2011, it was not the pivotal cause of the uprisings. Although both events were unexpected, and largely unforeseen, the absence of foresight does not preclude, with the benefit of hindsight, analysis and explanation for both events.

However, the main focus of the paper will be on the policy options rather than the underlying causes of the Great Recession of 2008 and the 'Arab Spring' popular uprising of 2011.

The plan of this chapter is as follows: section 4.2 examines briefly the principal factors that contributed to the discontent and ultimate eruption of popular unrest and regime change in some ACTs in 2011 and describes the main political and economic developments since 2011. Section 4.3 provides a general picture of the economic and political conditions currently prevailing in the ACTs and the immediate period prior to 2011. In section 4.4, the major challenges and in section 4.5 the policy options for the ACTs in terms of the dominant IMF/World Bank policy narrative are presented and evaluated while section 4.6 discusses some of the possible directions that an alternative policy narrative might take. Finally, section 4.7 offers a summary of the main points of the chapter, along with some concluding comments.

4.2 Factors contributing to the 'Arab Spring' uprisings

When, on 17 December 2010, Mohammed Bouazizi set himself alight, having been forced, through the experience of unemployment, to sell fruit in the street and then had his stand confiscated by the authorities, the effects of his actions would have extremely dramatic consequences. These consequences would manifest themselves not only in his own country, Tunisia, but also in several other countries in the so-called Middle East and North Africa (MENA) region. Bouazizi died on 4 January 2011 and, ten days later, the dictator Ben Ali fled the country. Over the course of a very short period, long-established authoritarian regimes in Egypt, Yemen and Libya, were also overthrown while widespread popular protests in other Arab countries, although not resulting in regime change, were seen as an acknowledgement by the governments of these countries of the need for political reform and economic transformation. The unexpected timing, as well as the ease with which popular protests (with or without external support) resulted in the overthrow of seemingly well-entrenched dictatorships, produced a plethora of comments and a voluminous academic literature on the topic.[4] A detailed account of these studies is beyond the scope of this paper, but a brief summary of the principal contributory factors leading to the popular unrest in the ACTs in 2011 is possible.

As Pollack (2011) puts it, "Like all great social upheavals, the Arab Spring was long in the making, and born of many intertwined causes. It might have happened at any time over the past two to three decades, but each passing brought new developments that made it that much more likely" (p. 2). Developments in the economic, social and political spheres all contributed to an intense sense of grievance across the Arab world that ultimately produced the eruption of popular anger in the winter and spring of 2011.

Of pivotal importance were developments in the economic sphere. For a variety of reasons, in the period 2000–10 growth rates in MENA countries averaged 4.7 per cent per annum, well below the average of 6.4 per cent achieved by low-and middle-income countries or the 9.4 per cent achieved by East Asian countries (see Yusuf, 2014). The slow growth produced and was associated with what Pollack (2011) calls "a raft of ulcerous economic liabilities: unemployment (especially among the outsized youth population); underemployment (especially among the middle class, whose education and status make them believe they deserve managerial or clerical job rather than driving a taxi or working in a restaurant); yawning wealth gaps; low levels of direct foreign investment outside the energy sector; meager non-energy exports; excessive dependence on the public sector for employment; rapid urbanization with inadequate infrastructure investment; and heavy outflow of capital, both human and financial" (p. 2). These economic developments although predating the Great Recession were undoubtedly accentuated and exacerbated by the onslaught of the Great Recession in 2008 which intensified feelings of hopelessness and insecurity. In addition to these economic developments, social as well as political developments were also significant contributory factors in bringing about the Arab Spring uprisings of 2011.

An increasing awareness in a globalized world of different political and economic realities elsewhere, partly the result of the development of modern communications and partly the result of direct conduct through foreign travel or tourism, added further to popular anger and frustration which was compounded by developments in the political sphere. Autocratic regimes, which had been in power for decades, not only failed to provide an optimistic developmental vision, but instead tolerated and encouraged corruption and rampant cronyism, which was largely responsible for the vast inequalities in income and wealth. Finally, the ability of authoritarian regimes to keep a tight control over dissent has been challenged by a new social development: the empowerment of dissenters in some 'Arab Spring' countries derived from the capacity to mobilize through the use of social media.

There are some significant differences in the way regime change has taken place in four of the six ACTs. The relatively swift collapse of the Tunisian and Egyptian regimes can be attributed to the relative homogeneity of their populations in contrast to Libya and Yemen and, to a greater extent, to Syria where the civil war is ongoing. Moreover the durability of the monarchies in Jordan and Morocco can be explained in terms of the way that their legitimacy is grounded on religion and historical associations between the state and ruling elites and to a measure of affection for the monarchs (Pollack, 2011).

The transition from dictatorship to democracy does not end with the overthrow of the autocratic regimes. As Owen (2013) points out, the first important step following a revolution is the drafting of a constitution. But who would draft the new constitution? In Tunisia and Egypt, it was decided that the new constitution was to be drafted by an elected constituent assembly. Elections, however, in the aftermath of decades of authoritarian rule invariably resulted in victory for the religious parties that are better organized and better able to mobilize their supporters. This political reality is reflected in the protracted process of drafting the new constitutions and the inordinate length and number of articles included in these constitutions. Once an article is inserted another one is deemed necessary to maintain a balance, and so on (Owen, 2013). The Tunisian constitution, completed in January 2014, for example, contains 149 articles. In Libya and Yemen committees have been appointed to draft a constitution, which (at the point of writing) is expected to be approved at a time not yet specified by the people in a referendum. The process of providing new constitutions in the Arab transition countries where regime change has taken place has been completed in Egypt and Tunisia, where new constitutions are now in place, but not yet completed in Libya and Yemen.

Of the six ACTs, only Tunisia has a democratically elected government based on a new constitution. In Egypt, the government of Mohamed Morsi – democratically elected also on the basis of a new constitution – has been overthrown by the military, although parliamentary elections are expected to take place during 2015. The political situation in Libya and Yemen remains turbulent and unstable whereas the monarchies in Morocco and Jordan remain stable and committed to reform.

4.3 An economic and political snapshot of ACTs

Before we examine the question of the policy options of ACTs in the aftermath of the Great Recession and the revolutions of the Arab Spring it will be useful to take a closer look at the overall economic and political picture before and after the revolutions (Yusuf, 2014).

4.3.1 Income per capita and growth performance

There is a great deal of variation in per capita GDP across the six ACTs. Yemen is in the low middle-income category, and Libya, due to its oil wealth, is classified as a high-income country. The other four are in the middle-income range, with Egypt having the lowest and Jordan the highest per capita GDP. With regard to economic growth, the ACTs averaged a growth rate of more than 4 per cent per annum between 2000 and 2010. Yemen had the lowest (4.1 per cent) and Jordan the highest (6.7 per cent) growth rates, which means that only Jordan surpassed the low- and middle-income average rate of 6.4 per cent and all of them fell short of the East Asian average of 9.4 per cent (admittedly somewhat biased in that it was inflated by China's involvement in the area).

4.3.2 Population size and structure

Egypt's population in 2015 is estimated to be 88 million, Morocco 33 million, Yemen 27 million, Tunisia 11 million, Libya 7 million and Jordan 6.6 million. The average annual growth of population is 1.9 per cent in Egypt, 2.9 per cent in Yemen, 2 per cent in Jordan and Libya, 1.2 per cent in Morocco and 0.9 per cent in Tunisia in the early 2010s. In terms of population structure, the ACTs currently have youthful population ranging from a proportion of the population under the age of 25 of 42.5 per cent in Tunisia to 59 per cent in Jordan. Consequently, the level of youth unemployment in the ACTs is high, even taking into account the low participation rates for women. Given the high fertility rates during the 1980s, the labour force will continue to expand rapidly well into the future.

4.3.3 Unemployment and job creation

Given the above demographic reality in the ACTs, even maintaining the current rates of unemployment will be problematic, requiring the creation of millions of additional jobs. According to some estimates (Kapsos, 2005) for the period 1991–2003, the global youth employment elasticity was 0.06, which means that employment increased by 0.06 per cent for every 1 per cent of GDP growth. Assuming an increase in the youth labor force of 0.5 per cent per annum, then with an elasticity of 0.06, the world economy would need an annual growth rate of 10 per cent in order to prevent an increase in youth unemployment. The average employment labour elasticities is significantly higher than the global average for the MENA region, which means that the MENA countries create more employment for every 1 per cent of GDP growth. However, this may not necessarily be good news if this involves the hiring of 'surplus' workers in the public sector or at the expense of adopting the latest technologies which tend to be capital-intensive.

4.3.4 Manufacturing and foreign trade[5]

The manufacturing sector as a share of GDP is low in Jordan, Tunisia, Morocco and Egypt and tiny in Libya and Yemen. With the exception of Jordan, its share has been diminishing in the ACTs between 2000 and 2010. Exports as a share of GDP and the export mix can be an indication of the degree of openness and the scope for export-led growth. In this regard, Egypt is the laggard, with an export to GDP ratio of 21 per cent; only Yemen has experienced a decline over this period – from 41 per cent in 2000 to 30 per cent in 2010. Libya, an oil exporter, used to be the leader with a 67 per cent rate; the others ranged from 33 per cent in Morocco to 49 per cent in Tunisia, with Jordan falling in between at 45 per cent. With the exception of Egypt, all countries are above the global average of 28 per cent and three exceed the East Asian average of 37 per cent.

As might be expected, Libya and Yemen are at the bottom of the list with only negligible merchandise exports, and their exports of Knowledge-Based Business Services (KBBS) are also negligible. Clearly, in the cases of Libya and Yemen, diversification and acceleration growth on the strength of non-fuel exports, although desirable, must, given the unstable political environment, remain a longer-term objective. The other ACT countries are better positioned, with Egypt again trailing with a 43 per cent share of manufactures in total exports, and a low and declining share of KBBS since 2000. Morocco, Jordan, and Tunisia are in a more comfortable situation, with the share of merchandise exports to total exports ranging between 66 per cent and 76 per cent. Insurance, financial services, or engineering services are absent from the ACTs' exports, and there is no significant presence in the market for global construction services. Morocco and Tunisia have modest exports to other KBBS; both have managed to increase the volume of exports by a sizable margin. Jordan, by contrast, has suffered a major decline. The global average for merchandise exports was 69 per cent and for KBBS was 45 per cent; East Asia was above the average for merchandise exports (79 per cent) and about level with regard to the export share of KBBS (43 per cent). Morocco, Jordan, and Tunisia have expanded their export-oriented manufacturing capabilities and now need to diversify and to increase domestic value added. They also need to strengthen the KIBS sector. Egypt is lagging behind in this respect. Except in Tunisia, where the weighted mean tariff rate was 16 per cent, the rates in the ACTs were below 10 per cent. Jordan had the lowest rate (5.2 per cent). Tunisia, Morocco and Egypt have each improved their World Bank Logistics Performance Index76 ranking since 2007, and in 2012, they ranked 41st, 50th and 57th, respectively. Yemen was a little further down, in 63rd place, with Jordan and Libya far behind (102nd and 137th from a total of 155 countries). Further gains would surely be helpful for all six ACTs, and reducing import lead times would facilitate participation in regional value chains (Yusuf, 2014, p. 22).

How did the political system in the ACTs respond to these economic conditions, which were exacerbated by the Great Recession? In the post-2008 period, in the face of declining economic growth, rising unemployment and worsening income and wealth inequalities,[6] for the political system prevailing at the time it was 'business as usual'. As discussed in section 4.2 above on the origins of the discontent that gave rise to the popular uprisings in 2011, the various authoritarian regimes in the 'Arab Spring' countries pursued the same policies whose primary purpose was the maintenance of autocratic and monarchical control through the establishment of a dominant public sector that controlled private sector activities and corruptly allocated resources to secure their hegemonic grip on the state and the economy (Iqbal, 2014).

The long-standing economic problems outlined above have become more acute since the onset of the political transitions in 2011. Not only popular expectations for better living standards have increased significantly, but at the same time the ACTs were faced with a serious economic downturn. The downturn was partly the result of transition-related disruptions, regional conflict, and an uncertain political outlook; and partly the outcome of an adverse external economic environment, particularly in Europe which had negative effects on confidence. The downturn has led to increased unemployment and to stagnation in living standards, and in all likelihood adversely affected the medium-term growth potential in some countries.

There is a wide gap between economic realities in ACTs and popular aspirations for an economic transformation that would produce swiftly a better future in terms of job creation and income generation. As noted above, demographic pressures indicate that, under current growth projections, unemployment is expected to continue to rise. At the same time, fiscal deficits and public debt have increased further, and international foreign exchange reserves have been run down, severely limiting the policy space for expansionary economic policies in the period ahead (IMF, 2014a).

In this setting, as the IMF (2014a) warns "the ACTs risk getting trapped in a vicious circle of economic stagnation and persistent sociopolitical strife. As economic realities fall behind populations' expectations, there is a risk of increased discontent, which could further complicate the political transitions, impairing governments' mandates and planning horizons and, consequently, their ability to implement the policies necessary to catalyze the much-needed economic improvement" (p. 3).

Which are these policies that are necessary in order to produce in the ACTs the much-needed and vital improvement in their economic performance?

4.4 The established narrative: the challenges and the policy options

There are, in the language of the IMF and the World Bank, significant 'challenges' facing all ACTs. Some of these 'challenges' are long-standing, while others are relatively new. Some new regimes, such as Tunisia, with a new popular mandate and commitment to political and economic reform, must confront and hopefully overcome all these old and new, predominantly economic, 'challenges'.[7] What are these 'challenges' and what are the policy options available according to the established IMF/World Bank narrative? In this section, we will provide a summary of the 'key challenges', the economic outlook and the policy options in the ACTs *from an IMF perspective*.

4.4.1 The challenges

The major economic problems currently facing the ACTs can be discussed, as noted above, under three different, but interconnected headings: The *unemployment* problem, the *indebtedness* problem and the problem of *structural reforms*. This is a familiar set of problems which the IMF/World Bank typically identifies for most, if not all the countries with which it deals. There is also an equally familiar set of policy prescriptions for countries seeking assistance from the IMF to tackle these problems.

Since these problems can be mutually reinforcing in nature they need to be addressed simultaneously since the failure to tackle them simultaneously can lead to a vicious circle of economic stagnation. Breaking this vicious circle is not always an easy undertaking. It is worth stressing, however, that a vicious circle can also be created by the very policy measures that are introduced in an attempt to break the vicious circle: savage austerity aimed at reducing public indebtedness may in fact increase public indebtedness! As the IMF (2013) acknowledged, somewhat belatedly, this was recently the case in Greece. We will return to this issue below, in our discussion of the policy options. We will consider, in no particular order, the nature of the three *challenges* – unemployment, indebtedness and structural reforms – as they apply in the six ACTs. It should be noted that the first two challenges are concerned with establishing macroeconomic stability and are, therefore, of more immediate concern to policy makers while structural reforms are perceived as a more medium- to long-term project.

4.4.2 The unemployment challenge[8]

Tunisia. The unemployment rate in Tunisia at the end of 2014 was 15.2 per cent and that for youth unemployment was over 40 per cent. With a decline in the growth rate in 2013, after a short-lived recovery in 2012, to 2.6 per cent and with 42.5 per cent of the population under the age of 25, the prospects for job creation and employment in Tunisia appear to be bleak. This growth performance must be seen in the historical context of a comparatively poor growth performance in the two decades prior to the 2011 revolution. Between 1990 and 2010, Tunisia, along with other MENA countries, achieved only low to moderate growth rates (well below the average growth rates of comparable economies in East Asia), while experiencing at the same time rapid growth in the size of the labour force. Under current demographic trends and annual growth projections for GDP, unemployment is expected to continue rising. If these assumptions are correct, it seems that the unemployment challenge is not susceptible to quick fixes.

Egypt. Real GDP growth was about 2 per cent in 2013/14, held back by the impact of the political transition on tourism and manufacturing sectors. As a result, the unemployment rate increased to 13.4 per cent.

Jordan. Despite an increasingly difficult regional environment, including the conflicts in Syria and Iraq, the macroeconomic situation has remained largely stable. Economic activity is slowly gaining momentum, with growth registering 3.2 per cent year-on-year in 2014 and expected to rise to 4 per cent in 2015. Unemployment in the first quarter of 2015, however, is 12.9 per cent, slightly higher than the 12.58 per cent average for the period 2007–15.

Morocco. In the first quarter of 2014, growth decelerated to 1.7 per cent (compared with the same period in 2013) pushed down by a return to normal cereal yields and weak growth in Europe. Nonetheless, some leading indicators point to a possible acceleration of activity as external demand picks up gradually. Unemployment, at 9.9 per cent in the first quarter of 2015, is higher than in the previous quarter but still below the average of 10.6 per cent for the period 1999–2015.

Yemen. The macroeconomic situation was relatively stable in 2013 before weakening in the first half of 2014. Growth in 2013 recovered to about 4.8 per cent – helped by a rebound in oil production. According to unofficial estimates, unemployment could be in excess of 30 per cent.

Libya. The 11-month blockade of Libya's oil facilities by federalist and tribal militias brought the country's oil output to a stop, depressing GDP by an estimated 14 per cent in 2013 and a projected 20 per cent in 2014. There are no reliable official statistics on unemployment but unofficial estimates put the unemployment rate for 2013–14 above 30 per cent.

4.4.3 The indebtedness challenge[9]

The debt problem in the ACTs has two components: an *internal* deficit in the government's fiscal balance and an *external* deficit in the country's current account. Below we examine the indebtedness challenge in each of the six ACTs.

Tunisia. Tunisia has, by international standards, relatively moderate levels of total public indebtedness. In 2013 total public debt as a proportion of GDP stood at about 45 per cent, only marginally higher than the pre-revolutionary average. The increase in total public indebtedness was largely the result of a significant rise in the budget deficit, which stood, in 2013, at 6 per cent of GDP, substantially higher than the pre-revolutionary average. In turn, the rise in the budget deficit was mainly due to the expansionary fiscal policies pursued in the aftermath of the Great Recession of 2008 and also the post-revolution increases in public expenditures, mainly on subsidies and public sector wage increases. While such expenditure hikes may have helped to boost aggregate demand and address urgent social needs and tensions the critical question with regard to the internal fiscal challenge is whether such deficits in the short and medium term promote or hinder economic growth.

With regard to the external deficit (about 8.2 per cent of GDP in 2013) the major impact of a persistently wide current account imbalance and declining capital inflows in the form of FDI, is on the exchange rate and the country's foreign exchange reserves. This puts further limits on the ability of policy makers to adopt expansionary economic policies. At the same time the role of the Central Bank in supporting the exchange rate and preserving the country's international reserves assumes, according to the IMF (2014a), crucial importance. The last two issues are of course equally pertinent for the rest of the ACTs, namely Egypt, Jordan Morocco, Yemen and Libya.

Egypt. The budget sector deficit in 2013/14 declined to 11.9 per cent of GDP on the back of an unprecedented level of grants (4.3 per cent of GDP) from the GCC countries. However, the underlying fiscal position (excluding grants) worsened to over 16 per cent of GDP and public debt has increased to over 90 per cent of GDP. In a context characterized by still large energy subsidies (about 6½ per cent of GDP) and fuel shortages, electricity outages have become increasingly frequent. Substantial financial disbursements and in-kind grants (oil shipments) from Kuwait, Saudi Arabia, and the UAE have helped to stabilize international reserves, although at a low level – just below three months' worth of imports.

Jordan. The central government's budget deficit, which stood, as a percentage of GDP, at 5.50 per cent, and the external current account deficit are projected to narrow in 2014–15, helped by lower international oil and food prices as well as expenditure reforms and the implementation of revenue-generating measures. Disruptions of gas flows from Egypt emerged, which probably damaged both the current and the fiscal accounts. Further escalation of the Syria conflict, which led to more refugees, strains further Jordan's limited resources. The protracted crisis in Iraq has negative implications for Jordan's exports and transit trade. The realization of any of these risks could also weaken confidence and have effects on external flows of foreign investment. Other general risks, which impact on all ACTs, include higher US interest rates and a slowdown of economic activity in emerging markets.

Morocco. In 2014 the authorities targeted a further reduction in the fiscal deficit – to 4.9 per cent of GDP from 5.5 per cent of GDP in 2013. Budget plans through August 2014 remains broadly consistent with this target, although the IMF suggests that developments will need to be monitored closely by the authorities as revenues are being affected by the slowdown in activity. The trade balance improved through August 2014 compared with the same period in the previous year, driven by a strong performance in newly developed sectors (mainly automobiles) and electronics, against a moderate increase in imports.

Yemen. The fiscal and current account deficits in 2014 increased only slightly despite a large decline in external grants. Accordingly, the underlying fiscal deficit narrowed substantially, reflecting a forced fiscal adjustment triggered by lack of financing and the determination of the authorities not to resort to borrowing from the central bank. According to the IMF (2014a), monetary policy remained 'prudent'. Macroeconomic balances worsened in early 2014 due to a wave of sabotage activities, leading to serious pressures on the fiscal and external sectors and disruption to economic activity, with GDP growth slowing down to about 1.9 per cent in 2014.

Libya. The large fiscal and trade surpluses of 2012 turned into deficits in 2013. The IMF (2014a) estimates that the government is expected to post a deficit in excess of 50 per cent of GDP in 2014 with the current account deficit exceeding 27 per cent of GDP. The twin deficits will take a toll on official reserves which are expected to decline by 22 per cent to 34 months of imports by the end of 2014.

4.4.4 The 'structural reform' challenge

'Structural reform' is a generic term referring to the need for change in long-standing activities, behaviour, practices and institutional arrangements that the IMF/World Bank do not like because it is considered that they are inimical to the promotion of growth and development. Of all the 'challenges' this appears to be the one least amenable to short-term solutions. Yet some of these reforms, if implemented quickly, could produce the kind of economic transformation that, according to the IMF/World Bank policy narrative, can make the task of managing the other 'challenges' of job creation and reduction in indebtedness considerably easier.

The list of structural reforms deemed necessary by the dominant policy narrative differs from country to country, but they typically fall into three broad categories: reforms in the public sector, reforms in the private sector and reforms in social security and welfare systems. The government is directly or indirectly involved in all three categories of the agenda for 'structural reforms'.

Reforms in the *public sector* usually involve demands for a reduction in its scope and size. These demands typically require a reduction in the number of public employees, changes in the composition of public expenditure away from generalized subsidies, the modernization of the banking and financial system and the privatization of public enterprises, which may include public banks. There is also a general expectation that the government will promote a business-friendly environment by cutting down on excessive regulations and bureaucratic 'red-tape' in the public sector.

The reforms in the *private sector* are concentrated mainly into efforts to reform the labour market. These involve the creation, through legal and institutional reforms, of what has come to be known as a 'flexible labour market'. The familiar slogan supporting these reforms is: 'if it is easy to fire workers it is easy to hire'. This means that under these reforms what workers regard as their hard earned rights come under threat.

The final category of expected structural reforms is closely connected with the implementation of reforms in the previous two sectors. The most vulnerable groups in society must be protected from the adverse effects of structural reforms in the public sector and labour market. The gradual reduction of generalized subsidies or the introduction of a more 'flexible' labour market would result in severe hardship for 'vulnerable' groups and, therefore, an alternative 'targeted' system of support must be put in place. On the other hand, the level of such support must not be too high as to discourage 'job search' among unemployed workers.

In all three areas of required 'structural reforms' of paramount importance is, of course, the implementation of measures to root out 'corrupt' practices and 'rent-seeking' behaviour in the economy and politics, which is connected to the broader objective of greater transparency and accountability and improved governance.

Given the perception that establishing macroeconomic stability is a more urgent task than the introduction of structural reforms, it is unsurprising to note that progress on the structural reforms front has been slow and uneven in the six ACTs countries considered in this paper. We will, therefore, not follow the same approach as with the *unemployment* and *indebtedness* challenges and discuss the *structural reform* challenge as it applies to each of the six ACTs. Instead we note the IMF (2014a) conclusion that "most ACTs have by now either started or announced ambitious reforms of generalized energy subsidies and other current expenditures to create space for better targeted social protection for the poor, and higher spending on infrastructure, healthcare, and education. These are important first steps in implementing the medium-term growth agenda. However, progress has been uneven across countries, and reforms of tax policy, civil service and public financial management remain quite slow. More attention is also needed in other areas, including banking and financial sectors, governance, business climate, and labor markets" (p. 3).

4.4.5 The policy options

According to the IMF/World Bank narrative, there are only a limited number of policy options that countries facing these challenges can adopt. Although these policies can be adopted voluntarily, they are usually adopted by countries as a condition for IMF support. The details are, of course, country-specific, but the generalities are very familiar. A typical 'menu' of policies usually includes the following prescriptions:

Establishing 'macroeconomic stability' in an indebted economy with high unemployment is an urgent policy priority. 'Macroeconomic stability' typically means giving priority to establishing a fiscal balance. An austerity programme aimed at rapid budget deficit reduction should be implemented immediately. The establishment of sound public finances would be a growth-enhancing strategy.

Fiscal consolidation should preferably be achieved primarily through public expenditure cuts than tax hikes. At the same time the revenue-raising capacity of the government should be enhanced through reforms to the tax collection systems.

Generalized food and fuel subsidies should be replaced by targeted social security nets.

Public enterprises should be privatized.

Foreign trade should be liberalized and regional co-operation encouraged and the financial system modernized.

Priority should be given to 'structural reforms' in the labour market, the civil service and the legal system.

As far as possible a 'business-friendly' environment should be promoted and cumbersome and bureaucratic regulations discouraging business and foreign direct investment (FDI) should be removed.

Such a programme is expected by the IMF (2014a) to produce short-run macroeconomic stability, which should, in turn, lay the foundations for rapid economic growth. Although not a sufficient condition, the acceleration of economic growth is a necessary condition for job creation and a reduction in unemployment. The underlying fundamental assumption in this policy agenda is that the primary engine in bringing about such an acceleration of economic growth in both advanced and emerging economies is the private sector of the economy: it is regarded by the IMF as the most efficient, dynamic, innovative and progressive sector capable of creating the conditions for acceleration of growth and lifting the country out of economic stagnation. There is, it is claimed, a considerable body of theoretical arguments and empirical evidence that support this vision: *that the best way forward is through the creation of the appropriate environment for* ***private sector-led growth***. The political transition from dictatorship to democracy offers the ACTs, according to the dominant policy narrative, a unique opportunity to set in motion a process of not only political and social but also economic transformation. What is meant by the term 'economic transformation' is perfectly clear: the creation of the conditions for private-sector led growth. The policy prescriptions outlined above follow from this vision.

According to the IMF (2014a), at this critical juncture for the ACTs, three economic policy priorities are essential: initiating measures enabling additional job creation in the near term to lessen the risk of a vicious circle; addressing what in the vocabulary of the IMF/World Bank are called 'macroeconomic vulnerabilities' to safeguard economic stability; and setting in motion necessary reforms to generate higher potential growth and job creation in the medium to long term.

The IMF (2014a) insists that near-term policies need to focus on quickly enabling job creation in order to lessen the adverse impact of the post-Arab-Spring economic downturns. Delays in the revival of private investment, in the context of impaired economic confidence, indicate a need for governments to shore up economic activity in the near term. Experience from other countries suggests that well-designed infrastructure projects can create jobs and lay a better foundation for private sector activity. With little room for the further widening of fiscal deficits in many countries, spending needs to be reoriented toward growth-enhancing and job-creating public investment that stimulates private sector activity, while protecting vulnerable groups through well-targeted social assistance.

In similar fashion to the second policy prescription by Williamson (1989), as discussed below, the IMF (2014a) recommends that the ACTs should introduce public expenditure reforms, which should involve redirecting social protection from expensive and inefficient generalized subsidies to transfers that better target the poor and vulnerable. In addition, containing public wage bills would reduce expenditure rigidities and support fiscal strategies for sustainability and private sector job creation. Revenue measures should focus on broadening the tax base and improving the efficiency of tax collection. Some ACTs also have room for raising income tax progressivity and increasing excise and property tax rates. Together, these policies would enhance equity while freeing scarce resources for priority expenditure in infrastructure investment, health, and education.

At the same time, near-term policies need to be anchored in medium-term policy frameworks that maintain and strengthen economic stability. With concerns about debt sustainability rising and fiscal balances and external reserves eroding, the IMF (2014a) maintains that countries need to anchor their fiscal policies in medium-term frameworks that safeguard macroeconomic stability and debt sustainability. In some cases, there may be room for scaling up deficits in the near term when adequate financing is available and in the context of medium-term adjustment programmes. The slower the pace of fiscal adjustment, the larger the financing needs will be, underscoring the need to anchor policies in credible medium-term consolidation plans; these will help secure the continued willingness of creditors to provide the necessary financing.

A familiar theme of this policy narrative is that a bold economic reform agenda will be essential for propelling private sector activity and fostering a more dynamic, competitive, innovation-driven, and inclusive economy. To achieve broad-based and sustainable growth, therefore, countries need to move gradually away from state-dominated to private investment and from protected and rent-seeking enterprises to export-led growth and value creation. Policies should aim at strengthening the revival of private sector confidence and laying the foundations for higher potential growth. A key goal will be to engineer a transformation for the public sector, a shift from providing privileges such as public employment, subsidies, economic rents, and tax exemptions, to providing basic economic services, adequate social protection, better governance, a level playing field for all economic actors, and a competitive environment for the private sector.

The IMF (2014b) believes firmly that countries will begin their efforts from different starting points and will have different reform objectives, but there are some common areas that should be covered: these include trade integration, business regulation and governance, labour market and education reform, improved access to finance, and better social safety nets (SSNs). Deepening trade integration can also offer significant benefits. In addition to the large potential direct gains of boosting exports and attracting productivity enhancing FDI, trade integration can serve as catalyst for reforms in other areas that will help countries to compete. Deeper trade integration will require better access to advanced economy markets. It will also involve carefully reducing further the ACTs tariffs and non-tariff trade barriers, and focusing on the increasingly important areas of trade facilitation and export promotion. Complex and burdensome business regulation needs to be tackled in order to unleash entrepreneurial activity and private investment. It is essential to improve the systems of checks and balances in domestic institutions to prevent the exercise of arbitrary discretion and non-transparent intervention, and to streamline business regulation with a view to cutting red tape and reducing informality and corruption.

Furthermore, the IMF (2014b) insists that institutional and regulatory reform should aim at reducing the scope for discretion, improving transparency, and strengthening institutional autonomy and accountability. Labour market and education reforms can provide incentives for hiring and participation in the formal private sector labour market. Countries should review labour market regulations with a view to reducing distortions that discourage hiring and skills-building, while ensuring an adequate level of social protection. Governments need to revisit their recruitment and compensation policies to ensure that hiring does not exceed needs and salaries do not bias jobseekers toward the public sector. Education systems should be improved and reoriented towards skills needed in the private sector. As these policies take time to yield tangible results, countries should consider employing active labour market policies to achieve quick improvements in labour market outcomes. The complexity of all these tasks requires, as will be discussed further below, careful prioritization and sequencing. Although countries differ in their starting conditions and will need to tailor their individual reform plans, the IMF (2014b) is convinced that the scope for macroeconomic and structural policies to support growth and maintain stability is substantial in all of ACTs.

At the same time, it should be recognized that the political transitions are at differing stages among the ACTs, and in some countries transitional governments have short horizons and limited mandates and therefore have less room to manoeuvre when setting in motion the policy reforms that the dominant narrative deems necessary. In addition, the administrative capacity to execute reforms differs among countries and is limited in some of them. Careful prioritization and sequencing of reforms is thus required to make efficient use of political capital and administrative capacity, and the complexity of the political transitions requires a flexible approach so that opportunities for reform can be seized as they arise. It will also be critical to identify those measures that can be taken quickly to produce strong effects, such as streamlining business regulation and improving the transparency of the budget process. Enacting this type of reform quickly would help strengthen confidence in the authorities' commitment to the reform process (IMF, 2014a).

During 11–12 May 2014, the IMF – jointly with the Arab Fund for Economic and Social Development and the Government of Jordan – hosted the conference 'Building the Future: Jobs, Growth, and Fairness in the Arab World' in Amman, Jordan. The IMF (2014b) provides a summary of the debate and reports that participants debated policies in four main areas: the top priority, according to the audience, was a strong and shared vision in each country to guide the economic future. Improving the composition of government spending to achieve more fairness, more efficiency, and, ultimately, more inclusive growth was also seen as important. Another policy priority was the promotion of greater transparency and good governance. Conference participants agreed that transparency and governance are areas where the region has to improve significantly and urged governments to establish more accountability vis-à-vis their citizens and strengthen the judicial system. This would also build credibility around their economic agendas and help attract investors.

Some conference contributors stressed the importance of creating more jobs for the youth and women. Others emphasized the need to change the perception of the state as chief employer and creating education systems that lead to productive employment. Participants emphasized the need to move away from a system of privileged access to a system of competition... The IMF is now in a dialogue with authorities across the region to translate this agenda into *policy recommendations tailored* to the context of each country (IMF, 2014b).

4.5 An evaluation of the narrative

The ultimate objective of this strategy is that of achieving rapid economic growth. The fundamental assumption of the strategy is that this objective is best achieved through measures and reforms that bolster the private sector of the economy. This strategy – and the assumptions on which the strategy is based – is considered to be appropriate not only for the ACTs, but for virtually all emerging and developing economies. What are the theoretical underpinnings of the strategy and is the claim of universal applicability justified?

The dominant paradigm in the discipline of economics is generally known as 'neoclassical' or 'neoliberal' economics.[10] It provides both a positive explanation of how the economy actually works and a normative model of how it *should* work. With the collapse of communism and the centrally planned economy as an economic model, the dominance of the neoliberal economic paradigm became complete. This was evident not only in academia but also in economic policy-making circles such as finance ministries and central banks and in international organizations such as the IMF and the World Bank. Its central message is that a free market economy is superior to any other known economic system and that, therefore, the best route to growth and prosperity for a country is the adoption of economic policies that promote and support free markets.

In fact, several tenets of neoliberalism have attained the status of 'axioms' or self-evident truths. To be fair, orthodox economists themselves have never described these tenets as 'axioms'. However, many so-called 'heterodox' economists who had consistently questioned these basic tenets have been brushed aside and totally ignored by both the academic and the policy-making establishments. These tenets therefore *appear* to be self-evident truths whose validity no serious (meaning mainstream) economist questions.

In the aftermath of the global economic crisis of 2007 and the Great Recession of 2008, although the dissenting voices in economics have become more vocal and their criticisms of mainstream economic theory and policy more pertinent and credible, they do not appear to have had a significant impact on either the academic or the policy-making orthodoxy. The commitment to the basic axioms of neoliberal economics by academics and policy makers remains largely unshaken. The following are some of the major, and relevant, 'axioms' of neoliberal economic theory (see, also, Arestis and González Martinez, 2015):

The public sector of an economy is inherently inefficient and the private sector inherently more efficient. This leads to the policy prescription of public sector cuts and privatization of public enterprises. Nationalization of any part of the economy is off the policy agenda.

Markets, including financial markets, are efficient and can be relied upon to produce an optimal allocation of resources. This leads to the policy demand for the creation of 'business-friendly' environment of low taxation and minimum intervention and regulation.

High rates of income taxation and welfare payments create disincentive effects to work effort. Therefore, both should be reduced. Alternatively, demands for higher taxes for the rich should be rejected as being counter-productive and destroying the potential for wealth creation.

Rising inequalities in income and wealth do not matter. There is a 'trickle-down' effect, whereby although the rich are getting richer the poor are better off in absolute terms. The familiar – and largely inappropriate – metaphor used in this context is of the tide that raises all boats, large and small.

By the same token reducing the power of trade unions by creating 'flexible' labour markets is also in the long-term interest of the workers because this will ultimately produce higher employment levels.

At the macroeconomic level, deficit spending by governments will 'crowd-out' private investment spending. Fiscal policy, therefore, as advocated by Keynesians to deal with recessions is ineffective. By the same token policies of fiscal austerity to deal with public indebtedness can be expansionary.

The above propositions are very similar to the ten policy prescriptions initially proposed by Williamson (1989; see, also, Arestis, 2004–05) that has come to be known, rather controversially, as the 'Washington Consensus'. The ten policy prescriptions of the 'Washington Consensus' can be outlined as follows:

1. Fiscal discipline: in effect, avoiding large fiscal deficits as a proportion of GDP.
2. A redirection of public expenditure priorities toward fields offering both high economic returns and the potential to improve income distribution, such as primary health care, primary education, and infrastructure.
3. Tax reform with a broader tax base and lower marginal tax rates.
4. Interest rate liberalization. Market-determined but moderate interest rates.
5. A competitive exchange rate.
6. Trade liberalization. Liberalization of imports, with particular emphasis given to eliminating quantitative restrictions (licensing, etc.); it should also be accompanied by trade protection to be provided by the introduction of low and relatively uniform tariffs.
7. Liberalization of inflows of foreign direct investment.
8. Privatization of state enterprises.
9. Deregulation. Abolition of regulations that impede market entry or restrict competition, except for those justified on safety, environmental and consumer protection grounds, and prudential oversight of the system.
10. Secure property rights.

The term 'Washington Consensus' provoked a great deal of controversy. It raised questions about its meaning, its validity, and record; and even its very existence.

With regard to the meaning of the term Williamson (1989) writes: "Th[is] paper identifies and discusses 10 policy instruments about whose proper deployment Washington can muster a reasonable degree of consensus. ... The paper is intended to elicit comment on both the extent to which the views identified *do* indeed command a consensus and on whether they *deserve* to command it. It is hoped that the country studies to be guided by this background paper will comment on the extent to which the Washington consensus is shared in the country in question. ... The Washington of this paper is both the political Washington of Congress and senior members of the administration and the technocratic Washington of the international financial institutions, the economic agencies of the U.S. government, the Federal Reserve Board, and the think tanks" (p. 1).

According to its author, the term 'Washington Consensus' refers to a set of policy recommendations supported by economists and policy makers in several Washington-based institutions such as the US Treasury, the Federal Reserve Board and the so-called 'Bretton Woods institutions' like the IMF and the World Bank. Fifteen years after the publication of his original policy list, Williamson (2004) claimed that he believed at that time "that views had pretty much coalesced on the sort of policies that had long been advocated by the OECD" (Williamson, op. cit., p. 2) and elaborated as follows on the meaning of the ten policy prescriptions. The context in which the first prescription was made was with regard to a region where almost all countries had run large deficits that led to balance of payments crises and high inflation. This hit mainly the poor, rather than the rich, who could protect their money by sending it abroad.

The suggestion of switching expenditure in a pro-growth and pro-poor way was *not* a prescription for all the burden of achieving fiscal discipline to be placed on expenditure cuts. On the contrary, the intention was "to be strictly neutral about the desirable size of the public sector, an issue on which even a hopeless consensus-seeker like me did not imagine that the battle had been resolved with the end of history that was being promulgated at the time" (Williamson, op. cit., p. 3).

The suggestion on tax reform was merely expressing a preference for the creation of a tax system that would combine a broad tax base with moderate marginal tax rates. The policy on liberalizing interest rates could have been formulated differently; and as Williamson (2004) suggests, "In retrospect I wish I had formulated this in a broader way as financial liberalization, stressed that views differed on how fast it should be achieved, and – especially – recognized the importance of accompanying financial liberalization with prudential supervision" (p. 3). Similarly, he acknowledges that the claim that a consensus existed on concerning competitive exchange rates was wishful thinking and that there were disagreement on the speed of effecting trade liberalization.

The liberalization of inward FDI specifically did not include comprehensive capital account liberalization, because such measure did or not command a consensus in Washington.

Privatization was a policy prescription, which originated as a neoliberal idea but had since won broad acceptance. Williamson (2004) admits that "We have since been made very conscious that it matters a lot how privatization is done: it can be a highly corrupt process that transfers assets to a privileged elite for a fraction of their true value, but the evidence is that it brings benefits (especially in terms of improved service coverage) when done properly, and the privatized enterprise either sells into a competitive market or is properly regulated" (p. 3).

The deregulation proposal's focus was mainly on easing barriers to entry and exit, rather than on doing away with regulations designed for safety or for environmental protection or attempting to prevent anti-competitive behaviour. Finally, the property rights prescription was mainly about providing the informal economy with the ability to gain property rights at acceptable cost.

Williamson (2004) felt it necessary to make the above clarifications in response to the way the term has been interpreted as purely a set of ideas supporting neoliberal 'market fundamentalism' imposed as a development strategy on unwilling developing countries. As Williamson (2004) puts it "Audiences the world over seem to believe that this signifies a set of neoliberal policies that have been imposed on hapless countries by the Washington-based international financial institutions and have led them to crisis and misery. There are people who cannot utter the term without foaming at the mouth" (p. 4).

The second set of criticisms relates to whether the Washington Consensus policy recommendations constitute a valid and successful development strategy. In this regard Stiglitz (2004) goes a step further and declares that the only consensus is that the Washington Consensus is a failed development strategy: "If there is a consensus today about what strategies are most likely to promote the development of the poorest countries in the world, it is this: there is no consensus except that the Washington consensus did not provide the answer. Its recipes were neither necessary nor sufficient for successful growth, though each of its policies made sense for particular countries at particular times" (p. 1). What Stiglitz (2004) means by the term 'Washington Consensus' was the oversimplified policy recommendations of the international financial institutions and the US Treasury produced during the 1980s and early 1990s before they acquired such negative connotations in both the Northern and Southern hemispheres and not the more subtle work of Williamson (1989, 2004). According to Stiglitz (op. cit.), whatever its original content and intention, the term – in the minds of most people across the world – has come to be associated with a development strategy that emphasizes privatization, liberalization, macro-stability (meaning mostly price stability) and a set of policies "predicated upon a strong faith – stronger than warranted – in unfettered markets and aimed at reducing, or even minimizing, the role of government. That development strategy stands in marked contrast to the successful strategies pursued in East Asia, where the *development state* took an active role" (p. 1; emphasis in original).

According to Stiglitz (2004), a broad criticism of the 'Washington Consensus' development strategy is that it has failed where it was implemented (Africa and Latin America) while a successful development strategy was implemented in countries that did not follow the Washington Consensus prescriptions (East Asia). Apart from the controversy concerning the success or failure of the strategy there are also several concrete objections, in principle, to the strategy advocated by the 'Washington Consensus'.

Critics point out that not all economists agree that free trade is always in the best interest of developing economies. A strict application of free trade and comparative advantage can leave developing economies producing primary products with low growth potential and high price volatility. As Stiglitz (2004) argues "There may be a broad consensus against 'excessive protectionism' that only serves the interests of special interests; but there is no consensus that rapid liberalization, especially in a country with high unemployment, will lead to faster economic growth. It may only lead to more unemployment. The usual argument that liberalization frees resources to move from unproductive protected sectors into more productive export sectors is unconvincing, when there are ample unutilized resources already available. In these cases, there is an emerging consensus: countries should be given scope to experiment, to use their own judgment, to explore what might work best for them" (p. 12). If countries promoted new industries, it may require both selective tariffs on cheap imports and also government subsidies. Too rapid trade liberalization might be counter-productive.

Equally counterproductive might be the inappropriate implementation of fiscal consolidation. Attempting to reduce budget deficits by cutting public expenditure and raising taxes in a recession may not only cause unnecessary economic hardship but may even cause negative growth rates which may result in an increase not a decrease in debt to GDP ratios. If fiscal consolidation impacts negatively on growth it will result in increased unemployment and poverty.

On the issue of privatization and de-nationalization critics questioned the ability of the private sector to combine superior efficiency without ignoring wider social objectives or that the privatization of natural monopolies will not simply create private monopolies detrimental to the public interest. On the policy of redirecting of public spending towards public sector activities like primary education, primary health care and infrastructure investment critics point out that invariably in practice such redirection has often been ignored in favour of more market-oriented policies, which have focused on less government intervention. Critics emphasize that financial deregulation has the potential to create credit crises and financial instability, as the global financial crisis of 2007 has demonstrated. We will return and elaborate on these issues when we discuss how the global financial crisis and the Great Recession affected the policy narrative with regard to the ACTs.

The final controversial issue in relation to the 'Washington Consensus' policy agenda is whether a consensus actually existed at the time of its promulgation or since. There are those who maintain that the ten policy recommendations command wide support, but only among the predominantly mainstream neoliberal academic economists and the technocratic establishment in Washington. Naim (2000) claims that no such consensus exists – even among mainstream economists – and that the 'Washington Consensus' should be renamed the 'Washington Confusion'. He writes "If this sample represents the Washington Consensus, then just imagine what a Washington Confusion would be like" (p. 3). Rodrik (2006), on the other hand, argues that there now exists an 'augmented' Washington Consensus, in which the original ten prescriptions are 'augmented' by a number of new prescriptions, such as the promotion of good corporate governance and anti-corruption legislation, the creation of flexible labour markets, support for World Trade Organization (WTO) agreements, establishment of financial codes and standards, 'prudent' capital account opening, non-intermediate exchange rate regimes, independent central banks/inflation targeting and the establishment of social safety nets (SSNs) in order to produce targeted poverty reduction.

The global financial and economic crisis of 2007, and the Great Recession that followed, re-ignited the debate about the 'Washington Consensus' policy agenda, especially in relation to policies imposed on the countries of the Euro Area periphery and to the policy options of transition economies in the Arab world. It has also re-ignited a more general debate, which had remained dormant for a number of years, regarding the workings of capitalism. The criticism and the questioning of the basic tenets of orthodox economic theory and the policy prescriptions that followed from these theories re-emerged and it has taken a variety of forms. In three specific areas the criticism is particularly pertinent.

First, the superior efficiency of the private sector and free markets, which was such a prominent feature of the 'Washington Consensus', can no longer be taken for granted after the sub-prime fiasco in the USA. The massive mismanagement of risk by the financial sector demonstrates clearly the folly of the strategy of de-regulation of the financial services sector. The experiment with 'light-touch' regulation has failed and it can no longer be regarded as a credible and reliable policy tool in either developed or developing economies.

Second, rising inequalities in income and wealth can no longer be regarded as part of the solution to the problem of stimulating growth. They have instead become part of the problem itself. Rising inequalities are objectionable not only on moral and ethical grounds but also on strictly economic grounds: the gap in aggregate demand resulting from the redistribution of income from the middle classes to the rich is filled by the financial sector with an ever-increasing level of private credit; and the 'search for yield' demanded by the very rich results in the taking of unacceptably high levels of risk by the financial sector with, as the world witnessed in 2007, disastrous consequences.

Third, in terms of macroeconomic stabilization the single-minded preoccupation of the established policy narrative with deficit reduction policies based, on the one hand, on the doctrine of 'expansionary austerity', and on the other hand on the existence of a so-called 'debt intolerance threshold', has come under severe attack from heterodox critics. 'Expansionary austerity' as a deficit reduction policy has failed in Greece and other countries of the Euro Area periphery and several studies (for example, Pescatori et al., 2014) have questioned the Reinhart and Rogoff (2009) claim that a particular debt threshold exists above which growth prospects are affected.

This debate is taking place not only in academic journals, but also in the mass media. It is fair to say that, unlike the previous major global economic crisis in the 1930s, the general public is much better informed about and possibly although not always has a better understanding of the different aspects of this debate between opposing schools of thought in economics.

We believe that this ongoing debate is significant, not because it will soon produce a definite resolution of all the theoretical and empirical disagreements in economics but because it raises doubts and uncertainties about the 'status' of these basic tenets of neoliberal economics. *Axioms that are questionable cannot remain axioms or self-evident truths forever.* The current IMF/World Bank policy narrative and its predecessor – the Washington Consensus' – can be seen in this light. It is a policy narrative which is based on some questionable axioms. This does not render the policy narrative entirely useless or the policy prescriptions wrong. What is being questioned is the 'one-size-fits-all' nature of the policy narrative. As Stiglitz (2004) noted in relation to the 'Washington Consensus', "there are some areas in which economic science has not yet provided sufficient evidence, sufficiently strong theory, or empirical evidence, to result in a broad consensus about what countries should do... Though it may not be possible to formulate simple prescriptions applicable to all countries, there may still be some principles, and a range of instruments, to be adapted to the circumstances of each country" (p. 12).

What this means is that any attempt to apply a set of rigid policy prescriptions to countries as diverse as Greece, Ireland, Portugal, Spain and the ACTs without adaptation to the needs and special circumstances of each country, is a mistake.

4.6 Is there an alternative?

The revolutions in the Arab World that began in January 2011 in Tunisia and spread throughout the region had their roots not only in demands for more democracy and participation, but also on a growing resentment with the prevailing economic environment, exacerbated by the Great Recession, in which job opportunities, especially among the young, were diminishing and corruption and inequalities growing. Since 2011, governments in the ACTs with varying degrees of success have been engaged in country-specific processes of political and constitutional reforms. At the same time they have also had to deal with the immediate problem of maintaining macroeconomic stability in a worsening international, regional, and domestic economic environment that adversely affected private sector confidence and growth. Although the focus on maintaining macroeconomic stability will remain a key policy priority in the short run, governments in the ACTs must not lose sight of the fact that an even bigger challenge remains: the actual implementation of the reform agenda. What kind of reform agenda should the ACTs implement in view of the fact that that there are significant financial gaps to be filled and, as is well known, financial support from international organizations comes with strings attached? Before attempting to answer this question, it is worth examining the nature and extent of help and assistance the ACTs are receiving from their external partners.

The IMF 'engagement' with the ACTs is as follows: Since the start of the Arab Spring in 20011, the IMF has approved a total of US$ 4.4 billion in disbursing programmes for Tunisia, Jordan and Yemen. Since July

2014, it also supports Morocco with a new Precautionary and Liquidity Line of US$5 billion. Moreover, the IMF is supporting Libya through a policy dialogue and is ready to enter programme discussions with Egypt should the authorities request such support. The Tunisian government is currently implementing an IMF-supported economic programme whose main objective is, according to the country's Finance Minister and Central Bank Governor, "to achieve short-term macroeconomic stability while laying the necessary foundations for supporting growth and protecting vulnerable groups" (IMF, 2014c). On 19 May 2015, the IMF announced that the request by Tunisia for a seven-month extension of the Stand-by Arrangement has been approved (IMF, 2015a). Similarly in Jordan the IMF (2015b) announced that programme performance remains broadly on course and that performance criteria were expected in end-March 2015 to be met. As a result, the completion of the sixth review made available to Jordan $196.5 million. In the Yemen the IMF granted a Rapid Credit Facility (RCF) in 2012, which was replaced in 2014 by a three-year Extended Credit Facility (ECF) aimed at supporting the country's reform agenda. The First Review mission under the ECF has, however, been postponed due to the deterioration in the political and security situation since early 2015 and the recent intensification of the armed conflict. Moreover, the IMF, in its continued effort to move forward the policy agenda in the ACTs, jointly organized the Amman Conference in May 2014 (see above); in addition, to positively responding to capacity development needs, such as those included through the programme pursued by the IMF–Middle East Regional Technical Assistance Center and the joint IMF/Kuwait training institute. Finally, in addition to ongoing advice through regular consultations, despite various security issues in several countries, the IMF undertook about 30 technical assistance missions and provided training to more than 400 participants from the ACTs in various courses in 2014. There is therefore quite significant involvement of the IMF in five of the six ACTs.

In addition to the IMF engagement the ACTs receive support in their economic transformation efforts from other external partners in the following areas. First, they received support in the form of external official financial assistance, which, since the beginning of the Arab Spring, amounted to around $80 billion. These disbursements have covered only a part of the ACTs financing gaps, notwithstanding significant contributions from the Gulf Cooperation Council (GCC) countries. It is expected that in the future greater and more stable financial support will be required to enable the ACTs in their fiscal consolidation effort. Increased public spending on infrastructure and basic services, assuming a gradual abolition of generalized subsidies, are essential for promoting growth and, therefore, a socially more acceptable fiscal consolidation. It is, of course, important to emphasize that future financial needs might be greater if conflicts in the region, spread further or intensify. Second, further progress with agreements to promote trade, harmonization of trade regulations convergence, and FDI will be needed. Assistance in the area is considered necessary in order to help build private sector-led recoveries and sustained growth for the ACTs. Progress in this area could provide a strong anchor for public confidence in the long-term sustainability of the economic transformations. Third, the reform process in the ACTs suggests a number of possible areas for further capacity-building technical assistance such as support of the reforms of public finance management, social safety nets, civil service, financial sectors (to improve access to finance for small- and- medium-sized enterprises), tax and customs policy and administrations, pensions, education and other social sector policies. In this regard, the Deauville Partnership's Transition Fund has so far helped with 53 projects with a total volume of $171.8 million as of September 2014 (IMF, 2014b).

As was noted above international financial support comes with conditions attached. These conditions relate to the appropriate policies that the creditors expect the countries that receive assistance to pursue. As was discussed at length above, the only game in town in terms of policy options for the ACTs is neoliberal orthodoxy.

Is there an alternative to the continuation of these IMF-supported programs which, to a greater or less extent, involves four of the six ACTs? Is there any possibility of deviating from the strategy of promoting and engineering a private sector-led growth, which, according to the IMF/World Bank narrative, is the best way of meeting the various economic 'challenges' currently facing the ACTs? In the light of the various criticisms of the neoliberal paradigm, briefly discussed above, is there any scope for an alternative strategy that takes note of these criticisms?

Although fundamentally the IMF/World Bank approach and outlook remains based firmly on the neoliberal paradigm there have recently been some shifts and changes in emphasis in certain aspects of the policy dimension, which are potentially very significant and noteworthy. Mr. Masood Ahmet, Director of the Middle East and Central Asia Department of the IMF, has recently declared that "with the benefit of hindsight, it has become clear that in past years we paid insufficient attention to growing socioeconomic imbalances and unequal access to economic opportunity... The Arab transitions have thus prompted us to step back and rethink our approach to economic policy recommendations for the countries undergoing transition" (IMF, 2014b, p. ix).

A rethinking is also taking place in the IMF's economic research department. First, Olivier Blanchard, the IMF's chief economist, has recently acknowledged that mistakes were made in the design of the Greek austerity programme: the fiscal multipliers were much more powerful than expected and the contraction in the economy much greater than expected (see Blanchard and Leigh, 2013). Second, a succession of very important IMF research papers deal with issue of inequality in a novel way, claiming that the effects of redistribution policies that reduce inequality are on the whole pro-growth (see Ostry et al., 2014).

The recent realization, therefore, that growing 'socioeconomic imbalances' or simply growing inequalities in income and wealth affected the dominant policy narrative in the following way: the IMF is now firmly committed to the objective of achieving 'inclusive growth' through its policy prescriptions. 'Inclusive growth' is, of course, interpreted in a variety of ways, but it is generally understood to mean a fairer distribution of the benefits of economic growth in the relevant economy.

How can the dominant policy narrative be adapted as to promote 'inclusive growth'? The IMF (2014b) attempts to answer this question as follows: "Realizing that the popular uprisings in the ACTs were born in part of a desire for more widespread and fairer distribution of economic opportunities, the IMF has increasingly focused on issues pertaining to inclusive growth. In particular, the IMF has recommended important economic reforms to reduce high structural unemployment and deliver a more equitable distribution of income, including enhancing business and investment conditions, increasing trade openness, improving the stability and access of the financial system, and improving social safety nets" (p. 9). The implication from the above quote seems to be that the best way of achieving 'inclusive growth' and a fairer distribution of the benefits of economic growth, remains the strategy that promotes private sector-led growth.

In addition to embracing 'inclusive growth' as the overarching objective of its policy agenda the post-Great Recession and post-'Arab Spring' policy narrative has now recognized that it must make two additional adaptations. First, there seems to be some shift in the rigid IMF position on 'expansionary austerity. It appears that it is now acknowledged that fiscal consolidation needs to proceed at a slower pace. In relation to the ACTs the IMF (2014a) has particularly recommended that "fiscal consolidation is pursued at a gradual pace to put fiscal balances on a sustainable path while limiting the adverse short-term effects on growth and unemployment" (p. 8). Second, it is now recognized that programme implementation is not a purely technocratic exercise. More focus is necessary on the political economy of reform. It is worth dwelling further on this last significant issue.

Successful political and economic transformations require a coordinated effort by all parts of a society. Political transformations create the opportunities for economic transformations, which, if successful, can re-enforce and strengthen the political transformation in a virtuous circle. What the IMF (2014b) is now acknowledging is that the design of the economic reform agenda cannot be done in a sociopolitical vacuum. Instead the ACTs need to focus on navigating the political economy of reform paying particular attention to the sequencing of reforms, with emphasis on early steps in areas with high payoffs. A flexible approach is required, and reform opportunities should be seized upon as they arise. Well-coordinated and stepped-up support from the international community is also essential.

The IMF (2014b) sets the scene with regard to the complexity of the task ahead. The ACTs embarked on a process that aims to achieve macroeconomic stability combined with structural reforms amidst a challenging sociopolitical environment. Policy makers throughout the ACTs are facing acute pressures to proceed urgently with the reforms while the sociopolitical environment challenges their ability to deliver them. Institutional uncertainty, such as the fact that a number of countries have yet to adopt new constitutions and elect governments with more than transitional time horizons, adds to the political risks and slows down the reform process which in turn delays the economic transformation agenda.

The famous prescription of the dominant policy narrative that 'short-term pain is necessary for long-term gain' has very little resonance with transitional governments or governments with short horizons and limited incentives to undertake reforms that have short-term political costs, irrespective of their future benefits. As the IMF (2014b) points out "transitional governments may find it difficult to implement subsidy reform or allow for exchange rate depreciation that would have negative income or balance sheet effects for some groups in the short term, even though these measures are necessary to strengthen inclusive growth in the future. Many reforms have important distributional impact, which can trigger early resistance" (p. 84).

Furthermore, the reform effort might be discouraged due to the power struggle between former elites and vested interests and newcomers which leads to increased political uncertainty and the slowing down of the reform process. Coalition governments which have been formed in a number of

ACTs, may also slow down the reform process due to the conflicting agendas of parties within the coalitions. A lack of experience among those new to government can present further obstacles to the design and implementation of reforms.

Finally, youth interests can no longer be taken for granted given the demographic reality in the MENA region, where youth make up the majority of the population. In the past Arab youth have traditionally borne a disproportionate share of the costs of economic adjustment. Any reform agenda in the ACTs needs to incorporate youth into the decision-making process, and to addressed youth needs and concerns explicitly.

In addition to the above complexities in the environment in which reforms must be implemented, the feasibility of reforms may also be constrained by limited administrative capacity to design and administer the reforms. The capacity of the reform system might become overloaded, thereby losing the ability to prioritize reforms. Essential but complex reforms may therefore not be feasible in the short term, and would require careful sequencing that includes investment in building the capacity to implement them.

The IMF, therefore, now acknowledges that there is no 'one-size-fits-all' approach and that a reform strategy for the ACTs must be tailored to the particular circumstances of each country as well as to the specific nature of the reforms. However, there are a number of important considerations that policy makers in the ACTs may wish to take into account when designing and implementing reforms. In other words, the political economy of reforms, according to the IMF (2014b), must consider the following factors.

First, policy makers must, in the IMF/World Bank language, take 'ownership of the reform agenda': "A strong case must be made for the benefits of reform. Gathering data and undertaking analytical work to explain poor outcomes, and identifying policies to improve them, are the first steps in a well-designed reform process. Highlighting the costs of the status quo and providing evidence of the benefits of reform across the different segments of the population can provide a compelling case for change" (p. 85).

Second, reform plans should be transparent and policy makers accountable for reform implementation. This can reduce the risk of reform paralysis in which reform is much discussed but never implemented. "To build momentum for reform, transparency about the whole reform process is essential. Policy makers' success will depend on listening to all stakeholders' views when formulating policy agendas.

This will require legal reforms to permit independent organizations to form without state approval" (IMF, op. cit., p. 85).

Third, a more participatory process will help identify areas of resistance or support for change: "Experience shows that involving a broader spectrum of society in the design of reform – along with a readiness to respond to concerns to the extent of modifying reform proposals – also fosters a sense of ownership for reform and can help hold back future opposition" (IMF, op. cit., p. 88).

Fourth, it is important for the success of the reform agenda to build coalitions: "Economic reform inevitably entails distributional consequences: losses for some – particularly those with vested interest in the status quo – in the short term, while generating broad benefits to the wider population only in the longer term. Gaining traction for reform – and ultimately succeeding in implementing it – depends to a great extent on a government's ability to build coalitions in support of change while addressing opponents' concerns about its distributional impact" (IMF, op. cit., p. 89).

Fifth, timing and sequencing of reforms are also of paramount importance. In a difficult and complex sociopolitical environment, it may be necessary to alter the timing of change, bringing forward some measures that can command sufficient support and to postponing others, since some progress is better than no progress at all. In this sense, it will be important to accept pragmatic deviations from what might be considered to be technically an 'optimal' path. IMF (op. cit.) suggests that "Policymakers may focus on low-hanging fruit or use small-step approaches, such as launching reforms on a limited scale and assessing them before expanding them. Examples include accepting a gradual approach to a tax increase or linking electricity tariff increases to improvements in service provision coverage" (p. 90). The introduction of exchange rate flexibility, on the other hand, is an example of a particularly difficult reform which can only be attempted by a newly elected government with a strong political mandate able to withstand the potential loss of political capital. Sequencing, therefore, means that initiatives that create tangible immediate benefits must be included in a reform agenda. In ACTs, it is clear that political support for the transitions is based on widespread expectations of improved economic opportunities for the majority of the population. It is vital, therefore, for the success of the reform agenda that initiatives are included which have a rapid impact and visible economic improvements and consider compensating in advance those vulnerable groups that stand to lose from the reforms.

Finally, of critical importance in the political economy of reforms is the role of communications. In section 4.2 above, the empowering role of modern communications and social networking in bringing about the political transformations during the 'Arab Spring' uprisings was particularly noted. Governments in the ACTs operating in a multi-stakeholder environment, in which a variety of interest groups voice their views and demands, it is important that governments are engaged with civil society through appropriate consultation and communication. "Effective communication needs to be an integral part of the economic reform process. Public communication campaigns should aim at increasing awareness of the planned policy changes, explaining the rationale and building buy-in for the proposed reforms, highlighting their benefits for society at large and for specific groups, and establishing realistic expectations about what can be achieved" (IMF, op. cit., p. 91). The task of effectively communicating the government's case for reform is considerably enhanced by the emergence of social media and the connectivity across media networks. A clear case for the overall benefits to society of reforms and of the inefficiencies and wastefulness of maintaining the status quo must be made. The IMF also believes that the communication strategy should also clarify the role of international financial institutions and the wider international community in supporting the reform process. An effective communication strategy must not only explain what government policy is but it must also make strategic choices of media for different messages and different audiences.

4.7 Summary and conclusions

Although a variety of underlying social, political and economic causes were responsible for the popular uprisings that shook the Arab World in 2011, there is little doubt that adverse developments in the economy, which the Great Recession greatly accentuated, were of pivotal importance. At the same time a political transition can create opportunities for economic transformation. The two developments can produce a virtuous circle whereby successful economic transformation can reinforce the political transition, which can, in turn, support further economic transformation. Unfortunately, as we saw above, this has not been the case in the experience of ACTs. Indeed, the experience with political transition, and consequently with economic transformation, varies significantly from country to country. It would be fair to say that there has been little transition to democracy and hardly any economic transformation. At one end of the spectrum in Libya and Yemen, although there has been regime change as a result of the 'Arab Spring' uprisings, there is hardly any meaningful political transition to democratic governance. Similarly, in Egypt the government lacks democratic legitimacy while Jordan and Morocco remain monarchies, albeit with democratically elected parliaments. Of the six ACTs, therefore, only Tunisia may fit the description of an Arab country in transition. Nevertheless, one thing that all ACTs have in common is a shared popular wish and expectation of an improved economic situation. How are these expectations to be fulfilled?

In this contribution we examined the political and economic reality of ACTs in the post-Great Recession period and the available policy options, as prescribed by the dominant IMF/World Bank policy narrative, in the world of the post-'Arab Spring' revolutions. These policy prescriptions are supposed to have undergone some modification following a rethinking of the dominant policy narrative in response to three recent developments: increased awareness of inequality issues; the failure of rapid fiscal consolidation in achieving deficit reduction; and the recognition that, in the area of reform implementation, a political economy approach is needed. Have these modifications significantly altered the policy options available to Arab transition economies?

With regard to the adoption of the 'inclusive growth' objective, one might be excused in thinking that nothing fundamentally changed in the policy narrative. The belief firmly remains that the best way of ensuring that the benefits of growth are fairly shared is by promoting private sector-led growth, shrinking the public sector and implementing 'targeted' reforms in SSNs. With regard to the so-called 'political economy' approach to the reform process, the overwhelming impression is that it simply represents a marketing exercise for the old narrative rather than any radical rethinking of the policy agenda. Its main concern is how to sell the policy narrative and persuade the public to adopt reforms. The public must be convinced that these reforms are, in their entirety, fundamentally sound and basically consistent with the free market neoliberal narrative. As far as the readiness to ease the speed of fiscal consolidations it is an encouraging sign that a genuine shift in the IMF position has taken place – a shift, incidentally, which may become more credible if an apology is offered for the savage and disastrous fiscal consolidation programme imposed on Greece, which still continues.

As far as alternative policy options are concerned, Arab Countries in Transition are not being offered a different choice from the one that existed prior to the Great Recession and the 'Arab Spring' revolutions. On the principle that 'whoever pays the piper calls the tune' an interesting development in recent years that runs counter to some of the more 'fundamentalist' tenets both of the 'Washington Consensus' and its successor, the IMF/World Bank policy agenda, is the significant investment by Chinese firms in developing economies in both Africa and Latin America. It appears that China's lending to developing countries recently surpassed that of the World Bank (see FT, 2015). The interesting thing about the Chinese approach is that it involves substantial investment in infrastructure and public sector investment; showing that in respect of economic development an interventionist approach can have a bigger return than leaving it to free markets. China, denied an enhanced role in the IMF, is now proposing the creation of the Asian Infrastructure Investment Bank (see, FT, 2015). Could such a development potentially provide a rival to the 'Washington Consensus' and the prevailing IMF/World Bank policy narrative concerning the role of markets and states in development? A possible 'Beijing Consensus', whatever that might turn out to be, can emerge in which case the neoliberal policy narrative might not be the only game in town.

It is certainly a positive development the acknowledgement by the IMF that their 'one-size-fits-all' approach to policy design and implementation was a mistake. It is now time to recognize that the 'all-or-nothing' nature of the policy prescriptions is also mistaken. It is indeed a mistake in the aftermath of the Great Recession to design an 'all-or-nothing' policy edifice based on a number of questionable axioms, as argued above.

Notes

1. The author is Associate Member of the Cambridge Centre of Economic and Public Policy, Department of Land Economy, University of Cambridge. He has previously taught at the University of Greenwich, University of Westminster, University of Middlesex and the School of Oriental and African Studies, University of London. He is grateful to Philip Arestis and Malcolm Sawyer for helpful comments. The usual disclaimer applies.
2. Policy options based on Islamic Economics are not considered in this contribution, not because they are unimportant but because they need a separate investigation and contribution altogether.
3. With the exception of Tunisia, describing the other five ACTs as 'democracies' is, of course, highly debatable.
4. A search for Arab Spring in May 2015 produced a list of 3,934 titles in Amazon. A similar search for the Euro Area crisis produced only 1,765 titles.
5. Tourism is an important, labour-intensive sector in terms both of earnings and employment growth. Unfortunately it is also a sector that is very sensitive to the security concerns of tourists.

6. There is a scarcity of reliable information on income and wealth inequalities in the Arab world. In this regard popular perceptions are more significant than hard data; see Alvaredo and Piketty (2014).
7. At the point of writing, in the case of Libya and Yemen, an even bigger 'challenge' is, of course, the absence of a central government!
8. Based on IMF (2014a).
9. Source: Trading Economics, available at: http://www.tradingeconomics.com/tunisia/government-budget.
10. See, for example, Arestis and González Martinez (2015).

References

Alvaredo, F. and Piketty, T. (2014) 'Measuring Top Incomes and Inequality in the Middle East: Data limitations and Illustrations with the Case of Egypt', *Economic Research Forum*, Working Paper 832.

Arestis, P. (2004–05) 'Washington Consensus and Financial Liberalization', *Journal of Post Keynesian Economics*, 27(2), 251–71.

Arestis, P. and González Martinez, A.R. (2015) 'The Absence of Environmental Issues in the New Consensus Macroeconomics is only One of Numerous Criticisms', in P. Arestis and M. Sawyer (eds), *Finance and the Macroeconomics of Environmental Policies*, Basingstoke: Palgrave Macmillan.

Blanchard, O. and Leigh, D. (2013) 'Growth Forecast Error and Fiscal Multipliers', IMF Working Paper, 13/1, January.

Financial Times (FT) (2015) 'China-led AIIB Attracts Rush of Applications', April. Available at www.ft.com/cms/s/0/94728d96-d82f-11e4-ba53-00144feab7de.html.

Iqbal, Z. (2014) 'The Arab Awakening: Determinants and Economic Consequences', *Middle East Institute*. Available at http://www.mei.edu/content/arab-awakening-determinants-and-economic-consequences.

IMF (2013) 'Greece: Ex-post Evaluation of Exceptional Access Under the 2010 Stand-by Arrangement', *IMF Country Report*, 13/15.

IMF (2014a) 'Arab Countries in Transition. Economic Outlook and Key Challenges', *Staff Papers*, October.

IMF (2014b), *Toward New Horizons. Economic Transformation Amid Political Transitions*, Washington, DC, IMF Staff.

IMF (2014c) 'Tunisia: Letter of Intent, Memorandum of Economic and Financial Policies, and Technical Memorandum of Understanding', *IMF Press Release*, March.

IMF (2015a) 'IMF Approves 7-Month Extension of the Stand-By Arrangement for Tunisia', *IMF Press Release No 15/229*.

IMF (2015b) 'IMF Executive Board Completes the Sixth Review Under the SBA for Jordan', *IMF Press Release No 15/185*.

Kapsos, S. (2005) 'The Employment Intensity of Growth: Trends and Macroeconomic Determinants', Employment Strategy Papers, Geneva: International Labour Organization.

Naim, M (2000) 'Washington Consensus or Washington Confusion', *Foreign Policy*, Spring.

Ostry, J.D., Berg, A. and Tsangarides, C.G. (2014) 'Redistribution, Inequality and Growth', *IMF Research Department*, February.

Owen, R. (2013) 'Historical Perspective on the Arab Spring', *Web Cast*. Available at http://www.wilsoncenter.org/event/historical-perspective-the-arab-spring.

Pescatori, A., Damiano, S. and Simon, J. (2014) 'Debt and Growth: Is there a Magic Threshold?', *IMF Working Paper*, February.
Pollack, N. (2011) *The Arab Awakening: America and the Transformation of the Middle East*, Washington, DC: The Brookings Institution.
Reinhart, C.M. and K.S. Rogoff (2009) *This Time is Different: Eight Centuries of Financial Folly*, Princeton, NJ: Princeton University Press.
Rodrik, D. (2006) 'Goodbye Washington Consensus, Hello Washington Confusion', *Journal of Economic Literature*, XLIV, 973–87.
Stiglitz, J. (2004) 'The Post War Washington Consensus', The Institute for Policy Dialogue.
Williamson, J. (1989) 'What Washington Means by Fiscal Reform', in J. Williamson (ed.), *Latin America Readjustment: How Much Has Happened?*, Washington, DC: Institute for International Economics.
Williamson, J. (2004) 'A Short History of the Washington Consensus', paper commissioned by *Fundación CIDOB* for a conference 'From the Washington Consensus Towards a new Global Governance', Barcelona, 24–5 September.
Yusuf, S. (2014) 'Middle East Transitions. A Long Hard Road', IMF Working Paper, 14/135.

5
The Impact of the Great Recession and Policy Responses in Latin America: Was This Time Different?

Fernando Ferrari-Filho
Universidade Federal do Rio Grande do Sul, Brazil
Luiz Fernando de Paula
University of the State of Rio de Janeiro, Brazil

Abstract: The 2007–08 international financial crisis and the 'Great Recession' (GR) affected the different regions of the world, including the emerging economies. In the case of most of the major economies of Latin America, the reduction of public external debt, the previous policy of international reserves accumulation and the reduction and improvement in the composition of public debt provided some policy space for the introduction of counter-cyclical policies. Consequently, governments could make use of counter-cyclical fiscal policy to face up to the effects of the IFC and GR, when on other occasions they made use of tightened policies. The countries' reaction to the crisis has varied with the use of different tools of economic policy. For instance, between 2011 and 2013, despite the operation of counter-cyclical policies, the economic growth showed great volatility in the economies of the region. In addition, there are a lot of concerns about the future performance of the economies of the region due mainly to the uncertainties related to the global economy.

Keywords: Great Recession; Latin America; counter-cyclical policies

JEL Classification: F63; O23; O54

5.1 Introduction[1]

The 2007–08 international financial crisis (IFC) was a crisis of globalized finance, meaning that a crisis in one specific segment of the financial system – specifically, the United States subprime mortgage market – eventually spread worldwide. The effects of such a crisis are not economically and socially neutral, especially because since 2009 the 'Great Recession' (GR) has affected the different regions of the world, including emerging economies.

As is well known, historical recent experiences of financial crisis in Latin America have been a succession of painful crises: the external debt crisis of the 1980s, the contagion of Mexican 1994–95 crisis and the contagion of Asian crisis, among others. However, on this occasion, the Latin American governments' policy responses to the contagion of global financial crisis and the GR were rather different. Why should this be the case? In most large countries of Latin America the reduction in public external debt, the previous policy of international reserves accumulation and the reduction and improvement in the composition of public debt, provided some policy space for the introduction of counter-cyclical policies. This meant that governments could make use of counter-cyclical fiscal policy to ameliorate the effects of the IFC, when on other occasions they had made use of tightened policies. The countries' reaction to the IFC and the GR has varied with the use of different tools of economic policies. Between 2011 and 2013, despite the counter-cyclical policies adopted by the main Latin American countries, the levels of economic growth in the region were very volatile. In addition, there are a lot of concerns about the future performance of the economies of the region due mainly to the uncertainties related to the global economy and the reduction of the policy space in greater Latin American economies.

The purpose of this chapter is to examine the consequences of the IFC and the GR in the main Latin America countries – Argentina, Brazil, Chile, Mexico and Venezuela[2] – and the implementation of counter-cyclical policies in these countries.

Following this introduction, the chapter is divided into three sections. Section 5.2 shows that the IFC and the GR both had a substantial effect on the economic dynamism of these countries, and also considers the reaction of the main Latin American economies to the environment of the IFC and the GR. Section 5.3 analyses the main counter-cyclical policies and their results implemented by the main Latin American economic euthorities (EA) to mitigate the impacts of the IFC and the GR. Finally, section 5.4 summarizes and presents some economic policy recommendations to assure macroeconomic stability – that is, sustainable economic growth, inflation under control and long-term fiscal and balance of payments equilibria – and to promote a consistent economic integration in the Latin America.

5.2 The consequences of the IFC and GR in the main Latin American countries and the reaction of their EA

The IFC crisis had a dramatic effect on economic activity, both in the developed countries and in the emerging economies, casting doubt on the very notion of the decoupling of emerging economies from developed countries. The developments from the crisis were observed not just in the financial system, but, most importantly, in the real realm of the economy. After a period of prosperity in the world economy running from 2003 to 2008, the United States, the countries of the Euro Area, Japan and some of the leading emerging countries, including the Latin American countries (Figure 5.1) went into recession in 2009. The scenario of economic downturn, shrinking trade flows and asset deflation that unfolded from September 2008 onwards caused the world economy to go into collapse.[3]

It should be stressed that the world recession in 2009 might have been much worse had it not been for the actions of the EA of both the G7 countries and the emerging countries that were taking an active part in mitigating the impacts of the IFC on the productive sphere of the economy. To that end, they implemented counter-cyclical fiscal policies

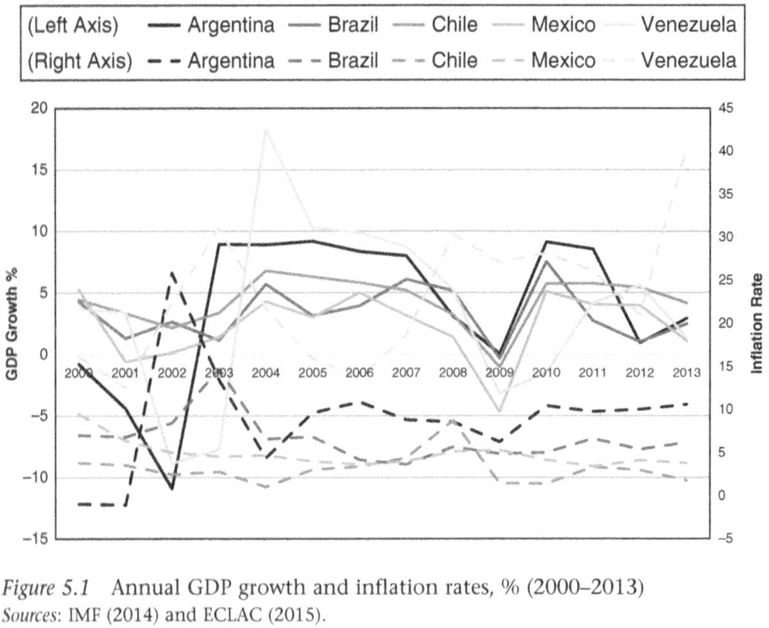

Figure 5.1 Annual GDP growth and inflation rates, % (2000–2013)
Sources: IMF (2014) and ECLAC (2015).

and expansionist monetary policies, mainly through the activities of their central banks as lenders of last resort, in order to reverse the steadily deteriorating state of expectations among economic agents. Indeed, governments of developed and emerging economies have responded to the 2007–08 IFC and the GR with a massive fiscal and monetary stimulus. In that regard, injections of liquidity and substantial interest rate reductions by central banks, along with fiscal incentives along 'Keynesian' lines, were important in reducing the impact of the crisis on the 'real economy' and seeking to restore agents' confidence in the workings of the markets.

The fact that the IFC was restricted to the developed countries, and the most emerging countries' fiscal and external situation was comfortable, led a number of analysts and policymakers to give credence to the hypothesis of a 'decoupling' of some emerging countries; that is, the notion that these economies would be able to sustain their dynamic performance and prove immune to contagion from the crisis. In 2008, moreover, the main concern among central banks, market analysts and multilateral organizations was with the inflationary pressures that emerging countries might suffer as a result of strongly rising food and oil prices.

However, particularly following the bankruptcy of Lehman Brothers in September 2008, economic agents' expectations as to the magnitude and development of the IFC changed dramatically. The crisis spread to the whole world economy by contagion effects, affecting credit and capital markets, as well as international trade, especially by countries dependent on the export of commodities, whose prices fell abruptly. In that context, some emerging countries experienced not just macroeconomic instabilities (in terms of economic activity or price volatility), but also situations of fiscal and external fragility, regardless of whether or not they had displayed, prior to the crisis, what were regarded as sound macroeconomic fundamentals.

The outcome was no different in Latin America: after a period of mini-boom of growth[4] (2003–08) arising mainly as a result of the commodities boom, by the end of 2008, most countries in the region had fallen into recession (from the last quarter of 2008 until the first quarter of 2009). The contagious crisis effect of the global financial crisis on the performance of Latin American economies was deep, short and synchronized, as can be seen in Figure 5.1. Indeed, in 2009 GDP growth in the region's main emerging countries was negative in Brazil, Mexico and Venezuela, while in Argentina and Chile the economic activity had dropped considerably as compared with 2008. Moreover, as Figures 5.2

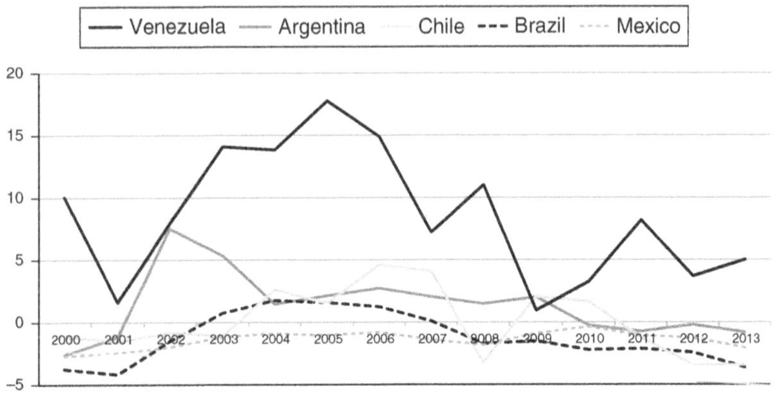

Figure 5.2 Current account/GDP, % (2000–2013)
Source: IMF (2014).

and 5.4 show, the trade balance and current account/GDP of the main Latin American countries had deteriorated substantially between 2008 and 2009 due to the fact that their most important trade partners, such as the United States and the countries of the Euro Area, had fallen into recession: the trade balance of Argentina, Brazil and Chile dropped, while the trade balance of Mexico and Venezuela improved; the current account deficits of Argentina, Brazil, Chile and Mexico worsened, while the current account surplus of Venezuela presented some volatility, but, at the end of the period, it had improved due to the increase in the price of oil. According to Figure 5.3, in general, commodity prices fell sharply by the end of 2008 – compared to the prices of the 2004–08 period – due to the GR that followed the financial crisis.

Another immediate channel of the contagion of global crisis was through the capital outflows in portfolio capitals, loans, foreign direct investment (FDI) and profit repatriation by transnational corporations.[5] Figure 5.4 shows that the balance of financial account reduced sharply in the aftermath of the Lehman Brothers bankruptcy, but it recovered quickly and strongly in Brazil and Mexico, the major economies of the region and also those that were the most integrated in financial terms. With regard to Argentina, one should consider the case after the renegotiation of the external debt in 2004–05, when its external indebtedness was reduced dramatically, and it did not obtain access to international financial market.

In principle, the IFC and the GR could cause inflationary pressures in the main Latin American countries, due to the sharp currency devaluation

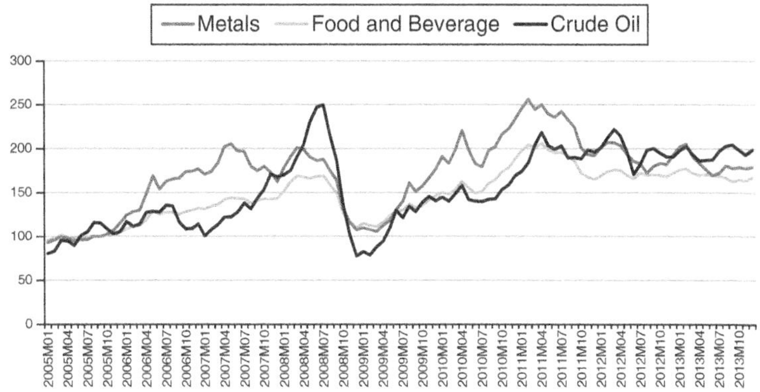

Figure 5.3 Commodity prices and oil prices, USD (2005–2013)
Source: IMF (2014).

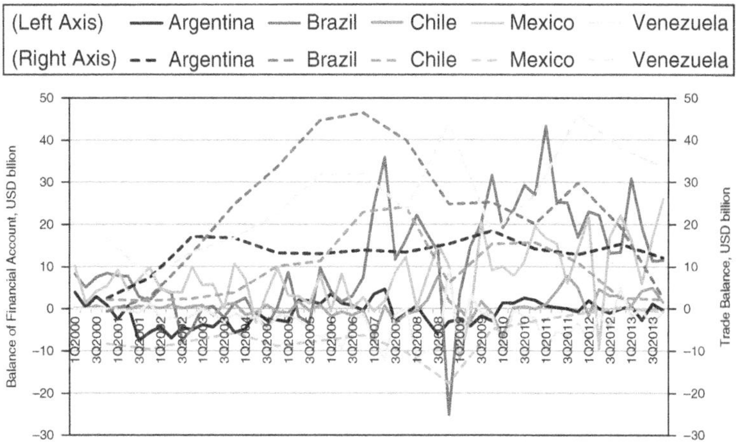

Figure 5.4 Balance of financial account and trade balance, USD billion (2000–2013)
Sources: ECLAC (2015) and World Bank (2014).

(against the dollar) during the contagion of the global financial crisis after the Lehman Brothers bankruptcy that would result in exchange pass-through effects. However, the recession that followed the financial crisis and the drop in the food and oil prices neutralized the inflationary effects of the devaluation and allowed the monetary authorities to implement an expansionary monetary policy (involving the expansion of monetary aggregates and/or a reduction in interest rates). The behavior of the inflation rate (consumer price index) before and after the crisis has been uneven across the economies: Argentina and Venezuela have much higher levels of inflation than Brazil, Chile and Mexico. In Venezuela, in particular, the inflation rate reached more than 40 per cent per year in 2013, and there is some concern about the likelihood of a future hyperinflation process (Figure 5.1). After the financial crisis, inflation increased in Argentina and Brazil and fell in Chile, while there was a more or less stable trend in Mexico. Brazil, Chile and Mexico adopted an inflation target regime under the conditions of a floating exchange regime, while Argentina operates a managed exchange rate with monetary targets and Venezuela, since January 2002, has implemented a dual exchange rate system.

Summing up, the IFC generated mechanisms by which it was transmitted to Latin American economies included: (i) the withdrawal of portfolio capital (with, incidentally, capital flight eventually affecting stock markets) and FDI; (ii) the interruption of credit, particularly for foreign trade; (iii) falling commodities prices; (iv) declining exports to developed countries; (v) volatile exchange rates; and (vi) rising levels of profit repatriation by transnational corporations.

Prates and Cintra (2009) argue that in previous crises, more precisely the external crises of the 1990s (Mexico, 1994–5, East Asia, 1997, Russia, 1998, and Brazil, 1998–9), most emerging countries implemented procyclical (restrictive) measures. This was in line with the principles of (and approved by) the International Monetary Fund (IMF), and was intended to regain the confidence of the financial markets as a necessary condition for foreign capital to flow back to those emerging economies. However, in view of the systemic nature of the present crisis emerging countries' EA decided that on this occasion such policies would be completely ineffective. Rather, they would contribute to aggravating the developments from the crisis by setting off a vicious circle of exchange depreciation, credit squeeze, asset deflation, and crises of effective demand and unemployment. In that light, these countries met the contagion effect by putting in place counter-cyclical measures to render their currencies less volatile, prevent balance of payments deterioration, assure liquidity for their domestic financial systems, stabilize prices and bring growth back on track.

Indeed, all the major Latin American economies, with the exception of Venezuela, experienced sharp recoveries in 2010 (Figure 5.1). Such a recovery was the consequence of a combination of external factors with domestic factors. The *external factors* are related to the recovery of the international trade by the middle of 2009, favoured by the recovery of the Chinese economy through the use of expansionary policies that once again increased the demand for basic goods; and the resumption of the capital inflows to emerging economies (including some Latin American countries) thanks to the expansionary monetary policy adopted by developed economies. The surge of capital flows, mainly in the modality of portfolio, contributed to the strong recovery of the capital markets in some important economies of the region, such as Brazil and Mexico.

The *domestic factors* are related to the successful implementation of counter-cyclical policies in Latin America. According to Paula et al. (2013, p. 235) economic policy responses included a large range of tools (see also Jará et al., 2009):

i. Central banks provided foreign currency liquidity to the private sector, to ensure both the continued operation of foreign exchange markets and the continued availability of external financing.
ii. External resources provided significant additional support to Latin American countries during the global financial crisis: the central banks of Brazil and Mexico established reciprocal currency arrangements with the FED, totaling US$30 billion each, while the IMF created Flexible Credit Line (FCL) financing facilities, which were used by Mexico (US$47 billion) and Colombia (US$10.5 billion).
iii. Some central banks, such as those in Argentina, Brazil, Mexico and Peru, increased the range of assets accepted as collateral to improve access to short-term funding. Many central banks (Colombia, Brazil and Peru) also relied heavily on lower banks' reserve ratio requirements.
iv. However, central banks delayed lowering interest rates until late 2008 or early 2009, due to concerns about inflationary pressures and the potential impact of the depreciation in the exchange rate; such behavior contributed negatively to economic growth in 2009.
v. Some countries made use of counter-cyclical fiscal policy, by reducing taxes to stimulate consumption (Brazil and Chile) and/or by the increase in public expenditures (Argentina, Brazil and Colombia).

One further counter-cyclical tool was the increase in the minimum wage that contributed to avoiding the fall in the real wage in a lot of countries and to moderate the reduction of consumption due to recession in the aftermath of the contagion of the crisis.

Reduced external vulnerability was the principal reason for the reasonable performance of emerging economies during the recent global financial crises; and it is associated with a set of factors, that includes: (i) lower current account deficits; (ii) floating exchange rates; (iii) a high level of foreign exchange reserves; (iv) reduced short-term external liabilities; and (v) capital account regulations in place (Ocampo, 2012). The combination of stronger external accounts, the accumulation of international reserves and the flexibility of the exchange rate showed that most emerging economies were prepared to face the contagion of the global crisis. According to IMF (2012, p. 132), "improvements in policymaking and the buildup of policy space in many of these economies account for the bulk of the increased resilience since 1990".[6]

In the case of the major economies of Latin America, in most countries the reduction of public external debt, the previous policy of international reserves accumulation (Figure 5.5), which had been possible due to the period of bonanza of commodities exports, and the reduction and improvement in the composition of public debt, with the increase of domestically-denominated debt, provided some policy space for counter-cyclical stabilization policies. The combination of the reduction of public external debt (external liabilities) with the increase in the foreign reserves (external assets) meant that most countries had a positive net balance in foreign currencies. So that the immediate and direct impact of the exchange rate devaluation on the public finances was positive, instead of negative, as had been the case on other previous occasions. Consequently, governments could make use of some counter-cyclical fiscal policy to face the effects of the financial crisis, when on other occasions they made use of tightening policies. Therefore, in contrast to former crises in Latin America, there were no financial crises in the region during the recent crisis.

Figure 5.6 shows that the ratio of the primary fiscal surplus over GDP, in all the economies analyzed in this chapter, with the exception of Venezuela, decreased in 2009 and recovered in 2010, which followed the economic recovery. According to CEPAL (2012, p. 17), fiscal policy in most Latin American economies had the following guidelines: (i) the 2003–08 period of economic growth was marked by generating fiscal primary surplus and the reduction of public debt – that is, before the external adversities of 2008–09 (Figure 5.6); (ii) in 2009, the stabilization of domestic demand through the increase of public expenditures (social programs, housing programs, the financing of small and medium-sized firms, infrastructure, and so on) and reduction of the taxes to stimulate consumption were active; and (iii) since 2010, implementation of tax reform (either revenues and expenditures sides) in some countries has played an important role in consolidating public finance. Fiscal deficits

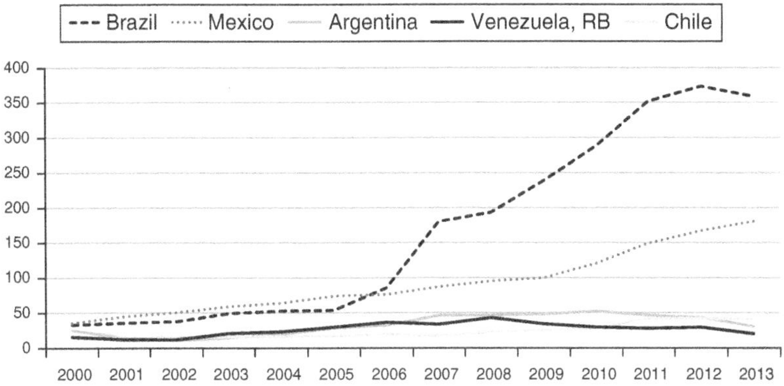

Figure 5.5 International reserves, USD billion (2000–2013)
Source: IMF (2014).

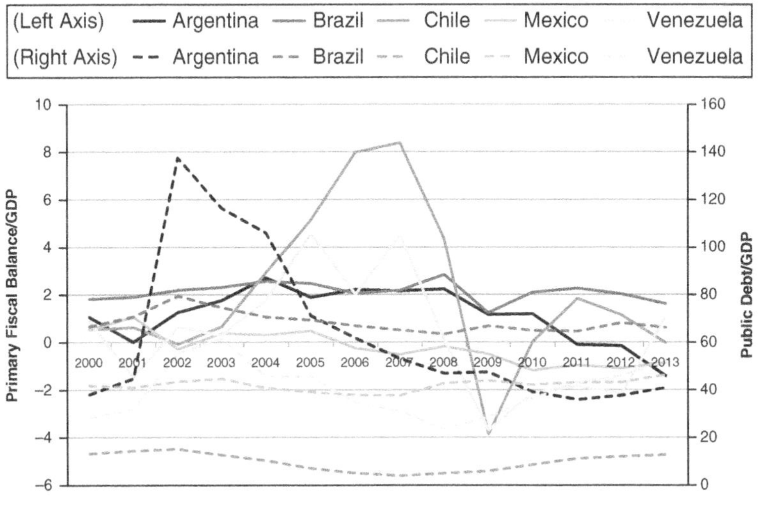

Figure 5.6 Public debt/GDP and primary fiscal balance/GDP, % (2000–2013)
Sources: IMF (2014) and World Bank (2014).

in Latin America (simple average) changed from –0.5 per cent of GDP in 2008 to –2.9 per cent in 2009, falling down again to –1.8 per cent in 2010 (CEPAL, 2012, p. 17).

As for monetary policy, although most economies (Brazil, Chile and Mexico) reduced interest rates during 2009, the management of the interest rate policy varied somewhat from country to country, with Chile adopting a more aggressive expansionary policy, and Brazil and Mexico implementing a more gradual policy. Venezuela had to deal with increasingly high levels of inflation, but even so their authorities adopted a more expansionary monetary policy. Argentina was the only economy of the selected countries that increased the central bank interest rate in 2009 (Figure 5.7). Other tools of monetary policy included reduction of reserve requirements on banking deposits and the implementation of some special credit lines by central banks (for instance, to finance exports). In some countries, like Brazil, where public banks have a high portion of the market share, these banks operated a counter-cyclical credit policy that helped to reduce the slowdown in the credit market. Indeed, thanks to the active role of public banks in some economies, the central banks' efforts to expand liquidity and the quick recovery of capital flows to emerging economics (including those in Latin America), domestic credit recovered rapidly and the temporary problems of liquidity in the banking sector had only a limited effect on economic activity in the region (CEPAL, 2014, p. 102). Figure 5.7 shows the behavior of the domestic credit/GDP ratio in Argentina,[7] Chile, Brazil, Mexico and Venezuela. In 2011–12, due to the slowdown of the world economy and greater uncertainty about the future, most economies adopted a more

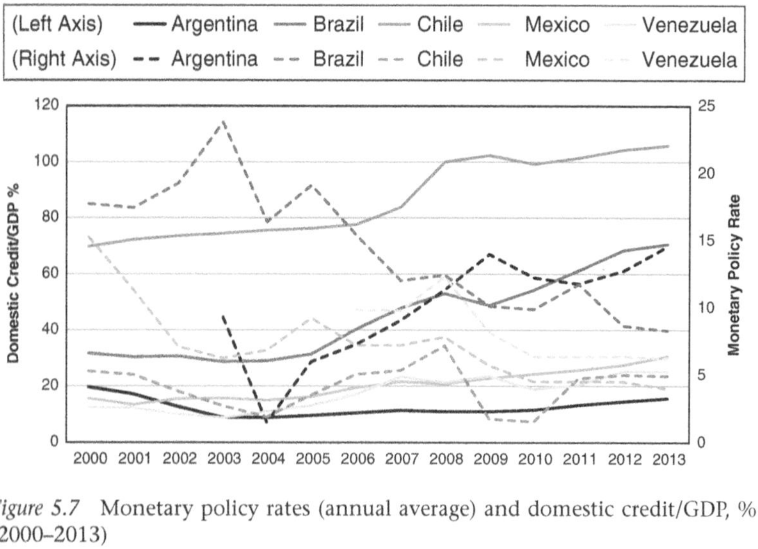

Figure 5.7 Monetary policy rates (annual average) and domestic credit/GDP, % (2000–2013)
Sources: ECLAC (2015) and World Bank (2014).

cautious and flexible monetary policy, with less variations and some reduction in the basic interest rate, combined with the implementation of macroprudential policies.

Finally, with regard to the exchange rate policy, although different strategies were adopted among the countries, no economy implemented a pure floating exchange rate management, but some combination of a flexible exchange rate with active intervention in the foreign exchange market, including a policy of foreign reserve accumulation. Venezuela was an exception in that its dual and later multiple exchange rate regime was implemented. Figure 5.8 (an increase in the rate means an appreciation in the rate, a decrease means a depreciation) shows that Chile and mainly Brazil had experienced appreciation of the real effective exchange rate (REER[8]) before the global financial crisis – in the case of Brazil this trend followed until 2011, and since then REER has depreciated – while Chile has had a more or less stable REER since 2006. Real exchange rate depreciated in Mexico before the crisis; and since 2010 Mexico has maintained a more or less stable trend. Argentina, following the big devaluation of 2001, under the context of a Convertibility Plan crisis, has adopted the target of a competitive exchange rate as one of the cornerstones of the economic policy – indeed, since 2004 REER has had a gradual trend for depreciation.[9] After the second quarter of 2009, the surge of capital inflows in various economies of Latin America resulted in a currency appreciation trend in most countries. Due to the

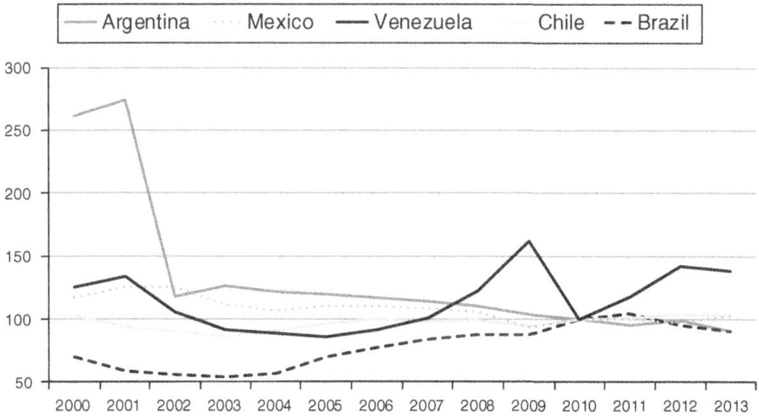

Figure 5.8 Real Effective Exchange Rate (2010=100) (2002–2013)
Source: BIS (2014).

application of continuous pressure on the exchange rate, Brazil implemented in 2010–11 some controls on capital inflows (with the use of a financial transactions tax) in order to reduce such pressure and to allow some currency devaluation. However, since 2013 capital flows in the region has shown more volatility due to the withdrawal of monetary stimulus measures in the United States and possible increases in the interest rate. Consequently, some monetary authorities have drawn on foreign reserves and with some changes in the macro-prudential regulations in order to mitigate exchange rate volatility.

Ocampo (2011) points out that the strengthening of Latin America to face the contagion of the global financial crisis was only possible due to the better performance of the balance of payments thanks to the exceptional external conditions that allowed some reduction in the external public debt and an increase in the foreign reserves, along with the benign international environment. However, the uncertainty about the recovery of the global economy and the slowdown in the rate of growth of the Chinese economy plus some domestic economic deterioration in some Latin American economies (high inflation, low GDP growth, increase of current account, deceleration of credit supply, etc.) seems to show that the policy space for implementation of counter-cyclical policies is reduced in the region.

According to CEPAL (2014, pp. 102–3), the economic environment in 2014 for the implementation of financial policies is somewhat different from those experienced in 2008–09: (i) the emergence of inflationary pressures in some economies (mainly in Argentina, Brazil and Venezuela) has put some pressure on monetary policy; (ii) the gradual, but imminent change in the FED monetary policy ('tapering') and consequent increase in the interest rates of emerging economies are resulting in a currency depreciation trend in Latin America, which can eventually increase domestic prices; and (iii) in some cases, the rapid growth in the credit supply can eventually put pressure on inflation and the external balance. However, the fiscal situations in Latin America are diverse and heterogeneous, and despite the wider deficit and the slowing economy, public debt has not risen in general (Figure 5.6).

Indeed, between 2012 and 2013, despite the counter-cyclical policies adopted by the main Latin American countries, economic growth showed great volatility in the economies of the region and there was an overall trend of some economic slowdown (Figure 5.1). In fact, economic growth has been uneven among the major economies of Latin America during this period: the average GDP growth in 2012–13 was, in the three major economies of the region, 1.9 per cent in Argentina, 1.8 per cent in Brazil and 2.7 per cent in Mexico, while it was 3.5 per cent in Venezuela and 4.8 per cent in Chile. Latin American economies continued to show some resilience to external shocks, although economic growth has shown clear signals of deceleration.[10] Since the 2008–09 crisis, domestic demand has been the main driver of growth in Latin America, while net exports made a negative contribution between 2010 and 2013. Indeed, weak growth in the developed economies and modest expansion in the emerging economies (especially China) can suggest that "boosting the region's external demand will be a slow and difficult process, which will limit the contribution of exports to growth" (ECLAC, 2014, p. 11).

With external demand weakening, most countries adopted policies of stimulus to domestic demand fuelled in part by monetary or fiscal policy measures that avoided a greater slowdown of the economic activity, but at the same time contributed to a deterioration in the current account deficits – as it was the case of Argentina, Chile, Brazil and Mexico (Figure 5.2). The current account deficit of Latin America widened from 1.8 per cent of GDP in 2012 to 2.5 per cent in 2013 as the imports of goods grew more rapidly than exports and the deficit on the services balances widened slightly due to tourism and transport (ECLAC, 2013, p. 8). More recently, the tendency of high current account deficits has weakened the stronger position of the major Latin American economies due to the reduction of external debt and foreign reserves accumulation.

In the next section we analyze the effects of the IFC and the GR on the economies of Argentina, Brazil, Chile, Mexico and Venezuela and the economic policy responses with their focus on the counter-cyclical policies.

5.3 Economic performance and the counter-cyclical policies of the main Latin America countries after the global crisis

5.3.1 Some structural characteristics[11]

It is useful to point out some structural features of the Latin American economies analyzed in this chapter. Brazil, Mexico and Argentina are the biggest economies in the region,[12] with a more diversified economy than either Chile or Venezuela, as they combine a productive structure with manufacturing, agriculture, mining and oil, while Chile and Venezuela have a much more specialized export sector.

Argentina belongs to the group of the economies focusing on 'agro-industrial exports' (agricultural products were responsible by 36 per cent of total exports in 2010–12) which also includes Paraguay and Uruguay, with the special feature of having a more diversified productive structure among these economies. The main destination of exports is the intraregional trade (41 per cent). Argentina had a long period of current account surplus due to the increase of exports (soya, cereals, wheat and manufacturing goods) caused by the improvement of the terms of trade and only in recent years has it experienced deficits. In particular, the Argentinean economy is subject to the external financing restriction since the Convertibility Plan crisis and the renegotiation of external debt,[13] and, more recently, with the problems related to 'vulture funds'. Another problem has been the increase of inflation – the official annual inflation rate has been around 10 per cent in 2010–13.

Brazil is, together with Mexico, the most diversified economy of the region. In contrast to Mexico, however, its manufacturing sector is mainly focused on the domestic market, while in Mexico '*maquiladoras*', those industries located next to United States, export consumer goods mainly to this latter country. Brazil, due to a set of features that include a medium-term trend for currency appreciation (2003–11), is suffering a problem of deindustrialization that has resulted in the reduction of manufacturing exports and the stagnation of the industrial sector. Consequently, the share of primary goods has increased in this country (21 per cent are agro industrial goods and 16 per cent is iron). Mexico shows the bigger concentration degree of exports in Latin America (78.7 per cent of exports to United States in 2010–12), and became very 'US-dependent', while Brazil presents one of the most diversified exports structure by destination. Both economies have exhibited moderate current account deficits for consecutive years, which have been compensated by FDI net flows, mainly in the case of Brazil. Indeed, Brazil and Mexico are among the most financially integrated economies in the region. Finally, Mexico's fiscal revenues are highly dependent on the income from basic goods: the relative share earnings of nonrenewable natural resources over public revenue was 33.4 per cent on average in the period 2009–12, whereas in Brazil the figure was only 6.3 per cent. Public finance has gradually deteriorated in Brazil and Mexico, with some increase in the public debt (42 per cent of GDP in Mexico and 66 per cent of GDP in Brazil in 2013). The combination of high interest expenditures with low GDP growth has contributed to some deterioration in the public debt.

Chile can be seen as part of the group of 'exporters of metals and minerals' which also includes Peru. This group has the main common feature of the high concentration in some export products (the exports of copper, for example, encompass 57 per cent of total exports of Chile), with some destination diversification, although Chile has the highest trade dependence on China in Latin America (23.5 per cent of total exports). Current account (percentage of GDP) was very high in Chile during the commodities boom (3.2 per cent on average in 2004–07), and more recently has shown a moderate trend to deficit (–2.3 per cent in 2012–13), due to the combination of fall in the price of copper with the increase of imports as a result of the increase of domestic demand. Because of the FDI inflows, the external financial needs have been low and eventually negative. The dependence of fiscal revenues from the basic goods income is high in Chile (16.5 per cent in 2009–12), although much lesser than the hydrocarbons export economies. Public debt, either domestic or external, has been maintained at low levels – respectively, 16.1 per cent and 2.8 per cent of GDP. As public indebtedness is low in Chile,[14] the main external vulnerability of the economy is related to the concentration of exports in a limited set of goods and some dependence to China.

Finally, Venezuela can be seen as part of the group of 'hydrocarbons exporter economies' which also includes Bolivia, Colombia, and Ecuador. The main feature of this group of economies is the very high concentration of exports in hydrocarbons and the high participation of these goods in the public revenues (39.8 per cent in 2009–12 in Venezuela). Oil exports represent 95 per cent of total exports of Venezuela and the main destination of the exports is the United States (36 per cent in 2010–12). The current account of balance of payments(percentage of GDP) has been very high due to the performance of oil exports: 13.1 per cent in 2002–08 and 5.0 per cent in 2010–13. Venezuela, a big exporter of oil, suffers typically from what is labelled in the literature 'Dutch disease' – that is, the chronic overvaluation of the exchange rate caused by the abundance of cheap natural resources compatible with a lower exchange rate than that which would pave the way for the other tradable industries. The main problem of Venezuela is the lack of diversification of productive structure and its high dependence on oil exports. Venezuela has also had the increasing problem of how to stabilize the economy: the inflation rate (CPI) has been higher than 20 per cent per year since 2008 and jumped to 56 per cent in 2013, raising some concern about the likelihood of a hyperinflation process to be in course in the next future.

5.3.2 Assessment of the economic performance and counter-cyclical policies

5.3.2.1 Argentina

Since the collapse of the 2001–02 Convertibility Plan,[15] Argentina has applied heterodox types of economic policies, which, in a context of international economic prosperity, high commodity prices, and domestic idle capacity, contributed to a vigorous recovery in Argentina's GDP in 2003–07 (8.6 per cent on average). According to Damill and Frenkel (2009), the macroeconomic regime based on the preservation of a stable and competitive real exchange rate (SCRER) was the main reason explaining the rapid growth experienced in Argentina, besides the commodities boom.

In 2008 and 2009, economic growth fell down to 1.5 per cent per year on average, and once again recovered in 2010 and 2011 (8.8 per cent on average) (Figure 5.1). However, GDP growth reduced substantially in 2012 and 2013 (1.9 per cent), a trend that has continued in 2014. As for the inflation behavior (Figure 5.1), the inflation rate exploded in 2002 (41.0 per cent), due to the huge exchange rate devaluation, and then reduced to 3.7 per cent in 2003, increasing since then (except in 2008), and has been maintained in high levels since 2010 (average of 10.6 per cent in 2010–13[16]).

Commodities boom combined with the currency depreciation resulted in a sustained current account surplus (percentage of GDP) of 3.1 per cent on average in 2002–09. Since then, deficit in current account has been low (no more than –1.0 per cent of GDP), but, as the economy does not have access to external financing, EA had to make use of international reserves and some measures to limit the access of domestic residents to the US dollar.

With the onset of the IFC, the Argentinean economy suffered, especially by the deterioration of terms of trade and the fall in external demand. Under such conditions, the Argentinian EA implemented fiscal and monetary stimulus packages designed to stabilize aggregate demand and temporarily assisting the more vulnerable social groups.

In terms of fiscal policy, the following measures were taken: (i) increased government spending, particularly in subsidies to the private sector and especially to the energy, transport and food industries; (ii) lower income tax rates on wage earnings; (iii) increased infrastructure expenditures and funding for programmes to combat poverty; (iv) adjustment of retirement contributions and benefit payments; and (v) reduction of taxes on agricultural exports, either to increase public sector revenue or to prevent those prices from being transferred to the domestic market (ECLAC, 2009a).

In 2009 public expenditure expanded significantly more than GDP, due to increases in wages, social security benefits and capital expenditures. In particular, transfers to private sector (including energy, transport and food subsidies) held at approximately 4 per cent of GDP[17] (ECLAC, 2009c, p. 74). Indeed, primary fiscal surplus not only was it reduced – from

2.2 per cent of GDP in 2008 to 1.2 per cent on average in 2009–10 – but also ran into deficit in 2011–13 (Figure 5.6). In 2009 the public debt increased slightly over the previous year's level to almost 50 per cent of GDP (Figure 5.6).

Monetary policy was managed on different approaches. In 2008, rapid growth in the economy and pressure from international prices, especially food prices, led the Central Bank of Argentina (CBA) to control the money supply and consequently raising the interest rate (Figure 5.7). At the end of 2008 and in 2009, a conflict in the agricultural sector led to some financial turmoil in the economy, basically due to the CBA's intervention in the foreign market. As a result, interest rates oscillated, with large fluctuations around periods of turbulence (ECLAC, 2009). In 2009, monetary aggregates expanded more slowly, and the CBA gradually increased the interest rate, while in 2010 monetary policy was relaxed in response to the uncertainty of the GR, introducing measures to expand liquidity and lowering the interest rate, thereby increasing the supply of credit from the financial system (Figure 5.7).

CBA intervened in the foreign exchange market, buying and selling foreign exchange as circumstances dictated, in order to maintain the level of the international reserves, which stood by US$48 billion in the end of 2009. Despite the considerable devaluation in 2008–09, exchange rate policy continued its trajectory of preserving a stable and competitive real exchange rate (Figure 5.8). Both the continuing trade surpluses and the policy of accumulating foreign reserves helped to stabilize the exchange rate market and assure a relatively comfortable external situation (current account deficits of -0.6 per cent of GDP on average in 2011–13), at least until recently. At the beginning of 2010 EA in Argentina decided to use international reserves for servicing external public debt. Indeed, according to ECLAC (2013b) "the external sector has been under strain since mid-2011, owning to a reversal in the energy balance ..., an appreciating real exchange rate, and a strong demand for foreign assets, as tends to occur in countries with a dual currency system in these circumstances" (p. 2).

Although Argentina's trajectory of sustained economic growth had been interrupted, the situation at year-end 2009 was that unemployment stood at 9 per cent, while inflation stood at 7.7 per cent. The decline in the agricultural output and industrial activity (mainly automobile production) was the consequence of falls in both the external and the domestic demand. By the end of 2009, signs of recovery were evident in the Argentinean economy, boosted by domestic demand and the renewed buoyancy of the Brazilian market.

In 2010–11, there was a strong recovery of the Argentinean economy basically due to the new commodities mini-boom and the expansionary monetary and fiscal policies implemented in 2009 and maintained in the following years. In particular, the demand for exportable goods recovered as a result of developments in agricultural product markets (strong recovery in grain harvests) and the better performance of major trading partners such as Brazil.

In terms of the exchange rate, EA intervened in the foreign exchange market to manage the nominal exchange rate to aim at, on the one hand, improving trade balance, and, on the other hand, to maintain inflation under control. With regard to inflation, this has been stayed at a high level since 2010, driven by a number of factors: the increase in international food prices, the nominal devaluation of the peso, and wage bargaining, as the perceptions of substantially higher inflation vis-à-vis the official rate has resulted often in the increase of real wages, which eventually contributes to a wage–price spiral.[18]

In 2011, while the government maintained an expansionary fiscal policy, the CBA decided to raise the interest rate. To avoid inflationary pressures, the exchange rate was geared to keep inflation under control by devaluing the currency more slowly than the rate of increase in domestic prices. By the end of the year the peso lost almost 8 per cent of its value and, as a consequence, there was a decline in foreign-currency deposits and, more importantly, a fall in the international reserves (Figure 5.5).

Throughout 2012, the government acted on two fronts: (i) it adopted domestic price regulation measures in the form of agreements with producers of certain goods and services and restrictions on food exports to keep inflation under control; and (ii) due to the deterioration in the trade balance, implemented measures to contain the erosion of international reserves. The main measures were: "(a) the introduction of foreign-exchange regulations, including restrictions on hoarding of foreign currency and on repatriation of profits by foreign firms; (b) the management of goods imports; and (c) the renationalization of a majority holding the oil company Repsol YPF" (ECLAC, Economic Survey for Argentina, 2013a, p. 2). As total external debt is not increasing, the lower level of external debt (28 per cent of GDP in 2013) can indicate that economic tensions in the Argentinean economy seen over the recent years and related to the balance of payments can have more to do with liquidity than external solvency.

Fiscal and monetary policies had contrasting features: while the CBA continued to increase the interest rate, the government decided to maintain the expansion of public spending in order to expand the economy, with the largest increases in social security benefits and current transfers to the private sector. Inflation rate increased in 2012 (10.8 per cent) and the GDP growth dropped to 1.0 per cent, due to contracting global economy (including Brazil) and falling agricultural output because of the drought.

During 2013, the government continued its strategy to contain the erosion of international reserves, adopting the following measures: "the regulation of import flows, tougher restrictions on foreign exchange for the purposes of hoarding and overseas tourism (which created a parallel exchange market) and the introduction of some limits on the repatriation of profits by foreign firms" (ECLAC, Economic Survey for Argentina, 2014a, p.2). Unlike the CBA, which implemented a contractionary monetary policy, the government, once again, maintained an expansionary fiscal policy (recording a primary fiscal deficit of –1.4 per cent in 2013), and "opted to fund this deficit by drawing on resources from the public sector itself, basically from the Central Bank of Argentina [CBA], the National Social Security Administration (ANSES) and the Bank of the Argentine Nation (BNA)" (ECLAC, Economic Survey for Argentina, 2014a, p. 3).

In terms of the exchange rate, in 2013 the peso had a substantial depreciation against the dollar, which, however, did not avoid some deterioration in the trade surplus – from USD 15.3 billion in 2012 to USD 12.1 billion in 2013 – as exports stagnated (a deterioration in the terms of trade and the stagnation of exports to Brazil). Furthermore, this depreciation had a negative impact on the inflation rate, due to the pass-through mechanisms. In response to the increase of inflation rate, at the end of 2013, "the government launched the Precios cuidados price-watch program, in which the national government, supermarkets, distributors and the main suppliers undertook to control the prices on a basket of 194 products, subsequently extended to 302 products" (ECLAC, Economic Survey for Argentina, 2014a, p. 5). Despite inflation problems, there was a partial economic recovery in 2013 (growth of 2.9 per cent per annum) pushed up by private consumption.

Preliminary data show that GDP growth dropped to –0.2 per cent in 2014 and the inflation rate rose to 24.2 per cent, because of the contractionary (and inflationary) effect of currency devaluation at the start of the year and the re-emergence of currency strains during the third quarter due to the judicial setback suffered by the country in its dispute with the so-called 'vulture funds' (ECLAC, 2014b).

5.3.2.2 Brazil

After the economic downturn in 2001 to 2003, the Brazilian economy recovered in 2004, pushed by the strong boom in commodities' exports that resulted from the greater rate of economic growth in the global economy, and the increase of the household consumption, due to both government stimulus to credit and the increase in the purchase power of the households, and the public investment, especially investment under the Growth Acceleration Program (*Programa de Aceleração do Crescimento*, PAC).[19] All these factors together eventually resulted in a mini-boom between 2004 and 2008, when the GDP grew 4.8 per cent on average (Figure 5.1).

In this scenario, Brazilian's EA underestimated the IFC. When fourth-quarter 2008 GDP was announced (–3.6 per cent), the figure cast doubt on the notion that Brazil was impervious to the effects of crisis. With the fall in all private components of demand, GDP growth fell to –0.3 per cent in 2009, before recovering strongly in 2010 (7.5 per cent) as a result of the counter-cyclical policies. In 2011, economic growth slowed (2.7 per cent), due to the depletion of idle industrial capacity and the impact of policies aimed at containing the surge in domestic demand and the resulting inflationary pressures. In 2012–13, in spite of the implementation of more expansionary policies, the economy slowed even more (1.8 per cent on average), pushed down by both investment and net exports, while consumption continued to expand, and employment levels continued to rise, albeit more slowly. The inflation rate, after falling to 4.3 per cent in 2009, rose to around 6.0 per cent on average in 2010–13.

The immediate impact of the 2008 crash on the Brazilian economy was the capital flight related to the portfolio investments and foreign loans; on the other hand, the reduction in foreign credit lines to resident banks and firms increased the liquidity constraints of some firms, including some main Brazilian exports firms that had been benefiting from interest-rate arbitrage involving foreign exchange derivatives. The reversal in the capital flows (Figure 5.4) exerted strong pressure on the exchange rate, which depreciated 42.6 per cent from 1 September to 31 December. Another important transmission channel of the IFC in Brazil was the domestic credit market, due to the impact of the reduction of the international credit operations (financing of exports) and, due to the overall deterioration of expectations about the future, the liquidity preference of the banks increased sharply, contributing to the slowdown of domestic credit.

Brazilian EA responded to the financial crisis by adopting a number of counter-cyclical measures (Barbosa, 2010; Paula et al., 2015): (i) in order to avoid the spread of the credit crunch, the Central Bank of Brazil (BCB) adopted a lot of liquidity-enhancing measures;[20] (ii) the BCB undertook interventions in the foreign exchange markets – selling US$23 billion of its foreign reserves in the last quarter of 2008 in the spot market and offering foreign exchange swaps in order to provide hedge against currency depreciation; (iii) state-owned banks were encouraged to expand their credit operations, compensating the deceleration in the credit supply by private banks; according to Montero (2014), "[m]ore than 83 percent of the growth available credit to the private sector in Brazil in 2008 and 2009 came from the public banks" (p. 127); and (iv) the Ministry of Finance implemented a lot of fiscal measures in order to stimulate aggregate demand: reduction in the industrialized products tax (IPI) burden on motor vehicles, consumer durables and construction items, and an increase in the duration of unemployment insurance. In addition, the BCB, with some delay, eased monetary policy by lowering the basic interest rate from 13.8 per cent in January 2009 to 8.8 per cent in September 2009.

ECLAC (2009) points out that Brazil was one of the Latin American countries to make use of a greater variety of tools to face the contagion effects of the crisis. According to Barbosa (2010), the delay in monetary policy to stimulate economic growth immediately after the 2008 crash had to be compensated by fiscal policy (primary fiscal surplus reduced from 2.8 per cent of GDP in 2008 to 1.2 per cent in 2009).

In 2009 the Brazilian economy suffered a recession due to the effects of the Lehman Brothers contagion – a decline of 0.2 per cent in GDP, pushed down by the sharp reduction in industrial output (–5.6 per cent). After the recession in the first semester of 2009, the economy recovered quickly in the second semester, and in 2010 the level of GDP growth was 7.6 per cent. Responding to the quick economic recovery and the consequent increase in the industrial capacity utilization, the investment rate increased from 17.0 per cent of GDP in the first quarter of 2009 to 20.5 per cent in the third quarter of 2010. A new surge of capital inflows to emerging economies began in the middle of 2009, and a further reason for such surge was the high differential between the internal and external interest rates – Brazil was one of the emerging countries that had a stronger trend of currency appreciation until 2011.[21]

By the end of 2010, with the fear of the increasing system risk of the financial system, due to the surge of capital inflows and the rapid increase in the supply of credit, the Brazilian government implemented some macro-prudential measures: (i) an increase from 8 per cent to 12 per cent in reserves requirements on sight and fixed-term deposits; (ii) an increase of minimum capital required for personal credit with maturity up to 24 months; and (iii) a rise in the tax on financial transactions (IOF) from 1.5 per cent to 3.0 per cent in all credit operations and an increase to 6 per cent in the IOF on new foreign loans with maturities of up a year.

The first three years of Dilma Roussef's government (2011–13) was marked, on the one hand, by the gradual worsening in the international scenario due to the Euro crisis and the decline in growth in emerging economies (including China), and, on the other hand, the introduction of some important changes in the modus operandi of economic policy, including the adoption of a more gradualist strategy on the part of the BCB to deal with inflation and the use of broader instruments of economic policy as a complement to the traditional tools.

After an initial period (the first semester of 2011), when EA adopted a more tightened economic policy in order to reduce aggregate demand to curb inflation acceleration, some counter-cyclical policies were implemented, due to the slowdown of the economy. Such measures included the change in the mix of economic policy (a reduction in the interest rate and the devaluation of the currency), that was expected to boost growth; credit stimulus and tax relieving to some sectors; and the implementation of capital controls. Finally, EA enhanced its commitment with fiscal austerity, understood as necessary to open space for the reduction in the interest rate.

The deterioration of the Euro crisis since September 2011 and the deceleration of the inflation due to the reduction in the commodities prices and in domestic demand, made possible a steady policy of reduction of the Selic (basic interest rate) that fell from 12.5 per cent per year in July 2011 to 7.5 per cent in August 2012. Furthermore, in order to curb the deterioration in the competitiveness of the manufacturing sector, in both external and domestic markets, BCB induced a currency devaluation of 30 per cent from July 2011 until May 2012.[22]

In 2012 EA adopted a counter-cyclical fiscal policy. The main fiscal tool was a tax exemption, which included the reduction of IPI on capital goods, exemption of the payroll in labour-intensive sectors, such as the construction and textile industry that was gradually extended to other sectors, and the reduction of IPI on some consumer durable goods in April 2012. Those fiscal measures aimed at reactivating the economy and increasing the competitiveness of the domestic industrial sector.

Over the period 2011 to 2013 economic growth was disappointing: average growth was only 2.1 per cent, while industrial output declined even more. All the components of demand decreased, but fixed capital contributed more of the decline. The poor economic performance was the consequence of both external and domestic factors. Although the economic situation of the Euro Area now seems to be not disruptive, the

Euro crisis affected the Brazilian economy mainly by the commercial side and by the deterioration of the entrepreneurs' expectations about the future of the world economy. More recently, the announcement of the end of 'quantitative easing' policy by the FED and its possible future change in monetary policy, capital flows to Brazil and Latin America have become more volatile (Figure 5.4).

On the other hand, investment rate increased in 2010–11 as firms were anticipating that economic growth would continue to be high – which did not happen. As a result, the capacity utilization rate of the industrial sector decreased, generating idle capacity that contributed to the slowdown of investments in 2012–13.

Exporters lost external markets due to the lack of competitiveness and low levels of external demand, while imports increased shifting part of the domestic industrial production – years of currency appreciation seem to be eroded by the competitive capacity of the domestic firms. Consequently, net exports did not contribute to higher growth. Household consumption was still high, but reduced gradually in consequence of the slowdown in the demand and supply of credit, due to the high level of the household indebtedness and non-performing loans.

Finally, public expenditures were not enough to compensate for the overall reduction in the aggregate demand. The Brazilian government hoped that the change in the mix of the economic policy (lower interest rate and more devaluated currency) together with some tax exemption to stimulate the demand and supply of goods, which would be enough to reach a robust economic growth. When it became clear that this was not the case, government sought to implement ad hoc measures to boost growth. Such action, however, was not well coordinated and lacked consistency (Paula et al., 2015).

Since the second half of 2012 there have been some changes in economic policy due to macroeconomic deterioration. First, the inflation rate began to increase in the end of 2012, with most pressure coming from services and food. Second, exchange rate became very volatile, reflecting both the uncertainties over the United States' monetary policy and the deterioration of the external accounts (current account of 3.6 per cent of GDP in 2013). Economic policy changes included the increase in the BCB basic interest rate from 7.25 per cent to 10.0 per cent between September 2012 and December 2013, and the reduction of financial transactions tax on overseas investments in Brazilian bonds to 0 per cent. In this context, the expectations of GDP growth for 2014 was only 0.2 per cent, while inflation reached almost the upper target of 6.5 per cent (6.4 per cent in 2014).

5.3.2.3 Chile

In recent years the dynamics of growth in the Chilean economy can be characterized by a 'stop-and-go' pattern, at the same time the country has had the highest GDP growth of the bigger economies of Latin America: the average growth rates were 2.9 per cent in 2001–03, 6.0 per cent in 2004–07, and 5.7 per cent in 2010–12, while the growth rates were 1.7 per cent in 2008, –4.7 per cent in 2009, and 4.2 per cent in 2013. This has resulted from a series of factors, such as energy scarcity, some inflationary pressures stemming from agricultural and mineral commodity price rises on the international market, and drought-related agricultural harvest loss. The onset of the IFC aggravated these problems and Chile's GDP fell by about 2 per cent. Inflation rate – one of the lowest of Latin America (average of 3.2 per cent in 2000–13, next to the inflation target of 3.0 per cent) – has also oscillated a lot (Figure 5.1). Indeed as one of the more open economies in the region, Chile's inflation is greatly influenced by imported goods.

As the path of GDP growth shows, the Chilean economy was substantially affected by the turbulence in the global economy in the fourth quarter of 2008 and the early months of 2009, when exports dropped sharply, in terms of both price and volume, and private spending in consumption (durable consumer goods) and investment fell abruptly.

The Chilean government's response to the crisis was to introduce a set of counter-cyclical measures which, consistent with the fiscal, monetary and exchange rate policies in place since the 2000s (intended to ensure macroeconomic stability and foster the build-up of foreign exchange reserves), were designed to mitigate the impact of the crisis on economic activity and the level of employment.

Of these counter-cyclical measures, fiscal measures had the greatest impact, either because they helped restore the level of domestic consumption and underpinned private investment or because they were responsible for reducing the government's fiscal surplus. Indeed, primary fiscal surplus fell from 5.7 per cent of GDP on average in 2004–08 to –3.9 per cent in 2009 and 0.0 per cent in 2010, increasing to 1.5 per cent on average in 2011–12 as economic growth and copper prices triggered a jump in tax revenues (Figure 5.6).

It is worth mentioning that, for several years, fiscal policy had been directed towards attaining a structural surplus to aim at generating "savings during boom periods when copper prices are high and GDP expands at above-trend rates" (ECLAC, Economic Survey for Chile, 2009, p. 121). According to Chilean EA, the idea of generating savings during boom times would enable the country to take counter-cyclical action in a context of economic growth below-trend level or of economic crisis.

From the start of the IFC, the EA used the counter-cyclical capacity that had been built up to take fiscal measures aimed at propping up employment levels, stimulating domestic demand and preventing poverty from rising. Chilean EA was able to implement counter-cyclical policies, which helped to counter external turmoil and gradually bring about conditions conducive to a resumption of economic growth in 2010 (ECLAC, 2009).

The fiscal measures comprised both budget measures, among them temporary tax reductions and increased income transfers to the poorest population groups, and non-budget measures, including fund transfers to state enterprises that provided credit guarantees, to state banks for capitalization, and to the state copper mining enterprise. More specifically, the income transfers to the poorest sectors of Chile's population took the form of (i) higher subsidies for home buyers (the existing housing subsidy was temporarily doubled and a new temporary subsidy introduced); (ii) expanded funding for small business finance and production, so that small businesses could access credit granted by commercial banks; (iii) tax rationalization measures to accelerate tax reimbursements to companies; and (iv) during the first quarter of 2009, low-income families were paid US$70 per family member. According to ECLAC (2009b, p. 81), the fiscal spending plan amounted to some US$4 billion, or roughly 2.8 per cent of GDP.

The Central Bank of Chile (CBC), despite the impact of the crisis on Chile's economy, initially maintained its restrictive monetary policy so that inflation would converge to its target values of between 2 per cent and 4 per cent. Furthermore, monetary policy continued to be geared towards an inflation target of 3 per cent per year on average for the medium term with a range of 1 per cent on either side. The inflation rate in 2009 was negative and was raised during the year 2010 as the economy recovered.

As the inflation target for 2008 was not met and the signs of recession began to be increasingly recurrent in early 2009, the CBC embarked on a process of more flexible and considerably lower interest rates: in December 2008 it was about 8 per cent and by December 2009 it had fallen to 2.5 per cent (Figure 5.7). The CBC also introduced more flexible compulsory deposit requirements. By the end of the first half of 2009, these measures had produced a slight recovery in the volume of credit, supported by low interest rates and reinforced by liquidity provision mechanisms.

In its exchange rate policy, the CBC continued intervening in the exchange rate market throughout 2008 and 2009, either to prevent the peso from appreciating or depreciating, or to buy exchange rate so as to strengthen Chile's foreign exchange reserves.

Initially, the CBC was not successful: by the end of October 2008, one month after the collapse of Lehman Brothers, the exchange rate depreciated by 38.5 per cent in nominal terms. However, at the end of 2008 and throughout 2009 the exchange rate reached levels comparable to those prior to the IFC.

Accordingly, in a context in which the exchange rate was being held stable in real terms (Figure 5.8), it added to a significant reduction in imports and a slight improvement in copper prices in the international markets, with the trade balance improving and the current account balance of payments reversing from a deficit in 2008 to a surplus in 2009 (Figure 5.2 and Figure 5.4).

In 2009, the government continued its expansionary fiscal policy (the primary fiscal target was reduced to 0.5 per cent of GDP) to boost the domestic market and the CBC decided: (i) to reduce the basic interest rate to a historic low of 0.75 per cent (Figure 5.7); and (ii) to adopt measures – for example, the swap programme was extended from one to six months – to increase liquidity in both pesos and dollars. Despite the expansionary monetary policy, the CBC continued to target annual inflation of 3 per cent per year. Even with these measures, in 2009 the GDP growth was only 0.1 per cent and the unemployment rate increased.

Throughout 2010, the fiscal target was reduced to 0 per cent of GDP. According to ECLAC (2011), "[t]he total expenditure of the consolidated central government climbed by 7% in real terms to reach 23.1% of GDP in 2010, reflecting the continuation of the counter-cyclical measures adopted in response to the global financial crisis, which had already pushed public spending up strongly in 2009" (p. 118).

Unlike fiscal policy, the CBC, after implementing counter-cyclical monetary policies in 2009, the basic interest rate was raised from 0.5 per cent in January 2010 to 3.25 per cent by December of the same year.

Despite the CBC's adoption of a floating exchange rate regime since the 1990s, the exchange rate performance, indeed, was operated in a similar manner to a 'dirty-floating' system, with little intervention by the CBC. Moreover, in 2010, due to the dollar depreciation in the global market, the peso experienced average nominal appreciation of 8.8 per cent over the 2009 value.

It is worth mentioning two additional factors that helped the recovery of the Chilean economy in 2010: first, due to the recovery of the international commodity prices, which also impacted on copper prices, as Figure 5.3 shows, the revenues of the National Copper Corporation (CODLECO) jumped by 87.7 per cent in real terms; and, secondly, the government continued to contribute to its sovereign funds and, as a result, there was a slight increase in foreign reserves (Figure 5.5).

In this context, ECLAC (2009) concluded, "[t]hanks to the capacities built up in previous years, the government was able to deploy counter-cyclical policies which helped to counter external turmoil and gradually bring about conditions conducive to a resumption of growth in 2010" (p. 87).

In 2011 and 2012, as a result of the economic recovery, the fiscal stimulus was reduced and public spending returned to trend values. The average GDP growth was around 3.2 per cent and, as a result, some inflationary pressure occurred. The CBC's response was immediate: monetary policy continued the gradual withdrawal of monetary stimulus and, as a result, at the end of 2011 the annual basic interest rate reached 5.25 per cent, while in 2012, "the annual nominal rates for consumer and commercial loans rose (...) to 27.8% and 9.5%, respectively" (ECLAC, Economic Survey for Chile, 2013, p. 2). During this year, the exchange rate, still based on a floating regime with some CBC interventions, experienced a significant appreciation. To avoid the impacts of the peso's appreciation on the returns of export and import-substitution sectors, the CBC intervened in the market with a programme of dollar purchases.

In 2013, the fiscal and monetary policies continued to be geared towards achieving structural balance in the medium term and targeting an annual inflation of 3 per cent. Despite the conditions of monetary 'austerity', domestic credit as a percentage of GDP increased almost 10 per cent when compared with the previous year (Figure 5.7). Moreover, the CBC maintained a free-floating exchange rate policy, with some intervention. At the end of 2013, the peso accumulated a depreciation of 11 per cent in nominal terms. In terms of economic activity, the GDP growth reduced from 5.6 per cent in 2012 to 4.1 per cent, in 2013, which is still a better performance than that found among the greater economies of Latin America (Figure 5.1).

It is worth mentioning that GDP growth in Chile after the contagion of the international crisis was pushed principally by domestic demand which, as we have seen, was well managed by EA. After the recovery of the trade surplus in 2010, as imports have grown more than exports, the balance of payments' current account dropped to –2.7 per cent of GDP on average in 2011–13.

5.3.2.4 Mexico

Before the IFC, the Mexican economy (in 2004–07) was growing at around 4 per cent per year and the annual average inflation rate was, on average, 4.1 per cent (Figure 5.1).

In 1999, Mexico adopted a flexible exchange rate regime and an inflation-targeting regime as a framework for the conduct of monetary policy. In terms of fiscal performance, there was a primary fiscal surplus from 2000 to 2005,[23] while from 2006 to 2008 there was a primary fiscal deficit (Figure 5.6). However, during this period, the EA managed the public debt to GDP ratio – from 2000 to 2008 the average ratio was around 40 per cent, as shown in Figure 5.6. In other words, before the contagion of the crisis, it seems that Mexican economy had presented consistent macroeconomic fundamentals.

However, as is well known, the Mexican economy is highly dependent on the United States economy, increasingly so since the economic integration between the two economies which occurred through the creation of the North American Free Trade Agreement (NAFTA), in 1994. For this reason, the effects of the financial crisis, which originated in the United States, has a significant impact on Mexico's export sector, considering that 85 per cent of the country's exports go to the United States. In addition to international trade, other channels of transmission of the global crisis included, to a lesser extent, declining foreign investment, tourism and remittances from workers abroad.

As a consequence, at the end of 2008 the economic growth dropped from 3.1 per cent in 2007 to 1.4 per cent per year and, consequently, the unemployment rate increased from 4.3 per cent in September 2008 to 6.4 per cent in September 2009. Moreover, the depreciation of the Mexican peso (almost 20 per cent from 2008 to 2009) caused inflationary pressures: the annual inflation rate, in December, reached 6.5 per cent. In 2009, the economy had shrunk by 4.7 per cent, a contraction which was greater than that experienced in 1995 after the *Tequila* crisis. After appreciating in real terms from 2005 to August 2008, the peso depreciated abruptly between October 2008 and March 2009 (16 per cent in real terms), and after this period a gradual appreciation emerged (ECLAC, 2009). According to ECLAC (2009b), "the global crises exposed [Mexican] structural deficiencies and its vulnerability to external shocks as well as the weakness and lack of resilience of its productive base and the limited maneuvering room there was for public policy to counteract the effects of those shocks" (p. 106).

Given the worsening economic situation in the world economy and the growing signs of its effects on the Mexican economy, the EA decided to implement counter-cyclical economic policies to boost the economy, although with more limited range compared to Argentina, Chile and Brazil.

In this way, the Bank of Mexico (Banxico) implemented measures to increase liquidity in the foreign currency market and in the banking system, such as: dollars were injected into the foreign currency market through extraordinary and daily auctions to aim at bringing down the exchange rate to its normal value; and Banxico reduced the basic interest rate by 375 basis points (at the end of the year the nominal interest rate was 4.5 per cent, according to Figure 5.7), and "established a guarantee programme through the development bank for short-term private lending" (ECLAC, Economic Survey for Mexico, 2009, p. 193).

At the same time, the EA opted to run fiscal deficits (from 2009 to 2013 the average fiscal deficit was around 1 per cent of GDP) to expand the economy, but this result was also due to the fact that public revenues sharply dropped as a consequence of the recession in 2009 and the fall of exports.

In 2010, the government continued to implement a counter-cyclical fiscal policy, with particularly large rises in social development spending and transfers to the states, while Banxico maintained its monetary expansionary policy. Throughout 2010, "international reserves were strengthened by the exchange-rate appreciation triggered by [the policy of reserve accumulation and] capital inflows" (ECLAC, 2011, p. 189).[24] At the end of the year, the Mexican economy had recovered from the recession of the previous year: in 2010 the GDP grew by 5 per cent, sustained by the dynamism of exports (pushed up by some recovery in the American economy) and with remarkable growth of the manufacturing sector and steadily declining unemployment rates. Such growth continued in the following two years (average growth of 4.8 per cent in 2010–12), while inflation was maintained more or less stable around 4.0 per cent per year, but above the annual inflation target of 3.0 per cent (with a range of 1 per cent on either side).

In 2011, the fiscal revenue increased in real terms, mainly because of the recovery of oil prices in the international market (Figure 5.4). As a result, despite the expansionary fiscal policy implemented by the government, the primary fiscal deficit to GDP was slightly reduced and the public debt/GDP ratio remained stable (Figure 5.6).

In terms of monetary policy, Banxico, on the one hand, did not relax the monetary policy, mainly due to the fact that inflation rate was above the target range, and, on the other hand, introduced some macroprudential policies, along the lines of the Basel III liquidity regulations, to avoid systemic risk in the financial system.

The currency market went through two distinct periods in 2011: in the first six months, there was a trend towards nominal appreciation, while from July to December, due to the Euro crisis, the peso was devalued. At the end of the year, the exchange rate depreciation reached 13.2 per cent and 6 per cent in nominal and real terms, respectively. Despite the high volatility of the exchange rate, the international reserves increased to US$148 billion (Figure 5.5).

In 2011, GDP growth reduced to almost 4.0 per cent, in part as a result of the global economic slowdown, which weakened external demand. Economic growth was driven by both exports and domestic expenditure growth. The widening current account deficit (1.0 per cent of GDP) reflected larger deficits on both the services account (payments for transport services) and the income account (higher interest payments and profit repatriations); a trend that followed and deepened over the following years.

In 2012, Banxico continued to focus its actions on price stability and, for that reason, monetary policy was less expansionary. Although the Banxico became a little bit conservative in terms of monetary policy, the government continued to run a fiscal deficit. As a result of the monetary austerity and a moderate fiscal deficit, at the end of year the inflation rate converged to the official target of 3 per cent.

To avoid some pressures on the exchange rate, Banxico "launched a system for selling up to US$ 400 million in daily auctions, at an exchange rate at least 2% above the previous business day's fix rate (peso depreciation)" (ECLAC, Economic Survey for Mexico, 2013, p. 3). Moreover, the international reserves continued to build up and by the end of December they reached US$163.5 billion.

In December of 2012, the Pact for Mexico was signed one day after the inauguration of the Enrique Peña Nieto administration (from the Institutional Revolutionary Party). This Pact, which brought interest in the Mexican economy among international investors, was based on a set of reforms to assure: economic growth, employment and competitiveness; security and justice; transparency, accountability and combating corruption; and democratic governance. In 2012, Mexico also "entered negotiations on the Trans-Pacific Strategic Economic Partnership Agreement" (ECLAC, Economic Survey for Mexico, 2013, p. 4) with the expectation of boosting market diversification.

By the end of 2012, GDP grew by 4 per cent, with the drop in external demand almost fully compensated by growth in domestic demand, especially investment.

In 2013, GDP growth rate dropped to 1.1 per cent due both to significantly slower growth in exports and also to more sluggish domestic demand, especially in terms of capital formation. The current account deficit was 2.1 per cent of GDP (Figure 5.2). With economic activity slowing heavily and inflation within the target range, the Banxico reduced the basic interest rate by 50 basis points, "after holding it steady at 4.5% for almost three years. This was followed by two further cuts of 25 basis points apiece in September and October, taking the rate to 3.5%" (ECLAC/Economic Survey for Mexico, 2014, p. 3).

At the same time, despite the promise of the new administration to announce a zero-deficit policy for the year and to maintain their fiscal responsibility, the government had to adjust this objective because economic activity was decelerating.

Regardless of the government's attempt to boost the economy, at the end of the 2013 the main Mexican macroeconomic indicators had deteriorated: the current account deficit increased, the exchange rate remained volatile with a trend of depreciation caused by the dollar strengthening on the international markets, and the GDP growth rate dropped.

5.3.2.5 Venezuela

Venezuela's economy is known to be highly dependent on oil exports and its government's revenues are connected with how oil prices perform on the international market. Accordingly, from 2005 to the end of 2008, when oil prices rose year on year (Figure 5.3), its trade balances were robust and growing (Figure 5.4); the current account surplus was 13.1 per cent of GDP on average in 2003–08 and GDP also posted robust growth rates. On the other hand, GDP growth experienced an enormous oscillation: GDP growth of 8.6 per cent on average in 2005–08, dropping to –1.5 per cent on average in 2009–10, recovering by 4.9 per cent on average in 2011–12, and dropping again in 2013 to 1.3 per cent (Figure 5.1). On the other hand, inflation is a huge concern in Venezuela: since 2007 it has been more than 20 per cent per year, exceeding 50 per cent in 2013.

Since Hugo Chávez first took office in 1999, oil revenues – especially those of the state oil enterprise, *Petróleos de Venezuela S.A.* (PDVSA) – have been fundamental to the strategy of galvanizing aggregate demand in the Venezuelan economy through the public sector by infrastructure investments and social spending. It is worth mentioning that throughout the Chávez government, many companies have been nationalized, such as energy and metallurgical firms, the Banco de Venezuela, and so on.

In 2008, aiming to reduce the high inflation rate, the Central Bank of Venezuela (CBV) implemented a monetary reform: the *bolivar* was introduced, the exchange rate was kept at 2.15 *bolivares fuertes* (BsF) per United States dollar in 2008, and the CBV adopted some restrictions on capital outflows.

The Venezuelan government adopted some measures to stimulate national production, including the continuation of the farm subsidies policy. A law for the reordering of the domestic liquid fuels market was passed in October 2008. Under this law intermediation in the supply and transportation of liquid fuels was made the state's prerogative and subsequently entrusted to PDVSA, its affiliates and the corresponding service stations.

The IFC and GR had a dramatic effect on the Venezuelan economy because: (i) the main partners of Venezuela went into recession; and (ii) between the fourth quarter of 2008 and the first quarter of 2009, the oil prices on the international market dropped abruptly. As a result, not only did the trade balance deteriorate, but the government revenues were reduced due to the dependence on oil revenues.

In view of declining fiscal revenues, the Venezuelan monetary authorities began to perceive a trade-off: either they would have to take measures to contain public spending by incorporating a pro-cyclical factor into fiscal policy or fiscal policies would have to be expanded to prevent continuing recession and unemployment.

Initially, the government opted for a fiscal adjustment, both because the public deficit had grown and because inflation accelerated to more than 30 per cent per year in 2008 (Figure 5.1). Accordingly, public expenditures, and in particular investment, were cut back, fiscal transfers were reduced, value added tax was raised from 9 per cent to 12 per cent and public sector wages were adjusted upwards, but below the yearly rate of inflation (ECLAC, 2009). EA believed that revenues should recover slightly, because the nationalization of certain oil and gas goods and service firms and others in the agricultural, banking and iron and steel industries would improve public sector accounts.

As regards monetary policy, one of the monetary authorities' main concerns was to bring the rising level of inflation under control. At the onset of the IFC, alarmed at the possibility that an inflationary shock might result from the global trend towards exchange rate devaluations, the monetary authorities adopted an essentially restrictive monetary policy characterized by high basic interest rates and higher levels of compulsory deposits to be held by banks, which reduced liquidity and credit in the economy.

In this context, the economic activity slowed during the last quarter of 2008 and in 2009 the GDP declined by nearly 3 per cent, when the drop in the overall demand (private consumption, investment and exports) was only partially offset by government consumption. In 2009, the worsening of fiscal situation was caused mainly by lower petroleum revenues and declining tax receipts, and since then the primary fiscal position has been a deficit of 1.8 per cent on average in 2009–13.

During 2010, while the central government fiscal deficit was lower than in 2009 as the decline in revenue (resulting from lower income tax collections and falling oil revenues) was less than the drop in spending, the CBV adopted measures to boost the economy. Thus, an expansionary monetary policy was implemented, the government intervened in the financial system to increase bank lending, 12 banks were nationalized, and the marginal reserve requirements rates for financial institutions were cut (from 23 per cent to 17 per cent).

In January 2010 the government devalued the BsF and established two exchange rates: BsF 2.6 (for authorized imports of food and medicine) and BsF 4.3 per dollar (for other imports authorized by the government).

Despite these measures, at the end of 2010 the economy continued its experience with recession: the GDP declined by 1.5 per cent.

In 2011, the government ran a primary fiscal deficit equal to 1.8 per cent of GDP, which was a slight improvement over the 2 per cent of deficit posted in 2010. The reason for this improvement was that revenues, due to the recovery of oil prices in the international market, increased more than public expenditure. According to ECLAC (Macroeconomic Report for Venezuela, 2012), "[t]otal central government revenue went from 19.5% of GDP in 2010 to 22.7% of GDP in 2011 ... oil revenue held steady at 6% of GDP" (p. 1). However, public debt continued to increase in 2011: it rose from 20 per cent to 25 per cent of GDP.

Monetary policy continued to be expansionary and the exchange rate was significantly depreciated (BsF 4.3). Due to high inflation in 2008–13 period, real effective exchange rate appreciated – according to ECLAC (2012, p. 2), being 43.6 per cent below the average recorded between 1990 and 2009.

In 2011 the CBV transferred USD 3.5 billion in international reserves to the National Development Fund (FONDEN), which is financed by PDVSA. Despite this transfer, the amount of international reserves at the end of the year was essentially the same nominal level as in December 2010 (Figure 5.5).

At the end of 2011, the Venezuelan economy grew by 4.2 per cent, driven by the expansion of public spending on the back of the high oil prices.[25]

In 2012, due to the high average price of the oil in the international market (it was around USD 100 per barrel in the first 10 months), the government decided to be more discretionary to allocate these extra-revenues and, consequently, public spending increase, including FONDEN. Moreover, a loan-for-oil agreement between China and Venezuela was created to finance the economic activity, mainly infrastructure.

In terms of monetary policy, it was more expansionary than in 2011. Under the context of expansionary fiscal and monetary policies, the government decided to adopt some non-traditional mechanisms to control inflation, such as, imports of consumption and final goods were encouraged and created a "law on fair costs and prices, which sets the maximum price for a number of products" (ECLAC, Macroeconomic Report for Venezuela, 2012, p. 1).

Considering that in 2012 Venezuela had a presidential election, the public investment increased – for instance, a housing programme was created: '*Gran Misión Vivienda Venezuela*' – and, as a consequence, the economy was boosted by public investments. It is worth mentioning that the expansion of domestic investments (public and private) more than offset the significant outflow of foreign direct investment, due to political and social elections during the election period.

High inflation during 2012 was responsible for the appreciation of the BsF. The exchange rate valuation was the one responsible for the deterioration of the trade balance. Consequently, the current account supply dramatically dropped, from 7.5 per cent, in 2011, to 3 per cent of GDP, at the end of 2012 (Figure 5.2).

Although 2012 was an emblematic year, the GDP growth rate was around 5.3 per cent, the highest rate since the beginning of the IFC, driven by the construction and services sectors; both of which were fueled by public spending funded by high oil prices and increased public borrowing (public debt over GDP increase from 28.6 per cent in 2009 to 46.0 per cent in 2012).

In 2013, fiscal and monetary policies were significantly expansionary.[26] According to ECLAC (Economic Survey for Venezuela, 2014), "[T]he greater abundance of liquidity [was] attributable to higher central government spending and the funding of State-owned enterprises via loans from the central bank" (p. 2).

The BsF was devalued from 4.30 to 6.30 against the United States dollar (losing 47 per cent of its value). Despite the devaluation, the Venezuelan currency remained overvalued, "since the real effective exchange rate in December 2013 was 47% less than the average seen from 1990 to 2009"

(ECLAC, Economic Survey for Venezuela, 2014, p. 3). In 2013, the economic growth substantially dropped: the GDP grew by only 1.3 per cent.

In summary, Venezuela's main economic problems of inflation and public sector imbalances have been apparent for some years, and the IFC merely aggravated them, principally because international liquidity became scarcer, reducing the influx of foreign capital to emerging economies, and because the price of oil fell considerably lately on the international market.

5.4 Conclusions and recommendations

This chapter has shown that the main Latin American countries – Argentina, Brazil, Chile, Mexico and Venezuela – were substantially affected by GR, confirming that there was no 'decoupling' process in the world economy. To different degrees all these economies were strongly affected by the global crisis and the GR that followed the crisis. With the exception of Venezuela, all the countries recovered strongly in 2010, with implementation of counter-cyclical policies, which were also favored by the recovery of the commodity prices by mid-2009. However, economic growth has oscillated a lot in recent years both because of the uncertainties related to the world economy and also because of some domestic issues related to the specificities of each of the economics examined for the purposes of this contribution.

The analysis of this chapter has also shown the efficacy of the counter-cyclical policies in a group of economies of Latin America, which depended, on the one hand, on the good governance of the macroeconomic policy. In most countries the reduction of public external debt, the previous policy of international reserves accumulation and the reduction and improvement in the public debt provided some policy space for counter-cyclical policies. On the other hand, it depended on the structural characteristics of each economy and its insertion in the international economy. For instance, Mexico, nowadays, has its economic dynamics strongly tied to the United States economy, and Venezuela's economy depends basically on oil exports – the prices of which have dramatically been falling more recently. The policy framework can also favor the implementation of counter-cyclical policies, as it is the case of fiscal policies in Chile, and the strong presence of state-owned banks in the case of Brazil.

The strengthening of Latin America to face the contagion of the global financial crisis was only possible due to the better performance of the balance of payments (current account surplus, foreign reserves accumulation, etc.) thanks to the exceptional external conditions before the global crisis of 2008. However, the uncertainty about the recovery of the global economy and the slowdown of the Chinese economy plus some domestic economic deterioration in some Latin American economies (high inflation, low GDP growth, increase of current account, and deceleration of credit supply, among others) seems to show that the policy space for implementation of counter-cyclical policies is somehow reduced in the region.

Given this scenario, and considering that there is no 'light at the end of the tunnel' for the solution of the GR, what should be done?

By way of conclusion, we suggest briefly some economic policy recommendations to assure macroeconomic stability and to promote a consistent and robust economic integration in the Latin American region that could be explored. To achieve this objective, it is suggested that: (i) monetary policies must explicitly consider the goal of employment stability, together with price stability; (ii) fiscal policy must prioritize public investment and social programs; and (iii) exchange rate policy must be designed to maintain a balance of payments equilibria. At the same time, it has been suggested that a Regional Market Maker in Latin America should be created[27] to boost the level of economic and financial integration in the region, and, on the other hand, it is necessary to consider recovery of the main state's functions, such as the inducer, financier and regulator of economic activity.

Notes

1. We are very grateful to Eduardo Kreibich and Luis Felipe Eick for research support.
2. The analysis considers Argentina, Brazil, Chile, Mexico and Venezuela, as overall proxies for the countries of Latin America, for two reasons: (i) these countries' Gross Domestic Product (GDP) represents almost 80 per cent of Latin America's GDP; and (ii) they are important to the region, both politically and economically.
3. According to the IMF (2014), the growth rates in 2009 of the United States, the Euro Area and Japan were, respectively, –2.4 per cent, –4 per cent and –5.1 per cent. Moreover, according to the World Trade Organization (2014) the volume of world trade shrank 12 per cent in 2009.
4. According to Ocampo (2011) in this period Latin America combined the highest economic growth since the post-war boom (until the 1970s) with positive social results in terms of reduction of poverty and inequality, favored unusually by: quick growth of trade, increase in the commodities prices and ample access to international financing at historically low costs.

5. It should be pointed out that there was not any financial/banking crisis within Latin American countries through, for example, bank purchases of 'toxic assets' or through inter-bank links with those of other countries.
6. Resilience is defined as the ability of the emerging economies "to sustain longer and stronger expansions and to experience shorter and shallower downturn and more rapid recovery" (IMF, 2012, p. 130).
7. It is important to mention that the monetary and financial systems of Argentina and Chile are the most deregulated compared to those systems of the other big economies of the region.
8. REER is the weighted average of a country's currency relative to an index or basket of other major currencies adjusted for the effects of inflation.
9. Venezuela was excluded from this analysis as the country implemented a complex multiple exchange rate system.
10. According to ECLAC (2015) data, the average GDP growth in Latin America in 2004–08 was 5.1 per cent per year, while it was 2.1 per cent in 2011–13. Preliminary data on 2014 indicates a GDP growth of only 0.1 per cent on average in the region.
11. Most data and relevant details of this section were extracted from CEPAL (2014, Chapter II).
12. The three countries – Brazil (41.7 per cent), Mexico (21.0 per cent) and Argentina (9.6 per cent) – represented together 72.0 per cent of the total GDP of Latin America in 2013.
13. From 2003 to 2005, after several proposals from the government of Argentina, payments of public debt (particularly external debt) to creditors was made at considerable discounts from nominal values. More specifically, in January 2005 it was proposed to swap old unpaid debt with a face value of USD 81.8 billion for new bonds with a maximum value of USD 41.8 billion.
14. Since 2001 Chile has adopted a counter-cyclical fiscal policy, based on the commitment to an announced goal of a medium-term structural balance as a percentage of GDP. The structural balance nets out the effect of the economic cycle (including copper price volatility) on fiscal revenues and constrains expenditures to a correspondingly consistent level. In practice, this means that expenditures rise when activity is low and decrease in economic booms.
15. In April 1991 Argentina implemented a stabilization plan called the Convertibility Plan, which consisted mainly of adopting a currency board-type exchange rate regime, which essentially anchored the Argentinean *peso* to the United States dollar.
16. One should be careful about the calculation of the inflation rate in Argentina due to changes in the methodology that have underestimated the real increase of CPI.
17. This figure has been maintained in 2011 13, according to ECLAC (2013b).
18. ECLAC (2012, p. 2) reports that average wages climbed by nearly 25 per cent in 2012.
19. The Brazilian government launched the PAC in January 2007 with three main objectives: to stimulate private investment; increase government investment in infrastructure; and remove the main obstacles to economic growth (bureaucracy, inadequate norms and regulation). For full details, see Brazil (2014).

20. Liquidity-enhancing measures included: (i) a reduction in reserve requirements that resulted in an expansion of liquidity of around 3.3 per cent of GDP in the money market; (ii) the creation of incentives for larger financial institutions to purchase the loan portfolios of small and medium banks; and (iii) an additional insurance deposit for small and medium banks.
21. From April 2009 to April 2011 Brazilian currency appreciated by 28 per cent.
22. Data obtained from BCB (2014).
23. In 2002, the primary fiscal balance showed a slight deficit.
24. At the end of December, the amount of reserves was about USD 113.6 billion (Figure 5.5).
25. Two extra budgetary funds account for a substantial proportion of public spending execution: the National Development Fund (FONDEN) – funded by contributions from *Petroleos Venezuela* (public oil firm) and by excess of central bank reserves – and the joint Chinese–Venezuelan fund.
26. The deficit of primary fiscal was equivalent to 2.2 per cent of GDP (Figure 5.6), up by 0.5 percentage points from 2012.
27. In view of the process of integration under way in Latin America, more specifically the UNASUR, it is important to institute a Regional Market Maker to (i) coordinate among countries' macroeconomic policies, (ii) foster discretionary fiscal transfers to reduce economic and social differences and integrate among countries' infrastructures, (iii) indicate a common trade policy and distribute the costs of achieving balance of payments equilibrium among the two groups of countries (those in deficit and those in surplus), (iv) propose that the system of local currency payments be generalized, and (v) set up and operate a reserve fund for countries to access when faced by external shocks, contagion from which may lead to exchange rate crises. For more, see Ferrari-Filho (2014).

References

Bank for International Settlements (BIS) (2014) *Statistics*. Available at http://www.bis.org (accessed in December).

Barbosa, N. (2010) 'Latin America: Counter-cyclical Policy in Brazil: 2008–09', *Journal of Globalization and Development*, 1(1), 1–12.

Brasil (2014) *Programa de Aceleração do Crescimento*. Available at http://www.brasil.gov.br/pac_(accessed in December).

Central Bank of Brazil (BCB) (2014) *Séries Temporais*. Available at http://www.bcb.gov.br (accessed in December).

Comisión Económica para América Latina y El Caribe (CEPAL) (2012) *Estudio Económico de América Latina y el Caribe 2012*, Santiago: CEPAL.

Comisión Económica para América Latina y El Caribe (CEPAL) (2014) *Estudio Económico de América Latina y el Caribe 2014*, Santiago: CEPAL.

Damill, M. and Frenkel, R. (2009) 'Las políticas macroeconómicas en la evolución reciente de la economia argentina', *Nuevos Documentos CEDES*, no. 65, Buenos Aires: CEDES.

Economic Commission for Latin America and Caribbean (ECLAC) (2009) *Economic Survey of Latin America and the Caribbean 2008–2009*. Available at http://www.eclac.org (accessed in December 2014).

Economic Commission for Latin America and Caribbean (ECLAC) (2009a) *Preliminary Overview of the Economies of Latin America and the Caribbean – Countries Reports*. Available at http://www.eclac.org (accessed in December 2014).
Economic Commission for Latin America and Caribbean (ECLAC) (2009b) *Preliminary Overview of the Economies of Latin America and the Caribbean – Countries Reports*. Available at http://www.eclac.org (accessed in December 2014).
Economic Commission for Latin America and Caribbean (ECLAC) (2009c) *Preliminary Overview of the Economies of Latin America and the Caribbean – Countries Reports*. Available at http://www.eclac.org (accessed in December 2014).
Economic Commission for Latin America and Caribbean (ECLAC) (2011) *Economic Survey of Latin America and the Caribbean 2010–2011*. Available at http://www.eclac.org (accessed in December 2014).
Economic Commission for Latin America and Caribbean (ECLAC) (2012) *Economic Survey of Latin America and the Caribbean 2012*. Available at http://www.eclac.org (accessed in December 2014).
Economic Commission for Latin America and Caribbean (ECLAC) (2013) *Economic Survey of Latin America and the Caribbean 2013*. Available at http://www.eclac.org (accessed in December 2014).
Economic Commission for Latin America and Caribbean (ECLAC) (2013a) *Preliminary Overview of the Economies of Latin America and the Caribbean – Countries Reports*. Available at http://www.eclac.org (accessed in December 2014).
Economic Commission for Latin America and Caribbean (ECLAC) (2013b) *Preliminary Overview of the Economies of Latin America and the Caribbean – Countries Reports*. Available at http://www.eclac.org (accessed in December 2014).
Economic Commission for Latin America and Caribbean (ECLAC) (2014) *Economic Survey of Latin America and the Caribbean 2014*. Available at http://www.eclac.org (accessed in December 2014).
Economic Commission for Latin America and Caribbean (ECLAC) (2014a) *Preliminary Overview of the Economies of Latin America and the Caribbean – Countries Reports*. Available at http://www.eclac.org (accessed in December 2014).
Economic Commission for Latin America and Caribbean (ECLAC) (2014b) *Preliminary Overview of the Economies of Latin America and the Caribbean – Countries Reports*. Available at http://www.eclac.org (accessed in December 2014).
Economic Commission for Latin America and Caribbean (ECLAC) (2015) *Statistical Information*. Available at http://www.eclac.org (accessed in January 2015).
Ferrari-Filho, F. (2014) 'A Regional Arrangement Proposal for the UNASUR', *Revista de Economia Política*, 34(3) (136), July–September, 413–32.
International Monetary Fund (IMF) (2012) *World Economic Outlook, October*. Available at http://www.imf.org.br (accessed in December 2014).
International Monetary Fund (IMF) (2014) *Data and Statistics*. Available at http://www.imf.org (accessed in December).
Jará, A., Moreno, R. and Tovar, C.E. (2009) 'The Global Crisis and Latin America: Financial Impact and Policy Responses', *BIS Quarterly Review*, June, 53–68.
Montero, A.P. (2014) *Brazil: Reversal of Fortune*, New York: Polity.
Ocampo, J.A. (2011) 'Como fue el desempeño de América Latina durante la crisis financiera global?', *Ensayos Económicos BCRA* 61/62, June.
Ocampo, J.A. (2012) 'Balance of Payments Dominance: Its Implications for Macroeconomic Policy'. Available at https://www.mtholyoke.edu/.../Ocampo_Macro_Mount_Holyoke.pdf (accessed in December 2014).

Paula, L.F., Ferrari-Filho, F. and Gomes, A. (2013) 'Capital Flows, International Imbalances and Economic Policies in Latin America', in P. Arestis and M. Sawyer (eds), *Economic Policies, Governance and the New Economy*, Basingstoke: Palgrave Macmillan, pp. 209–48.

Paula, L.F., Modenesi, A. and Pires, M.C. (2015) 'The Tale of the Contagion of Two Crises and Policy Responses in Brazil: A Case of (Keynesian) Policy Coordination?', *Journal of Post Keynesian Economics*, 37(3), 408–35.

Prates, D.M. and Cintra, M.A.M. (2009) 'Os países emergentes diante da crise financeira global', *Proceedings of II Encontro Internacional da Associação Keynesiana Brasileira*, Porto Alegre: AKB, CD-ROM.

World Bank (2014) *Indicators*. Available at http://www.worldbank.org (accessed in December).

World Trade Organization (WTO) *Statistics*. Available at http://www.wto.org (accessed in December).

6
An Eastern European Perspective on the Recent Financial Crisis and an Examination of Poland's Exceptionalism

Nigel F.B. Allington
University of Cambridge, UK
John S.L. McCombie
University of Cambridge, UK

Abstract: The article reviews the growth of the Eastern European countries after their transition and up to 2007 and then assesses the impact of the US financial crisis on them, making appropriate references to the growth of the South East Asian economies in the 1980s with which they share many features during their convergence process with the Western European economies. The macroeconomic policy responses are outlined and their success measured. The final part of the chapter looks specifically at Poland's experience on the grounds that it has been an exceptional economy both before and after the crisis for a number of reasons. These include the role of small and medium-sized enterprises, inward FDI, its low export/GDP ratio, tight financial regulations and the pursuit of macroprudential policies.

Keywords: Eastern European Economies, Growth, Financial Crisis, Poland's exceptionalism

JEL Classification: E02, E23, E60, E63, G01, G15

6.1 Introduction

This article examines the rise, fall and rise again of the Eastern European Economies (EEE), charting their transition from command to market economies, through the financial crisis and their subsequent recovery.[1] Their remarkable growth from the mid-1990s to mid-2000s came to an abrupt end following the Great Recession in 2008 when highly leveraged financial institutions in the US and Western Europe were forced to deleverage and revalue their toxic (heavily securitized) financial assets, leading to a freeze in the interbank and international capital markets. As world trade collapsed, the major impact on countries in Eastern Europe, South East Asia (SEA) and China registered as a severe drop in exports and thus in their economic growth. Whereas the growth rate in the EEE over the period 2004 to 2007 averaged 6.75 per cent, between 2008 and 2014, combining the crisis and post-crisis periods, it fell to an average of only 0.6 per cent. The worst-affected countries in 2009, the depth of the recession in the EEE, were the three Baltic States, Latvia, Lithuania and Estonia, followed by Slovenia, Hungary and Romania. Only Poland continued to grow in 2009, by a modest, but significant 1.6 per cent and indeed Polish growth over the crisis and post-crisis periods has averaged 3 per cent per annum, a remarkable achievement that has been labelled 'Poland's exceptionalism'. For comparative purposes, average annual growth in the Euro Area between 2004 and 2008 was 2.12 per cent and between 2009 and 2014 –0.2 per cent.

The paper proceeds as follows. Section 6.2 gives a brief account of the 2008 financial crisis; Section 6.3 assesses the position of the EEE before the crisis and Section 6.4 the impact of the crisis on them, including econometric evidence. Section 6.5 analyses the evolution of the crisis in the EEE in terms of the growth of credit, the impact of lending rates, foreign ownership of the EEE banks, the impact of the crisis on the banking sector (including the growth of non-performing loans), the holding of toxic assets by the banks, exchange rate policy during the crisis and the impact of FDI. Section 6.6 considers the macroeconomic policy responses to the crisis in the EEE. Section 6.7 focuses on the nature of Poland's exceptionalism before and after the crisis, including the key role of small and medium-sized enterprises, monetary and credit conditions, the ownership of its banks, the role of FDI and the foreign trade. Section 6.8 summarizes and concludes.

6.2 The Great Recession of 2008

The roots of the Great Recession can be located in the US subprime crisis and its aftermath, which has been represented as a classic insolvency crisis followed by a bank run (Reinhart and Rogoff, 2009). In an economic environment that combined low inflation with economic growth, the US and the Western European Economies (WEE) pursuing inflation targeting enjoyed low interest rates, which frequently fuelled a surge in household and corporate debt and led to excessive borrowing on the part of some Euro Area governments. Given low interest rates, US financial institutions, in order to make profits and satisfy their stockholders and employees, generated asset-backed derivatives, including mortgage-backed securities and collateralized debt obligations backed by loans to the subprime sector. The combination of securitization, asset insurance (credit default swaps), unsupportable credit ratings, and lax regulation of financial institutions enabled US financial institutions to sell these financial instruments to their counterparts in Europe and other US institutions. When the housing bubble in the US burst and these securities lost their value, the banks became insolvent. Governments in the US and also the heavily indebted ones in the WEE were forced to bail them out, creating layers of moral hazard and racking up even greater levels of debt. Unlike the SEA crisis, the epicentre of the current crisis has been the financial markets in the US and WEE, while the EEE have simply been a sideshow (Dietrich et al., 2011).

6.3 The Eastern European economies before the financial crisis

The rates of growth achieved by the EEE before the financial crisis compare favourably with those in SEA as they converged with the developed Western economies. After the trauma of their transition from planned to free market economies as growth collapsed, the process of social and economic integration post-1989 accelerated, culminating in the accession agreements with the European Union (EU) in 1993 and entry into the customs union in 2004. The reforms undertaken during this period included the liberalization of trade, the privatization of state-owned enterprises to encourage competition, the introduction of open capital markets, the creation of a stable macroeconomic regime including low and stable inflation, fiscal rectitude, the deregulation of labour markets, the protection of individual property rights and the reform of the tax system (Lütz and Kranke, 2013). Following the initial transition growth fell by –40 per cent in the Baltic States, the worst-affected economies, and by between –1 per cent and –25 per cent in the other EEE, although as is recorded by Svejnar (2002), the recovery came equally as quickly for most. As Aghion et al. (2010) noted, the key requirements for economic growth had already been identified in the Spence report (2008), including progressive education, trade, competition, labour market flexibility, and other growth-enhancing government economic policies, could all be found in all the EEE to a greater or lesser extent, although Hungary seemed to regress later. Like the SEA economies in the 1980s and early 1990s, the EEE were catching up with the advanced WEE utilizing their technology and investment capital including FDI. Their growth was underpinned by high levels of total factor productivity (TFP) supported by more competitive labour and final product markets, high levels of foreign trade and FDI, including structural and cohesion funding from the EU (Arrabitel et al., 2007).

There is disagreement over the drivers of growth in the EEE: Connolly (2012) argues that domestic demand determined their growth whereas Darvas (2011a) made the case for foreign trade. Connolly refers to pent-up demand under the conditions of state planning that, once released, drove growth higher while export volumes were insufficient to ensure that net exports had a significant growth effect. Rather, the increase in consumption and investment outpaced domestic savings and precipitated a growing deficit on the current account of the balance of payments, evident in most of the EEE. Then, with the liberalization of their capital accounts in the 1990s, substantial capital inflows intensified the financial linkages between the WEE and the EEE. In contrast, Darvas (2011a) compares the EEE with the SEA economies noting that both depended on foreign trade to drive economic growth to a similar extent with the identical result: a growing balance of payments deficit and dependence on foreign capital inflows. Both authors agreed that GDP growth and the current account were negatively correlated. Indeed, the rapid development of the financial sector in the EEE and the need for capital inflows accelerated their growth in the decade before the Great Recession with property and equity prices outperforming those in the WEE and the US (ECB, 2012). However, by 2007 the EEE had become vulnerable to external and domestic shocks working through a property bubble, increases in private external debt and high levels of borrowing in foreign currencies.

High levels of investment were needed by the EEE after the transition from state planning in order to replace obsolete capital and fuel a credit boom (Friedrich et al., 2010). Anticipating that TFP growth would increase with upgraded technology encouraging new investment, WE banks began to pursue long-term investment strategies in the region. As institutional quality and political stability increased, the risk premia previously attached to investments in the EEE fell. Estimates of TFP at the industry level by Benkovskis et al. (2012), incorporating the effects of higher international trade, non-constant returns to scale and aggregated TFP from industry to the macro level over the period 1996 to 2009, revealed that the Baltic States and Slovakia had the highest TFP, at 3 per cent and 4 per cent per annum respectively. The remaining EEE had TFP ranging from 1 per cent in Hungary to 1.4 per cent in Poland, 1.5 per cent in Bulgaria and 2.3 per cent in Slovenia with the differences attributable to a country's distance from the technology frontier, and whether the foreign investment supported greenfield-using new technologies or the acquisition of existing industrial plant using extant technologies. Not only did the former achieve higher TFP, but those countries with a fixed exchange rate also achieved higher levels of TFP growth, with the exception of the Czech Republic. These rates were twice those achieved by WEEs (an average of 2.4 per cent compared with 1 per cent) and only the UK and Sweden came close to the higher rates recorded in the EEE. In Poland, the Czech and Slovak Republics and Slovenia the highest levels of TFP growth were recorded in the manufacturing sectors, whereas in the Baltic States, Bulgaria, Hungary and Romania TFP growth was spread over a wider field. And TFP was mostly concentrated in the export sector.

A more nuanced view of growth in the EEE would conclude that their rapid growth reflected both an export orientation and expanding aggregate demand with higher levels of inward investment from the EU and other advanced economies leading to higher levels of TFP and therefore more sustainable economic growth over the longer term.

6.4 The impact of the financial crisis on the Eastern European economies

6.4.1 General comments

The bankruptcy of Lehman Brothers in September 2008 intensified the financial crisis in the WEE and the immediate impact was lower GDP growth in the EEE, which fell dramatically in some cases. International investors took fright as systemic risks increased and financial institutions began a process of rapid deleveraging, leading to the collapse of aggregate demand and a significantly lower demand for exports. In 2008 GDP growth started to slow in the Baltic States and Hungary. But it was the economies that experienced the fastest growth before the crisis that were the most severely affected in 2009, including the Baltic States, where GDP fell –17.7 per cent in Latvia, –14.8 per cent in Lithuania and –14.1 per cent in Estonia with somewhat lower negative growth rates of –4.5 per cent in the Czech Republic, –4.9 per cent in Slovenia and –5.5 per cent in Bulgaria (see Table 6.1). By 2010Q1, however, as there was a recovery in foreign demand, all of the EEE (with the sole exception of Romania) posted positive growth, with the Czech Republic and Slovakia growing again from 2008Q4. With the collapse in demand inflation, which had

Table 6.1 Growth of real GDP in the Eastern European economies, 2004–2014 (percentage change; minus signifies negative growth)

Country	2004	2005	2006	2007	2008	2009	2010	2011	2012	2013	2014
Bulgaria	6.7	6.4	6.5	6.4	6.2	–5.5	0.4	1.8	0.6	0.9	1.7
Czech R	4.7	6.8	7.0	5.7	3.1	–4.5	2.5	1.8	-1.0	–0.9	2.0
Estonia	6.3	8.9	10.1	7.5	-4.2	-14.1	2.6	9.6	3.9	0.8	2.1
Latvia	8.8	10.1	11.0	10.0	-2.8	-17.7	-1.3	5.3	5.2	4.1	2.4
Lithuania	7.4	7.8	7.8	9.8	2.9	-14.8	1.6	6.0	3.7	3.3	2.9
Hungary	4.8	4.0	3.9	0.1	0.9	–6.8	1.1	1.6	-1.7	1.1	3.6
Poland	5.3	3.6	6.2	6.8	5.1	1.6	3.9	4.5	2.0	1.6	3.3
Romania	8.5	4.2	7.9	6.3	7.3	–6.6	-1.1	2.3	0.6	3.5	2.9
Slovenia	4.4	4.0	5.8	7.0	3.4	–7.9	1.3	0.7	–2.5	-1.1	2.6
Slovakia	5.1	6.7	8.3	10.5	5.8	–4.9	4.4	3.0	1.8	0.9	2.4

Source: Eurostat; available at: http://ec.europa.eu/eurostat/data/database.

reached double-digit levels in the Baltic States and Romania, fell to an average of 2.6 per cent (from an average of 8 per cent in 2008). Only Latvia experienced deflation (price changes of -1.2 per cent) in 2010. In the wake of the crisis three countries – Latvia, Romania and Hungary – found it necessary to seek support from both the IMF and the EU. The IMF's Stand-By Arrangements were much more generous than the balance of payments support offered by the EU and involved less restrictive conditions (Lütz and Kranke, 2013).

Business cycles in the EEE had not converged before the crisis in 2008 and the Baltic States had unsustainable rates of growth driven by a combination of capital inflows and low interest rates supporting the growth of credit, leading to rising asset prices and a house price bubble. House prices increased by an average of 20 per cent a year in Bulgaria over a three-year period before the crisis, 25 per cent in Estonia, 21 per cent in Latvia and 15 per cent in Slovenia (the equivalent figures in Ireland and Spain, where the house price bubble was the largest in the Euro Area, were 8 per cent and 9 per cent, respectively). Strong wage growth in some economies, positive wealth effects and expansionary fiscal policies raised demand and growth, but also widened government budget deficits. In 2008 the Baltic States, Hungary, Poland and Romania broke the Stability and Growth Pact (SGP) cap for government budget deficits of –3 per cent, and Bulgaria, the Czech Republic, Slovenia and Slovakia joined them in 2009 (only Estonia had a deficit below that – at –2 per cent of GDP). Only Hungary broke the cap on government debt at 60 per cent of GDP with 71.9 per cent in 2008 and 78.2 per cent in 2009 and Slovenia breached the cap in 2013 (70.3 per cent) and again with 80.9 per cent in 2014. The increase in demand also raised inflation and led to a real appreciation of currencies in the EEE and growing deficits on the current account of the balance of payments. By 2008 all EEE had current account deficits, the worst being recorded by Bulgaria (with a deficit of 22.4 per cent of GDP), Lithuania and Latvia (at 13 per cent and 12.4 per cent, respectively) and Romania (11.5 per cent). However, by 2009 with the fall in exports accompanied by an even greater fall in imports, the Baltic States had moved into surplus and the deficits elsewhere had fallen – with the exception of the Czech Republic, where the deficit increased to 2.4 per cent of GDP (see Table 6.2). Nevertheless, with deficits on the current account the EEE, particularly Estonia and Latvia, became dependent on capital inflows financed by short-term capital flows that increased the level of debt denominated in foreign currencies. Given that foreign-owned banks had a dominant presence in the EEE, foreign loans in Euros were common, with currency risks elevated where countries had fixed exchange rates (Bulgaria, Estonia, Latvia and Lithuania).

The costs of borrowing increased in 2008 after the collapse of Lehman's and there was also a contraction of credit where it had been supplied previously by overseas lenders. Higher interest rates help to explain the contraction in output in the Baltic States and Romania. Where countries had relied more heavily on domestic sources of credit finance, as occurred, for example, in Poland, the Czech Republic and Hungary, the growth of credit slowed more moderately. Consequently, investment expenditure fell quite precipitously in the Baltic States, but in Poland it was sustained. The contraction in growth can also be linked to the fall in consumer expenditure, with Poland and Bulgaria the exceptions, but the decline in house prices and equities played a major role as households began to deleverage. Changes in consumption

Table 6.2 Current account balance in Eastern European economies (percentage of GDP; minus signifies a deficit)

Country	2004	2005	2006	2007	2008	2009	2010	2011	2012	2013	2014
Bulgaria	–6.3	–11.5	–17.3	–24.3	–22.4	–8.6	–1.5	0.1	–1.1	2.3	0.0
Czech R	–4.3	–1.0	–2.2	–4.3	1.9	–2.4	–3.7	–2.1	–1.6	–0.5	0.6
Estonia	–12.0	–8.7	–15.0	–15.0	–8.7	2.5	1.8	1.4	–2.5	–1.1	–0.1
Hungary	–8.3	–7.1	–7.1	–7.1	–7.2	–0.8	–0.3	–0.8	1.9	4.1	4.2
Latvia	–11.7	–11.8	–20.9	–20.8	–12.4	8.0	2.3	–2.8	–3.3	–2.3	–3.1
Lithuania	–7.6	–7.2	–10.4	–14.9	–13.0	2.1	–0.3	–3.8	–1.2	1.6	–0.4
Poland	–5.4	–2.6	–4.0	–6.3	–6.6	–4.0	–5.5	–5.2	–3.6	–1.3	–1.2
Romania	–7.5	–8.6	–10.4	–13.5	–11.5	–4.5	–4.6	–4.6	–4.5	–0.8	–0.5
Slovakia	–5.8	–7.3	–7.0	–4.8	–6.5	–3.5	–4.7	–5.0	0.9	1.5	0.2
Slovenia	–2.7	–1.8	–1.8	–4.2	–5.4	–0.6	–0.1	0.2	2.7	5.6	5.8

Source: Eurostat; available at: http://ec.europa.eu/eurostat/data/database.

were partly dictated by conditions in labour markets and in countries where labour markets were more flexible, such as the Baltic States, labour downsizing and wage reductions were applied rapidly, but elsewhere, including Poland, Hungary and the Czech Republic, where labour contracts were more rigid, the adjustment came mainly through slower wage progression as firms sought to keep skilled labour anticipating the resumption of growth. Thus, the combination of lower aggregate demand, reduced exports and lower demand for imported components led to a sharp reversal in the current account deficits in some countries, including Bulgaria, the Baltic States, Hungary and Slovenia (where the highest deficit in 2010 was 1.5 per cent in Bulgaria, while Estonia [temporarily] and Latvia moved into surplus – see Table 6.2).

The major impact of the crisis on the EEE was the result of the decline in exports. But there were significant country differences. Exports fell in 2009 by 24 per cent in Estonia, and between 17 per cent and 10 per cent in Slovenia, Slovakia, Hungary, Latvia, Bulgaria and the Czech Republic. By contrast, Poland, which was less dependent on exports, experienced a fall of 6 per cent and Romania 2 per cent. The fall in export demand was partially mitigated by the fall in the nominal effective exchange rate and the greatest reversal came in those countries with flexible exchange rates – notably Poland, Hungary and Romania. The major industries where exports fell were in the capital goods and intermediate goods sectors, particularly those linked to the motor vehicle supply chain. These goods were exported to the WEE and the policies adopted by governments there, such as public investment in infrastructure and car replacement schemes, had spillover effects on the EEE. The Baltic States and Poland also had strong trade links with Russia and the Commonwealth of Independent States as well as other EEE.

Some EEE experienced capital outflows as investor confidence waned and financial institutions began a process of deleveraging, including the Baltic States, Bulgaria and Romania. FDI also fell in most EEE in 2009 (with the exception of Poland) and the reduction started two years later in Estonia (when the most substantial falls occurred). Hungary experienced the largest reversal in FDI, down by 2.6 per cent in 2009 and 16.2 per cent in 2010, while Slovenia (0.7 per cent) and Latvia (0.25 per cent) also suffered FDI reductions in 2009.

6.4.2 Econometric tests of the impact of the crisis and the specific vulnerabilities of the EEE

In an empirical analysis of the impact of the financial crisis on the output of the EEE, Furceri and Zdzienicka (2011) assessed the period

1989 to 2008 using an autoregressive equation with distributional lags and employing two methodologies. First, they employed a market pressure index (MPI), building on research by Kaminsky and Reinhart (1999). They incorporated pressure from the change in the real effective exchange rate and (declining) foreign exchange reserves that accounted for several previous financial crises. Secondly, Furceri and Zdzienicka used the IMF crisis database to construct a dummy for three types of financial crises (banking, debt and currency) comparing the real effects of a financial crisis on the EEE and the advanced WEE, taking into account structural heterogeneities and the impact of their macroeconomic policy responses. The authors examined country size and openness, foreign capital inflows (including FDI), financial development, credit expansion, the foreign liabilities of indigenous banks and a number of macroeconomic variables including exchange rate regimes, government expenditure, interest rates and IMF support packages.

They estimated the financial crisis would have a long-term impact on the EEE and WEE with output lower by 1 per cent after one year, but perhaps by as much as 12–17 per cent five years after a financial crisis. And that the impact was greater on the EEE because they were more vulnerable and smaller economies where banking crises had been more frequent. These vulnerabilities included the exposure of their banks to currency and maturity mismatches, disruption to the international capital markets and bank panics as well as the sudden cessation of capital flows. The most appropriate macroeconomic policy responses, they concluded, were fiscal ones that dealt more immediately with the crisis, whereas monetary policy would make a more modest contribution because of the variable length of the monetary transmission mechanisms. In addition, countries with floating exchange rates were less affected by a financial crisis because monetary policy was not constrained by the policy trilemma. In the event, it was the Euro Area economies that suffered a more prolonged long-term contraction in their growth because of the alignment of their financial and sovereign debt crises, while the EEE recovered after two years, even if the Czech Republic and Slovenia experienced a double-dip recession in 2012–13.

Turning to vulnerability indicators, six were identified by Gallego et al. (2010) based on the study carried out by Kaminsky and Reinhart (1996). They were (1) *market sentiments* – assessed positively by financial markets until the crisis because of the EEE strong economic ties with the US and the WEE, but which deteriorated during the financial crisis; (2) *external vulnerability* – which worsened because of higher levels of external debt with some of it in foreign currencies; (3) *banking sector* – this indicator deteriorated because deposit growth did not match the growth of credit forcing the banks to rely more heavily on foreign funding, with the exceptions of Poland and the Czech Republic; (4) *fiscal position* – stronger than that of the WEE before the crisis with the exception of Hungary (which had debt at 67 per cent of GDP), although six countries were subject to the excessive deficit procedure; (5) *monetary indicators* – including credit growth that expanded, growing money supply (M2) and a house price bubble in several countries; and, finally, (6) *real indicator* – given that inflation was stable and nominal interest rates falling or negative, industrial production rose and exports expanded in the EEE.

Gallego et al. (2010) tested whether these vulnerabilities were a good predictor of financial and other crises by regressing them on financial conditions and then real conditions. The dependent variable in the first case was the Emerging Market Bond Index (EMBI) and, in the second, the rate of real GDP growth. In the EEE, the monetary indicator drives the EMBI, but EMBI spreads after the crisis were not correlated with either the banking or external vulnerability indicators. With regard to real GDP growth, this variable was less affected where the external and real vulnerabilities were small – in particular, a strong banking sector provides protection from a severe recession, as do strong public sector (mainly fiscal) indicators. The authors concluded several vulnerabilities had become critical for some EEE. The key ones were the external and banking sectors and aspects of the monetary indicators, including the growth in bank credit: the fiscal and nominal indicators were indicators of greater macroeconomic stability. Unfortunately, the general picture does not reveal any individual country differences nor the dynamics of the indicators.

Furthermore, in a paper examining the role of liquidity conditions and sudden falls in investors' appetite for risk, Chudik and Fratzscher (2011) use a global VAR methodology, including variance decompositions and Generalized Impulse Response Functions that accommodate the diversity of the transmission process. They conclude that liquidity constraints are more powerful determinants of the transmission of the global crisis in advanced economies, whereas declining propensities for risk-taking explain the transmission in emerging markets like the EEE and, surprisingly, those in the WEE. The financial side of the economy bore the brunt of the adjustment in the advanced economies while in the EEE it was the real side of the economy.

The falls in GDP growth were largest in countries with highly leveraged financial systems that experienced more rapid credit growth before the crisis (Berkmen et al., 2009), reflecting the banking vulnerability criterion. Countries with pegged exchange rate systems and large levels of foreign trade suffered the largest falls in their GDP, extending the external vulnerability criterion. Latvia and Estonia pegged their currencies to the Euro in preparation for entry into EMU while Bulgaria and Lithuania formed a currency board with the Euro for the same reason. Interestingly, in the Baltic States the balance of payments on the current account improved dramatically compared with the pre-crisis period as imports fell faster than exports. Thus in conclusion, the sensitivity of the EEE to the financial crisis should be linked to three key factors: capital flows and financial integration, over-dependence on foreign trade and the remittances of migrants (Darvas, 2011b).

Despite their clear macroeconomic and financial vulnerabilities, the EBRD (2009) argued that the financial crisis took time to affect the EEE because foreign capital inflows held up, and the cost of borrowing fell while credit and output growth continued throughout 2007, after the initial disruptions to international financial markets. Eventually, however, credit growth retreated because of tighter lending standards imposed by the regulators in the EEE (and the banks), as a result of concerns over the preceding credit boom and the collapse of Lehman's.

An explanation for the change in fortunes remains contentious, but the study carried out by the EBRD (2009) suggests a number of explanations. First, capital flows switched to safer havens in developed economies including the WEE, penalizing the EEE and other transition economies. This emerged from the belief that the crisis would ultimately have a greater impact on the more vulnerable transition economies. The 'safe haven' effect can be linked to considerable financial support from governments in WEE for their own banks, not to the strength of the banks or the effectiveness of the regulatory authorities in the WEE. Secondly, the capital reversal could have been a manifestation of a general fall in capital flows as the crisis intensified. Syndicated bank lending by the largest 156 international lenders to the private sector in the EEE reached a high of US$51 billion in the first half of 2007, but fell the following year after the collapse of Lehman's. What the data show is that lending in WEE increased, whereas their loans to the transition economies fell by 50 per cent (from 18 per cent to 9 per cent of all their loans). These changes took place, however, against a dramatic fall in the volume of lending (75 per cent in emerging markets and 50 per cent in the home country); and global deleveraging seems to account for the general fall in loans to transition economies. Somewhat ironically lending to emerging markets fell most where Western banks received financial support from their own governments.

Because export markets remained firm, the tighter financial conditions did not lead to a decline in output until after September 2008. However, exports contracted sharply in 2008Q4 and growth in the export-dependent economies, particularly the Czech Republic, Hungary and Slovakia, fell. This contraction in exports can be linked to the decline in manufacturing in the WEE the main trading partners of the EEE. And this was accompanied by a 'sudden stop' in cross-border banking flows between the WEE and EEE, a combination of a drop in trade credit provided by banks and a decrease in remittances by labour working abroad.

6.5 Key factors in the evolution of financial crisis in the Eastern European economies

6.5.1 General comments

The key factors include: the growth of credit to the private sector; connected with this were the level of lending rates; lending by foreign banks, including the impact of Recommendations S and T in Poland and the Vienna Initiative 2.0; the impact the financial crisis had on the banking sector and the subsequent growth of non-performing loans; the degree to which the banks were exposed to toxic assets created by US financial institutions; the impact of FDI on the EEE and, finally, the impact of their exchange rate policy. These are examined in the following subsections.

6.5.2 The growth of credit to the private sector

As Reinhart and Rogoff (2009) established, the financial crisis in the EEE represents a classic bank-inspired credit boom-and-bust cycle and one accompanied by a deficit on the current account of the balance of payments. A credit boom, with all its associated negative consequences, emerged first in Latvia and Estonia and was followed in 2007 by a reduction in bank lending leading to a collapse in consumption and investment and a severe drop in output. Output growth in 2008 in Estonia was –4.2 per cent and in Latvia –2.8 per cent with both exhibiting negative growth before the rest of the EEE. Lehman's bankruptcy exacerbated the emerging credit crunch as international liquidity dried up. Despite the severity of the ensuing crisis and mirroring events during the earlier banking crisis in SEA in 1997, the crisis in the EEE abated after two years. And while the private sector incurred most of the debt, it was the public sector that had to adjust to mitigate the fallout. Thus, by 2010Q3 growth had returned to all EEE (with the exception of Romania) and only one bank had failed: Parex Bank, a domestically owned bank in Latvia which, having raised its finance through short-term borrowing on the European wholesale markets, found itself unable to refinance its loans.

Firms in the EEE mainly borrowed from banks to finance their investment so the share of bank assets in total assets exceeded 85 per cent while corporate equity markets remained small. The expansion of credit and its subsequent decline has been identified as the major contributory cause of the financial crisis (Åslund, 2012). How the rate of bank credit to the private sector (BCPS) to GDP evolved across the EEE was examined by Cottarelli et al. (2005) for the period covering their transition. They determined that the ratio rose most in Bulgaria, Estonia and Latvia (11 per cent, 22 per cent and 17 per cent, respectively) between 1998 and 2002. The authors then allocated the transition economies to three different groups differentiated by their BCPS ratios. The first group, the so-called 'early birds', had an average BCPS ratio that increased by more than 1.5 per cent between 1998 and 2002 fuelled mainly by the growth in deposits and the concomitant fall in credit extended to government. These economies include Bulgaria, Estonia, Hungary, Latvia, Poland and Slovenia. In 2001 and 2002 the BCPS ratio for this group of six rose on average by 29 per cent and 32.6 per cent respectively. Four, Estonia, Latvia, Poland and Slovenia also financed their credit expansion by borrowing overseas.

The second group, the 'late risers', only experienced a rise in their BCPS ratio to levels above 1.5 per cent after 2001, again financed by a rise in deposits and included Lithuania amongst the EEE. In 2001 and 2002, the BCPS ratio for this group rose by 11.6 per cent and 14.2 per cent, respectively. Finally, the 'sleeping beauties' witnessed a fall in the BCPS ratio after earlier bank loans had been written off including the Czech and Slovak Republics, whose ratios had fallen by 15 per cent and 20.1 per cent, respectively, and Romania where the ratios had stabilized. The balance sheet of the banks in this group expanded in line with the growth of GDP and in 2001 and 2002 the BCPS ratios rose on average by 21.9 per cent and 20.9 per cent respectively.

The composition of bank credits differed between the groups. Among the 'early birds', credit increased to the corporate and household sectors, but in the case of the 'sleeping beauties', credit to the corporate sector declined (with the exception of Romania, where it remained stable), and it also grew at a slower rate to households. The conclusion drawn by the authors was that institutional factors and those originating within the banks themselves were responsible for these changes – rather than the behaviour of the borrowers. Furthermore, the rapid growth in credit did not represent some 'catching-up' process and neither did the position of most 'early birds' depend on their ability to borrow overseas. Rather, growth in the BCPS ratio reflected domestic savings, although in the cases of Estonia and Latvia overseas borrowing was important. Other contributing factors included the fall in lending to the public sector (crowding-in), the progress of structural reform and the level of private ownership of the banks and legal protection afforded to creditor institutions. All these factors made a positive contribution to the growth of the BCPS ratio. The authors speculated that they might be expected to contribute to an elevated ratio in the foreseeable future given that the BCPS ratio in the EEE before the crisis remained below that recorded in the WEE (the averages were 22.9 per cent and 95.3 per cent respectively in 2001).

While Cottarelli et al.'s (2005) paper considers credit growth up to 2002, Aydin (2008) takes the analysis to 2005 specifically for the Central and Eastern European economies, although he adopts a different methodology so the two papers should be regarded as complementary. Aydin (op. cit.) considers the impact of the progressive increase in the foreign ownership of EEE banks on the availability of credit using a fixed effects panel estimation model for the period 1990 to 2005 covering the 59 largest banks. The 1990s and 2000s are considered separately so the results from the latter period are of most relevance and cover the period of rapid economic and financial growth. The foreign banks were drawn to the EEE by their faster economic growth and higher interest rates in the 2000s, although these factors could not explain the developments in the 1990s. Austrian and German banks had acquired large stakes in the EEE banks and the Scandinavian countries took stakes specifically in banks in the Baltic States. Consequently, the business cycle in the WEE, the policy responses of their governments, and the Euro Area's monetary policy all had a major impact on the operation of the Area's banks and consequently their operations in the EEE.

An attempt was made in the period leading up to the crisis to determine how close the EEE were to an equilibrium level of credit. Examining credit growth in the EEE, Ėgert et al. (2006) estimated equilibrium levels of credit for small, open economies (out-of-sample panel) and transition economies (in-sample panel) opting for the former given that the coefficient estimates for the transition economies were unstable. Credit growth in the Czech Republic, Hungary, Poland, Slovakia and Slovenia is determined by credit to the public sector, inflation, the spread between lending and deposit rates, financial liberalization, and competition in the banking sector. In the Baltic States, Bulgaria and

Romania credit growth depends on GDP per capita. Also, where house prices were already relatively high, this preceded a further increase in the availability of credit. The economies that undershoot the equilibrium level of credit growth are Lithuania, Poland and Romania while the rest were found to be close to the upper level of the equilibrium.

6.5.3 The impact of lending rates

Linked to the growth of credit, lending rates charged to borrowers across the EEE decreased dramatically between 2005 and 2007, underpinning the boom in cheap credit (de Haas and Knobloch, 2010). Domestic banks relaxed their lending standards as they could access cheap funding from foreign banks and the collateral ratios for new mortgage lending declined (EBRD, 2009). In response, the more conservative regulators in Poland, Romania and the Baltic States tightened the required loan-to-value (LTV) ratios for their financial institutions in early 2007. But notwithstanding this adjustment, the absence of credit bureaus created problems for the banks that could not check the creditworthiness of potential borrowers, many of whom had made multiple loan applications to different banks. And in some EEE the inadequate pay for regulators led to the appointment of inexperienced technical staff and unsatisfactory levels of supervisory expertise and operation. The final problem, mirroring developments in SEA, was the extent of borrowing in foreign currencies where interest rates were low, encouraging high levels of largely unhedged borrowing. Any exchange rate risk was ignored, or assumed away because some countries had direct pegs to the Euro or adopted a currency board linked to the Euro in preparation for their entry into the Euro Area. Finally, intense competition between the banks stimulated rapid credit growth irrespective of any necessary safeguards. However, between 2008Q4 and 2009Q1 the flow of capital to the EEE contracted significantly, causing domestic banks to reduce their lending immediately. Consequently, house prices fell and the proportion of non-performing loans increased.

6.5.4 The lending patterns of foreign-owned banks

With the increase in the foreign ownership of banks in the EEE the expansion of domestic credit depended on the way these banks operated and also the economic conditions in the home country. Foreign banks from mainly WEE increased the availability of credit more than domestic banks and also made use of international capital markets. In this regard, Poland was different because foreign borrowing by its banks was severely limited by so-called Recommendation S, and subsequently

Recommendation T (examined further below). By increasing the level of competition, foreign-owned banks increased the total amount of credit available, but also improved the efficiency and quality of financial transactions. There were drawbacks, however, including selective lending to the safest borrowers and the potential for sudden credit stops if economic conditions deteriorated in the home country, with the possibility that foreign banks might even pull out of the country completely.

The EEE avoided a full-blown currency and banking crisis due to the Vienna Initiative 2.0 (2009) that required collective actions by public and private sector stakeholders (including the European banks themselves) that agreed to coordinate their response to the financial crisis (Berglof et al., 2009 and EBRD, 2009). The Vienna Initiative 2.0 meant that the major foreign banking groups maintained support for their subsidiaries in the EEE. Statistically, Berglof et al. (2009) demonstrated that countries with high levels of foreign bank ownership experienced smaller capital outflows, although foreign banks were largely responsible for the credit growth and external debt in the EEE before the crisis and that these factors contributed to the reversal in economic growth. The EBRD (2009) confirmed that reversals in bank lending experienced by the EEE were much smaller than predicted on the basis of the historical relationship between the flow of capital to these countries and measures of international risk aversion. Thus lending by foreign banks through their local branches and subsidiaries remained stable compared with direct lending from the foreign bank in the home country while lending by domestic banks in the EEE fell much more.

In a recent econometric assessment of the relationship between bank ownership and credit growth de Haas et al. (2014) found that foreign-owned banks reduced their rate of credit growth by an average of 5.2 per cent in 2010 when private domestic banks reduced theirs by an average of 19.9 per cent. Average annual credit growth by foreign-owned and domestic banks had been 41 per cent before the crisis. Credit growth fell most in the years 2008, 2010 and 2011, but in 2009 (the Vienna Initiative 2.0 year) the decline ceased in Poland, even if elsewhere this initiative made little difference. The mixed results reported by the authors are confirmed in de Haas and van Lelyveld (2014). Banks in the EEE appear, therefore, to be in a governance void with neither the home country of the parent bank, nor the host country, exercising appropriate supervisory powers over the banks with the exception of Poland.

Foreign-owned banks had lower credit growth in the 2000s than their privately-owned domestic counterparts. The latter were part of larger conglomerates which raised their capital through a domestic 'client bank' with whom they had a longer-term relationship, while the foreign banks were more selective in their lending, looking for high-worth companies. Nevertheless, the foreign banks borrowed more extensively on the international capital markets to finance their lending in the EEE and such interbank lending became more significant overtime. In fact, credit growth attributable to foreign-owned banks reflected the size of the parent bank (the larger the parent bank the greater the expansion of credit), and the larger their interbank liabilities the greater the growth in credit.

Growth of credit was linked to the growth of the money supply M3 by the ECB, indicating that credit was partly funded by markets from within the Euro Area (Caporale et al., 2009). A fall in the profitability of the parent bank did not adversely affect the growth of credit, but an increase in the operating costs of the subsidiary did. Finally, credit growth expanded with an upturn in the business cycle in the home country, but there was no evidence that the growth of credit fell if the home country experienced a recession. Indeed, when interest rates spreads narrowed on lending within the home country, profit opportunities were still available from the higher spreads in the EEE. Thus the speculation of Cottarelli et al. (2005) that the growth of credit up to the 2007 financial crisis was sustained by the progressive increase in foreign ownership of banks in the EEE seems to have been borne out. Nevertheless, despite the expansion of the activities of foreign-owned banks, privately-owned domestic banks continued to have a significant effect on the expansion of bank credit.

6.5.5 How the crisis impacted on the banking sector and the growth of non-performing loans

After the bankruptcy of Lehman's the price of banking stocks were in free fall in the EEE, a worse movement than that experience by banks in the Euro Area (Dietrich et al., 2011). Most banks in the EEE were believed to be at risk of insolvency because their parent banks were expected to withdraw funds to recapitalize themselves. However, the position is much more complex than this. Refinancing became more difficult and credit supplies fell between late 2008 and early 2009. But because of the greater relative prosperity of the EEE and the potential for profits the flow of capital continued, particularly to Poland and the Czech Republic. So any fall in lending is attributable to the depreciation of the local currency not the withdrawal of financial support. Consequently, only Latvia and Lithuania experienced both a pre-existing and continuing decline in capital inflows. Clearly foreign banks performed a stabilizing role in the EEE by keeping their lines of financing open and active.

With the financial crisis, credit conditions deteriorated sharply and even came to an halt (Mihaljek, 2010). This reversal emerged on the supply side from tighter global credit conditions, the slowdown in capital inflows, increased risk aversion on the part of banks and falling demand for credit as aggregate demand collapsed. Rising unemployment and falling real wages impaired borrowers' debt servicing capacity and increased the share of non-performing loans (NPL). The average level of NPL in 2011 was 11 per cent, but in Latvia and in Lithuania 20 per cent and in Bulgaria and Romania 15 per cent in Poland was middling with 8.8 per cent reflecting tighter conditions on loans and Slovenia had the lowest level at 5.3 per cent. NPLs were mainly attributable to households rather than corporations as they had been in the SEA economies during the 1997 crisis. And the econometric evidence is clear that the collapse in GDP in the EEE drove the rising levels of NPL (Skarica, 2014; and Klein, 2014). High provisioning for NPL by the banks subsequently reduced their profitability lowering the return on equity from late 2008 further compromising the banks' capacity to lend.

6.5.6 The exposure of Eastern European banks to toxic assets and investor confidence

Five EEE, Estonia, Latvia, Lithuania, Bulgaria and Romania, were overheating prior to the crisis of 2007 and there followed a credit boom-and-bust cycle leading to a current account crisis (Åslund, 2012). An obvious direct cause of the financial crisis could have been changes in the prices of toxic assets in the portfolios of their financial institutions as it had been for WEE banks (Gallego et al., 2010; ECB, 2012). Fortuitously, the EEE had limited exposure to exotic subprime derivatives (mortgage-backed securities and collateralized debt obligations), partly due to their more limited financial sophistication, but principally because domestic lending opportunities presented more profitable opportunities and banking regulations in several countries were tighter than those in either the US or WEE. The most important effects were indirect, therefore, through the deterioration in foreign investors' confidence in the foreign exchange, equity and housing markets in the EEE. These had a major impact, with capital outflows and downward pressure on asset prices, creating a liquidity crunch in the money and debt markets and lower consumption and investment. Nevertheless, the EEE did not have to devalue following and crisis, including those countries that pegged their exchange rates in order to join EMU (Bulgaria, Estonia, Latvia and Lithuania), that also had the largest deficits. Instead they pursued 'internal devaluations', cutting public expenditure and wages that coincidently helped to reduce their current account deficits.

Those economies with floating exchange rates found that depreciating exchange rates drove inflation higher and posed a challenge for banks with larger lending portfolios in foreign currencies and also unhedged borrowers. The crisis impacted on financial institutions through deteriorating credit quality, increasing volumes of NPL that reduced their profitability and problems over capital flows from parent banks despite the existence of the Vienna Initiative 2.0. Money market rates consequently rose, reaching their highest levels in the Slovakia in 2007 and in Lithuania, the Czech Republic, Hungary, Poland and Romania in 2008 clearly linked to the size of their government's budget deficits. Even though the spread on Euro Area sovereign debt started to narrow from March 2009, interest rates remained above pre-crisis levels.

6.5.7 Exchange rate policy and growth during the crisis

The disruptive effect of the financial débâcle sparked by the US subprime crisis was greater on the EEE than on other areas, including SEA and China, and their recovery was much slower. While some economies had vibrant manufacturing industries and sound macroeconomic fundamentals, others were more vulnerable exhibiting credit, consumption and housing booms leading to higher current account deficits. The crisis therefore caused a correction that might have been anticipated beforehand and which changed the growth path of some of the EEE. In addition, their exchange rate policies had a considerable impact on their prospects for future growth.

Some EEE pegged their exchange rates against the Euro, including Estonia, Bulgaria, Latvia and Lithuania, and as a consequence their convergence with the Euro Area took the form of inflation rather than currency appreciation. The credibility of the exchange rate meant that borrowing in foreign currencies increased because interest rates on Euro-denominated loans were lower and in some cases real rates became negative. This served to increase the credit boom as well as those in consumption, construction and housing. The consequence of these developments included rising wages, higher inflation and a growing deficit on the current account.

Those EEE with floating exchange rates received FDI inflows mainly into the manufacturing sector, while those with fixed rates had a higher concentration in the financial and housing sectors. This has implications for the competitiveness of the economies and obviously their industrial capabilities. The reduction in the growth of credit had a major impact on the three Baltic States. But despite the severity of the crisis none of the EEE changed their exchange rate regimes. To deal with the crisis, the pegged exchange rate countries opted for internal devaluation with the emphasis on price and wage cuts the latter, particularly in the public sector where the cuts have been dramatic and accepted with equanimity (Åslund, 2010). The deficits on the current accounts were corrected in the process, but problems with the competitiveness of their economies remained unresolved.

Real wage increases exceeded productivity growth in several EEE in the early 2000s and this problem was acute for those with pegged exchange rates (Darvas, 2011b). Countries with floating exchange rates, with the notable exception of Romania, did better and Poland, Slovakia and the Czech Republic recorded falling labour costs in manufacturing: a similar internal devaluation had occurred in Germany in the late 1990s. Those EEE with pegged exchange rates also had expanding non-tradable sectors where there was a competitiveness gap; the exchange rate under purchasing power parity and adjusted for the Balassa–Samuelson condition, had become overvalued. In consideration of these points, it is generally recognized that all of the EEE needed to improve their competitiveness following the crisis if permanently higher unemployment is to be avoided, most especially in the countries with pegged rates. Competitiveness can also be improved beyond adjustments in prices and wages through the development of better infrastructure (where the EEE are lagging behind their WEE counterparts), fully functioning and competitive markets and improvements in their capacity to absorb Western technology. This presumes that they are not yet in a position to engage in domestic innovation in the immediate future. Greater flexibility on the part of the EU towards the interpretation of the Maastricht criteria for euro entry would also be helpful, especially in terms of membership of the Exchange Rate Mechanism II. Any premature fixing of the exchange rate could damage the catch-up process with the WEE and some countries, including Poland, have asked for derogation from ERMII entry as a condition for EMU.

6.5.8 The role of foreign direct investment into the Eastern European economies

The contribution of FDI to growth in the EEE cannot be underestimated. They opened their banking sectors to international investors to attract capital, increase technical know-how and to improve corporate governance, efficiency and competitiveness. Accession into the EU in 2004 fostered greater capital inflows and progressive financial integration led to an increase in foreign ownership in the banking sector that boosted credit growth and fuelled a pre-crisis boom (Lane, 2008). By 2008 foreign banks owned 80 per cent of the EEE banking assets with major shareholdings by Austrian, German, Italian and French banks and by Scandinavian banks – in particular, in the Baltic States (Gardó and Martin, 2010). The largest share of capital inflows as a percentage of GDP came from FDI and in 2004 the four largest recipient countries were: Bulgaria 10.2 per cent, Romania 8.5 per cent, Estonia 8 per cent, and Slovakia 7.2 per cent) Abiad et al. (2007). By 2007 the top four recipients were Bulgaria 29.4 per cent, Estonia 12.4 per cent, Latvia 8.1 per cent and Romania 5.8 per cent, but during the crisis these rates collapsed with the exception of Estonia where the only blip came much later in 2011. These FDI flows were favoured by EEE governments because they were less volatile and more beneficial to economic growth (von Hagen and Siedschlag, 2008).

Using dynamic panel analysis, Carstensen and Toubal (2004) examined two sets of variables affecting FDI in the EEE. First, *traditional variables*, market size, trade costs, plant and firm-specific costs and secondly, *transition-specific variables*, privatization measured by the share of private businesses in total businesses, the methods of privatization and various risk factors linked to each country. Both sets of variables had a significant impact on FDI. The market potential, low relative unit labour costs, corporate tax rates, level and methods of privatizations, legal, political and economic environment all had a positive and robust impact on FDI. Skilled labour helped to attract FDI because it was important in the implementation of innovative production technologies and the adoption of WEE business culture. The EEE integration into the EU creating a larger internal market with lower trade costs and improved transportation links also attracted FDI into their economies.

In several of the EEE their central banks were institutionally less developed and thus not successful in managing capital inflows and reining in credit growth where necessary, and in limiting the growth in foreign-currency-denominated debt in the early 2000s. Thus, rapid GDP growth was largely based on domestic demand and financed in the main by capital inflows which generated large external imbalances in the EEE already highlighted (Gardó and Martin, 2010). However, the expansionary effects of capital inflows was partially offset by tighter fiscal policy, although this had limited success (von Hagen and Siedschlag, 2008). Also, the FDI inflows only covered the current account deficits in the Czech Republic, Poland, and Bulgaria, whereas

Romania had a balance of payments surplus as a result of strong capital inflows. The Czech Republic, Poland, Slovakia and Slovenia managed to avoid overheating, but Hungary continued with fiscal expansion and sustained higher inflation as a result. Inflation therefore increased with the worst-affected countries Bulgaria and the Baltic States. As wages and house price rose, the economies became less competitive and experienced widening current account deficits. Add to this the financial crisis and the result is collapsing output and rising unemployment. The largest increases in unemployment occurred in the Baltic States and Slovakia, where rates peaked in 2010 above 15 per cent (19.5 per cent in the case of Latvia), remaining elevated until 2014 with only the Czech Republic, Hungary and Romania returning to the average rates they had experienced before the crisis.

A sudden stop in foreign capital inflows arising from a fall in exports from the EEE was accompanied by an outflow of FDI which brought the economies to the brink of their own financial crisis as their current account deficits became unsustainable. Using the sudden stop in capital inflows to date the financial crisis in the EEE, Gallego et al. (2010) nominated September 2008 the date at which Lehman's entered bankruptcy. Evidence that the crisis appeared to be more severe in economies that were either export-oriented or exhibited financial vulnerabilities was deduced by, amongst others, Connolly (2009), Goldstein and Xie (2009), Åslund (2010) and Myant and Drahokoupil (2010). The fast pace of financial and trade liberalization had not been matched by a sufficient structural transformation in their economies or any significant improvement in their levels of productivity growth.

6.6 The macroeconomic policy responses to the crisis in the Eastern European economies

The major responses involved adjustments to fiscal and monetary policy, although some internal devaluations also occurred. The fiscal policy responses differed between the EEE depending on their fiscal balance before the crisis and those countries that received support from the IMF had to adhere to specific tax and expenditure strictures, including reducing the size of the public sector, lowering the wage bill, limiting welfare payments including pensions and lower capital investment. Measures to reduce tax evasion and to widen the tax base formed the revenue side of the required adjustments. Lithuania and Bulgaria's deficits expanded to 4.2 per cent and 9.1 per cent of GDP respectively in 2009/10; the Czech Republic's peaked at 5.5 per cent in 2009; Poland's was elevated above the SGP limit before the crisis and rose to 7.6 per cent in 2010; Romania's and Slovakia's peaked at 8.9 per cent and 7.9 per cent respectively in 2009; Slovenia's reached 5.9 per cent in 2009. Only Poland and Slovenia's deficits did not fall below the SGP limit by 2013, –4 per cent and 14.9 per cent respectively. Slovenia's deficit ballooned in 2013 because of the recapitalization of its banks to avert an international bailout although the deficit fell to –4.9 per cent in 2014 as the banks recovered and tax revenues began to rise.

Poland and the Czech Republic allowed automatic fiscal stabilizers to operate unimpeded and tightened fiscal policy by raising VAT in the case of the Czech Republic and some reduction in discretionary government expenditures in Poland. Nevertheless, public investment increased in Poland due to structural and cohesion funding available from the EU and private investment responded to lower corporation taxes (from 27 per cent to 19 per cent). In seven of the EEE excessive deficit procedures were put in place as their deficits breached the Maastricht fiscal rules and this constrained their room for manoeuvre, but in 2011 Bulgaria's deficit fell below the target, followed by Latvia and Hungary in 2012 and the Czech Republic, Lithuania and Romania in 2013. Slovakia was never subject to the procedure, but reached the target in 2013 after pursuing a proactive fiscal policy, whereas Poland remained above the target for most of the 2000s and Slovenia's deficit, having been below the Maastricht target before the crisis, remained elevated above it between 2009 and 2013. Only Slovenia (80.9 per cent 2014) and Hungary (76.9 per cent) still break the debt target of 60 per cent of GDP.

Turning to monetary policy, very low interest rates and credit growth meant that several countries, those with fixed exchange rates, the Baltic States and Bulgaria, experienced higher inflation before the crisis and, in the presence of Mundell's (1968; Obstfeld and Taylor, 1997) impossible trinity, necessarily followed a restrained monetary policy.[2] Rising real interest rates in Latvia and Lithuania may even have impacted negatively on their growth in the early part of the crisis. Those countries less dependent on external financing and also experiencing lower imbalances, including the Czech Republic, Hungary, Poland and Romania that were inflation targeters, had lower inflation and introduced lower interest rates in 2008 when the crisis struck and systemic risks increased with the collapse of Lehman's. The Czech Republic and Poland also benefitted from currency depreciation. Reductions in interest rates were delayed in Hungary and Romania because of the risks to inflation and the potential for international investors to withdraw financial support to firms and households. There was also the potential for a conflict between monetary and fiscal policy – fiscal tightening and simultaneous monetary loosening. The contraction in interbank lending and rising risk premia plus capital flight meant that the potential for an active monetary policy in most EEE became severely restricted.

6.7 The economic performance of Poland during the financial cisis: Poland's exceptionalism

6.7.1 General comments

Poland's transition was painful, but short-lived. Real GDP fell –14 per cent between the end of 1989 and 1991, but for the rest of the 1990s GDP growth averaged over 5 per cent per annum. In the 2000s, before the crisis, GDP growth averaged 4.5 per cent and the country grew throughout the crisis at a respectable average rate of 3.1 per cent. Unemployment, on the other hand, had remained stubbornly high until the financial crisis in 2008 falling to a low of 7.1 per cent, before rising again and averaging 9.5 per cent down to 2014. Poland has a much higher involuntary unemployment rate, a lower rate of long-term unemployment, and a much higher rate of temporary employment than the Euro Area. Inflation has remained within the target of 2.5±1 per cent since 2002 with elevated rates in 2008, 2011 and 2012 of 4.2 per cent, 4.3 per cent and 3.7 per cent, respectively, no more than 0.7 per cent to 0.2 per cent above the target. In 2013 and 2014, however, with lower oil and food prices, inflation fell to 0.9 per cent and 0.0 per cent, respectively, and averaged –0.225 per cent in the first four months of 2015, but interest rates have been reduced to counter this threat from deflation and further cuts are expected in mid-2015. Investment has averaged 20 per cent of GDP per annum throughout the 2000s, which compares favourably with Hong Kong, Taiwan, Malaysia and the Philippines, but only two-thirds that of Korea and half that of China. The rate of savings, on the other hand, is less than that of any SEA economy and explains the necessity for FDI and other sources of potentially destabilizing inward capital flows. Although exports are less important to Poland's economic growth, the growth of exports averaged 7.5 per cent per annum during the 2000s and 5.2 per cent after the crisis year of 2008. The deficit on the current account of the balance of payments, common to all EEE, was muted in Poland and financed by structural funds from the EU and FDI. The deficit as a percentage of GDP averaged –3.9 per cent between 2000 and 2007 and the same rate between 2008 and 2014. Poland has been subject to the EU excessive deficit procedure, but the primary deficit averaged 1.7 per cent in the 2000s before the crisis and 2.5 per cent after the crisis so no particular cause for concern until the Fiscal Compact takes effect. It should leave the procedure by 2016. The level of debt as a percentage of GDP has remained well below the Maastricht cap, averaging 16.5 per cent throughout the 2000s and then rising to an average of 20 per cent after the crisis. Poland is therefore a remarkable economy, as Table 6.3 illustrates.

Poland was the only EEE to register positive GDP growth throughout the crisis years (averaging 3.1 per cent). Growth fell in 2009, but improved in 2010 and 2011 (to 3.7 per cent and 4.8 per cent, respectively), before falling to 1.8 per cent in 2012, 1.7 per cent in 2013 before rising to 3.3 per cent in 2014. The IMF (2014) forecasts that growth will average 3.5 per cent between 2015 and 2020. Growth was supported by strong domestic consumption, averaging 60 per cent of GDP in the 2000s (linked to increasing disposable incomes and falling unemployment). During the crisis, Poland's unemployment rate was relatively lower than that of the majority of the EEE, only the Czech Republic and Romania had lower rates. (Many new jobs have been created in the manufacturing sector since September 2013.) Polish unemployment is also lower than that in the Euro Area countries.

Positive employment growth is linked to the growth of small and medium-sized enterprises (SMEs) and generous EU and EBRD grants for public investment. In 2010, for example, the Polish Agency for Enterprise Development (PAED) reported that SMEs played a crucial role in the growth of Poland's GDP in terms of employment and consumption, but, equally importantly, made a major contribution to exports. SMEs contributed 46.9 per cent to Poland's GDP in 2008 (microenterprises employing 0–9 workers generated 29.8 per cent of the total, small and medium-sized enterprises employing between 10–49 workers generated 7.3 per cent and 9.8 per cent, respectively). Employment in the SME sector grew by 6.4 per cent in 2009.

According to PAED (2010), seven out of ten workers were employed in small enterprises in 2008. Analysis of the subcategories of SMEs showed that microenterprises reported employment growth of 3.7 per cent, small enterprises 18.6 per cent, medium-sized enterprises 4.9 per cent and large enterprises 4.5 per cent. However, the employment participation rate in Poland remained below the WEE rates by as much as 11 per cent, but during the crisis rose to within 5 per cent of the WEE average. Poland, therefore, enjoys a job-creating recovery.

Table 6.3 Economic data for Poland, 2000 to 2014 (percentage; minus signifies a deficit)

	2000	2001	2002	2001	2002	2003	2004	2005	2006	2007	2008	2009	2010	2011	2012	2013	2014
Real GDP	4.3	1.2	1.4	1.2	1.4	3.6	5.1	3.5	6.2	7.2	3.9	2.6	3.7	4.8	1.8	1.7	3.3
Investment	24.5	20.5	18.4	20.5	18.4	18.8	20.4	19.6	21.5	24.8	24.3	20.2	21.0	22.2	20.6	19.1	20.3
Saving	18.8	17.6	15.7	17.6	15.7	16.3	15.0	17.1	17.6	18.5	17.8	16.2	15.5	17.1	17.1	17.7	19.0
Inflation	10.1	5.5	1.9	5.5	1.9	0.8	3.5	2.1	1.0	2.5	4.2	3.5	2.6	4.3	3.7	0.9	0.0
Imports	15.5	–5.3	2.8	–5.3	2.8	9.6	8.1	6.3	18.1	15.8	9.4	–12.4	14.0	5.5	–0.6	1.8	8.7
Exports	23.2	3.1	4.8	3.1	4.8	14.1	4.9	9.7	15.6	10.2	7.0	–6.3	12.9	7.9	4.3	5.0	5.6
Unemployment Rate	16.1	18.2	19.9	18.2	19.9	19.6	19.0	17.7	13.8	9.6	7.1	8.2	9.6	9.6	10.1	10.3	9.0
Deficit Structural	–4.0	–4.9	–5.3	–4.9	–5.3	–6.0	–5.6	–3.4	–4.8	–2.6	–4.2	–7.1	–7.6	–5.5	–3.8	–3.3	–3.2
Deficit Primary	0.0	–2.2	–2.1	–2.2	–2.1	–3.2	–2.6	–1.2	–1.4	0.2	–1.5	–4.7	–5.1	–2.4	–1.1	–1.5	–1.3
Debt	6.9	13.9	13.4	13.9	13.4	17.6	15.1	15.8	14.9	10.1	9.9	14.7	19.8	24.4	25.6	29.0	22.1
Current Account	–6.0	–3.1	–2.8	–3.1	–2.8	–2.5	–5.4	–2.6	–4.0	–6.3	–6.6	–4.0	–5.5	–5.2	–3.6	–1.3	–1.2

Source: IMF; available at: http://www.imf.org/external/pubs/ft/weo/2015/01/weodata/weoselgr.aspx.

6.7.2 Monetary policy, credit conditions and the real estate market in Poland

The expansion of credit in Poland was relatively lower than that in the other EEE. The Polish Central Bank (PCB) kept interest rates at 6.11 per cent in 2008 (a high rate compared with those set the Federal Reserve in the US of 1.92 per cent that year or, indeed, the rate set by the ECB). The higher rate aimed to control inflation and in Poland rates were generally kept higher and for longer than might have been desirable for investment. Interestingly, fitting a Taylor Rule to Poland's interest rate decisions shows that these were consistent with the Rule as were those in the Czech Republic and Hungary (Maria-Dolores, 2005). The results were confirmed by Clarida et al. (1998) and then just before the crisis by Frömmel and Schobert (2006). Poland's inflation targeting clearly operated in a way that was consistent with the Rule.

The credit to GDP ratio in Poland rose precipitously from 25 per cent in 2004 to 50 per cent in 2009 and posed a risk to financial stability, a problem exacerbated by the expansion in lending in foreign currencies. However, the proactive intervention of the Polish authorities largely mitigated this risk. Earlier in 2007 the Polish Banking Supervision Authority (KNB) had published an Act on Liquidity Risk Management resulting in the volume of lending by Polish banks being lowered twice whereas the regulatory authorities in the other EEE largely ignored the risk. The Polish authorities also passed so-called Resolution Number 386 in 2008 imposing binding liquidity standards on all Polish domiciled banks, whether foreign or otherwise, through effective moral suasion alone.

Furthermore, the resolutions of the Commission on Banking Supervision (KNB) divided assets and liabilities by liquidity and stability in order to manage liquidity risk in Poland. There were four groups of assets: core liquidity, supplementary liquidity, assets of limited liquidity and unique assets. Liabilities were grouped into three broad categories: regulatory capital, stable and unstable external funds. Quantitative and qualitative benchmarks for liquidity were established for all banks with any shortfall to be notified to the authorities and adjustments to restore the benchmark level implemented immediately. By December 2010, in fact, all banks met the requirements (Kruszka and Kowalczyk, 2011). The combined effect of this Resolution put a cap on lending to the corporate sector in particular, effectively limiting moral hazard (and in the process of averting risk corporate lending fell 3 per cent in 2009 and 2010). Loans to the household sector showed the largest growth, rising 21 per cent per annum between 2004 and 2008 – almost twice the rate of growth of loans to the corporate sector.

The volatility of capital flows into Poland, but also into the Czech Republic and Romania, did not warrant IMF-sanctioned capital flow management (CFM) measures as a result of an evaluation of the key determining macroeconomic criteria undertaken by Chowdhury and Keller (2012), including: exchange rate undervaluation, the inadequacy of foreign exchange reserves and a positive output gap. Poland had a floating exchange rate that exhibited neither under- nor over-valuation (misalignment of between –7 per cent and +5 per cent, averaging –2 per cent), more than adequate reserves (a ratio of reserves to short-run debt, the current account deficit and international reserves of 84 per cent or US$100 billion in October 2014) and inflation that had declined from 4.3 per cent in 2011 and growth in bank credit stabilized at a manageable 6 per cent pa.

Between 2004 and 2007 real estate prices in the capital, Warsaw, advanced by more than 100 per cent. Property purchasers in Poland generally benefitted from rising incomes, the easy availability of credit, modest bank margins and, despite the exchange rate risk, the progressive substitution of cheaper foreign currency loans for zloty loans. However, the increase in demand in the real estate sector was coupled with limited supply-side flexibility as property developers reduced their planned investment projects in 2001 for the following three- or four-year time horizon as bank loans became scarcer. Tighter supply, therefore, combined with growing demand resulted in rising prices that suppressed some demand. With a LTV on new mortgages of 80 per cent from 2017 the risk of a house price collapse will be reduced.

6.7.3 Foreign ownership of Polish banks and their financial position, including investment in risky assets

Polish banks had been acquired by foreign financial institutions during the privatization process. In 2009, Poland had 49 banks, 18 branches of foreign banks, 576 cooperative banks and 1,800 credit unions (Kruszka and Kowalczyk, 2011). Foreign owners held major shareholdings in 37 commercial banks, accounting for 68.1 per cent of the total assets in the banking sector. By 2009, Italy controlled 13.3 per cent of banking sector assets, followed by Germany 10.4 per cent, Netherlands 8.6 per cent and France 5.8 per cent. This has proved to be a sufficiently diversified ownership structure to reduce the degree of exposure to economic events in a single country, but not, of course, a Euro Area-wide crisis.

Foreign currency-denominated lending by Polish banks increased as a result of the combination of financial market liberalization and greater foreign investment. Parent banks and the international capital markets provided the inflow which was smaller, but, more importantly, less volatile than that offered to other EEE. FDI was the most stable part of the inflow with one-third going to manufacturing underpinning an accelerated rate of productivity growth. Critically, in the early phase of the financial crisis, foreign parent banks did not transfer liquid assets home; instead, they increased the value of their investment liabilities significantly in 2009 and 2010, contradicting the findings of de Haas and van Lelyveld (2014). The combined strength of the Polish economy and the robustness of the regulatory regime account for this degree of support. And Poland became one of the first countries in the region to regulate foreign exchange (FX) lending through Recommendation S for the management of credit risk.

Recommendation S on Good Practices Regarding Mortgage-Secured Credit Exposures was introduced by the Polish Commission for Banking Supervision in June 2006 and consisted, inter alia, of two elements: (1) It required higher creditworthiness when customers applied for a residential loan in a foreign currency; and (2) It set high standards for disclosing FX-related risks. Banks were advised to offer a Polish zloty loan first, but when the customer insisted on a FX loan they were required to disclose risks associated with FX borrowing risks and a simulation for repayments given specified levels of zloty depreciation and increases in interest rates. The Recommendation was amended in January 2011 with the introduction of maximum levels of loans-to-value ratios, a maximum 25-year repayment period and a cap on repayments at 33 per cent of borrowers' monthly income (Zettelmeyer et al., 2010). This Recommendation also required banks to maintain higher household debt-servicing capacity and lower loan-to-value ratios for consumer and mortgage borrowing denominated in foreign currencies. Additional measures had been taken by the Polish authorities the previous February (2010) through Recommendation T to restrict foreign borrowing by customers with low income using stress-testing analysis (cases where debt repayment would exceed 50 per cent of monthly income). In contrast with the moral suasion of Recommendations S and T, in March 2010 legally binding rules were introduced with the risk weighting attached to retail borrowing in foreign currencies raised from 75 per cent to 100 per cent. These were unprecedented changes, but highly effective measures and the regulatory authorities in the WEE and the UK in particular could learn much from them.

At the beginning of the financial crisis, Polish banks had strong financial fundamentals, including above-average levels of capitalization and consequently survived it rather well. The Polish Financial Services

Authority (PSFA) persuaded the banks not to distribute their 2008 profits to strengthen their balance sheets: the profit retention rate achieved was 100 per cent and this provided a crucial cushion. The capital adequacy ratio for all banks stood at an impressive 12.5 per cent in 2009 and 14.9 per cent in 2014 with Tier 1 capital set at 13.7 per cent, well above the legal requirement. In contrast, the core capital ratio in Western banks had been 2 per cent before the financial crisis and this will only rise to 13 per cent under voluntary Basel III rules. And these will not be fully implemented until March 2019, although the minimum capital requirement will be phased in from 2014. The 13 per cent includes 4.5 per cent common equity, 6 per cent Tier 1 capital and a 2.5 per cent mandatory capital buffer. A further 2.5 per cent counter-cyclical buffer is entirely discretionary.

The Polish Financial Supervision Authority (KNF) guided Polish banks on investments in derivatives and other exotic financial instruments. As a consequence of this guidance and close regulation, toxic assets represented only 0.2 per cent of total financial sector assets at the beginning of the crisis in 2007. Toxic assets did not, therefore, destabilize the Polish banking sector as they had done their counterparts in the US and the UK as well as in many Euro Area countries. The KNF also undertook its own stress tests of Polish banks alongside the ECB's Comprehensive Assessment and established to their own satisfaction that they were resilient to financial shocks.

Poland also organized Flexible Credit Line support from the IMF from May 2009 which was renewed in July 2010 and again in January 2013 (IMF, 2015). While the total amount available in Special Drawing Rights has increased over this period, no drawings have taken place. However, this precautionary measure has enabled Poland to proceed with corrective macroeconomic policies without fear of a speculative attack. Once again this has confirmed the economic foresight of the Polish authorities.

6.7.4 Foreign direct investment in Poland

Poland was one of the region's biggest beneficiaries of inward FDI as a direct result of its macroeconomic and political stability before the financial crisis and it continued to receive FDI both during and after the crisis. It had a significant impact on TFP as noted above. Four key factors attracted FDI to Poland: the ready availability of skilled low-wage labour (a low ratio of labour costs to productivity), high yields on investments, plentiful natural resources and, finally, its pivotal geographical position in Europe, including a long contiguous border with Germany, a major market for Polish goods and a source of investment funds. The major sources of FDI have been Germany (16 per cent of the total), Netherlands (also 16 per cent), Sweden (13 per cent), Luxembourg (11 per cent); in terms of the number of investment projects supported in 2011, 36 originated from the US, 15 from the UK, 14 from South Korea and a further 13 from China. As a destination for FDI, a Europe Attractiveness Survey undertaken by Ernst and Young in 2013, Poland ranked first, ahead of the Czech Republic. In 2012 FDI created over 13,000 jobs supported and 148 new projects (some 22 per cent up over the previous year).

In 2007 the inflow of FDI peaked at US$23bn (on a par with the levels found in Ireland and Sweden). With the emergence of the crises, however, it fell 37 per cent to US$15bn in 2008 and a further 13 per cent to US$13bn in 2009. Nevertheless, it recovered in the following year to US$14bn and US$21bn in 2011 when the stock of FDI had reached 42 per cent of GDP. The major sectors receiving FDI were manufacturing, food processing, electronics and telecommunication, followed by financial services, real estate and retailing. Leven (2012) established that the stability of the financial sector and the housing market together accounted for the rebound in FDI in 2011 (in 2008 mortgages represented 10 per cent of Poland's GDP compared with 18 per cent in the Czech Republic and some 70 per cent in the US). Furthermore, Poland had become a major centre for outsourcing and off-shoring for a large number of multinationals in the critical medium-to-large technology sectors. This development can be linked to the existence of several large cities with well-developed infrastructure and highly competitive operating costs attracting many multinationals. However, despite the apparent robustness of the economy, 2012 witnessed another reversal in FDI as the inflow fell to US$6bn. This represented a drop of 71 per cent attributable in large measure to the Euro Area crisis, but it is expected to be a one-off outflow of capital as the economies of major donors return to growth. This renewed inflow will be facilitated by extensions to existing Special Economic Zones and the development of new ones by the Polish Information and Foreign Investment Agency and the more favourable taxation of corporations.

6.7.5 A measured role for foreign trade

Poland sustained only a modest drop in economic growth at the lowest point in the crisis as global aggregate demand collapsed because the share of exports in GDP (at 33 per cent in 2004) was low compared with that of other EEE. Even though this ratio had risen to 45 per cent by 2012, other EEE were more vulnerable to a downturn in trade because they still had much higher ratios than Poland. The comparable figures for the Czech Republic and Estonia in 2004 were 49 per cent and 69 per cent, respectively, and in 2012 78 per cent and 90 per cent, respectively. Polish exports were more diversified, with the major markets being Germany, other EEE and the Commonwealth of Independent States, meaning that this diluted the risks of a downturn unless it were truly global. Poland, in fact, together with the Czech Republic, Hungary and Slovakia, have developed a particularly robust and diversified supply chain. The potential impact of economic developments more recently in Germany, where growth has slowed, have been exaggerated, according to Elekdag and Muir (2013), who tested the proposition using the IMF's Global Integrated Monetary and Fiscal Model. The EEE, and Poland more specifically, are far more open to shocks from the global economy while Germany provides an anchor for stability in the region.

The growth of exports fell, but imports declined even more – from $176.17bn in 2008 to $49.2bn in 2009 – with the combined effect reducing the trade deficit to –4 per cent of GDP (from –6.6 per cent the year before). The depreciation of the Polish zloty over the same period raised the competitiveness of Polish exports, even if the cost of imports rose. Consequently, the price of consumer goods using imported components increased by almost 10 per cent with the expected inflationary consequences.

Andrle et al. (2013 and 2014) examine the spillover effects of the financial crisis in the Euro Area on Poland in terms of output growth, inflation and the dynamics of interest rates given that half the country's exports are destined for the zone and 60 per cent of the banking sector is controlled by the Area's institutions. The authors use a semi-structural, forward-looking two-country model incorporating cyclical dynamics with real and financial links built in. Their results highlight the susceptibility of the Polish economy to external shocks and indicate that 50 per cent of output volatility and 25 per cent of the country's cyclical inflation dynamics can be explained by developments in the Euro Area alone with flexible exchange rate emerging as playing a crucial stabilizing role over the business cycle. Thus, Poland, and those countries with flexible exchange rate regimes, are more insulated from recent adverse developments in the Euro Area.

6.8 Summary and conclusions

This chapter analysed the impact of the financial crisis on the EEE which experienced an economic boom and bust followed by renewed growth, albeit at a reduced rate. Unlike the WEE, this recovery had been predicted by econometric estimation on the basis of an examination of past crises in transition economies. Their rapid GDP growth had been driven by expanding and essentially unsustainable levels of credit expansion connected to large inflows of FDI, strong growth in world trade and income, a ready export market and easy global liquidity conditions. Growth, as predicted by the neoclassical growth models, was converging with that in the WEE and between 2007 and 2015 five of the EEE joined the Euro Area having satisfied the Maastricht nominal convergence criteria. Slovenia, the first to join, entered EMU just before the Great Recession in 2007. Slovakia joined at the depth of the Recession in 2009 and Estonia followed in 2011. Latvia (2014) and Lithuania (2015) joined as the crisis began to dissipate. That the EEE had been resilient up to 2008Q3 was due to their vulnerability indicators, identified above, being benign with strong fiscal and monetary positions accompanied by favourable international financial market sentiments. Large FDI inflows and rapid credit growth were perceived to be manageable and supportive of the catch-up process with the WEE, while downside risks were contained.

The period of resilience ended with the collapse of Lehman Brothers in late 2008. The prices of stocks, fixed income securities and houses fell in parallel with the decline in world economic growth and trade that impacted severely on the EEE exports. This led to contraction in investment and a decrease in private consumption, accompanied by an increase in unemployment. Credit and deposit growth decreased rapidly and banks were confronted with increasing levels of non-performing loans and lower levels of profitability, but not the growing degree of insolvency experienced by their WEE counterparts which had purchased large volumes of toxic US assets. Policymakers could not pursue structural reforms during the financial crisis because the financial markets were in turmoil and the political climate was hostile. The freeze in international capital markets, for example, prevented any further privatizations. One important issue in the context of the EEE was whether the financial crisis would lead to the cessation of necessary economic policy and structural reforms to correct for institutional shortcomings. Fortunately, the size of the EU and the attraction of entry into EMU continued to act as a powerful incentive for the EEE to continue on the reform path by reinforcing the message of the benefits from the single market programme and supportive macroeconomic policies in both the WEE and the EEE. Against this optimistic backdrop, the improved outlook for growth after 2009Q3 reinvigorated the reform process.

Poland's positive GDP growth throughout the 2000s, and in 2009 in particular, was supported by large and resilient domestic consumption linked to an increase in disposable income and a rising employment rate, limited exposure to the decline in world trade, low levels of exposure to the most severely affected EE and WEE, a flexible exchange rate regime (which facilitated Poland's adjustment to external shocks) and stringent regulations in the monetary and financial sectors. The positive role played by SME and generous EU and EBRD grants for infrastructure investment also made significant contributions to Poland's growth. The favourable geographical distribution of the financial crisis between non-EU countries from Poland's perspective and investment in research and development-enhancing productivity growth protected its economic growth. Poland has proved throughout the 2000s, and particularly during the period of the financial crisis, that it deserves the epithet of an 'exceptional economy'.

Notes

1. The Eastern European economies are: Bulgaria, the Czech Republic, Estonia, Hungary, Latvia, Lithuania, Poland, Romania, Slovak Republic and Slovenia.
2. The 'impossible trinity' refers to the impossibility of a government achieving simultaneously a fixed exchange rate, open capital markets and an independent monetary policy. Only two of the three are possible at any one time.

References

Abiad, A., Leigh, D. and A. Mody (2007) 'International Finance and Income Convergence: Europe is Different', IMF Working Paper 07/64, Washington, DC: International Monetary Fund.

Aghion, P., Harmgart, H. and N. Weisshaar (2010) 'Fostering Growth in CEE Countries : A Country-Tailored Approach to Growth Policy', EBRD Working Paper No. 118, London: European Bank of Reconstruction and Development.

Andrle, M., Garcia-Saltos, R. and G. Ho (2013) 'The Role of Domestic and External Shocks in Poland: Results from an Agnostic Estimation Procedure', IMF Working Paper No. 220, Washington, DC: International Monetary Fund.

Andrle, M., Garcia-Saltos, R. and G. Ho (2014) 'A Model-Based Analysis of Spillovers: The Case of Poland and the Euro Area', IMF Working Paper 14/186, Washington, DC: International Monetary Fund.

Arrabitel, O., Heinz, F., Martin, R., Przybyla, M., Rawdanowicz, L., Serafini, R. and T. Zumer (2007) 'Determinants of Growth in the Central and Eastern European EU Member States – A Production Function Approach', ECB Occasional Paper No. 61, Frankfurt: European Central Bank.

Åslund, A. (2010) *The Last Shall be the First – The East European Financial Crisis*, Washington, DC: Peterson Institute for International Economics.

Åslund, A. (2012) 'Lessons from Reforms in Central and Eastern Europe in the Wake of the Global Financial Crisis', PIIE Working Paper 12/7, Washington, DC: Peterson Institute for International Economics.

Aydin, B. (2008) 'Banking Structure and Credit Growth in Central and Eastern European Countries', IMF Working Paper 08/215, Washington, DC: International Monetary Fund.

Benkovskis, K., Fadejeva, L., Stehrer, R. and J. Worz (2012) 'How Important is Total Factor Productivity for Growth in Central, Eastern and Southeastern European Countries?', Working Paper No. 5, Department of Latvijas Banka, Vienna Institute for International Economic Studies and Foreign Research Division of Oesterreichische Nationalbank.

Berglof, E., Korniyenko, Y., Plekhanov, A. and J. Zettlmeyer (2009) 'Understanding the Crisis in Emerging Europe', EBRD Working Paper, no. 109, London: European Bank for Reconstruction and Development.

Berkmen, P., Gelos, G., Rennhack, R. and J. Walsh (2009) 'The Global Financial Crisis: Explaining Cross-Country Differences in the Output Impact', IMF Working Paper 09/280, Washington, DC: International Monetary Fund.

Caporale, G., Rault, C., Sova, R. and A. Sova (2009) 'Financial Development and Economic Growth: Evidence from Ten New EU Members', Discussion Paper no. 940, London: Brunel University.

Carstensen, K. and F. Toubal (2004) 'Foreign Direct Investment in Central and Eastern European Countries: A Dynamic Panel Analysis', *Journal of Comparative Economics*, 32(1), pp. 3–22.

Chowdhury, I. and L. Keller (2012) 'Managing Large-Scale Capital Inflows: The Case of the Czech Republic, Poland and Romania', IMF Working Paper 12/138, Washington, DC: International Monetary Fund.

Chudik, A. and M. Fratzscher (2011) 'Identifying the Global Transmission of the 2007–2009 Financial Crisis in a GVAR Model', *European Economic Review*, 55(3), pp. 325–39.

Clarida, R., Galí, J and M. Gertler (1998) 'Monetary Policy Rules in Practice: Some International Evidence', *European Economic Review*, 42(6), pp. 1033–67.

Connolly, R. (2009) 'Financial Vulnerabilities in Emerging Europe: An Overview', BOFIT Working Paper, no. 3, Helsinki: Bank of Finland.

Connolly, R. (2012) 'The Determinants of the Economic Crisis in Post-Socialist Europe', *Europe–Asia Studies*, 64(1), pp. 35–67.

Cottarelli, C., Dell'Ariccia, G. and I. Vladkova-Hollar (2005) 'Early Birds, Late Risers, and Sleeping Beauties: Bank Credit Growth to the Private Sector in Central and Eastern Europe and in the Balkans', IMF Working Paper 03/213, Washington, DC: International Monetary Fund.

Darvas, Z. (2011a) 'Beyond The Crisis: Prospects For Emerging Europe', *Comparative Economic Studies*, 53(2), pp. 261–90.

Darvas, Z. (2011b) 'Exchange Rate Policy and Economic Growth After the Financial Crisis in Central and Eastern Europe', *Eurasian Geography and Economics*, 52(3), pp. 390–408.

de Haas, R. and S. Knobloch (2010) 'In the Wake of The Crisis: Dealing with Distressed Debt Across the Transition Region', EBRD Working Paper no. 112, London: European Bank for Reconstruction and Development.

de Haas, R., Korniyenko, Y., Pivovarsky, A. and T. Tsankova (2014) 'Taming the Herd? Foreign Banks, the Vienna Initiative and Crisis Transmission', *Journal of Finanical Intermediation*, 24(3), pp. 325–55.

de Haas, R. and I. van Lelyveld (2014) 'Multinational Banks and the Global Financial Crisis: Weathering the Perfect Storm?', *Journal of Money, Credit and Banking*, 46(1), pp. 333–64.

Dietrich, D., Knedlik, T. and A. Lindner (2011) 'Central and Eastern European Countries in the Global Financial Crisis: A Typical Twin Crisis?', *Post-Communist Economies*, 23(4), pp. 415–32.

Ėgert, B., Backė, P. and T. Zumer (2006) 'Credit Growth in Central and Eastern Europe: New (Over)Shooting Stars?', ECB Working Paper no. 687, Frankfurt: European Central Bank.

EBRD (2009) *Transition Report: Transition in Crisis*, London: European Bank for Reconstruction and Development.

ECB (2012) *Convergence Report*, Frankfurt: European Central Bank.

Elekdag, S. and D. Muir (2013) 'Trade Linkages, Balance Sheets, and Spillovers: The Germany-Central European Supply Chain', IMF Working Paper 13/210, Washington, DC: International Monetary Fund.

Eurostat (2015) http://ec.europa.eu/eurostat/data/database.

Friedrich, C., Schnabel, I. and J. Zettelmeyer (2010) 'Financial Integration and Growth – Is Emerging Europe Different ?', EBRD Working Paper no. 123, London: European Bank for Reconstruction and Development.

Frömmel, M. and F. Schobert (2006) 'Monetary Policy Rules in Central and Eastern Europe', Discussion Paper no. 341, School of Economics and Management, University of Hannover.

Furceri, D. and A. Zdzienicka (2011) 'The Real Effect of Financial Crises in the European Transition Economies', *Economics of Transition*, 19(1), pp. 1–25.

Gallego, S., Gardó, S., Martin, R., Molina, L. and J. M. Serena (2010) 'The Impact of the Global Economic and Financial Crisis on Central Eastern and South Eastern Europe (CESEE), and Latin America', Occasional Paper Series, Banco de Espana, Madrid.

Gardó, S. and R. Martin (2010) 'The Impact of Economic and Financial Crisis On Central, Eastern and South-Eastern Europe: A Stock Taking Exercise', ECB Occasional Paper Series, no. 114, Frankfurt: European Central Bank.

Goldstein, M. and D. Xie (2009) 'The Impact of the Financial Crisis on Emerging Asia', paper prepared for the conference on 'Asia and the Global Financial Crisis', sponsored by the Federal Reserve Bank of San Francisco Santa Barbara, 18–20 October.

IMF (2014) *Economic Outlook: Legacies, Clouds, Uncertainties*, Washington, DC: International Monetary Fund.

IMF (2015) http://www.imf.org/external/pubs/ft/weo/2015/01/weodata/weoselgr.aspx.

IMF (2015) *Republic of Poland: Assessment of the Impact of the Proposed Flexible Credit Line Arrangement on the Fund's Finances and Liquidity*, Washington, DC: International Monetary Fund.

Kaminsky, G. and C. Reinhart (1996) 'The Twin Crises: The Causes of Banking and Balance of Payments Problems', International Finance Discussion Papers no. 544, Board of Governors of the Federal Reserve System, March.

Kaminsky, G. and C. Reinhart (1999) 'The Twin Crises: The Causes of Banking and Balance-of-Payments Problems', *American Economic Review*, 89(3), pp. 473–500.

Klein, N. (2014) 'Non-Performing Loans in CESEE: Determinants and Impact on Macroeconomic Performance', IMF Working Paper no. 13/72, Washington, DC: International Monetary Fund.

Kruszka, M. and M. Kowalczyk (2011) 'Macro-Prudential Regulation of Credit Booms and Busts: The Case of Poland', Policy Research Working Paper, no. 5832, Washington, DC: World Bank.

Lane, P. R. (2008) 'The Macroeconomics of Financial Integration: A European Perspective', Discussion Paper no. 265, Institute for International Integration Studies, Trinity College, Dublin.

Leven, B. (2012) 'The Impact of Global Recession on FDI – Poland's Case Study', *International Journal of Business and Social Science*, 3(13), pp. 60–6.

Lütz, S. and M. Kranke (2013) 'The European Rescue of the Washington Consensus? EU and IMF Lending to Central and Eastern European Countries', *Review of International Political Economy*, 21(2), pp. 310–38.

Maria-Dolores, R. (2005) 'Monetary Policy Rules in Accession Countries to EU: Is the Taylor Rule a Pattern?', *Economic Bulletin*, 5(5), pp. 1–16.

Mihaljek, D. (2010) 'The Spread of the Financial Crisis to Central and Eastern Europe: Evidence from the BIS Data', in R. Matousek (ed.), *Banking and Financial Markets in Central and Eastern Europe after 20 Years of Transition*, London: Palgrave Macmillan, pp. 5–31.

Mundell, R. (1963) 'Capital Mobility and Stabilisation Policy Under Fixed and Flexible Exchnage Rates', *Canadian Journal of Economics and Political Science*, 29(4), pp. 475–85.

Myant, M. and J. Drahokoupil (2010) *Transition Economies: Political Economy in Russia, Eastern Europe, and Central Asia*, London: Wiley-Blackwell.

Obstfeld, M. and A. M. Taylor (1997) 'The Great Depression as a Watershed: International Capital Mobility in the Long Run', National Bureau of Economic Research, Working Paper 5960.

PAED (2010) *Enterprise the Polish Way*, Warsaw: Polish Agency for Enterprise Development.

Reinhart, C. and K. Rogoff (2009) *This Time is Different: Eight Centuries of Financial Folly*, Princeton, NJ: Princeton University Press.

Skarica, B. (2014) 'Determinants of Non-Performing Loans in Central and East European Countries', *Financial Theory and Practice*, 38(1), pp. 37–59.

Spence, M. [and twenty others] (2008) *The Growth Report: Strategies for Sustained Growth and Inclusive Development*, Commission on Growth and Development, Washington, DC: World Bank.

Svejnar, J. (2002) 'Transition Economies: Performance and Challenges', *Journal of Economic Perspectives*, 9(1), pp. 3–28.

von Hagen, J. and I. Siedschlag (2008) 'Managing Capital Flows: Experiences from Central and Eastern Europe', ADB Institute Discussion Paper no. 103, Tokyo: Asian Development Bank Institute.

Zettelmeyer, J., Nagy, P. and S. Jeffery (2010) 'Addressing Privtate Sector Currency Mismatches in Emerging Europe', EBRD Working Paper no. 115, London: European Bank for Reconstruction and Development.

7

China Confronts the Great Recession: 'Rebalancing' Neoliberalism, or Else?

Dic Lo
SOAS, University of London, UK

Abstract: This paper posits that China's economic transformation since the turn of the century has tended to converge to what can be called the Golden Age Model. Characteristic of the model is rapid growth in productive investment, and therefore productivity and wage growth, underpinned by the institutional nexus of 'Big Business, Big Labour, and Big Government'. The convergence to the Golden Age Model has been seriously hindered by neoliberal-oriented policies over the past few years, so much so that there is a real danger of the Chinese economy being subject to the full rigour of the Great Recession. The prospects for the future depend, thus, on the rivalry between the political-economic forces behind the two models. And the outcome of the rivalry will be of fundamental importance given the fact that China has already become a globally significant centre of production, holder of financial resources, and carrier of outward direct investment.

Keywords: China, economic transformation, Golden Age Model, neoliberalism

JEL Classification: O11, O53, P26

7.1 Introduction

In 2008–09, amid the unfolding of the US financial crisis and the ensuing Great Recession worldwide, China's good economic performance (and its role in sustaining world development) was widely praised by both domestic and international public opinions. Optimism over the future prospects prevailed. Now, by 2014–15, things have changed and pessimism seems to have become predominant. Indeed, the actual economic performance since 2012 has declined substantially: there has been a slowdown in economic growth, the development of property bubbles, an accumulation in financial risks and debt burdens, the threat of deflation, the policy dilemma faced by the state, and so on. This atmosphere of pessimism seems to have reached its culmination in March 2015 when, in the National People's Congress (the Parliament), the government officially announced its target of annual economic growth for 2015 at the rate of 7 per cent – down from the actual rate of 7.4 per cent in 2014, which had been the lowest for more than two decades.

There is a specific policy line that has thus been promoted by the media, the international establishments, and sections of the Chinese authorities. This centres on the pair of notions of 'restructuring' and 'rebalancing'. Restructuring implies policy measures of austerity and market reforms, for coping with the accumulated financial risks. Rebalancing, meanwhile, is meant to sustain an acceptable pace of economic growth. This focuses on raising internal demands vis-à-vis external demands, and raising consumption at the expense of investment in internal demands. The 'New Normal', a catchphrase that has by now become central to official discourses, is the underpinning of this policy line. The dominant interpretation of this catchphrase goes in the following way: that the dynamism of long-term economic growth has already been seriously weakened, so much so that rapid economic growth is no longer sustainable – even an acceptable pace of growth requires obtaining 'reform dividends'.[1]

In a sense, this catchphrase can be understood as the latest version of the 'China story' in line with the Washington Consensus. It contends that the model of China's economic growth over the previous three decades was not intrinsically sustainable in the first place, that fundamental restructuring and rebalancing are needed in order to make growth sustainable, and that any deviation from such restructuring and rebalancing is unreasonable and will only result in disasters. The conclusion thereby follows: the restructuring and rebalancing, and Chinese economic transformation in general, must be in the direction of converging to the neoliberal model, that is, the model of a financialized free market economy.

How valid is this 'China story'? And how reasonable is the policy made on the basis of this story, not only for coping with financial risks but also for promoting long-term economic (and social) development? Note that the emphasis on restructuring and rebalancing, instead of state expansionary policy, is tantamount to dismissing the strategy of 'growing out of debts'. Yet it is precisely this strategy ('expanding public investment to stimulate growth, thereby reducing debts') which helped China to escape from its economic predicament in the period 1998–2001, following the East Asian financial and economic crisis. And the condition of public finance in 2008 or in 2014, in terms of the much lower ratio of public debts to GDP as well as the existence of public assets to back up the debts, was in fact far superior to that in 1998.[2]

Viewed more closely, the essence of the strategy of 'growing out of debts' is to stimulate economic growth by means of debt-financed government investment in infrastructure, hoping that the resulting economic growth will be more than proportionate to the growth in debt – thereby leading to decreases in the debt-to-GDP ratio. This strategy was antithetical to the policy recommendations of the Washington institutions, which typically call for austerity in the form of cutting back on government expenditures and liquidating unviable commercial banks. In the event, the strategy proved very successful in bringing the Chinese economy out of the difficult conditions in the period 1998–2001. What appeared to be unexpected, however, is that the strategy also helped to produce the outcome of the trend of development known as '*guo jin min tui*' ('the state sector advances, whilst the private sector retreats'), simply because of the close relationship between government investment and the expansion of state-owned enterprises.

Long term, as will be explained and argued below in this chapter, Chinese economic transformation from the late 1990s to the present day has been in fact in opposition to the rationale of market-driven restructuring and rebalancing. In view of its structural dynamics and institutional attributes, it has rather tended to converge to what can be termed the 'Golden Age Model', that is, the model of social and economic development that prevailed in advanced capitalist countries in their Golden Age (circa 1950–1973). It is the neoliberal orientation of state policies since 2008 that has fundamentally undermined this convergence. The future prospects for China's economic transformation thus hinge on the rivalry between the political-economic forces behind the two contrasting models.

The objective of this chapter is to look into the future prospects for Chinese economic transformation, based on an integrated analysis of both the major policy issues over the years of the Great Recession and the underlying long-term structural-institutional dynamics. Specifically, the chapter seeks to analyse the dynamics, and actual developmental performance, of the process of Chinese economic transformation from the turn of the century until the present time. On this basis, it further seeks to clarify the developmental implications of the rivalry between the alternative scenarios as represented by the two indicated models.

This chapter is organized in seven sections, of which this introduction is the first. Section 7.2 depicts the main aspects of Chinese economic performance during the Great Recession. This is meant to provide the general background for the subsequent theory-based, in-depth analyses. Section 7.3 summarizes the main arguments of the mainstream interpretation of the 'New Normal', and contrasts the arguments with the reality. Section 7.4 then turns to analyse the efficiency and sustainability of the prevailing, capital-deepening path of economic growth, highlighting both its advantages and its limitations. Section 7.5 relates the attributes of the growth path to the boarder structural-institutional nexus. It is submitted that the coherence of the growth path and the nexus exhibits a strong tendency of converging to the Golden Age Model. Section 7.6 returns to analyse the issues of short-term performance and policies. It highlights the likelihood that the indicated convergence could be blocked by the 'neoliberal turn' in the policy arena since the outbreak of the Great Recession. Section 7.7 summarizes and concludes the chapter.

7.2 Chinese economic performance during the Great Recession

Chinese economic performance during the Great Recession appears to be respectable, at least by international comparison. It is the case that the annual rate of output growth fell sharply, from an average of 10.6 per cent in the years 2002–11 to levels that are in the range between 7 per cent and 8 per cent in the latest years of 2012–14. This slowdown in growth is more serious than that in the previous downturn in 1998–2001, the years when China was hard-hit by the East Asian financial and economic crisis. And the recorded growth rate of 7.4 per cent in 2014 is the lowest recorded since the early 1990s. Nevertheless, such a growth rate is still sufficient to achieve the target of doubling the size of the economy over the next ten years.

In terms of international comparisons, in the period 2008–13, the expansion of China's per capita GDP appears to have substantially outpaced all other comparable economies ('comparable', that is, whether in terms of level of development or size of the economies). The scale of expansion is 63 per cent for China, 26 per cent for the average of all low-and-middle-income economies, and less than 1 per cent for the group of high-income economies. Other members of the BRICS grouping – that is, the grouping of representative 'emerging economies' composed of Brazil, Russia, India, China and South Africa – have varied scale of expansion, but all of them are substantially below those of China: 35 per cent for India, 14 per cent for Brazil, 10 per cent for Russia, and 5 per cent for South Africa. In view of this performance, it seems appropriate to judge that, at least up until the end of 2014, there was no trace of the Great Recession in China.

But is the pace of expansion of the Chinese economy, in its own right or relative to comparable economies, set to last over the long term? Or is the sharp growth slowdown since 2012 a symptom of the long process of expansion approaching its termination? These are the crucial questions which this paper seeks to answer in the subsequent sections. The economic performance itself gives little clue as to the answer to this question. The concern repeatedly expressed by the Chinese state leadership over the threat of deflation, for instance, is no more than based on inferences from the short-term performance of price movements. It is the case that the general price level has fallen sharply since 2011, with the investment price index falling to near-zero growth and the producer price index falling into the region of negative growth. But this is not at all unprecedented. The price fall in 2008–09 was steeper than this time round. Even the previous experience of deflation, in the years 1998–2002, did not result in prolonged economic stagnation. There is not sufficient evidence, therefore, to suggest that the ongoing growth slowdown is to persist into the long term.

To answer the aforementioned questions requires ascertaining whether the ongoing growth slowdown represents a cyclical movement, or a long-term trend. It requires putting the short-term performance in long-term (and theoretical) perspectives. The remaining part of this section is purported to depict some further characteristics of the short-term performance that are considered to be of long-term importance, thus serving to provide the general background for the subsequent theory-based, in-depth analyses.

A commonly adopted approach is to examine the process of rebalancing in the Chinese economy over the years of the Great Recession. In this regard, there are discernible complexities. At one level, internal demand substituting for external demand seems to have taken effect, as it is evident in the sharp decrease of net exports as a proportion of aggregate expenditures: from the previously highest level of 8.8 per cent in 2007 down to 2.4 per cent in 2013. Insomuch as this substitution is due to the weakening of the international competitiveness of Chinese manufacturing exports, multiple factors are likely to have been at work, most notably the appreciation of the Chinese currency and the rising costs of production in China (the appreciation in the real exchange rate is likely to have been greater than the appreciation in the nominal exchange rate, in view of the rising labour costs during this period). Meanwhile, at another level, the expected rebalancing in the domestic front – consumption substituting for investment – has not occurred. In fact, the opposite has actually been the case: Consumption as a proportion of aggregate expenditures has continued to decrease, whereas the investment share of aggregate expenditures has continued to increase. The consumption shares have remained at below 50 per cent levels from 2007, compared with the 50 per cent-plus levels for most of the years in 1993–2006 and the 60 per cent-plus levels for all the years in the period 1978–92. These trends of evolution might point to some important forces being at work in the Chinese economy.

One possible reason for the continuous decrease in the consumption share of aggregate expenditures concerns income distribution. Specifically, as is in line with well-established economic theories, and as has been widely perceived as the reality in China, the continuously declining share of labour compensation in national income has been held responsible for the decrease in consumption as a proportion of aggregate expenditures.[3] The labour share of national income decreased continuously, from a level of almost 60 per cent in 1992 to exactly 50 per cent by 2005. Thereafter, the share has always stayed at below-50 per cent levels – the decrease has accelerated over the years of the Great Recession. In this connection, there are two points of note regarding the implications of this trend of evolution. First, even if the causal relationship between labour compensation and aggregate consumption is established, it need not lead to the outcome of the slowdown of economic growth. It only defines the character of the growth path, rather than determining the pace of growth. The pace of growth itself depends on the efficiency of the resulting investment-led growth path. This will be analysed in details in the subsequent sections. Secondly, insofar as the declining labour share is a distributive issue, it needs to be placed in the boarder context of Chinese political economy. It is the state that has remained the major capital owner in China, and, at least legally and in principle, the state is representative of the people. Again, this political-economic issue will be discussed later in the subsequent sections.

The preceding discussion helps to clarify the evolving character of the 'demand regime' of Chinese economic growth. Turning to the 'productivity regime', it is noted that the investment-led growth path has been associated with visible and substantial progress in this respect. A simple, input-side indicator is research and development (R&D) expenditure as a proportion of GDP. Data from the World Bank's *World Development Indicators* (accessed 30 March 2015) indicate that the ratio for China in the year 1996 was of the value 0.6. It then increased continuously, reaching a level of 1.4 by 2007, and then increasing further to the level of 2.0 by 2012. The pace of increase exceeded the average of all low-and-middle-income economies, by a wide margin, where the value of the ratio was 0.9 in 2007 and 1.2 in 2001. Expressed as a ratio to the same indicator of all high-income economies, the Chinese figures were 26 per cent, 61 per cent and 85 per cent, respectively, for the years 1996, 2007 and 2012. A process of rapid catching-up is clearly evident.

Meanwhile, another important aspect of the development of the productivity regime concerns investment in infrastructure. Tremendous expansion of investment in infrastructure has always been a salient characteristic of Chinese economic development, particularly at times of downturn. In the years of the Great Recession, from 2008 until the present time, the investment focused on building up a network of railways that is of world importance in terms of its frontier technology, that is, the high-speed rail system. Rapid development has persisted throughout the years of the Great Recession. In a similar manner, the tremendous expansion of the internet-using population has continued unabated in recent years – far outpacing the average of low-and-middle-income economies, and rapidly catching up with the standards of high-income economies. In terms of the indicator of internet users per 100 people, Chinese performance was on a par with the average of all low-and-middle income economies in 1999: both being 0.7, in comparison with the number of 20.3 for high-income economies. By the year 2006 the figures for China, all low-and-middle income economies, and high-income economies, increased to 10.1, 8.4, and 56.5, respectively. Thereafter, China far outperformed the rest of the developing world and caught up rapidly with the advanced countries. By 2013, the figures for the three entities had increased to 45.8, 29.1, and 78.2, respectively. The Chinese figure was equivalent to 59 per cent of high-income economies, compared with that of 37 per cent for all low-and-middle-income economies.

What has been the role of policy efforts in the actual economic performance depicted above? What policies have been used, and in what measures? To verify the association of policy efforts and the achievements and shortcomings of China's actual economic performance during the Great Recession, it is necessary first to consider the state of public finance in the perspective of its long-term evolution. Figure 7.1 shows the trends of government revenue and expenditure, expressed as ratios to GDP. One point is clear from the figure: that the government ran sizeable deficits by substantially increasing its expenditures in the years 2008–14. This suggests that the government did make efforts to

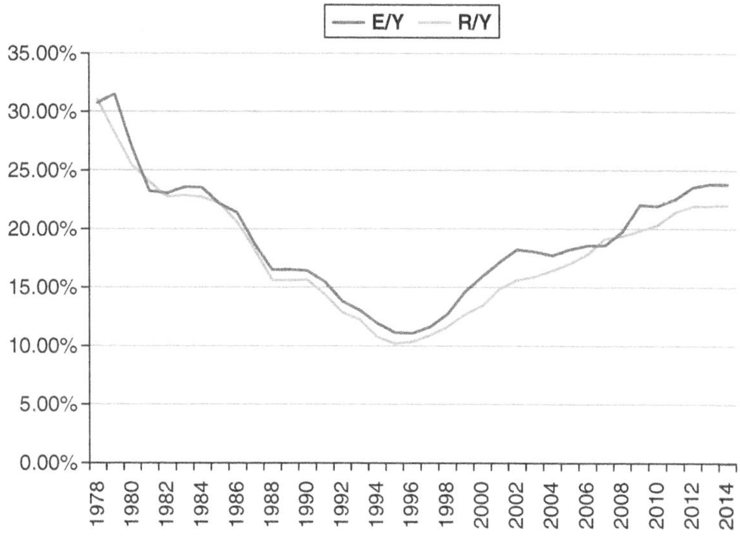

Figure 7.1 Government revenues and expenditures (as ratios to GDP, %)
Note: R = revenues; E = expenditures; Y = GDP.
Sources: *China Statistical Yearbook* 2014; and *Statistical Communique on the National Economy and Social Development in 2015*.

stem the adverse impact of the Great Recession. The employment of the policy efforts can be seen as a repeat of the actions it took in successfully bringing the economy out of the adverse impact of the East Asian financial and economic crisis, that is, the strategy of 'growing out of debts', which entailed massive government investment in infrastructure for the purpose of stimulating economic growth. Yet the fact that the repeat endeavour this time round is substantially smaller in scale than the previous one, as is indicated by the smaller scale of the deficits relative to the size of the economy, indicates the limit of government efforts in accounting for the actual economic performance since 2008.

In contrast to direct government fiscal policy, indirect monetary and financial tools seem to have played a more important role in accounting for the actual performance of the Chinese economy since 2008. It is spectacular that the M2 money supply increased from a stock that is equivalent to 150 per cent of GDP in 2007 to 193 per cent in 2014. The stock in 2014 was three times that in 2007. Meanwhile, it is even more spectacular that the stock of total social financing to the real economy (TSF) increased from an equivalent of 127 per cent of GDP to 206 per cent. The stock in 2014 was 3.9 times that in 2007 (Figure 7.2).

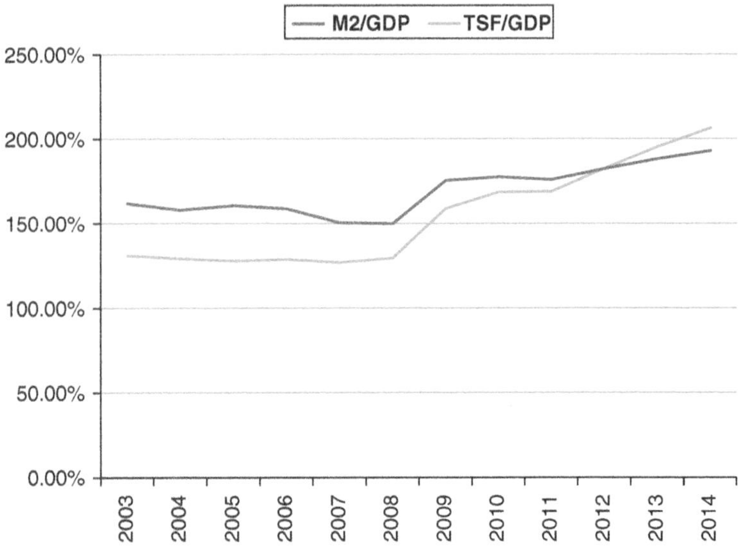

Figure 7.2 Money supply (M2) and stock of total social financing to the real economy (TSF), as ratios to GDP

Notes: M2 definition of money supply and TSF are year-end outstanding figures. The initial stock of TSF, for the year-end of 2003, is IMF estimate.

Sources: *China Statistical Yearbook* 2014; and *Statistical Communique on the National Economy and Social Development in 2015*; IMF (2014) 'People's Republic of China: 2014 Article IV Consultation', IMF Country Report no.14/235.

A process of tremendous financial expansion was at work during this period. It was also a process of financial innovation, given the fact that from 2012 onwards an expanding share of the stock of TSF does not fall into the scope of the money supply in its hitherto broadest measure.

Concerning the Chinese 'shadow banking' sector, an official estimate of the total scale put it at a level of around 10 per cent of GDP as of early 2014.[4] In this connection, the scale of local government debts has also attracted widespread concerns. Based on the data obtained from the official auditing of a sample of local governments, estimates of the total scale as of 2012 year-end varies between 23 per cent and 29 per cent of GDP. In comparison, central government debts at that time were equivalent to 14.5 per cent of GDP. Thus, as of 2012 and 2013, total state sector debts as a ratio to GDP probably exceeded 50 per cent. This is substantially below the 70 per cent-plus levels in the time of the East Asian crisis, but, at any rate, it is still a rather serious problem.[5]

From the depictions above in this section, it can be concluded that the Chinese economy has performed reasonably well in the years 2008–14, but it is not at all free of problems, either short-term or long-term. The continuous improvement in its productive capacity offers an optimistic outlook. Yet the possibility still cannot be ruled out that the growth slowdown might well be a long-term trend. The threats of deflation and excessive monetary expansion might be short-term issues, but they could still undermine the potentials of long-term development. All of these do not imply that the government has been taking a hands-off approach. What they do suggest is that, to account for the actual performance and to ascertain the future prospects for long-term development, one needs to consider the broader structural-institutional context within which the government plays its role in the economy.

7.3 The 'New Normal' of the Chinese economy: claims and realities

The interpretation of the catchphrase the 'New Normal' is diverse, its theoretical underpinning is obscure, and the analyses and judgements thereof are made from a range of intellectual-political orientations. Nevertheless, it is possible to identify a mainstream interpretation that is composed of six interrelated arguments.[6] The first three, essentially neoliberal-oriented, arguments are:

- First, the accumulation of financial risks and debt burdens is the result of the weakening of the growth dynamism of the productive sector – rising cost, low efficiency, excess capacity, and so on, ultimately showing up in the form of decline in profitability.
- Secondly, the weakening of growth dynamism has been mainly caused by the exhaustion of 'demographic dividends', that is, the growth slowdown in the supply of 'cheap labour'.
- Thirdly, fundamental market reforms ('reform dividends') will be needed to maintain an acceptable pace of growth, because the Chinese economic system is grossly inefficient. Past economic growth has been achieved despite, not because of, this system.

At a more concrete level, concerning the exhaustion of the dynamism of economic growth, three further arguments can also be discerned:

- Fourth, the dynamism behind Chinese economic growth over the previous three decades is not 'cheap labour' per se, but rather the 'super-exploitation of labour' – and this super-exploitation has now reached its (social and physical) limit.

- Fifth, underconsumption: because of super-exploitation, the Chinese economy has been in a constant state of worsening imbalances. Consumption as a proportion of national income has continued to decrease, making economic growth increasingly dependent on investment and export.
- Sixthly, because relying on investment as the ultimate driving force of economic growth has its intrinsic limits, export dependence has become characteristic of the Chinese economy. And the Great Recession worldwide implies that this reliance can only cause severe impact on Chinese economic growth.

Consider Argument One. This is advanced not only by neoliberals but also by a number of Marxist scholars. Neoliberal economists typically consider capital flows from the productive sector to speculative activities, in pursuit of profits, as perfectly normal and as an indication of allocative efficiency. Insofar as bubbles emerge to threaten the economy, they argue that this must be caused by market distortions, and that therefore market liberalization is the answer. The Marxist scholars typically follow the theoretical tradition of Henryk Grossman in arguing that financial expansion is the outcome of a decline in profitability in the productive sector. Hence, they have reached the same pessimistic judgement over the state of the Chinese economy.[7] But the judgement does not appear to fare well in the light of the existing evidence. Taking industry as representative of the productive sector, its profitability is far from undergoing a trend of secular decline. If anything, there has been a rising trend since the late 1990s and the economic downturn in recent years has not fundamentally reversed this trend. The industrial profit rate, defined as the ratio of total pre-tax profits to total capital (that is, the net value of fixed assets plus circulating capital), increased continuously from the hitherto lowest level of 6.2 per cent in 1998 to the highest level of 18.0 per cent in 2011, before declining only slightly to 15.2 per cent in 2013.

Nor are Arguments Two and Four sufficiently and empirically grounded. As will be explained below, in terms of the character of economic growth, Chinese economic transformation during the era of market reforms can be divided into two periods. In the first half of the era, from the late 1970s until the mid-1990s, economic growth was associated with a process of labour-intensive, consumption-led industrialization. Then, in the second half of the era, from the mid-1990s until the present time, a process of capital-deepening, investment-led industrialization has characterized economic growth. It is easily observable that, throughout the entire reform era, the immediate driving force of economic growth has always been improvement in labour productivity, rather than the growth in labour supply. Between 1978 and 2013, for more than three decades, per worker GDP grew at a very fast rate of 8.3 per cent per annum in real terms. And there is a trend of acceleration of growth, evident in the increase of the average annual real growth rate from 6.7 per cent in the period 1978–92 to 9.3 per cent in the period 1993–2013 (Table 7.1).

Conceptually, there can be three different sources of improvement in labour productivity. The first possible source is a lengthening of per-worker working hours and increasing work intensity, that is, increasing the exploitation of labour. Given the physical limits to workers, it is unlikely that this source has significantly accounted for the productivity improvement of that pace and duration, as indicated in Table 7.1. The second possible source is the transfer of labour from the rural-agricultural sector to industry-services, the latter being characterized by much higher levels of productivity. This is likely to have been of importance; existing estimates put it as high as accounting for 40 per cent of actual improvement in labour productivity (Dorrucci et al. 2013). But, note that this process of labour transfer is almost a uniquely China phenomenon on the world scale over the era of globalization. The existence of surplus labour in the rural-agricultural sector, a structural characteristic of many developing economies, is only a necessary condition for the transfer. The transfer has been associated with a fast process of industrialization-urbanization in China, which necessarily entails sufficient productive investment. The third possible source is technological progress. Productive investment, by raising the capital–labour ratio, is likely to have been the main source of improvement in

Table 7.1 Average growth rate of real GDP and total labour employment (%)

	(a) **Real GDP**	(b) **Total employment**	(a)–(b)
1978–2013	9.77	1.47	**8.30**
1978–92	9.39	2.67	**6.72**
1993–2013	10.02	0.72	**9.30**
1993–2002	9.83	1.03	**8.81**
2003–13	10.18	0.45	**9.73**

Source: *China Statistical Yearbook* 2014.

labour productivity associated with technological progress. Conceivable mechanisms include embodied technical change, as well as dynamic efficiencies such as learning by doing, economies of scale and scope, and organizational efficiencies.

Rapid growth in productive investment, and with it the persistent rise in the investment–GDP ratio, is one of the salient characteristics of Chinese economic transformation over the reform era (Figure 7.3). This characteristic is at any rate spectacular on the world scale: the ratio of gross capital formation to GDP has been well above 35 per cent in most years. It is also noteworthy that since the mid-1990s the pace of investment growth has tended to accelerate. In other words, a capital-deepening path of economic growth has prevailed since then – in contrast to the labour-intensive path in the first twenty years of the reform era. The concurrent acceleration of productivity growth, as

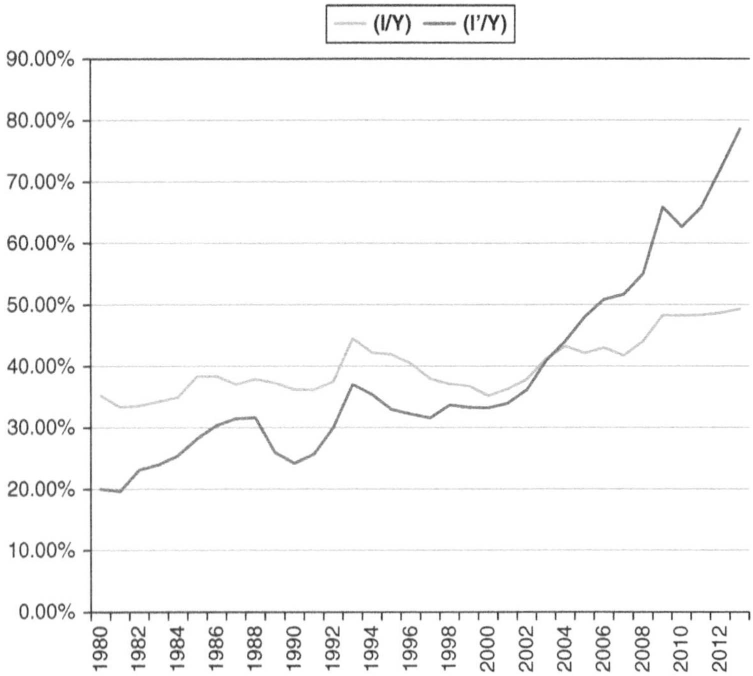

Figure 7.3 Investment–GDP ratio (%)
Note: I = gross capital formation; I′ = total fixed asset investment; Y = GDP.
Source: *China Statistical Yearbook* 2014.

indicated above in Table 7.1, appears to indicate the efficiency advantage of this capital-deepening path.

In this connection, and before moving on to discuss the sustainability and developmental implications of the capital-deepening growth path (Argument Five), it will be helpful to deal with the aforementioned Argument Six concerning export dependence. There are indeed serious concerns associated with this latter argument. One concerns the so-called 'global imbalances': that China's sizeable current account surplus is a symptom of the fact that its economic growth is structurally dependent on the demand of the world market. Top US financial officials such as Ben Bernanke and Lawrence Summers have asserted that 'global imbalances' were crucial conditions for the eruption of the financial crisis, and have concluded that China was a cause of the imbalances.[8] Another concerns China's accumulation of huge official foreign exchange reserves: it suggests the inability of domestic demand to absorb the economic surplus that underpins the reserves, and hence the need for supporting foreign (chiefly US) consumers as a means for absorbing China's economic surplus.[9]

The notion of export dependence is actually analytically akin to the neoliberal theory of export-led growth. It implies that the sustainability of economic growth hinges on a comparable pace of export expansion – or even on continuously increasing the ratio of trade surplus to the national output. But this judgement clearly contradicts the reality. Trade surplus as a share of China's aggregate expenditure has generally been modest. It is only in the years 2004–07 that the share became large by international comparison, reaching the peak level of almost 9 per cent in the year 2007. In fact, in the ten years or so before 2004, and the years after 2007, the share did not exceed 3 per cent most of the time. And the trade deficit was predominant earlier, in most years of the first half of the reform era – that is, 1978–92. In view of these numbers, it is hard to claim that export dependence is a structural characteristic of the Chinese economy.

Scholars such as Akyüz (2010) and Zhu and Kotz (2011) have argued that the gross measure of net exports might understate China's export dependence, because some of the imports are destined for domestic consumption, and that it is necessary to take into account the possible crowding-in effect of exports on domestic investment and consumption. These arguments might contain elements of truth. Yet they have to be balanced by a perhaps even more significant factor. This is the fact that China's trade surplus has been mainly accounted for by processing trade – that is, international trade characterized by China importing parts and components, assembling into finished products, and re-exporting the products to the world market. Indeed, for most of the years since the early 1990s, the surplus in processing trade has even exceeded the total surplus of China's foreign trade. And the contribution of processing trade to the Chinese economy has been relatively modest. A rough estimate can be computed by assuming that the domestic value-added ratio of processing trade is equal to the ratio of net-to-gross export. This ratio stood at 45 per cent at its peak in the year 2009, and the value-added so computed is only equivalent to 5 per cent of GDP in that year. This is hardly compatible with the proposition of export dependence. What can be more reasonably inferred from this observation is that the Chinese economy is in fact of a dualistic structure. The sector of processing trade is no more than an enclave, and it is not really large enough to lead to export dependence for the Chinese economy as a whole.

In the subsequent sections we turn to a detailed discussion of the remaining two Arguments – Five and Three.

7.4 The sustainability and developmental implications of capital-deepening growth

As indicated above, with the exception of the years 2004 to 2007, Chinese economic growth has been underpinned by domestic rather than external demand. Within domestic demand, the share of consumption in aggregate expenditure has decreased continuously. It decreased from 60 per cent-plus in the first half of the era (1978–92) to 50 per cent-plus in the second half (1993–2007), and further to below-50 per cent levels after 2007. Yet all these do not necessarily imply that economic growth has thereby been bogged down in a state of underconsumption. After all, rapid economic growth has been sustained over more than three decades in the reform era, or at least almost two decades from the mid-1990s onward, amid the prevalence of capital-deepening industrialization. The crux is that investment growth has been fast enough to more than compensate for the relative sluggishness of consumption growth.

Theoretically, there is no certainty regarding the sustainability, or otherwise, of such a growth path that is based on 'producing investment goods for producing investment goods' (the so-called 'Feldman–Manalanobis–Domar model'). There is some certainty, however, that for this growth path to be sustainable, it requires a fast enough pace of technological progress to offset the tendencies of diminishing marginal productivity of capital and diminishing demands for the existing products.[10] The question of sustainability, therefore, is ultimately an empirical question. And, as indicated in the previous section, with reference to Table 7.1, productivity growth in the Chinese economy has been very fast since the late 1970s and particularly since the mid-1990s.

Compared to the labour-intensive path of economic growth, the capital-deepening path since the mid-1990s has achieved not only faster productivity growth but also better results in social development. It has been more, rather than less, favourable to consumption growth. Table 7.2 shows the real growth rate of total consumption and investment. In the period 1978–92, the average annual growth rate of consumption (deflated by the consumer price index) was 8.7 per cent, close to the investment growth rate (deflated by the investment price index) of 8.9 per cent. Entering the period 1993–2002, consumption growth remained at the same rate of 8.7 per cent, amid the acceleration of investment growth to reach a high rate of 11.1 per cent. Thereafter, in the period 2003–13, consumption growth also accelerated to reach a high rate of 10.4 per cent, although not as high as the 14.6 per cent rate of investment growth. At any rate, looking at the long-term trends, it is perfectly justified to say that an average annual real growth rate of consumption by 9.2 per cent for the entire period of 1978–2013 cannot be judged as unsatisfactory. The record in 1993–2013 and especially in 2003–13 indicate that the capital-deepening path of economic growth has been associated with the acceleration, rather than the slowdown, of consumption growth. In other words, the gains in economic growth have been successfully translated into raising the living standards of the society as a whole.

Productivity improvement and accelerated consumption growth have also been associated with an enhanced capacity of the economy in job creation, defying the capital-deepening character of the growth process. In the Chinese statistical system, agricultural labour is assumed to be

Table 7.2 Consumption and investment: average annual real growth rates (%)

	Consumption	Investment
1978–2013	9.22	11.26
1978–92	8.73	8.87
1993–2013	9.56	12.89
1993–2002	8.65	11.06
2003–13	10.39	14.58

Note: Consumption and Investment (that is, gross capital formation) are both components of aggregate expenditures. Their real growth rates are calculated by using the consumer price index and fixed asset investment price index, respectively, as the price deflators.
Source: *China Statistical Yearbook* 2014.

in full employment. To verify the job creation capacity of the economy needs to look at the transfer of labour from agriculture to industry and the services sector. In the period 1978–92, employment in the secondary and tertiary sectors increased, on average, by 11.2 million persons a year. The number increased to 12.1 million in the period 1993–2013. And, in the sub-period 2003–13, the number was 14.5 million, indicating a trend of acceleration of growth.

The agricultural share of employment has registered an even faster pace of decrease since the mid-1990s. In the later period of 2005–12, the agricultural share of employment decreased by a hefty 13.3 percentage points. This was accounted for mainly by the acceleration of labour absorption by the secondary sector (that is, industry plus construction), whose share of employment increased by 7.8 percentage points over the same period. The fact that there were still problems with urban unemployment was due to the even more rapid pace of urbanization during this period: agricultural employment decreased, on average, by a hefty magnitude of 11.9 million people a year, compared with the figure of 2.9 million a year in 1993–2004 and that of a net increase of 7.4 million a year in the period 1978–92.

Finally, capital deepening and productivity improvement, together with changes in the social-political environment, has further resulted in rises in labour compensation from the late 1990s onward – a reversal of the trend of persistent stagnation that occurred in the previous period. This reversal is clearly evident in the comparison of the trend of the average annual real growth rates of the wage rate in the urban-formal sector (*cheng zhen zhi gong*) and that of per capita real GDP. All the way from the late 1970s to the late 1990s, wage growth lagged persistently behind the growth of per capita GDP. This divergence reached its most serious stage in the years of mass privatization and mass layoffs in 1993–97, when the slowdown in wage growth was accompanied by an acceleration in per capita GDP growth. It is from 1998 onward that the wage growth has outpaced per capita GDP growth. Meanwhile, beside the performance of the urban-formal sector, data from the National Bureau of Statistics, as well as from various surveys, indicate that the wage rate of secondary and tertiary employees as a whole has also registered rapid growth in recent years.

The trend of rising wage rates, in conjunction with the rapid growth in productivity and employment, suggests a healthy pattern of economic and social development. Achieving the twin targets of sustained rapid economic growth and compensation-enhancing employment expansion has always been the prime objective of China's state leadership and the demand of the society as a whole. From the analysis above, it is evident that the twin targets have been essentially achieved since the turn of the century. This is in contrast to the situation in the first half of the reform era, where rapid economic and employment growth was associated with sluggish growth in labour compensation. The transition from labour-intensive growth to capital-deepening growth since the mid-1990s has substantially speeded up the growth in labour compensation, while sustaining – indeed accelerating – the rapid productivity and employment growth. This is a far cry from the dominant, neoliberal interpretation of the 'New Normal'.

7.5 China converging to the 'Golden Age' model'?

Simultaneous growth in productivity and the wage rate, and in consumption and investment, are precisely the defining characteristics of the development model in advanced capitalist economies in the Golden Age of 1950–73. Central to the model is the existence of a series of structural-institutional conditions that underpin persistent growth in productive investment.[11]

Theoretically, the structural dynamics of the model manifests itself in two crucial aspects. In production, the model requires parallel growths in the capital–labour ratio and labour productivity. In distribution, it requires parallel growths in labour productivity and the wage rate. The combination of these two aspects results in stable shares of labour and capital in total output, which results, in turn, in parallel growths in consumption and output. The end result is a stable profit rate, which is the foundation of the persistent growth in productive investment (and therefore economic growth) – at least in a capitalist setting.

What will happen if the required conditions do not hold? In the realm of distribution, a balance tipping to the wage rate could lead to profit squeeze, while that tipping to labour productivity could lead to underconsumption or over-accumulation. Either way, the result could be investment stagnation and therefore the slowdown of economic growth. In the realm of production, labour productivity growth is a necessary condition for growth in the capital–labour ratio. To sustain this necessary condition requires enhancing work intensity and gaining economies of scale, along with truly technological change. To make it a sufficient condition requires restrictions on allocation outlets of resources that are alternatives to productive investment (that is, the predominance of speculative financial activities in the economy).

The structural dynamics reported above require, correspondingly, a particular set of institutional arrangements as its underpinnings. Both for enhancing work intensity and gaining economies of scale, the existence of 'Big Business', that is, large-scale enterprises in oligopolistic markets, is required. But 'Big Labour', that is, collective bargaining, would then be needed as a countervailing force – in order to ensure wage growth catching up with productivity growth (and hence consumption growth catching up with output growth). Insofar as wage growth lags behind, 'Big Government', that is, the welfare state, will need to come out as the remedy. Government promotion of productive investment, and restriction on alternative allocation outlets, is also needed insofar as productivity growth is insufficient to induce productive investment (hence role of the 'Military-Industrial Complex', state-owned enterprises, and so on).

The structural-institutional nexus characterized above does not necessarily ensure long-term economic growth and near-full employment. Even if growth of consumption and investment do occur, the effect of the nexus still depends on the potential of productivity improvement. Theoretically, this potential hinges on two conditions: the balance between consumption and investment growth, and the appropriate technological-organizational condition. Historically, the Golden Age Model does have the tendency to generate the outcome of excessive investment and underconsumption. This characteristic is similar to that of the Feldman–Manalanobis–Domar model of economic growth. In the circumstances where product innovation is not fast enough to counteract this tendency, outward investment becomes an important solution. With regard to the technological and organizational aspect, both theoretically and historically, the weakening of growth dynamism is typically associated with the bureaucratization of the institutional arrangements of 'Big Business, Big Government, and Big Labour'.

At any rate, the Golden Age was characterized by sustained rapid economic growth and near full employment over a long period of time – although it is likely to have been the exception rather than the norm in the history of capitalism. The associated economic model is a far cry from the free market model of neoliberalism that has prevailed in our times, that is, the era of globalization. The Golden Age Model is not simply a matter of entailing intensive and extensive state intervention in the economy in the form of 'Big Government'. It is a system of outright suppression of the working of 'factors markets', defying the requirement for flexibilities in the labour and capital markets. In contrast, the era of globalization is also an era of financialization, where speculative financial activities have gained increasing predominance in the economy. The requirement for providing capital the maximum freedom to move around in pursuit of maximum profitability, and hence the freedom to dissociate itself from the productive sector, is antithetical to the Golden Age Model.[12]

What is the relevance of the Golden Age Model, and the neoliberal free market model, to late development? The existing literature on late development has been dominated by the debate over the role of the state, and specifically of state industrial policy, in promoting industrialization and economic growth. The renowned debate over comparative advantage-following (CAF) versus comparative advantage-defying (CAD) strategies, is a case in point (see the exchange in Lin and Chang, 2009). But analysing the CAF-CAD characteristics of structural change might be insufficient for establishing the role of industrial policy. Theoretically, it could be argued that a CAF path of structural change is in line with the principles of the market, that is, principles of relative scarcity, although it begs the question as to whether the market in reality can actually produce such outcome. Even so, it does not follow that a CAD path of structural change must be the product of state intervention, or, more specifically, of state industrial policy. In a world of increasing returns and demand-led productivity growth, the demand regimes matter in shaping the path of structural change. Meanwhile, the industrial policy literature is also about the conditions for the working of alternative strategies. In particular, there is the further debate on the developmental state versus crony capitalism. The analysis of the conditions within which one set of characteristics – short-term profit orientation, long-term developmental concerns, as well as rent-seeking and crony capitalism – dominate the others, is necessary for establishing the role of the state in the process of late development.

The same caution is needed when judging the efficacy of the neoliberal doctrines in their promotion of the free market model. The canonical policy doctrine of the Washington Consensus with respect to industrialization, of 'trade regime neutrality', hinges on the assumption that technological transfer, and thereby economic development, is an automatic outcome of the market. This doctrine is consistent with standard neoclassical growth theory. But, even within neoclassical economics, the mainstream of theories of endogenous technological change suggests that technology is mainly the product of investment, and business investment typically premises on some degree of exclusive rights over the utilization of the product. Hence, technological development necessarily requires the existence of a policy-institutional environment that is not confined to the market.[13]

More recently, a modified position from the Washington institutions has been advocated by the then World Bank chief economist Justin Yifu

Lin, and shared by economists like Dani Rodrik and Joseph Stiglitz. The central proposition is that structural change in line with the principle of comparative advantage (that is, CAF) might not always materialize, because of market failures in delivering the necessary technological development. There thus follows the need for some forms of market-friendly government intervention to foster industrialization. It requires government actions to overcome the failures of the market, as an entity, in realizing the principle of the market – the principle of comparative advantage, and of relative scarcities in general (see Lin 2010).

Yet another position that distances further from the orthodoxy is the theories of industrial policy, associated with the work of Amsden (1989), Chang (1994) and Wade (1990). The central proposition is that industrialization is more than realizing the principle of comparative advantage, given the importance of dynamic increasing returns and economies of scale and scope in economic development. Hence, there is the need for market-supplanting government intervention to foster industrialization, that is, to deliberately distort the market in order to promote technological development. The precise means can vary, but the general point is for the government to create 'economic rents' (in a clearly-defined duration), which are awarded to firms with good performance in technological and economic development (Chang 2009).

Finally, the position of theories of the 'national innovation system', most clearly framed by Lazonick (2004, 2009), puts technological development at the centre of industrialization. The central proposition is that, in the era of information revolution, the precondition for late development is the building up of not just production capacity as such, but rather the innovation capability for absorbing, assimilating, and improving upon imported technology. This requires the existence of a range of long-term oriented business institutions, in addition to government promotion.

It is of note that, for the various positions summarized above, there is a progressive shift from pure theory to realism. The Washington Consensus and the modified positions from the Washington institutions implicitly assume a pure market – that is, the market of Walrasian general equilibrium analysis as typically presented in standard microeconomic textbooks – within which productivity-improving structural change takes place. The theories of industrial policy and the 'national innovation system', in contrast, are more aware of the complex and shifting nature of the world market in reality. In particular, in recent years, there has emerged an influential contention that the process of globalization, including North–South economic relations, has been increasingly shaped by financialization (Wade 2006, 2008). The rising predominance of speculative financial activities implies a tendency of short-termism, that is, capital is increasingly forced to minimize fixed investment and demand 'flexibility' in the productive sector (especially in labour employment).

From the perspective of developing economies, therefore, solely relying on the working of the market might make it difficult for their industries to move out of the assembling stage, and to move up the value-added ladder. More important, in the context of financialization and the associated pressing demand for flexibility, developing economies need to find the appropriate ways to raise their productivity sufficiently fast in order to avoid being stuck in the 'race to the bottom' type competition in the world market.[14] The imperative thus arises for a holistic approach in achieving late development, that is, the need for a coherent structural-institutional nexus that is oriented towards productive investment. This brings the discussion back to the appropriateness of the Golden Age Model, contra the neoliberal free market model, for late development – specifically for China in the face of the Great Recession.

Turning to China, and with reference to the two rival models characterized above, a question naturally arises: what has accounted for the sustained rapid growth in productive investment, and, therefore, the prevalence of the capital-deepening path of economic growth? Undoubtedly, this has been in large measure related to the leading role of the state in the economy, so much so that the structural-institutional nexus of the economy has come to be known as 'state capitalism/socialism, Chinese style'. The arrangement of the system of public finance has been geared towards promoting infrastructure investment. The research and development of frontier and strategic technology have been driven mainly by state promotion or inducement. State banks, which have continued to dominate Chinese finance as a whole, have been instrumental to productive investment. Finally, state-owned enterprises (SOEs) have hitherto continued to be the main carriers of the structural dynamics of Chinese economic transformation as characterized above. The trend of development dubbed *guo jin min tui* (the state sector advances, while the private sector retreats), which has been visible since the late 1990s, testifies to this situation.[15]

Compared with Chinese economic entities of other types of ownership, SOEs, by their nature, are in a much better position to fit with the prevailing path of capital-deepening growth. After more than three decades of reform (in particular, the mass privatization drive in the 1990s), what remain of Chinese SOEs today are mostly, large-scale, capital-intensive, and technologically advanced enterprises. A pattern of specialized division of labour is thus in existence between SOEs and non-SOEs, where the latter are mostly labour-intensive enterprises. It is observable that, in industry, SOEs' capital share has tended to exist their output share. The opposite is the case when their share of employment is compared to their output share. And both of the two discrepancies have largely widened since the late 1990s. By 2012, SOEs accounted for approximately 55 per cent of fixed capital, 14 per cent of labour employment, and 35 per cent of value-added in Chinese industry as a whole. The capital–labour ratio of SOEs was 7.5 times that of non-SOEs in that year.

Outside of industry, in the rest of the Chinese economy, the pivotal role of SOEs has hitherto also appeared to be firmly established. The annual survey by the business association the China Enterprise Confederation reveals that, in 2012, up to 62 per cent of the largest 500 firms (both industry and non-industry) by sales values were SOEs. Of the top 40 firms, all but one (number 39) were SOEs. The sales value of SOEs within the top 500 was, on average, 2.78 times that of non-SOEs. Moreover, in the same year, 86 Chinese firms (mostly SOEs) entered the rank of top 500 in the world. This number was 24 more than Japan's and was equal to the combined number of Germany, the UK and France.[16]

Back to the broader picture of 'state capitalism/socialism, Chinese style', in addition to promoting productive investment, state orientation towards constructing a welfare state has been evident and indeed has made tremendous progress since the turn of the century. Within a ten-year period, 2003–13, a publicly-funded healthcare system was (re-) established to cover almost the entire population. Provision of affordable housing for the urban low-income people, mostly immigrants from rural areas, has also been on the government agenda. Most far-reaching, there has emerged a new policy line that emphasizes labour compensation-enhancing economic growth, rather than growth based on 'cheap labour'. Policy measures of this nature have included increasing the protection of labour rights, the enforcement of proper employment contracts, the implementation of minimum-wage legislation, and the promotion of the establishment of trade unions in business establishments of all kinds including subsidiaries of transnational corporations.

It is of note that, from the late 1970s up until the turn of the century, the Chinese state leadership basically adopted a laissez-faire approach towards labour employment, particularly outside the state sector. This is evident in the declining influence of the only existing official trade union the All-China Federation of Trade Unions. Union members as a proportion of the total of employees within the secondary and tertiary sectors decreased from 49 per cent in 1981 to 29 per cent in 2000. The situation has changed since then. As a proportion of the total of employees with the secondary and tertiary sectors, union membership climbed back to a level of 36 per cent in 2005 and then further to 53 per cent by 2013. The rebound in unionization owes much to the enforcement by the central government of the stipulation that enterprises of all types of ownership are required to allow for the setting up of unions or for workers joining unions. This requirement has for a long time been sternly resisted by local governments, by private employers, and, most notably, by foreign capital-funded enterprises. Yet, from the point of view of the state leadership, this is essential to the promotion of collective bargaining over labour compensation. And collective bargaining is, in turn, considered to be indispensable for establishing an economic growth path that enhances labour employment compensation.

The prevailing structural-institutional nexus in the Chinese economy deviates fundamentally from the neoliberal ideal of the free market economy. Yet the paradox is that the nexus has simultaneously achieved the following outcomes, all on unprecedented scales: rapid output and productivity growth, rapid expansion in consumption, rapid increases in job creation, and rapid rises in the wage rate. All these have provided the necessary material conditions for broader social development: the fundamental enhancement of the power of labour, the reconstruction of a publicly funded comprehensive healthcare system, and the acceleration of the process of urbanization. Thus, the assertion that this nexus must be dismantled, and that China must take the neoliberal policy prescriptions for its future economic transformation, does not appear to be convincing at all.

7.6 The neoliberal turn and politics

The Neoliberal Model, or the model of the free market economy, holds the promise of the 'natural path of development', meaning in every point of the path there is optimality in resources allocation. The three generations of the policy doctrines of the Washington Consensus – market and trade liberalization, the privatization of public assets and services, and financialization of the economy – all centre on this promise. But there is a question concerning the consistency of the policy doctrines. Specifically, is speculation tantamount to productive investment, and market liberalization tantamount to financial liberalization?

Much has been said about the benefits that have been brought to China from its market reform and, particularly, its integration into the world market. Indeed, it is generally agreed that China's fast productivity growth over the era of globalization owes much to the technology transfer and industrial relocation from the advanced capitalist countries. This almost-consensus view is analytically akin to the neoliberal theory of export-led growth. It is also consistent with the critical theory of undercutting, which posits that because of the fact that China has absorbed an exceedingly large share of the transferred technology and relocated industry, the rest of the developing world has had difficulty in transcending the predicament of de-industrialization.[17]

In view of the intrinsic contradictions of the world capitalist economy as proposed in the relevant critical literature, however, the indicated technology transfer and industrial relocation are not necessarily conducive to world development – not even to the economies that receive the technology and industry. The crux is that technology transfer and industrial relocation from the advanced countries is motivated by profitability decline, and ultimately by demand deficiency in their home markets. The transfer and relocation are bound to create new productive capacity in the recipient economies. Hence, for the world economy as a whole, the transfer and relocation in effect amount to delaying rather than solving the problem of over-accumulation, and the problem is prone to become increasingly serious in subsequent periods. In this context, late developing economies that integrate themselves into the world market by means of receiving the transfer and relocation will bear the brunt of world economic crises or severe fluctuations once the problem of over-accumulation could no longer be delayed (Harvey 2005, 2010). In this light, the so-called global imbalances can be understood as a result of the technology transfer and industrial relocation. The cost inflicted on China in the global imbalances and the resulting financial crisis and economic recession can be understood as the price for the way through which China integrates itself into the world market.

Central to the transition in the advanced capitalist world from the Golden Age to the era of neoliberal globalization is the financialization of the economy. This process is characterized by the rising predominance of speculative financial activities, which also implies capital increasingly dissociating from the productive sector. Financialization thus embodies an intrinsic contradiction: the speculative pursuit of profits tends to crowd out productive activities, thereby resulting in systemic demand deficiency and undermining the sources of profits. Yet, despite the intrinsic contradiction, the paradox is that financialization has actually been sustained for a prolonged period, at least up until the outbreak of the crisis in 2007. Key to resolving the paradox is the concept of 'accumulation by dispossession' as developed by Harvey (2005, 2010), that is, cheapening productive inputs by means of neoliberal policies at both the national and international levels. Put another way, capital accumulation in the era of globalization is based mainly on the incorporation of productive resources that had been previously outside the capitalist world economy. The policy doctrines of the Washington Consensus – particularly those concerning the liberalization of international finance – are means to serve this ultimate end of accumulation by dispossession. The sustainability of capital accumulation, therefore, hinges on the balance between the damages caused by speculative financial activities, on the one hand, and the supports provided by dispossessing activities, on the other hand.

But the process of financialization is prone to accelerate over time, just like any other speculative activities. The financial crisis that erupted in 2007–08 and the Great Recession that followed are unlikely to reverse the process of accumulation by dispossession. To the contrary, advanced capitalist countries have the incentives to press for the acceleration of this process. It is conceivable that, even in the circumstance that the financial crisis and the Great Recession are to persist, assertions such as 'we need more globalization, not less' are likely to be back in vogue in the international arena in the future. These are precisely what have been recommended to China in the name of restructuring and rebalancing under the New Normal.

In China, neoliberal resistance to the production-oriented structural-institutional nexus depicted in the preceding section, takes the form of the sporadic emergence of financial bubbles. This reflects the inclination of capital to evade state restrictions on speculative activities and, more fundamentally, to dissociate itself from productive investment in order to pursue short-term profits. Since 2008, financialization and the expansion of speculation have indeed largely weakened the dynamism of the Chinese economy in its convergence towards the Golden Age Model. What have prevailed are asset bubbles, systematic risks, and austerity in policy orientations.

A case in point is the ballooning property bubble. This can be gauged by looking at the trend of expansion of total fixed-asset investment (*FAI*), which broadly encompasses property investment (*PI*) and gross capital formation (*GCF*). More precisely, by definition, $FAI = (GCF - SSI - IAI) + PI + IV$, where SSI = small-scale investment, IAI = intangible asset investment, and IV = inventory investment. Given that *SSI* and *IV* are of very small magnitudes in recent years, the difference between fixed asset investment and gross capital formation can thus serve as a somewhat underestimated measure of property investment. As was already indicated in Figure 7.3, before 2004, *GCF* persistently exceeded *FAI* by a substantial margin. The situation has been reversed since then, with *FAI* in excess of *GCF* reaching a gigantic magnitude of around 30 per cent of GDP in 2013. Conversely, the fact that the ratio of *GCF to GDP* remained basically unchanged in the years 2009–13 suggests that bubble-type property investment might have crowded out productive investment, and this might have in a large measure accounted for the slowdown in economic growth in recent years.

The judgement that the property investment boom might have been a bubble is reinforced by looking at the evolution of 'total social financing to the real economy' (TSF). This indicator encompasses bank loans and a wide range of alternative forms of financing, carried out by a wide range of non-bank financial institutions. In the years 2003–08, the ratio of TSF to GDP remained basically unchanged. Thereafter, it surged from 129 per cent in the fourth quarter of 2008 to reach 207 per cent by the first quarter of 2014. And the increases were mainly accounted for by non-bank financing activities. In comparison, because most banks are under much tighter government controls and regulations, controls over bank lending are also much tighter than other forms of finance – although unregulated shadow banking activities by the banks have also become a serious issue in recent years. It is thus to some extent reasonable to infer that, in a relative sense, bank lending is more supportive of productive investment and less prone to be involved in financial bubbles. This being the case, the evolution of the scale and composition of TSF suggests that an increasingly significant proportion of financial resources have been allocated to non-productive activities. This inference is made clearer if the focus is placed on the increments of the components of TSF. Whereas the increments of net bank lending as a proportion of GDP have remained at basically the same level of around 15 per cent all the times, the increments of TSF as a proportion of GDP have increased from 16.7 per cent in 2002 to 22.2 per cent in 2008 and then further to 30.4 per cent in 2013. Taking into account that a sizeable proportion of bank lending probably also leaks out of productive investment via shadow banking, at least half of TSF probably has been allocated to non-productive uses in recent years. No wonder, therefore, there have been complaints from productive enterprises of widespread shortage of financial supports since 2011.

Such is the policy line after 2008, which has been aimed at rebalancing, restructuring, and reaping 'reform dividends'. The danger imposed by the property bubble is not only a tendency of 'crowding out' productive investment, but also a tendency towards debt and financial crises. In the face of this latter danger, since 2013 the Chinese government has focused its efforts on 'deleveraging'. One influential interpretation of this policy line posits that it is the productive sector, rather than the financial sector, that has caused the current predicament. It is claimed that the attractiveness of productive investment has tended to diminish due to demand imbalances and factor market rigidities associated with the prevailing capital-deepening growth path. It is further claimed that fundamental financial liberalization should help to both correct the imbalances and promote the better allocation of resources. Thus, a reorientation of the structural-institutional nexus of the Chinese economy towards the neoliberal model, after all, is claimed to be the only correct direction (Dorrucci et al. 2013; IMF 2014, 2015; OECD 2014; World Bank 2012).

Are there elements of truth with the promise of the neoliberal doctrines, and, more generally, the promise of the convergence to the financialized free market model? In view of the actual experience of world development under globalization, these promises do not seem to hold. The era of globalization has actually been associated with very unsatisfactory developmental progress. Between 1980 and 2013, the average annual real growth rate of per capita GDP for all low-and-middle-income economies combined is 2.8 per cent. This pace of growth is slower, rather than faster, than the rate of 3.0 per cent over the previous decades of the 1960s and 1970s. Moreover, in the 1980–2013 period, there was actually a trend of serious uneven development within the developing world. East Asia experienced a tremendous acceleration of economic growth, over and above the respectable performance pre-1980. South Asia exhibited a similar trend, albeit of a substantially smaller scale. The average annual growth of low-and-middle-income economies outside East Asia and South Asia is close to the very modest rate of 1 per cent, for fully 33 years. It is no exaggeration to call the era of globalization, especially the 1980s and 1990s, the 'lost decades of development'. And the development lost occurred 'in spite of policy reforms', that is, in spite of the worldwide reforms aimed at converging to the neoliberal model.[18]

There has been, in a sense, somehow an uprising even within the Washington institutions against the fully-fledged neoliberal model. What has been promoted by the less-than-fundamentalists since the late 1990s is something like the free market model plus market-friendly government interventions minus financialization. This promotion owes much to lessons derived from East Asian development. The so-called Post Washington Consensus, coined and promoted by Stiglitz (1996, 1998) at the turn of the century, is based on the theory of information-type pervasive market failures, particularly the unavoidable failures of the financial market. Otherwise, it is desirable – indeed indispensable – for developing economies to integrate themselves into the world market, as is claimed to be exemplified by both the miracle and crisis in East Asian development. Bhagwati (2004, chapter 13) delivers essentially the same message when, using East Asia as the chief example, he advocates 'free trade, but not free capital flows'.

Lin's (2010, 2013) promotion of the policy doctrines of what he calls the New Structural Economics (NSE) represents the latest attempt of the less-than-fundamentalists. Financialization has no role to play in the NSE doctrines. Instead, what has been promoted is a return to the first-generation doctrine of the Washington Consensus, centring on free market and free trade. And the promise thereof is, once again, the stages-approach to comparative advantages, that is, the 'natural path of development'. It is claimed that this promise has successfully materialized in the East Asian experience, in the form of the 'flying-geese pattern of international development', and that the same pattern can be achieved in the broader developing world. It is precisely with this understanding that Lin has been sanguine on Chinese economic growth under the 'New Normal', and on world development amid the rising importance of China as a capital and technology supplier to other developing economies (particularly to Africa). In his view, Japan, South Korea, and the like, at the time when their per-capita income level was as China's today, continued to enjoy another twenty years of fast growth. Such a normal pattern, or natural path, is most likely what China is heading on today. Indeed, Lin has repeatedly asserted that, if China is going to enter an era of the 'New Normal', the normalcy of this era is such that it will still have an average annual growth rate of 8 per cent in the next twenty years.[19]

But is the notion of the 'natural path of development' trustworthy, and does the East Asian miracle set a sufficiently realistic precedence for China today? The aforementioned trend of uneven development across the world must cast doubt on the natural path. Note that this trend is very serious in the era of globalization, but much less so in the Golden Age. There must be some fundamental changes on the world scale, which have resulted in the uneven development. Invoking the notion of the 'natural path', or the 'flying-geese pattern' is thus unconvincing for backing the prediction that China is to repeat the East Asian miracle in the future.

Meanwhile, at a different and more specific level, Lin's views on China still appear to have some validity. This concerns the central importance of productive investment in economic development all the way from the Golden Age until the present time. Along with its outstanding growth performance, East Asia also stands out in the developing world regarding productive investment. According to information from *World Development Indicators* (accessed 30 March 2015), East Asia's gross capital formation, as a proportion of GDP, increases substantially from an average of 27 per cent in 1960–80 to 37 per cent in 1980–2013. The performance of all low-and-middle-income economies combined (including East Asia) is much less impressive, in terms of both absolute levels and the magnitudes of increases: it increased from 23 per cent to 28 per cent. Somehow, compared with the rest of the developing world, East Asia has been more capable of maintaining and increasing the high investment rates, in the context of an increasing financialized and speculative world economy. And it should be noted that, in this regard, China has had the best performance even within East Asia. Its gross capital formation as a proportion of GDP increases from an average of 30 per cent pre-1980 to 40 per cent. Given this outstanding developmental performance, it is really difficult to find a convincing economic justification for China to move down the route of financial expansion, at such a tremendous pace, since 2008.

The persistent financial expansion, and the flows of capital to the bubble sectors, might well be the result of policy orientations. It is arguable that this is a case of the 'Greenspan Put, Chinese style'. As the banks and the Chinese economy as a whole have been held hostage by speculative capitals, the government has had to be exceedingly cautious in order not to let the bubbles go burst. The result is continuous crowding out of productive investment. If policy measures aimed at coping with financial risks are based on the mainstream interpretation of the 'New Normal', the dynamism for the Chinese economy to converge to the Golden Age Model can only be fundamentally weakened. Policies in the name of 'obtaining the reform dividends' – reducing productive investment (the story of excess capacity), suppressing the wage rate (the story of excessive rise in labour cost), dispossessing SOEs (the story of inefficient SOEs), resisting state industrial policy (the story of market distortion), etc. – are all antithetical to the convergence.

Stiglitz (2010) points out, with respect to what has just been discussed, that the essence of the 'Greenspan Put' is the privatization of profits and the socialization of costs. In other words, this is to protect the interests of financial speculators at the expense of the general public.

This seems the normality of politics in the age of neoliberalism. In China, the orientation towards neoliberalism is evidently shared by a wide spectrum in the domestic social, economic and political establishments. The challenge from all these neoliberal forces, domestic and international, pushes to the forefront the question as to what social-political conditions will be needed for sustaining and improving upon the existing structural-institutional nexus that tends to converge to the Golden Age Model. It is well-known that what underpinned the Golden Age Model of the advanced capitalist countries in the 1950s–1970s was social-democratic politics. A political arrangement containing similar attributes might thus be needed for China – particularly for preventing the neoliberalization of state power and policy orientation, for preventing the bureaucratization of the state sector, and for preventing the financialization of the economy as a whole.

7.7 Summary and conclusions

The Washington Consensus view on 'rebalancing' in the Chinese economy focuses on substituting internal demands for external demands, and, within internal demands, substituting consumption for investment. The related view on 'restructuring' focuses on cutting back on economic establishments that are not in line with principles of the market, that is, principles of comparative advantage, private property rights, and free finance. It is claimed that such rebalancing and restructuring can only be achieved via neoliberal reforms, particularly via the systematic liberalization of internal and external finance. And it is promised that such rebalancing and restructuring will make Chinese economic growth more efficient and sustainable, while also helping the world economy to move out of the Great Recession.

What has actually happened deviates fundamentally from the neoliberal model. Since the turn of the century, the prevailing capital-deepening path of economic growth has been associated with accelerating productivity and consumption growth, as well as accelerating employment and wage growth. In the institutional dimension, this growth path has been mainly underpinned by the working of the state sector, that is, the nexus of the government (industrial policies and the welfare state), state-owned enterprises and state-controlled banks. Essentially, this structural-institutional nexus embodies a range of important attributes of the Golden Age Model, which had its three main pillars known as 'Big Business, Big Labour, and Big Government'.

The rivalry between the two models in China has reached an acute stage in recent years. State policies in line with the Golden Age Model – promoting productive investment and labour compensation – have made significant achievements, particularly in terms of withstanding the adverse impact of the worldwide Great Recession. Yet the policies have also been significantly resisted and hijacked by speculative financial interests (including sections of the state itself) in the form of redirecting financial resources to the bubble sectors. By causing the precipitation of financial resources, and threatening to generate financial crises, the speculative interests clearly seek to reshape state policies in pursuit of the neoliberal model. This rivalry thus puts Chinese economic transformation at a crossroads.

The outcome of the rivalry will be of fundamental importance not only for China itself but also for the broader world. Today, China has already become a globally significant centre of production, holder of financial resources, and carrier of outward direct investment. It is of note that a major aspect of the process of accumulation by dispossession in the era of neoliberal globalization has been the very large-scale incorporation of Chinese labour into the world market. According to the IMF (2007), weighing countries' labour force by their export-to-GDP ratio, the effective global labour supply quadrupled between 1980 and 2005, with East Asia contributing about half of the increase. Over this period, there has also been an accelerating trend of massive relocation of industry and jobs from the rest of East Asia and beyond to mainland China. That is to say, more than half of the increase in the labour force that produces for the world market came from China in the period 1980–2005. By the same indicator of employment adjusted by the export-to-GDP ratio, as of year-end2005, China's share of the world total of workers producing for the global market reached 25 per cent.

If China is to converge to the Golden Age Model, rather than the neoliberal model, Chinese labour is most likely to become increasingly organized. This will help to largely strengthen the power of the global working class as a whole. Globalization based on accumulation by dispossession is thus likely to encounter increasingly strong resistance. If the ongoing worldwide Great Recession is mainly a product of neoliberalism, the resistance is likely to indeed help world development moving out of the predicament. Long term, it will facilitate the redirection of the world economy towards a path of social and economic development that is more stable, humane and just than what has actually prevailed.

Notes

1. For the mainstream analysis of Chinese economic growth in the years of the Great Recession, and the recommendation of standard neoliberal policies, see IMF (2014, 2015) and OECD (2014). For recommendation of policy for long-term economic reform and development, see World Bank (2012). The production of these reports has had significant contribution by sections of the Chinese authorities. The World Bank report, for example, was in fact jointly authored by the Bank and the Centre of Development Research, which is a ministry under the Chinese State Council (the cabinet).
2. See Lin (2013, chapter 7) on China's policy responses to the 1997–1998 East Asian financial and economic crisis. This is in the context of drawing up lessons from world developmental crises under globalization and appropriate policy responses. For a more elaborate account of the Chinese policy responses, and the long-term importance of the strategy of 'growing out of debts', see Lo (2001).
3. See Simarro (2011) for an analysis of the relationship between the labour share of national income, aggregate consumption, and economic growth in China. Continuous decrease of the labour share is an established observation. Its negative impact on consumption growth is almost a consensus judgement. Nevertheless, whether or not these have dragged on economic growth remains unclear.
4. Chinese shadow banking is mainly composed of entrusted loans, trust loans, bank acceptance, net corporate bond financing, and non-financial enterprise equity. These together with bank loans form total social financing to the real economy (TSF). The IMF (2015) summarizes the dynamics behind the expansion of TSF in China: "(I)n the wake of the global financial crisis, policies were implemented to encourage credit-intensive investment. This fuelled a boom in housing construction and lifted debt-to-GDP ratios from 100 percent of GDP in 2007 to more than 200 percent in 2014, with less well-regulated shadow banks providing two-thirds of the increase" (p. 14).
5. Local government debts data from http://www.infzm.com/content/94503; central government debt data from *China Statistical Yearbook 2014*; shadow banking data from http://www.chinanews.com/gn/2014/03-06/5920282.shtml. Note that because local government expenditures have mainly focused on infrastructural investment, their debts have been mostly backed by existing assets of varied qualities.
6. For neoliberal-oriented interpretations of the 'New Normal', and associated policy recommendations, see Garnaut et al. (2014), Lu and Cai (2014), OECD (2013), and Woo (2012). Chinese official documents have frequently made use of this catch phrase since 2014, but there does not seem to exist officially a definite interpretation and a clear elaboration on its policy ramifications.
7. For an analytically Marxist work of this kind, on the Chinese economy and speculative bubbles, see Gaulard (2013). See also Li (2008, especially chapter three). For a Marxist contention that the productivity growth of the Chinese economy has been mainly based on super-exploitation of labour, see Piovani (2014).
8. In the international media, the most outspoken commentators that blame China for causing, or prolonging, global imbalances and thereby the

financial crisis are Martin Wolf (*Financial Times*, 17 November 2009 and 8 December 2009) and Paul Krugman (*New York Times*, 31 December 2009 and 14 March 2010). See the summaries and criticisms of these assertions by McKinley (2009) and Petras (2009).

9. For the story of China embodying export dependence, see Zhu and Kotz (2011) and Akyüz (2010); for attempts to relate export dependence to underconsumptionism, and further to super-exploitation, see Hung (2009).
10. Fransman (1986) provides perhaps the most thorough and incisive review of the literature on the Feldman–Mahalanobis–Domar model and related growth theories. It is highlighted that the efficiency and sustainability of the model can only be empirically determined, depending on technological progress. See also the formal presentation of the characteristics and dynamics of model in Dutt (1990). For a review of the relevance of the theories to Chinese economic development from the mid-1990s onwards, see Lo (2012, chapter 6).
11. In the relevant literature, there exist multiple interpretations of the structural dynamics and institutional attributes of the advanced capitalist economies in the Golden Age. This chapter draws mainly on Bowles et al. (1985) and Glyn et al. (1990), which basically synthesize the theoretical framework of the Social Structure of Accumulation School, the Profit-Squeeze school, and the Regulation school. For comparison, see Cairncross and Cairncross (1992), particularly the chapter by Kindleberger, which summarizes the work of mainstream neoclassical economics and US Keynesianism on the economics of the Golden Age.
12. See Glyn (2006) concerning the systemic trend of financialization and its destructive impact on world development in the era of neoliberal globalization. See also Wade (2008), focusing on the implications for developing economies.
13. See Lo (2012, chapter 2) for a review of the literature on late industrialization, especially with respect to the role of industrial policy, the developmental state versus crony capitalism, and the broader structural-institutional arrangements.
14. See Lo (2012, chapter 2) on the demand for 'flexibilities', logical of financialization, on the productive sector in the context of globalization.
15. See Lo and Wu (2014) on the role of state industrial policy in promoting the development of strategic industries and technological innovations, and Lo et al. (2011) on the role of state-controlled banks in sustaining the growth of productive investment. On *guo jin min tui* (the state sector advances, whilst the private sector retreats), see Xie et al. (2012). There exists a substantial body of studies that highlight the conducive role of the state in the process of Chinese economic transformation; see, e.g., Felipe et al. (2010), Gabriele (2010), Heilmann (2009), Kotz (2005), and Poon (2009).
16. For the 2012 data of top 500 Chinese firms, released by China Enterprise Confederation on 31 August 2013, see http://www.guancha.cn/economy/2013_08_31_169453.shtml.
17. The neoliberal establishments have tended to view China's developmental record in a favourable light, taking it as a manifestation of the notion of 'the natural path of development', i.e., labour-intensive, export-oriented industrialization. Left-wing scholars, in contrast, tended to assess the experience in a negative way. Hart-Landsberg and Burkett (2004) and Harvey (2005)

contended that the experience can be summarized as 'Chinese super exploitation of labour under-cutting the world working class as a whole'. Arrighi (2007) and Glyn (2006), whilst agreeing with the thesis of under-cutting, did not take the thesis of super-exploitation as well. They rather tended to consider that the under-cutting was due to much faster labour productivity growth in China than other developing economies. Palley (2006) provides a synthesis of the critical and neoliberal stories of China, in the sense that his analysis is identical to the neo-liberal story whereas his policy conclusions are a mix of the two.

18. 'The lost decades: developing countries' stagnation in spite of policy reform 1980–1998', this is actually the title of Easterly (2001), a rarity as a World Bank research paper.
19. Lin (2010, 2013). For its insistence that, following the preceding experiences across East Asia, China has all the potential of achieving an annual average of 8 per cent economic growth in the next 20 years, see http://news.xinhuanet.com/fortune/2014-10/23/c_127133547.htm and http://www.getinews.com/news-9270748-Still-8-percent-economic-growth-potential-in-the-new-normal:-Justin-Lin.html. At the level of economic theory and development policy, Fine and van Waeyenberge (2013) provide an incisive critique of Lin's New Structural Economics – arguing that Lin's work is still strictly within the paradigm of the Washington Consensus, particularly in terms of its ignorance of the worsening environment for world development caused by financialization.

References

Akyüz, Y. (2010) 'Export Dependence and Sustainability of Growth in China and the East Asian Production Network', Research Paper no. 27, Geneva: South Centre.

Amsden, A.H. (1989) *Asia's Next Giant: South Korea and Late Industrialization*, New York: Oxford University Press.

Arrighi, G. (2007) *Adam Smith in Beijing: Lineages of the Twenty-First Century*, London: Verso.

Bhagwati, J. (2004) *In Defense of Globalization*, Oxford: Oxford University Press.

Bowles, S., D. Gordon and T. Weisskopf (1985) *Beyond the Wasteland: A Democratic Alternative to Economic Decline*, London: Verso.

Cairncross, F. and A. Cairncross (1992) *The Legacy of the Golden Age: The 1960s and Their Economic Consequences*, London: Routledge.

Chang, H.-J. (1994) *The Political Economy of Industrial Policy*, London and Basingstoke: Macmillan

Chang, H.-J. (2009) 'Industrial Policy: Can We Go Beyond an Unproductive Confrontation?', Annual World Bank Conference on Development Economics, Wsahington, DC: World Bank.

Dorrucci, E., G. Pula, and D. Santabárbara (2013) 'China's Economic Growth and Rebalancing', Occasional Paper Series no. 142, Frankfurt am Main: European Central Bank.

Dutt, A.K. (1990) *Growth, Distribution, and Uneven Development*, Cambridge: Cambridge University Press.

Easterly, W. (2001) 'The Lost Decades: Developing Countries' Stagnation in Spite of Policy Reform 1980–1998', Working Paper no. 27272, The World Bank. www.worldbank.org.

Felipe, J., U. Kumar, N. Usui, and A. Abdon (2010) 'Why China Has Succeeded – and Why It Will Continue to Do So', Working Paper no. 611, The Levy Economics Institute.

Fine, B., and E. van Waeyenberge (2013) 'A Paradigm Shift That Never Will Be? Justin Lin's New Structural Economics', *Competition and Change*, 17(4), 355–71.

Fransman, M. (1986) 'Machinery and Economic Development', in M. Fransman (ed.), *Machinery and Economic Development*, Basingstoke and London: Macmillan.

Gabriele, A. (2010) 'The Role of the State in China's Industrial Development: a Reassessment', *Comparative Economic Studies*, 52, 325–50.

Garnaut, R., L. Song, and Cai F. (2014) 'Reform and China's Long-term Growth and Development', in L. Song, R. Garnaut and F. Cai (eds), *Deepening Reform for China's Long-term Growth and Development*, Canberra: Australian National University Press.

Gaulard, M. (2013) 'Changes in the Chinese Property Market: an Indicator of the Difficulties Faced by Local Authorities', *China Perspectives*, 2, 3–14.

Glyn, A. (2006) *Capitalism Unleased: Finance Globalization and Welfare*, Oxford: Oxford University Press.

Glyn, A., A. Hughes, A. Lipietz and A. Singh (1990) 'The Rise and Fall of the Golden Age', in S. Marglin and J. Schor (eds), *The Golden Age of Capitalism: Reinterpreting the Postwar Experience*, Oxford: Clarendon Press.

Hart-Landsberg, M., and P. Burkett (2004) 'China and Socialism: Market Reforms and Class Struggle', a special issue of *Monthly Review*, July–August.

Harvey, D. (2005) *A Brief History of Neoliberalism*, Oxford: Oxford University Press.

Harvey, D. (2010) *The Enigma of Capital and the Crises of Capitalism*, London: Profile Books.

Heilmann, S. (2009) 'Maximum Tinkering Under Uncertainty: Unorthodox Lessons from China', *Modern China*, 35(4), 450–62.

Hung, H.-F. (2009) 'American's Head Servant? The PRC's Dilemma in the Global Crisis', *New Left Review*, 60, 5–25.

IMF (2007) *World Economic Outlook*, April, Washington, DC: IMF.

IMF (2014) 'People's Republic of China: 2014 Article IV Consultation – Staff Report', IMF Country Report No.14/235, Washington DC: IMF. Available at http://www.imf.org/external/pubs/ft/scr/2014/cr14235.pdf.

IMF (2015) *Regional Economic Outlook: Asia and Pacific – Stabilizing and Outperforming Other Regions*, May, Washington DC: IMF.

Kotz, D.M. (2005) 'The Role of the State in Economic Transformation: Comparing the Transition Experiences of Russia and China', Working Paper 2005–04, Department of Economics, University of Massachusetts, Amherst.

Lazonick, W. (2004) 'Indigenous Innovation and Economic Development: Lessons from *China's Leap into the Information Age*', *Industry and Innovation*, 11(4), 273–94.

Lazonick, W. (2009) *Sustainable Prosperity in the New Economy?*, Kalamazoo, MI: W.E. Upjohn Institute for Employment Research.

Li, M. (2008) *The Rise of China and the Demise of the Capitalist World Economy*, London: Pluto.

Lin, J.Y. (2010) 'New Structural Economics: a Framework for Rethinking Development', World Bank Policy Research Working Paper series, no. 5197.

Lin, J.Y. (2013) *Against the Consensus: Reflections on the Great Recession*, Cambridge: CUP.

Lin, J.Y. and H.-J. Chang (2009) 'Should Industrial Policy in Developing Countries Conform to Comparative Advantage or Defy It? A Debate between Justin Lin and Ha-Joon Chang', *Development Policy Review*, 27(5), 483–502.

Lo, D. (2001) 'China after East Asian Developmentalism', *Historical Materialism*, 8, 251–62.

Lo, D. (2012) *Alternatives to Neoliberal Globalization: Studies in the Political Economy of Institutions and Late Development*, Basingstoke and London: Palgrave Macmillan.

Lo, D., G. Li, and Y. Jiang (2011) 'Financial Governance and Economic Development: Making Sense of the Chinese Experience', *PSL Quarterly Review*, 64(258), 267–86.

Lo, D., and M. Wu (2014) 'The State and Industrial Policy in Chinese Economic Development', in J.M. Salazar-Xirinachs, I. Nübler, and R. Kozul-Wright (eds), *Transforming Economies: Making Industrial Policy Work for Growth, Jobs and Development*, Geneva: International Labour Office.

Lu, Y., and F. Cai (2014) 'China's Shift from the Demographic Dividend to the Reform Dividend', in L. Song, R. Garnaut, and F. Cai (eds), *Deepening Reform for China's Long-term Growth and Development*, Canberra: Australian National University Press.

McKinley, T. (2009) 'Will Pinning the Blame on China Help Correct Global Imbalances?', *CDPR Policy Brief*, no. 2, Centre for Development Policy and Research, School of Oriental and African Studies, University of London.

OECD (2013) 'The People's Republic of China – Avoiding the Middle-income Trap: Policies for Sustained and Inclusive Growth', Paris: Organisation for Economic Cooperation and Development.

OECD (2014) 'Interim Global Economic Assessment', Paris: Organisation for Economic Cooperation and Development. Available at http://www.oecd.org/eco/economicoutlook.htm.

Palley, T.I. (2006) 'External Contradictions of the Chinese Development Model: Export-led Growth and the Danger of Global Economic Contradiction', *Journal of Contemporary China*, 15(46), 69–88.

Petras, J. (2009) '"Global Imbalances" Versus "Internal Inequalities" (Understanding the World Economy)', unpublished paper. Available at http://petras.lahaine.org.

Piovani, C. (2014) 'Class Power and China's Productivity Miracle: Applying the Labor Extraction Model to China's Industrial Sector, 1980–2007', *Review of Radical Political Economics*, 46(3), 331–54.

Poon, D. (2009) 'China's Evolving Industrial Policy Strategies and Instruments: Lessons for Development', Working Paper series 2009–02, Trade and Industrial Policy Strategies, Pretoria, South Africa.

Simarro, R.M. (2011) 'Functional Distribution of Income and Economic Growth in the Chinese Economy, 1978–2007', working paper number 168, Department of Economics, SOAS, University of London. Available at http://www.soas.ac.uk/economics/research/workingpapers/.

Stiglitz, J.E. (1996) 'Some Lessons from the East Asian Miracle', *The World Bank Research Observer*, 11(2), 151–77.

Stiglitz, J.E. (1998) 'More Instruments and Broader Goals: Moving Toward the Post-Washington Consensus', WIDER Annual Lectures 2, Helsinki: UNU/WIDER.

Stiglitz, J.E. (2010) *Freefall: America, Free Markets, and the Sinking of the World Economy*, New York: W.W. Norton.

Wade, R.H. (1990) *Governing the Market: Economic Theory and the Role of Government in East Asian Industrialization*, Princeton, NJ: Princeton University Press.

Wade, R.H. (2006) 'Choking the South', *New Left Review*, 38, 115–27.

Wade, R.H. (2008) 'Financial Regime Change?', *New Left Review*, 53, 5–21.

Woo, W.-T. (2012) 'China Meets the Middle-income trap: the Large Potholes in the Road to Catching-up', *Journal of Chinese Economic and Business Studies*, 10(4), 313–36.

World Bank (2012) *China 2030: Building a Modern, Harmonious, and Creative Society*, Washington, DC: World Bank.

Xie, F., A. Li and Z. Li (2012) '*Guo jin min tui*: a New Round of Debate in China on State Versus Private Ownership', *Science and Society*, 76(3), 291–318.

Zhu, A. and D.M. Kotz (2011) 'The Dependence of China's Economic Growth on Exports and Investment', *Review of Radical Political Economics*, 43(1), 9–32.

8

The Political Economy of Inequality and Boom–Bust Cycles in Turkey: Before and After the Great Recession

Özlem Onaran
University of Greenwich, UK
Cem Oyvat
University of Greenwich, UK

Abstract: There has been a remarkable continuity in the main characteristics that determined the growth regime in Turkey over the last two decades despite seemingly significant political changes. This neoliberal speculation and finance-led growth regime has proved to be both socially and economically unstable, as shown by the post-Great Recession developments as well as the recent history of Turkey, which is marked by regular boom-and-bust cycles. In the recent global crisis, Turkey experienced one of the severest recessions in 2009 – deeper than that observed in other major emerging economies. The recovery since 2009 is as fragile as before. In the last decade insecurity has increased among all segments of the working people bar the poorest. Turkey's growth model dependent on cheap labour, speculative financial capital inflows, a construction boom and a high trade deficit, would have experienced a crisis sooner or later even without the impact of the Great Recession.

Keywords: Turkey, boom–bust cycles, Great Recession, inequality

JEL Classification: E24, E25, E6

8.1 Introduction

This paper aims to discuss the implications of the growth pattern in Turkey for inequality and labour in the post-1980s period, and to contextualize the developments since the Great Recession within the longer-term structural problems of the country. The adjustment of wages and changes in functional income distribution in favour of capital has played a central role in relieving the pressures over profits during Turkey's integration to the global economy since the 1980s. Furthermore the episodes of currency crises resulted in further distributional shocks at the expense of labour. Turkey's post-1980 growth pattern has been dependent on speculative financial capital flows and has been marked by continuous cycles of boom and bust, as in the cases of the crises of 1994 and 2001 and, most recently, the Great Recession of 2008–09. The distributional outcomes of these crises have not been neutral for labour vs capital.

This chapter discusses the dynamics behind these distributional shocks and also their persistence by analysing the trends in wages, employment, and income distribution, the distributional and labour market consequences of financial crises and boom-and-bust cycles following capital flows, and the consequences for the growth regime in Turkey. The main hypothesis of the paper is that there has been a striking continuity in terms of the distributional policy of different governments from the 1980s to the 2000s. The major institutional and political changes after the 2001 crisis have not led to any disruption in the neoliberal policies or the anti-labour (pro-capital) incomes policy of Turkey. The lack of an industrial policy, and the dependence on low wages to maintain competitiveness, and hence dependence on imports and speculative capital inflows for growth has been the common problems in economic policy in the neoliberal era. These policies have been unable to solve the structural problems of Turkey. It is for this reason that Turkey has experienced the effects of the Great Recession more strongly than many other emerging economies, and still remains fragile in the aftermath of the crisis.

Risks due to both domestic and international financial fragility have been creating new economic turbulences in Turkey since 2006. Given its structural problems, Turkey would have had a currency crisis and recession even without the impact of the global crisis. The Great Recession was simply the final shock that turned turbulences into a deep recession in 2009. Turkey has experienced the crisis deeper than other emerging markets due to its heavy reliance on foreign capital inflows as well as the delayed policy responses of the Justice and Development Party (AKP) government[1] and the Central Bank of the Republic of Turkey to the crisis. In the aftermath of the Great Recession, Turkey has been one of the most fragile emerging markets to the reversals of capital flows following planned changes in quantitative easing in the USA.

The rest of the paper is organized as follows: Section 8.2 discusses the growth regime, the centrality of capital inflows, the boom–bust cycles in Turkey, and the impact of the Great Recession on the levels of economic growth. Section 8.3 discusses the trends in inequality in terms of both functional income distribution, with a focus on the share of wages and personal income distribution, and comparing the effects of the currency crises of 1994 and 2001 with the effects of the Great Recession, and also discussing the political economy behind the ongoing support to the current policies in Turkey despite the Great Recession. Section 8.4 deals with the employment and unemployment trends. Section 8.5 discusses the labour market institutions and their link to inequality. Section 8.6 presents the link between rising inequality and low growth in Turkey by shedding light on the wage-led character of the growth regime. Finally, section 8.7 summarizes and concludes.

8.2 Speculation-led growth regime in Turkey, the boom–bust cycles and the Great Recession

Turkey experienced a major structural change in the 1980s, shifting from an import-substituting industrialization strategy to an export-oriented growth model through the implementation of an orthodox structural adjustment programme, along the lines typically prescribed by the IMF and the World Bank (Onaran, 2009a). The programme is regarded as 'orthodox' in terms of its strong reference to neoclassical economic theory as well as the 'shock therapy'-style reversal in the development strategy and also the strongly pro-capital redistributive policy stance. Since then, the strategy of various governments has been guided by economic policies that include the dismantling of government regulations in financial, goods and labour markets, as well as an openness to trade, foreign direct investment and financial capital flows. Pro-capital redistribution of income accompanied by a military coup in 1980 and a change in the labour code was a major factor that facilitated the export-oriented strategy. A drastic initial decline in the wage share in the early years of the structural adjustment programme, as we will discuss in more detail in section 8.3 below, moderated the competitive pressures over capital at a time of increased exposure to international markets. The promise of these policies has been that liberalized markets and specialization in the comparative advantages of the country will increase efficiency, exports, and growth, attract foreign capital, and that the positive effects will eventually 'trickle down' to provide fairer distribution, where each factor of production receives a return consistent with its marginal productivity; eventually the returns to labour would also increase.

After the initial phase of liberalization in domestic markets and foreign trade, Turkey also liberalized its capital account in 1989 as the second stage of its integration to the world economy. The capital flows consisted mostly of volatile portfolio investments and short-term credit, with the share of foreign direct investment (FDI) in total financial account being limited to a range of 10–20 per cent apart from several exceptional years of FDI, like 1989, 2002, and finally 2006–08. Speculative and short-term capital inflows have led to a fragile growth pattern and created phases of boom, which were then typically followed by a bust (Yenturk, 1999; Onaran, 2007a).

Shortly after the liberalization of the capital account in 1989, the accumulated risks associated with a high current account deficit, combined with the mismanagement of the domestic borrowing policy by the government, which had the unfeasible obsession to try to reduce the interest rates on the eve of the elections in 1993, ended up triggering a massive capital outflow in 1994. This first currency crisis after the liberalization of the capital account led to a depreciation of the currency by 23.9 per cent in just one year and a severe recession with GDP declining by 6.1 per cent in 1994.

It was not long before the international investors started to take advantage of the deflated asset prices in the stock and bond markets and the low exchange rate risk that came with the already depreciated currency (Onaran, 2009a). The capital inflows continued during much of the 1995–2000 period. At the end of 1999, Turkey repeated the former mistake of many other developing countries by adopting a currency peg in 2000 as part of an anti-inflation programme. However, the experience of 2000 showed that the use of the exchange rate as a single nominal anchor was only partially successful in controlling inflation, as had also been the case in many other countries, and the decline in inflation was not sufficient to prevent a significant real appreciation of the currency by –15.9 per cent in just one year (2000). At the same time, the current account deficit reached 3.7 per cent of GDP. The questions regarding the sustainability of the current account deficit, accompanied by financial risks in the private banking sector, invited a series of pessimistic speculative expectations, and Turkey experienced an even more severe crisis in 2001.[2] In 2001, the overall capital outflow amounted to 8.5 per cent of GDP; and GDP itself decreased by 5.7 per cent.

Overall, the strategy of integrating Turkey into the world economy was based mainly on increasing competitiveness via a sharp decline in wages. This has led to a significant contraction of domestic demand, as will be discussed in more detail below. However, this policy was unable to stimulate a higher growth potential via higher investment.

The dramatic financial crisis of 2001 and its implications for wage and employment losses were certainly one important aspect in the election victory of the AKP in 2002. All three establishment parties of the ruling coalition during the crisis were excluded from the parliament, since the electoral support for each of them was below the 10 per cent threshold. Despite the political break with the legacy of the former establishment, the AKP government continued to pursue a solely neoliberal programme, serving the interests of the large-scale domestic capitalists as well as international investors.

Indeed, the economic policy stance of the government remained along the same lines as the previous coalition's programme after the crisis, which was also supported by the IMF. Economic policy in general was a relatively uncontested area between the government, business circles, and the military elite, despite the political conflicts between them (Onaran, 2009a). Nevertheless, AKP's aim of creating and supporting a more conservative and Islam-oriented capitalist class[3] and bureaucratic cadres also provoked the old ruling elite establishment, including the major corporations of Turkey, the military and the former bureaucrats, who tried to maintain their own power in politics and their share in the wealth of the country.

The government developed a discourse that built on a selective narrative of economic statistics, in particular high growth with low inflation for a long period, and maintaining FDI inflows at historical highs. However, these statistics disguise the fragility as a result of the high current account deficit and the levels of domestic and external private debt, the question about the sustainability of the capital flows, the inability of the economy to create sufficient jobs, and the persistent levels of inequality and poverty. The so-called 'success' of low inflation was achieved at the expense of declining real wages, which barely recovered since the 2001 crisis, as we will discuss in more detail below. The obsession with inflation as the sole target of macroeconomic policy and ignoring employment and incomes policy is also part of a conscious anti-labour policy stance. Most importantly, the high growth performance proved to be hiding the deep structural problems involved with debt-led growth, and was sure to be reversed with or without the global Great Recession. Last but not least, Turkey failed to combine FDI policy with industrial policy during the 2000s as well as before; the very low share of FDI in manufacturing made productivity, technology, employment, or wage spillover unlikely. Hoping that FDI would be a safe means of financing the huge current account deficit also proved to be unrealistic in an environment of global credit crash and collapse in investment after the Great Recession. These points are the evidence of a continuity of the neoliberal policy package from the 1980s to 2000s.

By and large, the economic policy stance of the government secured the support for the large-scale employers' organization to AKP despite hesitations due to political pressures from the military establishment. The balance of power changed significantly after 2008, and AKP emerged as the winner in its battle with the military and juridical establishment after steering and winning a series of major lawsuits against high-ranking officers over alleged military coup d'état plans.

It is true that after the 2001 crisis, Turkey enjoyed an uninterrupted and high-growth era, with a 7.2 per cent average annual rate of growth in GDP in the period 2002–06.[4] High capital inflows prompted by the high real interest rates offered by Turkey were the determining source of finance for achieving this growth rate; however, it had little impact on the levels of real investment. The deflated prices in the asset markets and the immediate and the substantial depreciation of the currency following the 2001 crisis not only lowered asset prices once again in terms of foreign currency, but also decreased the likelihood of further depreciation over the coming period, and even created the possibility of an appreciation after the overshooting of the exchange rate in the summer of 2001. That provided a favourable environment for international portfolio investors. Additionally, the being an accession country and the prospects for EU membership was a significant factor in securing the capital flows in the period after 2001.[5] In that period, there were also significant inflows of FDI, which were facilitated by the EU anchor, the political push for privatization or deregulation and by the high rates of depreciation of the local currency, which led to a dramatic decline in asset prices. The result of this new wave of capital inflows was typically a continuous appreciation of the currency; at the end of 2006 the current account deficit reached a historically high level of 6.0 per cent of GDP. Nevertheless, the market sentiments celebrated this period as a completely new era, where the EU anchor was playing an important role in decreasing political risks, and creating the potential for a higher FDI and financial capital inflow. The optimists also emphasized that the current account deficit was financing new private investments, which would eventually improve competitiveness and exports. The government mostly cited the effect of increasing oil prices in 2006 as an excuse for the increase in the current account deficit, and seemed to place a particular trust in the corrective capacity of the flexible exchange rate system, which was implemented in parallel with a policy of inflation targeting after the 2001 crisis, to tame speculative expectations. Meanwhile, little attention was paid to the increased foreign debt of the private sector, and the exchange rate risk that it was exposed to.

The optimism about the start of a new era in the Turkish economy was already being disturbed by the global turbulences in the world economy in May–June 2006 (Onaran, 2006). At that time, the concerns centred around the effects of a possible recession in the US on the emerging economies via the contraction in export markets, a decrease in the appetite for risk and increase in the perceptions of risk, and, consequently, increased volatility in the private capital flows towards 'riskier' markets. At this time Turkey and Hungary were identified as being among the most vulnerable countries due to their high degree of indebtedness, a large share of foreign currency-denominated debt, exchange rate overvaluation, high external financing needs, and their dependence on capital flows (Goldstein, 2005).

The initial shock in 2006 faded away slowly, but Turkey subsequently remained fragile to other shocks (Onaran 2006 and 2007a). With regard to the real economy, the risks of dependency on volatile international flows had already been demonstrated by the immediate slowdown in growth in the third quarter of 2006, which continued into 2007. The high growth performance of the years after 2002 is presented as an indicator of success by the ruling AKP; however, the fragility of this period was tested severely by the turbulence in the global financial markets – particularly after July 2007. By the time that the global financial turmoil started in 2007, Turkey was already among the short list of countries to be affected the most. The current account deficit, which was 6.0 per cent as a ratio to GDP in 2006, only moderately decreased to 5.8 per cent of GDP in 2007 despite slower growth; and remained at 5.5 per cent in 2008.

The dependency of the country on external finance became an increasingly serious problem during the global credit squeeze in 2008. The speculation and finance-led growth model once again proved to be economically unsustainable. With significant capital outflows in Autumn 2008, the recession started in the fourth quarter of 2008, dragging down the overall growth rate for 2008 to 0.7 per cent. Table 8.1 shows the growth rate of GDP and its components during the Great Recession. Turkey had one of the severest recessions in 2009 with a contraction of 4.8 per cent – deeper than that experienced in other major emerging economies (Öniş and Güven, 2011). Accordingly, between 2007 and 2009, GDP per capita in Turkey contracted by 3.3 per cent, which was significantly

Table 8.1 Annual and quarterly growth rate (%) of Gross Domestic Product and its components

	2008 Q1	2008 Q2	2008 Q3	2008 Q4	2009 Q1	2009 Q2	2009 Q3	2009 Q4	2010 Q1	2008	2009
Gross Domestic Product (GDP)	7.0	2.6	0.9	–7.0	–14.7	–7.8	–2.8	5.9	12.6	0.7	–4.8
Consumption Expenditures of Households (C)	5.7	0.6	–0.4	–6.7	–10.2	–1.7	–1.9	5.0	7.9	–0.3	–2.3
Consumption Expenditures of Government (G)	5.5	–3.4	2.6	2.8	5.3	–0.1	5.1	18.2	0.5	1.7	7.8
Gross Fixed Capital Formation (I)	7.3	–2.0	–8.7	–18.7	–27.9	–24.5	–18.2	–4.2	17.2	–6.2	–19.0
Exports of Goods and Services (X)	13.0	4.3	3.8	–8.2	–11.1	–10.8	–5.2	7.2	–0.8	2.7	–5.0
Imports of Goods and Services (M)	14.0	2.0	–3.8	–24.9	–31.0	–20.6	–11.7	11.0	22.0	–4.1	–14.3

Note: Quarterly growth rates measure growth compared to the same quarter of previous year.
Source: TUIK.

worse than the average growth in GDP per capita in lower-middle and upper-middle-income countries. Table 8.2 presents the growth performance of different country groups before and after the Great Recession.

The higher rate of contraction in Turkey during the Great Recession relative to other emerging economies is partly related to the lack of capital account regulations in Turkey. For the selected emerging economies Table 8.3 exhibits the capital inflow, capital outflow, foreign exchange and financial sector specific regulation indices reported by Erten and Ocampo (2013). The indices show that in 2007 the regulations on capital inflows and outflows in Turkey were significantly lower compared to the other emerging economies such as China, India, Russia, Malaysia and Thailand. The lack of regulation in capital flows can partially explain Turkey's relatively larger current account deficit/GDP ratio before the Great Recession, as the capital inflows provided a greater space for Turkey to increase the investment–saving gap. As a consequence, Turkey experienced a stronger boom cycle driven by capital flows in the run up to the Great Recession. This made Turkey's economy more fragile to sudden reversals in capital flows than was the case for the other emerging economies, as it significantly raised Turkey's dependency on the foreign financial inflows.

The difference between the crisis of 2009 and the former crises in Turkey was that it was part of a global financial crisis. As international surplus capital was in search of safe havens in its escape from the toxic assets in the headquarters of international finance in the US and Europe, there was, at the very beginning of the crisis (from July 2007 until mid-2008), a wave of volatile and shorter-term capital inflows to emerging markets, including Turkey, which were soon followed by outflows. The previous hopes that Turkey's capital inflows were now more stable proved to be wishful thinking as the share of FDI inflows in capital inflows decreased rapidly to 12.7 per cent in 2010, amidst a global collapse in investment; this ratio stands at the same level as of 2014.

Due to the global nature of the Great Recession, which made it different from an isolated currency crisis, the nominal depreciation was more limited, and this was later followed by an appreciation; overall, by the end of 2009 the Turkish lira (TL) had depreciated by 27.9 per cent with respect to the US dollar and 9.6 per cent with respect to the Euro compared with its level in August 2008. The pass-through from devaluation to inflation was also lower than in previous crises due to the global deflationary environment.

Moreover, unlike the economic crisis in 2001, the Great Recession did not cause significant damage to the banking sector in Turkey. In 2000,

Table 8.2 The average annual growth of GDP per capita in different country groups with respect to income level (162 countries)

		1990–2002	2002–2013	2002–2007	2007–2009	2009–2013
All Countries	Lower income	1.48	3.18	3.44	2.77	3.14
	Lower-middle income	0.66	3.15	4.27	1.43	2.70
	Upper-middle income	1.16	2.81	4.68	–1.39	2.73
	Higher income	1.70	0.82	1.94	–2.84	1.31
Countries that are not fuel dependent	Lower income	1.10	3.08	2.98	2.79	3.42
	Lower-middle income	0.88	2.93	3.93	1.10	2.67
	Upper-middle income	1.47	2.81	4.78	–1.52	2.67
	Higher income	1.87	1.12	2.29	–2.42	1.49
Turkey		**1.44**	**3.54**	**5.49**	**–3.33**	**4.67**

Notes: The countries were classified accordingly to World Bank's classification in World Development Indicators. The countries were classified based on their classification in 1990 for 1990–2002 and on their classification in 2002 for 2002–13. Turkey promoted from lower-middle-income to higher-middle-income group in 2003 and is still in the higher-middle-income group. The fuel dependent countries are 22 countries whose major export good is indicated as fuel in any of the IMF's World Economic Outlooks for 2002–14.
Source: Own calculations based on World Development Indicators.

Table 8.3 The average annual growth of GDP per capita (2007–2009), pre-crisis current account surplus/GDP and the level of capital account regulations in the selected emerging economies

	Average annual growth of GDP per capita (%, 2007–09)	Current Account Balance/GDP (%, 2007)	Indices measuring capital account regulations in 2007			
			Capital inflow regulations	Capital outflow regulations	FX-related regulations	Financial sector specific restrictions
Brazil	1.46	0.1	0.25	0.58	0.75	–
China	8.85	10.1	1.00	1.00	1.00	0.67
India	4.77	–0.7	0.92	1.00	–	1.00
Indonesia	3.86	2.4	0.58	0.50	1.00	0.33
Malaysia	–0.19	15.4	0.75	1.00	0.75	–
Mexico	–2.93	–1.4	0.42	0.50	1.00	0.67
Russia	–1.44	5.6	1.00	1.00	0.50	0.33
S. Africa	–0.08	–6.7	0.50	0.92	0.75	0.67
Thailand	–0.10	6.3	0.83	1.00	0.75	0.67
Turkey	**–3.33**	**–5.8**	**0.08**	**0.33**	**0.75**	**0.00**

Note: The capital account regulation indices range between 0 and 1. The absence of regulations in all selected categories are coded as 0 and the presence of regulations in all selected categories are coded as 1.

Source: Authors' own calculations based on World Development Indicators, Erten and Ocampo (2013).

there were 61 commercial banks in Turkey; however, this number fell to 40 in 2002 as many of the banks went bankrupt during the economic crisis (Marois, 2012). By contrast, between 2007 and 2010 the number of commercial banks in Turkey only fell from 33 to 32. The stronger structure of the banking sector is partially an outcome of new regulations in the banking sector introduced as part of the structural reforms implemented following the economic crisis of 2001 (Bakır and Öniş, 2010). Moreover, the reduction in the number of banks in the early 2000s created a more oligopolistic banking sector. Unlike the European banks, the banks in Turkey were not investors in the CDO markets, but rather experienced only the traditional liquidity, credit, and open position risks associated with the Great Recession. Additionally, the bank managers increased the work intensity in the branches, in turn increasing the pressure on bank employees. Between 2004 and 2009, the number of bank branches increased by nearly 50 per cent, whereas the growth in employment was only 36 per cent during the same period. As a result, the ratio of labour costs to the banks' overall balance sheet decreased from 1.9 per cent in 2002 to 1.4 per cent in 2009, that is, around half their 1999 level (Marois, 2012). These factors increased the average returns in the banking sector and contributed to shield the existing banks from the negative impacts of the Great Recession.

Yet the Great Recession did have a very negative effect on the Turkish economy in several different ways. First of all, as a reflection of large current account deficits, the private savings/GDP ratio in Turkey was around 4.4 per cent less than the private investments/GDP ratio in 2007 (Yükseker, 2013). This meant that capital inflows were an important source of finance for bank credits in Turkey. Therefore, the significant decline of capital inflows in 2008 and 2009 suddenly restricted the availability of domestic credits (Uygur, 2010), which were crucial for domestic investments. Secondly, the high volatility in capital inflows generated uncertainty for the private investors and reduced their confidence (Cömert and Çolak, 2014). The real sector confidence index of the Central Bank,[6] which was reported as 110.5 in December 2007 declined to just 58.5 in November 2008. The decline in economic confidence, together with a tightening in the availability of domestic credits, decreased the gross fixed capital formation by 6.2 per cent in 2008 and 19 per cent in 2009 as can be seen from Table 8.1. Considering that the gross fixed capital formation in 2007 had a share of 25.2 per cent in overall GDP, its contraction was a major source of reduction in Turkey's GDP during the Great Recession.

The Great Recession also caused a temporarily decline of 20 per cent in Turkey's export revenues through the period 2007Q4–2008Q3. The main reason behind this decline was the collapse of demand in the EU countries, as Turkey's exports relied heavily on the EU-28 (Uygur, 2010). Turkey's heavy dependency on the EU exports was an outcome of the Customs Union agreement signed between Turkey and the EU, which became effective in 1996. During the Great Recession, the EU-28's share in total exports declined from 56.6 per cent in 2007 to 46.2 per cent in 2009.[7] Accordingly, a proportion of exports shifted to Middle Eastern, Asian and African countries. AKP government's trade policies, including the mutual easing of visa requirements and bilateral trade agreements between Asian, African and Middle Eastern countries, also helped to increase diversification in the country's export markets (Öniş and Güven, 2011).

Imports of goods and services also declined by 4.1 per cent in 2008 and 14.3 per cent in 2009, which slightly eased the Great Recession's negative outcomes on Turkey. The contraction in GDP significantly reduced the level of imports, as the pre-crisis production in Turkey was highly dependent on imports of intermediate and capital goods (Yeldan et al, 2012). Moreover, Turkey is a major importer of energy (oil, natural gas and coal) so the massive decline in oil prices reduced the energy imports of Turkey from US$5.1 billion in July 2008 to US$1.9 billion in April 2009 (Uygur, 2010).

The policy responses of the AKP government and the Central Bank of Turkey to the Great Recession were very limited during the months of the recession (Uygur, 2010; Öniş and Güven, 2011). Although the Great Recession began to damage Turkey's economic growth in the third quarter of 2008, the AKP government remained optimistic in its future growth forecasts, and did not implement any serious counter-cyclical policies until late 2008.[8] The consumption expenditure of the government increased only by 1.7 per cent in 2008, and the primary budget surplus declined slightly – from 4.2 per cent in 2007 to 3.5 per cent in 2008 (Uygur, 2010). That fiscal policy response was very weak compared to the fiscal stimulus in Argentina, Brazil, Russia and South Korea that constituted around 5–6 per cent of their GDPs in 2008 (Öniş and Güven, 2011).

In late 2008, the AKP government finally started to implement significant counter-cyclical policies. In December 2008, the maximum limit of export rediscount credits of the Eximbank in Turkey was doubled from $500 million to $1 billion and the eligibility criterions for Eximbank credits were also eased (Uygur, 2010). From March 2009 onward, the AKP government introduced tax cuts on real estate, vehicles and many consumer goods, including electronics, white goods, office equipment and furniture – these tax cuts continued until the end of September 2009. On the labour side, a public subsidy programme supporting part-time employment was implemented in January 2009. Moreover, a new scheme against unemployment was introduced in June 2009. According to that scheme, private investments on import-dependent industries and in economically backward regions were subsidized by the government through tax cuts, cheap credits and social security premium reductions (*Cumhuriyet*, 2009, 3 June). Although, these measures mostly aimed to recover the losses of entrepreneurs, they still supported Turkey's recovery through increasing consumption expenditure of the government by 7.8 per cent in 2009 (Table 8.1).

The policy response of the Central Bank of Turkey was also delayed during the first months of the Great Recession. During the summer of 2008, the Central Bank of Turkey continued its emphasis on inflation targeting. It increased its policy rate from 15.3 per cent in May 2008 to 16.8 per cent in June 2008, and maintained this until November 2008 (Uygur, 2010). Nevertheless, as the declining demand eased the concerns on inflation, the Central Bank of Turkey reduced the policy rate significantly – from 16.8 per cent in November 2008 to 6.3 per cent in October 2009 (Cömert and Çolak, 2014). Moreover, starting from late 2008, the Central Bank of Turkey stopped accumulating foreign exchange reserves and started to drain its reserves by selling US$15 billion in the second half of 2009. Similar to fiscal policies of the AKP government, the late monetary policy response of the Central Bank of Turkey also delayed the recovery of the Turkish economy.

The recovery since the Great Recession is as fragile as the growth regime dependent on capital flows and marked by boom and bust cycles in its past three decades. Following the Great Recession, Turkey implemented a few macroprudential measures – a gradual increase in reserve requirements, restrictions on consumer loans, and the introduction of credit-growth caps. Nevertheless, these measures were very limited compared to the capital account regulations that other emerging economies such as Brazil, India and Indonesia introduced (Erten and Ocampo, 2014). As a result, growth in Turkey continued to be highly dependent on speculative financial capital inflows and the financial sector grew significantly faster than the industrial sector. Figure 8.1 shows the share of information, communication and industry sectors as compared to the share of financial and insurance services in GDP. The production share of information, communication and industry sectors in GDP, which had stood at 28.2 per cent in 2007, increased only slightly, to 28.8 per cent in 2013. During the same period, financial and insurance

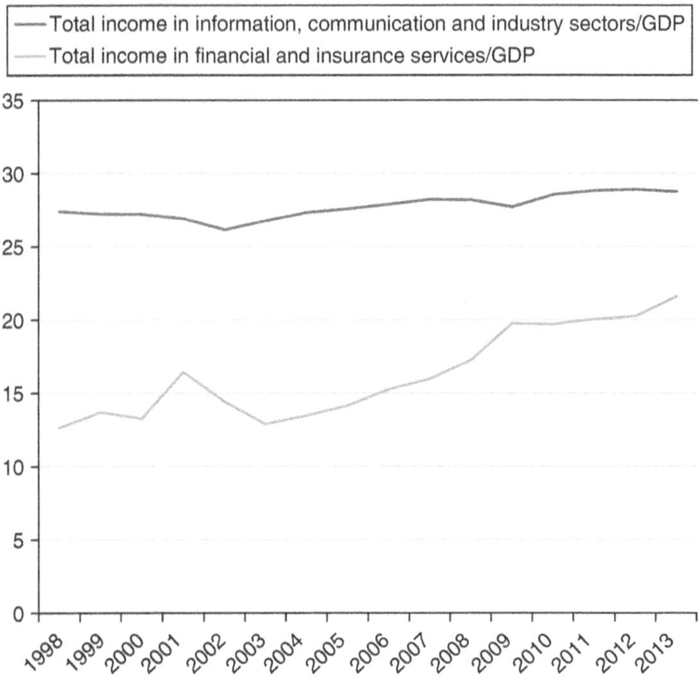

Figure 8.1 Total income earned in financial and insurance services and information-communication and industry sectors as a share of GDP (1998–2013, %)
Source: Own calculations based on data supplied by TUIK.
Note: Financial and insurance incomes include financial intermediation services indirectly measured.

services continued their ongoing significant growth and their share in GDP jumped from 16 per cent to 21.6 per cent during the period 2007–13. Moreover, Turkey's production is significantly dependent on the imports of intermediate and capital goods (Yeldan, 2013a). Between 2009 and 2013, the share of imports in GDP increased from 25 per cent to 29 per cent.[9] The imports of intermediate and capital goods constituted greater than 85 per cent of those imports[10] (Yeldan et al., 2012). A genuine developmentalist industrial policy was noticeably absent from AKP's economic policy mix.

AKP took pride in having paid off the last instalment of its debt to the IMF in 2013. However, the foreign debt of the private sector reached previously unseen levels; in the last decade firms in Turkey borrowed increasingly more in the international financial markets (Yeldan, 2013b). Growth was driven by debt accumulation on the part of both private firms and households. Short-term private debt/GDP ratio more than doubled and stood at 18.4 per cent by 2014; with the long-term private debt/GDP ratio at 19.0 per cent.[11] Karacimen (2012) shows that household debt also increased significantly from 7.3 per cent in 2003 to 37.7 per cent in 2009 as a ratio to household income.

In 2006, Onaran had (2006) asked "Can 'it' happen again?" to remind the risk of a Minskian bust due to a shock followed by a sudden shift in expectations and capital outflows. It *happened* again in 2008–09. The next bust and crisis in Turkey is not a question of 'if' but 'when', and the international financial investors will make that decision, as is the case in all economies dependent on capital inflows. The foreign capital outflows from Turkey in 2013 following the rise in political instability was already a signal in this direction. As major protests erupted against the government's authoritarian regime at the Gezi Park in Istanbul, the government labelled the protests a conspiracy of the international actors and the 'interest rate lobby', and in response to the wave of capital outflows the government initiated an official inquiry about the sales of shares in the stock market, particularly by the foreigners. Recep Tayyip Erdoğan, the then Prime Minister, has been in conflict with the Turkish Central Bank ever since regarding the bank's attempts to moderate capital outflows by increasing interest rates. Sadly, this concern about capital outflows has not turned into a genuine interest in regulating capital flows, but an excuse to support a conspiracy discourse to shed doubts on an authentic social movement.

A further wave of volatility in capital flows came after the announcement of the US Federal Reserve Board that they could consider gradually phasing out the quantitative easing programme (the injection of money into the markets) in the summer of 2013. The aggressive expansionary monetary policy of the world's major central banks since 2008 has helped to maintain capital inflows to emerging markets such as Turkey, offering high speculative returns. The negative effect of the announcement of the Fed on international capital flows was similar across the world, but the effect was particularly marked in Turkey. Overall nominal depreciation of the Turkish lira (TL) with respect to the US dollar reached 95 per cent and the currency also 61 per cent with respect to the Euro between August 2008 and 2014. Accounting for inflation, the real exchange rate depreciated by 10.1 per cent in 2014 compared to 2008. March 2015 saw further volatility in capital outflows from Turkey and the exchange rate due to the expectation of increases in the US interest rates; again Turkey has been one of the most affected emerging economies with strong pressures on the exchange rate. The pass-through effect of depreciation is increasing inflationary pressures and also bringing about a slowdown in output, and the world demand remains weak after the recession; the positive effects of depreciation on exports remain limited. The imported intermediate input content of export goods is also moderating the competitiveness effects of depreciation. The pressure of President Erdoğan to keep interest rates low in an effort to maintain the popularity of the party ahead of the Summer elections, who accused the governor of the Central Bank, Erdem Başçı by 'selling out the homeland' to the 'interest-rate lobby', has contributed to uncertainty and capital outflows (*The Economist*, 2015).

In the meantime, the EU anchor has completely lost its relevance for Turkey after the Great Recession. The relations with the EU cooled subsequent to the 2004 EU enlargement. After the Great Recession, the loss in appetite for further enlargement on the part of the EU coincided with AKP's reorientation towards the US as well as the Middle East internationally, and the establishment of a clearly more authoritarian regime domestically. This removed one anchor that was often referred to in the financial markets regarding the stability of the capital flows to Turkey.

Overall, Turkey's level of fragility after the Great Recession is a continuity of its long-lasting structural problems related to a speculation-led/debt-led growth model that is dependent on capital inflows and susceptive to boom–bust cycles. This model takes the country through endogenous cycles of optimistic and pessimistic expectations stability and instability à la Minsky.

8.3 Inequality and wages during the boom–bust cycles and the Great Recession

This section of the paper discusses the trends in inequality during the boom–bust cycles in Turkey, and in particular compares the effects of the currency crises of 1994 and 2001 with the effects of the Great Recession. Then we present the reasons behind the ongoing support behind the current policies in Turkey despite the devastating effects of the Great Recession and persisting inequalities.

We first start with changes in functional income distribution, that is, the distribution of income between wages and profits. Evidence from the currency crises in emerging economies during the period of 1994–2001 after the liberalization of the capital account shows that the labour share declines in all countries that have experienced currency crises during the two or three years following the crisis (Onaran, 2007b and 2009a); and this decline in labour share then compensates for the increase in financial costs due to higher interest rates or depreciation for industrial firms. Evidence also suggests that industrial firms find the chance to increase their returns from financial activities (Istanbul Chamber of Industry, 2003).

Strikingly, the whole era of Turkey's liberalization and integration into the world economy since 1980 has been a period of decline in the wage share. While the race to the bottom in the wage share has been a global trend, the decline in the labour share in Turkey has been the highest in the G20 countries along with Mexico (Onaran and Galanis, 2014).

Indeed, the major negative shock to labour's share took place in the early phase of neoliberal structural adjustment in 1980; the recoveries in the later stages were minor and short-lived, and were reversed by financial crises of 1994 and 2001. Turkey, which based its international competitiveness during the era of liberalization on low wages, experienced a significant decline in the manufacturing wage share.

The short period of increase in the wage share following the significant labour mobilizations during 1989 to 1991 was reversed by the 1994 crisis. The crises of both 1994 and 2001 led to a clear and long-lasting decline in the wage share in Turkey. After the crises of 1994, the fall in the wage share continued also in 1995, with a cumulative decline of 27.0 per cent compared to 1993. A strong economic recovery took place immediately after the currency crises of 1994 and 2001, with production returning to its pre-crisis level within a year; however the fall in the wage share continues for much longer. The slow recovery in the wage share in Turkey after the 1994 crisis was again reversed in 2001. The shock in 2001 was more dramatic: the wage share continued to decline throughout the eight years that followed, including 2008, which also includes five years of AKP regime. The decline finally amounted to a cumulative fall of 22.0 per cent in 2008 compared to 2000.

The initial year after the currency crises is always associated with a decline in the wage share, and the percentage decrease in the wages greatly exceeds the rate of decline in production during the currency crises. After a crisis, declines in private sector wages follow as the fear of job losses grows in the face of possible downsizing or bankruptcies. Employers' organizations push labour unions to accept dramatic wage cuts or compulsory unpaid leave to avoid job losses. Eventually, profits are restored and when the crisis is long past, it is labour that carries the burden of adjustment. The crisis also creates a hysteresis effect that destroys the bargaining power of labour for a long period afterwards. The trauma of the crisis and the ultimate need to keep the export sector competitive becomes part of the employer discourse. The unions have a hard time to recover following the loss of employment after the crisis; the remaining members often find themselves burdened with increased debt and dramatic losses in living standards, which does not facilitate militant bargaining even after the crises. This is a common destiny shared by labour in other countries as well: Diwan (2001) defines crises as episodes of distributional fights, which leave 'distributional scars'.

Overall, the major source of the decline in the wage share during the currency crisis years is the decline in real wages, which owes itself in part to the inflation shock due to depreciation and in part to a loss in the bargaining power. Figure 8.2 shows the real wage index (deflated by CPI) in manufacturing industry.

Employment has also declined in all crisis years, with the exception of 1980, when the crisis was associated with the military coup, which also banned lay-offs (Onaran, 2009b). During all of the crisis years, the decline in the real wage is much higher than the change in employment, the difference reaching rather dramatic levels during the 1994 and 2001 crises. This difference indicates that the wages adjust relatively flexibly to changes in the labour market conditions. During the crises both productivity and real wages decline, with the latter decreasing at a significantly

Figure 8.2 Real Wage Index, 1973–2013 (1979=100, deflated by CPI)
Source: Own calculations.
Note: We are extending the real wage data in Onaran (2009) based on the Annual Survey of Employment, Payments, Production and Tendencies in Manufacturing Industry, which is available only until 2001, and by using the percentage change in Real Earnings Data in the Quarterly Manufacturing Survey, which is available until 2008, and the percentage change in the Gross Wages–Salaries Index in manufacturing industry reported in the Industrial Labour Input Indices, which starts from 2005 onwards on a quarterly basis; the latter reports nominal changes, which we deflate by the inflation in CPI.

higher rate. Following the crisis years, productivity recovers, but real wages continue to decline for three more years after the crisis.[12] The rate of decline in real wages following the 1994 and 2001 crises have reached 30.0 per cent and 24.5 per cent, respectively, in three years. The recovery after 2004 was negligible, and before the Great Recession hit in 2009 and as of 2008 real wages were still 14.2 per cent lower than in 2000 and 34.3 per cent lower than their peak level in 1991.

In addition to the decline in overall growth of the economy and bargaining power of workers during a crisis, inflationary shocks during these currency crises set the stage for the decline in wages and thereby labour's share (Onaran, 2009b). Due to the high import dependency of Turkey, depreciation creates a large increase in the price of the imported goods, and thus in overall input costs. The pass-through effect of currency depreciation on prices generates dramatic increases in inflation, albeit at lower rates than the nominal depreciation. The magnitude of this shock is related to the import dependency of the economy and the oligopolistic power of the firms to pass on import price changes to consumers. These shocks are not only unexpected, but also difficult for the workers to reflect to their wages due to the magnitude of the shock. The workers confronted with the threat of job loss during a crisis mostly fail to pass the consequent price shocks to their nominal wages. In the meantime, utilizing the imbalance of power relations, the firms compensate for the increase in input costs by a decline in labour costs. The rate of depreciation of the Turkish lira against the dollar reached as high as 169.5 per cent and 96.0 per cent in 1994 and 2001, respectively. The outcome was a radical deterioration in the real wage, and consequently the wage share, during currency crises. Estimation results indicate that a 10 percentage point increase in the depreciation rate leads to a 2.2 percentage point decrease in the growth rate of the wage share (Onaran 2007a). Indeed, similar episodes were also experienced during the early phase of opening up in the early 1980s, which was accompanied by huge devaluations of the domestic currency with the aim of achieving higher international competitiveness. The reverse of this story was also true during episodes of capital inflow, and currency appreciation, when employers became more accommodating towards wage demands. The 1989–93 episode is a case in point. However, this was soon disturbed by the currency crisis in 1994.

The recession in 2009 was another major shock to wages, and in this case nominal wages declined by 3.2 per cent. Furthermore, different from the currency crisis, in the deflationary global environment of the Great Recession, the inflation rate did not hike as much, remaining limited to 6.2 per cent. That overall limited the real wage loss by 8.9 per cent in 2009. There have been some gains in real wages in the following years, but again compared to the peak in 1991, real wages are still 18.6 per cent lower, and are just 5.3 per cent above their level in 1979 before the structural adjustment programmes, despite the significant increases in productivity over the course of almost three decades.

The 2009 recession was also unique in the sense that the fall in labour productivity was higher than the fall in real wages, and that hence wage shares moved counter-cyclically, that is, increased, during 2009. The currency crisis experiences of Turkey and other developing countries, with high inflationary shocks and a consequently pro-cyclical wage share, is quite different from the experience in a recession without a major devaluation, as has been the case during the Great Recession. After 2009, the wage share nevertheless declined during the recovery during 2010–11, and the recovery since 2012 has been dismal. Overall, the wage share in 2013 was 37.1 per cent, and was still dramatically lower than the wage share at its peak in 1991 (by a rate of 55.0 per cent), 21.8 per cent lower compared to 2000, and even 34.8 per cent lower than its level in 1979. Apart from the crisis episodes, the recovery in the wage share is also very weak.

One interesting puzzle is the widespread support for the ruling government in Turkey despite the decline in wages during the Great Recession and the reduction in wage shares during the post-crisis period. Interestingly, the discontent about the government manifested itself in mass protests in summer 2013, but the starting point for this protest was not explicitly economic inequality or wage stagnation. The obvious injustice and police brutality in Gezi Park in May 2013 was the final straw in a long process of accumulation of discontent against an authoritarian government, their social policies pushing for a conservative Islamic-lifestyle threatening in particular women and the youth, criminalization and imprisoning of oppositional groups ranging from seculars to Kurds, socialists, and trade unionists, and last but not least neoliberal policies, which increasingly commercialized public services, created areas of rent for large corporations, and destroyed the ecological environment. 27 May, and the mobilizations that followed, marked a historic moment for the collective memory of the movements in Turkey. This has been ever since the spontaneous mobilization of a new generation, which has been brought up by the conservative neoliberal authoritarian AKP regime for a decade. It has been a source of inspiration given the creativity and sense of humour of the young people involved. It has been a broad movement bringing together first time activists of all ages – young and old, trade unions, civil society organizations, and political groups from a wide spectrum.

Despite the mass protests, it is also true that Turkey is deeply divided in terms of the sentiment about the AKP regime, and there is still a significant level of support for the government, even following the Great Recession. The AKP government was firstly elected with 34.3 per cent support in 2002 and it increased its votes to 46.6 per cent in the general elections of 2007. Despite the significant economic contraction during the Great Recession, AKP's share of votes declined only slightly – to 39 per cent – in the local elections of 2009. With these results, AKP declared victory in 45 of the 81 main cities, including Istanbul and Ankara. Moreover, the AKP government quickly regained its political support during the post-Great Recession period, increasing its share of votes to 49.8 per cent in the general elections of 2011.

AKP's election successes in the post-Great Recession period can be attributed to several factors. First, the AKP government gained massive control over the Turkish media, which partially shielded AKP from possible criticisms on its economic policies during the Great Recession. In Turkey, a large part of the media companies are also involved in economic activities other than media and they benefit from the government contracts (Buğra and Savaşkan, 2014). According to the report of Freedom House (Corke et. al, 2014), this led to crony capitalist relationships between entrepreneurs in the media sector and the AKP government, which reinforced the self-censorship in the Turkish media. A large number of journalists in Turkey were fired for speaking out against the AKP government. Moreover, dozens of journalists were imprisoned under broadly defined anti-terrorism laws, which also reduced the amount of criticism on AKP. AKP's control over media helped Erdoğan to build a discourse on the effects of the Great Recession and supported his claim that Turkey "will be the country that would be least affected from the crisis... The crisis will pass Turkey at a tangent" (NTV, 21 April 2009).[13]

Secondly, the government has managed to play the religious card, especially through the headscarf dispute, with its efforts to remove the ban against the headscarf for female students at universities. Such strategies helped the government to shift the emphasis from living standards to identity, and sustain hopes in the majority of the working people that, once economic stability can be maintained, the benefits would indeed trickle down to the majority eventually.

Thirdly, the capital flows to emerging economies increased significantly in the 2000s (Vasudevan, 2009; Akyüz, 2012), which generated booms that would lead to higher growth rates in the emerging economies, including

Turkey. During the 2002–13 period the average growth in GDP per capita more than doubled in lower-, lower-middle- and upper-middle-income countries compared to the 1990–2002 period, as reported in Table 8.2. The growth of GDP per capita in Turkey followed a similar trend, with the average annual growth in GDP per capita increased from 1.44 per cent in 1990–2002 to 3.54 per cent in 2002–13. This is particularly an outcome of high growth rates in the boom periods, as the average annual growth in GDP per capita were 5.49 per cent and 4.67 per cent between 2002 and 2007 and 2009–13 respectively. The higher growth rates observed after the economic crisis of 2001 were conceived as AKP government's success in economic policy, rather than being attributed to the influence of changing global trends. Therefore, the 3.3 per cent decline in GDP per capita between 2007 and 2009 had only a mild impact on the level of support for the AKP.

Fourthly, from a political economy perspective, there are important distributional dynamics in the background of both the discontent about the regime as well as the support for it. AKP has initiated redistribution towards the poorest of the society via both populist in-kind transfers of food and coal, in particular in the eve of the elections, as well as some institutional pro-poor changes.[14] The AKP government centralized the three existing social security funds (Emekli Sandığı, SSK, Bağ-Kur) in a single institution (Social Security Institution) and all employees started to access the same health coverage as the government employees who previously had had the largest and best-quality coverage (Tekgüç and Atalay, 2015). Moreover, a larger part of unemployed and informally employed individuals received a 'Green Card', which grants partial access to public health services. Indeed, the AKP government aims to privatize the health services through subsidizing private healthcare. Accordingly, the share of General Practitioner doctors in private healthcare services increased from 5.5 per cent in 2002 to 16.6 per cent in 2012 (Tekgüç and Atalay, 2015). Nevertheless, at the present time the role of private healthcare services is still small in Turkey. Moreover, the healthcare services are mainly financed by public social security funds. These policies increased access for the poor and the informal sector workers. Furthermore, the share of social transfers, in particular transfers other than pensions and survivors' benefits, have doubled as a ratio to GDP – from 0.9 per cent in 2006 to 1.8 per cent in 2010; as of 2013 they constitute 1.5 per cent of GDP.[15] The relative poverty rate (the ratio of individuals below 50 per cent of the median value of the consumption expenditures per equivalent individual) declined from a level of 18.5 per cent in 2002 to 16.0 per cent in 2011.[16]

Minimum wages have also received a significant boost in real terms, increasing from 0.6 as a ratio to the median wage of full-time workers in 2002 to 0.7 in 2012 (0.7 as of 2013), and minimum wages as a ratio to average wages increased from 0.3 in 2002 to 0.4 in 2013.[17] Albeit still at a low level, the increase in minimum wages is remarkable.

During 2002–13 the Gini coefficient in Turkey also decreased according to the official statistics, as can be seen from Table 8.4. The Gini coefficient measuring income inequality between households declined from 0.440 in 2002 to 0.400 in 2010 and stayed at a constant level of 0.400 over the period 2010–13.[18] According to the official statistics, the Gini coefficient did not also significantly change during the Great Recession as it slightly increased from 0.406 in 2007 to 0.415 in 2009 before falling back to 0.400 in 2010. Nevertheless, these statistics should be interpreted with caution, as Gini coefficient data is not entirely reliable. Between 60 and 67 per cent of total income in Turkey cannot be captured by household budget or income and living conditions surveys.[19] Moreover, during the period of 2005–06 the Gini coefficient increased by 0.05 points; which is a sign of poor-quality data according to the quality standards that Deininger and Squire (1996) introduced for income distribution data.[20]

Nevertheless, there are factors that would reduce the Gini coefficient during the period from 2002 to 2013. According to data from household

Table 8.4 Gini coefficient values for Turkey (2002–2013)

	Urban	Rural	Total
2002	0.440	0.420	0.440
2003	0.420	0.410	0.420
2004	0.390	0.420	0.400
2005	0.380	0.370	0.380
2006	0.415	0.406	0.428
2007	0.394	0.375	0.406
2008	0.395	0.378	0.405
2009	0.405	0.380	0.415
2010	0.389	0.379	0.402
2011	0.394	0.385	0.404
2012	0.391	0.377	0.402
2013	0.392	0.365	0.400

Note: Gini coefficient values on 2002–2005 are based on Household Budget Surveys. In 2006, Turkstat changes its methodology and starts to use Income and Living Conditions Surveys for estimating the Gini coefficients. Unlike Household Budget Surveys, Income and Living Conditions Surveys construct panel data.
Source: TUIK.

budget or income and living conditions surveys, the share of revenues from transfers in total income increased significantly – from 17.5 per cent in 2002 to 22.2 per cent in 2013.[21] The growth in the share of transfers did not stop during the Great Recession. Indeed, the share of revenues from transfers in total income increased from 18.2 per cent in 2007 to 19.6 per cent in 2009. The higher share of transfer revenues possibly contributed to a decline in the Gini coefficient based on household income and kept the Gini coefficient at lower levels during the Great Recession. Moreover, the higher minimum wage/average wage ratio and the reduction in the share of informal activities would redistribute the inequality within labourers and hence reduce the overall inequality.

Overall, there has been a redistribution of income towards the poorer since 2002. However, the source of this redistribution was the income losses of the organized blue-collar and white-collar/professional working people rather than taxes on corporate profits and the rich. This redistribution helped to increase the profits of the employers without hurting the poorest further. Between 2006 and 2013 there were increases in the share of both the bottom 40 per cent and the top 20 per cent within the total wage income, whereas the share of the middle 40 per cent decreased.[22] The share of the bottom 40 per cent of the households within the total wage income increased from 10.7 per cent in 2006 to 12.0 per cent in 2013;[23] and the share of the top 20 per cent of the households within the total wage income increased from 51.7 per cent in 2006 to 53.1 per cent in 2013, while the share of the middle 40 per cent decreased from 37.6 per cent in 2006 to 34.9 per cent in 2013. This may also explain in part the diverse class composition of the mass, albeit shaky, electoral support for the AKP.

In the last decade insecurity has increased for all segments of the working people, with the exception of the poorest. Interestingly, this dynamic of redistribution under a conservative neoliberal regime shows a remarkable resemblance to the trends in Brazil. In the case of Brazil, the governing Workers Party, a progressive party quite different from AKP, has implemented some pro-poor policies such as child benefits to the poor families and an unprecedented increase in the minimum wage (Fishlow, 2011; Neri, 2010). The AKP government's approach was a very hostile approach on labour movements and unions and its continuous aim of deregulating the labour markets.

8.4 Employment and unemployment

Contrary to the promises of neoliberalism, after almost three decades of extensive liberalization in Turkey, functional income distribution is changing at the expense of labour, as shown above. Moreover, the persistence of high unemployment and a slowdown in the employment creation capacity of the economy goes hand in hand with lower labour costs (Onaran, 2009a). Thus, falling labour costs are not necessarily creating more employment in contrast to the neoliberal thesis. This is particularly remarkable since it is taking place at a time when the labour market is becoming increasingly flexible, as will be discussed in more detail below. Indeed, this pattern is not specific to Turkey; the stagnation or decline in manufacturing employment can also be observed in Eastern Europe or Latin America (Onaran, 2008; Pollin et al., 2004). This pattern shows that the increase in global competition has generated a decline in the employment creation capacity of economic growth, particularly in manufacturing.

The post-2001 recovery in Turkey has been particularly devastating for labour due to the jobless growth pattern that has dominated the 2000s. After the 2001 crisis, the unemployment rate hiked to 8.5 per cent in the country compared with a rate of 6.6 per cent in 2000, and the effect was heavier in the urban areas as can be seen in Figure 8.3.[24] Urban unemployment increased to 11.9 per cent in 2001 and jumped further to 14.6 per cent in 2002. The recovery started only five years after the crisis, and it was very short-lived. The Great Recession reversed the recovery, and

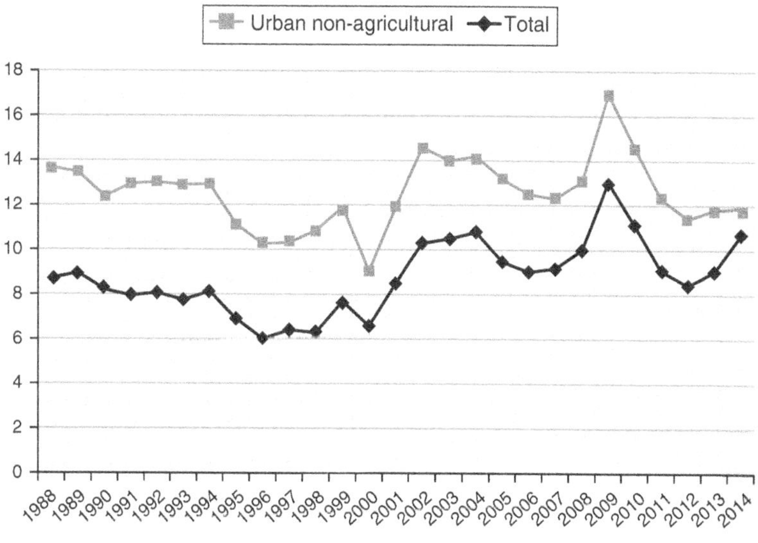

Figure 8.3 Unemployment rate in Turkey (1988–2014, %)
Source: TUIK.

unemployment started to increase again in 2008, hiking to 13.1 per cent in 2009 with non-agricultural urban unemployment reaching 17.0 per cent. As of July 2015, the seasonally adjusted unemployment rate is as high as 10.4 per cent in Turkey (according to last available data at the time of writing by the Turkish Statistical Institute (TUIK)).

Another important issue is the increasing number of discouraged workers. Unemployment rates reflect only the rate of unemployed as a ratio to labour force. However Turkey also experienced an increase in the numbers of discouraged workers, who are ready to work, but do not look for jobs, because they do not have any hope of finding one, after the crisis. Since these people are regarded as non-participant, they are not recorded as unemployed; thus the unemployment numbers is disguising important information. Among the male residing in urban areas, the share of discouraged workers to the non-participant male working-age population was just 1.2 per cent, and, after a hike in 2004, it reached 4.4 per cent as of 2012 after falling only to 3.8 per cent in 2013. If we compare the discouraged workers to non-participant male working-age population excluding the retired, students, disabled, and those, who have not defined their reason, this ratio is as high as 44.7 per cent as of 2009, and as of 2013 it is still at 36.8 per cent. In 2001 it was only 5.6 per cent.

The problem of unemployment is even more severe among women and young people. The rate of unemployment reached an astonishing rate of 18.5 per cent for young urban men, and 27.9 per cent for young women (15–24 years old) in 2013. Among the unemployed of all age groups, 20.8 per cent of urban men and 30.7 per cent of urban women have been unemployed for more than a year. It is unsurprising that the mass mobilizations in summer 2013 coincided with a time of record high youth unemployment and increasing levels of precariousness. This is a new generation, who feels insecure about the future, working, if at all, with fixed-/short-term contracts, or part time without a choice, at times in the informal sector, most often for low pay, and usually in jobs not appropriate to their education levels and aspirations.

Among the urban women the rate of unemployment (in the non-agricultural sector) was 17.3 per cent in 2013. Moreover, the labour force participation rate of urban women in the same year was strikingly low: only 28 per cent. As a consequence of the very low female labour force participation rates, Turkey has a very low employment rate as a ratio to its total working-age population: for example, only 43.9 per cent of the urban working-age population was employed in 2013. The crisis of 2001 has led to an increase in the female labour force participation rate, which stood at just 17.2 per cent in 2000. This has been basically a survival strategy by the households, relying on precarious female employment, particularly in households, where the male breadwinner lost his job (Baslevent and Onaran, 2003). However, this increase was also accompanied by a hike in the female unemployment rate from 13.0 per cent in 2000 to 16.6 per cent in 2001 and further to 18.7 per cent in 2002. The 2009 recession was a further shock with the urban female labour force participation rate increasing to 22.3 per cent, along with an unemployment rate of 21.5 per cent.

The gender-based division of labour, the dismal supply of affordable social services for childcare, and the low wages in the labour market lead to the exclusion of many women from paid work. Turkey is not making full use of the productive capacity of its female population. A phenomenal indicator of the anti-women policy stance of the government is its call for women to give birth to at least three children, and its attack on women's right to abortion and birth control in an environment where the urban female labour force participation is at a level which bears no resemblance to those observed in a developed country. Even if the women who do not have a paid market job are still productive through the invisible domestic work, that is reflecting only part of their productive capacity, and leading to severe inequality problems because of the exclusion of the women from economic and social life as well as political decision-making processes. However, it is not enough to simply encourage women to participate in the labour market. Turkey has to combine an employment-targeting macro policy with policies targeting higher employment rates for women. This will continue to be one of the significant issues in the process of Turkey's economic and social development.

8.5 Labour market institutions and flexibility

In Turkey, and also other developing as well as developed countries, low rates of employment growth are often cited as evidence of labour market rigidities. However, the analysis of labour market outcomes of structural adjustment above shows that labour has borne the whole burden of the economy's adjustment to the neoliberal outward-oriented growth model (Onaran and Yentürk, 2002).

Throughout the structural adjustment history of Turkey, changes in labour legislation have contributed significantly to losses in labour's share. Turkey changed its Labour Law in 2002, going further in the direction of a low road labour flexibility strategy (Taymaz and Özler 2003).

The new legislation has been instrumental in changing the labour environment in a number of ways. First, it provides a legal basis for part-time and fixed-term employment. The employers are expected to lower labour costs by switching to fixed-term contracts and sub-contract labour. Secondly, it reduces the cost of layoffs for the employers. Thirdly, it reduces the coverage of employment protection by excluding those establishments employing fewer than thirty workers. Following the new labour law, the part-time employment rate increased from 6.6 per cent in 2002 to 8.1 per cent in 2007. Nevertheless, the rising unemployment in the Great Recession led to a greater growth in the part-time employment rate and fed the precariousness in the labour markets. By 2010, the part-time employment rate in Turkey reached to 11.5 per cent and increased further to 11.8 per cent in 2012 (ILO, 2015).

The low levels of trade unionization reject the claim of the employer organizations and the neoliberal observers that unions are a source of rigidity and thereby unemployment. The unionization rate varied between 11 per cent and 58 per cent, and the collective bargaining coverage varied between 10 per cent and 20 per cent in the early 2000s; even taking into account these considerable sectoral variations these were very low rates (Ilkkaracan and Levent, 2006). However, union power has continued to deteriorate significantly under the AKP regime. Union density has more than halved from 9.5 per cent in 2002 to 4.5 per cent in 2012, and now stands at the lowest among the OECD countries – lower than the figures in Eastern Europe or Mexico and Korea.[25] During a decade of AKP rule, the amount of workers working for outsourced companies has more than tripled reaching to above 1.5 million.

The AKP government's approach to the labour movements is also very hostile. The AKP government suspended several large-scale strikes in glass, tyre and metal industries on the grounds of 'national security' concerns (Oyvat, 2011; *Hürriyet*, 12 March, 2014). Moreover, despite the labour unions' demands, the AKP government did not permit the May Day demonstrations in 2003–08 and 2013–14 to be conducted in Istanbul's main square – Taksim. During the May Days in 2007, 2008 and again in 2013 and 2014, the AKP government prevented labour union's demonstrations in Taksim Square through police violence and 'protected' the Taksim area by cancelling a significant part of public transportation services in Istanbul to prevent access. The restrictions on the labour movements contributed a decline in the real wages during the Great Recession and the stagnation of real wages during the post-Great Recession.

Health and safety regulation violations have also increased under the AKP regime, with almost a thousand workers dying in workplace accidents

(Tellioglu, 2014). Dr Ahmet Tellioglu, a workplace doctor at a major factory in Istanbul, who has been sacked recently because of his objection to serious health hazards in the practices of the factory, has stated that "anyone who is just above the poorest or earning just above the minimum wage, thus any working person, who has something to loose, feels increasingly more insecure in Turkey today" (Onaran, 2013, p. 2).

There is also a large informal sector, which is not covered by the labour code. Recently, there have been some improvements in terms of a decline in informal employment. During 2002–14, the share of informal employment in the total employment declined from 52.1 per cent to 35 per cent[26] as can be seen in Figure 8.4. It is worth noting that the fall in informal employment went along with more deregulation in the labour market and a fall in the power of trade unions, and

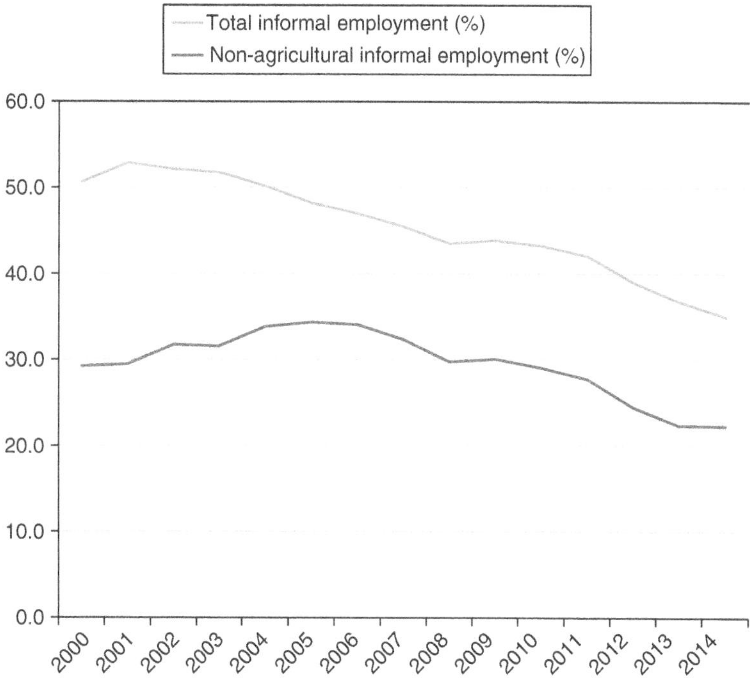

Figure 8.4 Total and non-agricultural share of informal employment in Turkey (2000–2014, %)

Note: Persons who are not registered to any social security institution are considered as informally employed.

Source: Own calculations based on TUIK's data.

an overall pro-capital shift during this period. Moreover, the share of informal employment in non-agricultural employment in Turkey has an inverted U-shaped shape; hence it increases slightly during 2000–05 and declines thereafter. Overall, the non-agricultural informal employment share declines from 31.7 per cent in 2002 to 22.3 per cent in 2014. The inverted-U shape of the non-agricultural informal employment share is consistent with the cross-country analyses of Rauch (1993) and Elgin and Oyvat (2013). Moreover, the share of self-employment and unpaid family workers in non-agricultural employment also decreased from 19.1 per cent to 13.5 per cent during 2003–13.

Despite improvements, there is still a sizable level of informal employment. Indeed, the decline in informal employment stopped temporarily in 2008 and 2009 (Figure 8.4) as during the Great Recession, informal employment was possibly a survival strategy for many employees. Although the informal sector seems to be generating employment, it leads not only to loss of tax income but also to a low productivity production structure.

Another survival strategy that poor households developed against the consequences of the Great Recession was the return of migration to the rural areas, although the agricultural sector was not one that benefited from the pre-crisis boom. Indeed, the annual growth in agriculture was only 0.2 per cent between 2002 and 2007.[27] The lack of growth in agriculture was an outcome of IMF and World Bank policies implemented in 1999 and 2001/2002 (Aydın, 2010). Following the economic crisis in 2001, the price of subsidies for agricultural goods, and the support for agricultural cooperatives, were eliminated in Turkey and replaced with direct income support for farmers. The change in agricultural regime significantly reduced the agricultural subsidies that the small- and medium-scale farmers receive.[28] Moreover, following the letter of intent given to IMF in 1999, the agricultural markets in Turkey were extensively liberalized and the imported cheap food products subsidized by the developed countries became increasingly available. As a result, the imports of agricultural and food products increased from $2.6 billion in 1999 to $2.9 billion in 2002 and then expanded further to $7 billion in 2007.[29] To summarize, due to the liberalization in agriculture and reduction in agricultural subsidies, the benefits of economic growth between 2002 and 2007 were not realized by small-scale farmers. Indeed, the share of rural population below the poverty line slightly increased from 34.5 per cent in 2002 to 40 per cent in 2004 and reduced back to 34.8 per cent in 2007.[30] Moreover, the share of agricultural income in GDP as a ratio to the share of agricultural employment declined by 15.5 per cent between 2003 and 2007.[31] The relative decline in agricultural incomes also led to de-peasantization as the share of agriculture in total employment decreased significantly from 34.9 per cent in 2002 to 22.5 per cent in 2007.[32] Nevertheless, the deterioration of economic growth caused by the Great Recession stopped the de-peasantization trend in Turkey and stimulated a reverse migration of labour towards the agricultural sector. The total agricultural employment that had experienced a consistent declined between 2001 and 2007, increased from 4.5 million workers in 2007 to 4.8 million workers in 2009 following the Great Recession. The growth in agricultural employment continued several years after the Great Recession, and the the level of employment in the agricultural sector reached 5.4 million workers in 2011. The share of agriculture in total employment increased consistently – from 22.5 per cent in 2007 to 23.1 per cent in 2009 and then 23.3 per cent in 2011.[33] The growth in agricultural employment was an outcome of massive increase in non-agricultural unemployment following 2007 (as reported in Figure 8.3) rather than growing rural incomes or increasing government support for agriculture. Indeed, similar to the economic crises in 2001, the government responded to the Great Recession by cutting the subsidies for agriculture further (Bağımsız Sosyal Bilimciler, 2011). The real value of agricultural government subsidies declined by 29.6 per cent between 2007 and 2009.[34] Consistently, the rural areas impoverished significantly during the Great Recession. The share of rural population below the poverty line increased from 34.8 per cent in 2007 to 38.7 per cent in 2009.[35]

8.6 The effect of distribution on investment and growth

The structural weakness of the Turkish economy, which made it particularly fragile during and in the aftermath of the Great Recession, is related to its weak investment performance and its reliance on capital inflows for growth. Investment is the major driving force that creates demand and thus employment. Despite an increasing profit share in the Turkish economy, the level of investment has remained weak. Evidence shows that there is no statistically significant effect of higher profit share on private investment (Onaran and Galanis, 2014; Onaran and Yentürk, 2001). The increase in profits has been increasingly channelled to financial investment rather than investment in physical capital and machinery. Even the largest 500 industrial firms in Turkey have a high and increasing share of net interest and financial income in their total revenues (Istanbul Chamber of Industry, 2003).

On the contrary, the negative effect of the rise in the profit share on consumption is very strong and more than offset the net export effects, which are also strong. Overall, econometric estimations by Onaran and Galanis (2014) show that the partial effect of a 1 percentage point increase in the profit share leads to a 0.49 percentage point decrease in consumption as a ratio to GDP, and only a 0.28 percentage point increase in net exports; incorporating the multiplier effects as well, a 1 percentage point increase in the profit share leads to a 0.5 percentage point decrease in the growth of GDP. The negative impact is even higher in the environment of global 'race to the bottom'. The growth regime in Turkey is significantly wage-led (Onaran and Stockhammer, 2005; Onaran and Galanis, 2014); thus, when wages are suppressed both production and investments are suppressed, and thereby employment (Onaran and Aydıner, 2010). Turkey's neoliberal economic policies since 1980 in the last 45 years have generated a vicious circle of lower wage share, lower investment, low competitiveness, import dependency, lower and volatile and jobless growth. This is the structural weakness behind the strong impact of the Great Recession in Turkey.

8.7 Summary and conclusions

Turkey's growth regime is marked by an acute dependence on speculative capital inflows and the subsequent boom-and-bust cycles. Lack of industrial policy, dependence on low wages for competitiveness, and hence dependence on imports and capital inflows for growth, has substantially limited the transformation of the productive structure of Turkey. The Great Recession brought the risks and detrimental long-term consequences of Turkey's dependence on financial capital flows once again to the forefront. Turkey would have experienced a crisis sooner or later even without the Great Recession. Due to its inherent structural weaknesses, Turkey has been one of the emerging economies to be most severely affected by the Great Recession. Similarly, since 2013, Turkey has been severely affected by the reversal in capital flows in response to the planned changes in quantitative easing in the USA.

Dependence on global export markets and the destructive effects of speculative capital flows make it harder for countries like Turkey to preserve a stable development path. In order to be able to realize the possible benefits of international demand, and generate a not only sustainable but also egalitarian industrial restructuring, a combination of industrial and trade policy as well as incomes policy is required.

Notes

1. In the beginning of the 2000s, a group that is separated from the Islamic 'National Vision' movement generated a new movement around Justice and Development Party (AKP) under the leadership of Recep Tayyip Erdoğan. Similar to the 'National Vision', AKP adopted a conservative view and frequently used Islamist references. However, unlike the anti-Western 'National Vision', this new Islamic movement sympathized with Turkey's EU membership, securing the political relationships with the USA and NATO and the flows of international capital. (Balkan et al., 2014). Following the economic crisis in 2001, AKP came to power as a majority government in 2002, and has remained in power since then (see, also, footnote 3 below).
2. See Yeldan (2002), Akyuz and Boratav (2003) and Uygur (2001) for a more detailed discussion.
3. In the present day AKP has tight relations with the Independent Industrialists' and Businessmen's Association (MÜSİAD), which has a strong Muslim background. Indeed, it is widely thought that MÜSİAD is an abbreviation for 'Muslim Businessmen's Association'. In an interview conducted by the *Milliyet* newspaper (10 April 2004), the first chairman of MÜSİAD, Erol Yarar, accepts that this common knowledge reflects the position of MÜSİAD well. He says that "being called as Muslim Businessmen's Association never disturbed me. Indeed, this is an honour for us".
4. This corresponds to 5.9 per cent growth in per capita GDP.
5. In the period after 2001, EU turned into an important anchor in partnership with the IMF to determine the direction of economic change as well as to signal the credibility of the programs to the international investors (Öniş and Bakır, 2005; Ataç and Grünewald 2006). The targets of IMF programmes and the steps to be taken to fulfil the economic conditions of membership overlapped, and EU's role, in terms of auditing Turkey, began to include economic aspects in addition to political ones.
6. The real sector confidence index is based on the Central Bank's surveys conducted among managers in the manufacturing sector. The surveys include questions on managers' perception of current and future production, sales, prices, employment, stocks, costs, capacity utilization, inflation and credit interest rates (TCMB, 2015).
7. Own calculations based on data supplied by Turkish Statistical Institute (TUIK).
8. The most destructive effects of the Great Recession are realized after the fourth quarter of 2008 following the collapse of Lehman Brothers in mid-September 2008. Nevertheless, the fragility and expectations of crisis in the US economy already started to reduce the US GDP during the third quarter of 2008. According to the US Bureau of Economic Analysis's data, the seasonally adjusted economic growth in the US was –1.9 per cent and –10.7 per cent for GDP and gross private domestic investment respectively. The expectation of an economic crisis in the US also affected the Turkish economy. The real sector confidence index of the Central Bank already went down from 110.5 in December 2008 to 94.6 in August 2009 and to 86.4 in September 2009. Accordingly, GDP growth declined to 0.9 per cent in the

third quarter of 2008 from 7.0 per cent in the first quarter of 2008 (Table 8.1). Also the gross fixed capital formation collapsed by 8.7 per cent in the third quarter of 2008 compared to the same quarter of the previous year.

9. Own calculations based on data supplied by the Turkiye Istatistik Kurumu (TUIK).
10. In 2011, the share of intermediate goods in total imports was as high as 71.9 per cent, while the shares of consumption and capital goods in total imports were 15.5 per cent and 12.3 per cent respectively (Yeldan et al., 2012).
11. Own calculations based on data supplied by the Turkish Central Bank.
12. The only exception is the 1981 recovery in wages after the military coup of 1980.
13. "The crisis will pass Turkey at a tangent" was a motto that Erdoğan used frequently, and which became popular in the mainstream media (see, for example, *Sabah*, 27 November 2010; *Sabah*, 15 December 2008; *Yeni Şafak*, 27 December 2010).
14. According to Eder (2013), the decentralized and non-systematic structure of the poverty aids also support creation of crony economic and political chains. First, a large part of these aids are supplied by local municipalities, which are also allowed to use private services and charities for various services and funding. Nevertheless, the funding supplied by charities can also function as a substitute for bribery that would have a return on an infrastructure investment bid. Second, in-kind transfers of coal and food serve as a tool of political patronage. These in-kind transfers are inherently unstable and are not granted citizens as a social right.
15. Data supplied by TUIK on distribution of annual incomes by types of income.
16. Own calculations linking the poverty data before and after 2006 supplied by TUIK.
17. Own calculations based on data supplied by http://stats.oecd.org.
18. The income inequality in Turkey has historically been lower than the majority of the Latin American and Sub-Saharan African countries. The Latin American and Sub-Saharan countries have a colonial history, which led to inegalitarian agrarian structures and concentration in the control of natural resources. Contrarily, Turkey was not colonized by European countries; it is relatively resource poor and the land Gini coefficients in Turkey have been lower than the land Gini coefficients in the majority of the Latin American and Sub-Saharan African countries. This also kept the income Gini coefficients in Turkey at lower levels (Oyvat, 2014).
19. Own calculations based on data supplied by TUIK. Data problems on the estimation of inequality are commonly observed in the developing economies. According to Ravallion (2003)'s estimates for developing countries, the consumption per capita from the national accounts deviates largely from the per capita expenditures based on national sample surveys.
20. In their cross-country income inequality database, Deininger and Squire (1996) classify the inequality data as doubtful if Gini coefficients differ by 0.05 or more than 0.05 compared to the closest observation.
21. Own calculations based on TUIK's household budget and income and living conditions data.
22. Own calculations based on data supplied by Turkish Statistical Institute (TUIK) on distribution of annual incomes by types of income.

23. The increase in the share of bottom 40 per cent wage earners is partially due to homogenization of labour markets followed by higher economic growth in 2000s, and a fall in the share of informal employment, as we will discuss in more detail below.
24. Data in the rest of this section are based on Household Labor Force Surveys by the Statistical Institute of Turkey.
25. Data supplied by http://stats.oecd.org.
26. This is consistent with Porta and Shleifer (2014) who exhibit that the informal employment share in total employment is larger for poorer countries.
27. Own calculations based on data supplied by TUIK.
28. In the second half of 2000s, the AKP government partially shifted away from the agricultural policies of 2001/2002 and reintroduced the previously eliminated agricultural subsidies with pre-2007 election concerns (Aydın, 2009).
29. Own calculations based on data supplied by TUIK.
30. TUIK's calculations of poverty rates based on TUIK's poverty line.
31. Own calculations based on data supplied by TUIK.
32. Own calculations based on data supplied by TUIK.
33. Own calculations based on data supplied by TUIK.
34. Own calculations based on consumer price index and the value of government subsidies on agriculture (in current Turkish Lira prices) supplied by TUIK and Bağımsız Sosyal Bilimciler (2011) respectively.
35. TUIK's calculations of poverty rates based on TUIK's poverty line. The poverty rates based on poverty lines are not calculated since 2010, due to the methodological revision.

References

Acemoğlu, D. and Robinson, J. (2013) 'The Political Economy of Turkey. Why Nations Fail'. Retrieved from http://whynationsfail.com/blog/2013/2/27/the-political-economy-of-turkey.html.

Akcay, C. (2008) 'Turkey Weekly Macro Comment', Yapi Kredi Bank, Strategic Planning and Research Section, mimeo.

Akyüz, Y. (2012) 'The Boom in Capital Flows to Developing Countries: Will It Go Bust Again?', *Ekonomi-tek*, 1(1), pp. 63–96.

Akyüz, Y. and Boratav, K. (2003) 'The Making of the Turkish Crisis', *World Development*, 31, pp. 1549–66.

Atac, I. and Grünewald, A. (2006) 'Turkey's Political Economy between Crisis and Strong Growth: Discussion of the Europeanisation Dynamics in Turkey', paper presented at ESA Workshop, Vrije Universiteit Amsterdam, August–September.

Aydın, Z. (2010) 'Neo-Liberal Transformation of Turkish Agriculture', *Journal of Agrarian Change*, 10(2), pp. 149–87.

Aydın, Z. (2013) 'Global Crisis, Turkey and the Regulation of Economic Crisis', *Capital & Class*, 37(1), pp. 95–109.

Bağımsız Sosyal Bilimciler (2011) 'Derinleşen Kriz ve Türkiye Ekonomisine Yansımaları: Ücretli Emek ve Sermaye'. Retrieved from http://www.bagimsizsosyalbilimciler.org/Yazilar_BSB/BSB2011.pdf.

Bakır, C., and Öniş, Z. (2010) 'The Regulatory State and Turkish Banking Reforms in the Age of PostWashington Consensus', *Development and Change*, 41(1), pp. 77–106.

Balkan, N., and Balkan, E. and Öncü, A. (2014) 'Foreword', in N. Balkan, E. Balkan and A. Öncü (eds), *The Neoliberal Landscape and the Rise of Islamist Capital in Turkey*. Oxford: Berghahn Books.

Baslevent, C. and Onaran, Ö. (2003) 'Are Women in Turkey More Likely to Become Added or Discouraged Workers?', *Labour*, 17(3), pp. 439–58.

Buğra, A., and Savaşkan, O. (2014) *New Capitalism in Turkey: The Relationship Between Politics, Religion and Business*, Cheltenham: Edward Elgar Publishing.

Corke, S., Finkel, A., Kramer, D.J., Robbins, C.A. and Schenkkan, N. (2014) *Democracy in Crisis: Corruption, Media, and Power in Turkey*, Freedom House Special Report.

Cömert, H., and Çolak, M.S. (2014) 'Can Financial Stability be Maintained in Developing Countries after the Global Crisis: The Role of External Financial Shocks?', ERC-Economic Research Center, Middle East Technical University, no. 1411.

Cumhuriyet (2009, 3 June) 'İşverene teşvik paketini seçme hakkı'. Retrieved from http://www.cumhuriyet.com.tr/haber/diger/65540/isverene_tesvik_paketini_secme_hakki.html.

Deininger K. and Squire L. (1996) 'A New Data Set Measuring Income Inequality', *World Bank Economic Review*, 10(3), pp. 565–91.

Diwan, I. (2001) 'Debt as Sweat: Labor, Financial Crises, and the Globalization of Capital', mimeo. Available at http://info.worldbank.org/etools/docs/voddocs/150/332/diwan.pdf.

Eder, M. (2013) 'Deepening Neoliberalization and a Changing Welfare Regime in Turkey', in C. Rodriguez, A. Avalos, H. Yilmaz, A.I. Planet (eds), *Turkey's Democratization Process*, London: Routledge.

Elgin, C., and Oyvat, C. (2013) 'Lurking in the Cities: Urbanization and the Informal Economy', *Structural Change and Economic Dynamics*, 27, pp. 36–47.

Erten, B., and Ocampo, J.A. (2013) 'Capital Account Regulations, Foreign Exchange Pressure and Crisis Resilience', Initiative for Policy Dialogue Working Paper Series.

Erten, B., and Ocampo, J.A. (2014) 'Turkey's Hot-Money Problem', Project Syndicate, 4 April. Retrieved from http://www.project-syndicate.org/commentary/bilge-erten-and-jose-antonio-ocampo-show-why-domestic-macroprudential-regulations-cannot-replace-capital-account-management.

Financial Times (18 March 2014) 'Turkey: The Erdogan–Gulen Showdown'. Retrieved from http://www.ft.com/cms/s/0/1b1d4ea0-ab8e-11e3-8cae-00144feab7de.html#axzz3UEqIm2LV.

Fishlow, A. (2011) *Starting Over: Brazil Since 1985*, Washington, DC: Brookings Institution Press.

Goldstein, M. (2005) 'What Might the Next Emerging-market Financial Crisis Look Like?', Institute for International Economics, Working Paper Series, No. 0 5–7.

Istanbul Chamber of Industry (2003) *Turkey's Top 500 Industrial Enterprises*, Istanbul: ICI.

Ilkkaracan, I. and Levent, H. (2006) 'The Role of Labor Market Institutions in Management of Economic Crises: The Case of Collective Bargaining and Wage Setting in Turkey', paper presented at EAEPE Annual Conference, İstanbul, November 2006.

ILO (2015) *Key Indicators of the Labour Market*, 8th edition. Available at http://www.ilo.org/empelm/what/WCMS_114240/lang--en/index.htm.

Karacimen E. (2012) 'Political Economy of Consumer Debt in Developing Countries: Evidence from Turkey', paper presented at the 9th Annual Conference of Historical Materialism, 8–11 November, London.

Marois, T. (2012) *States, Banks and Crisis: Emerging Finance Capitalism in Mexico and Turkey*, Cheltenham: Edward Elgar Publishing.

Milliyet (10 April 2004) 'Muhafazakâr MÜSİAD, Metroseksüel olabilir mi?'. Retrieved from http://www.milliyet.com.tr/2004/04/10/business/abus.html.

Neri, M.C. (2010) 'The Decade of Falling Income Inequality and Formal Employment Generation in Brazil', in *Tackling Inequalities in Brazil, China, India and South Africa: The Role of Labour Market and Social Policies*, Paris: OECD Publishing.

NTV (21 April 2009) 'Erdoğan: Kriz teğet geçer, 2010'da toparlanırız'. Retrieved from http://www.ntv.com.tr/arsiv/id/24959014.

Onaran, Ö. (2002a) "Adjusting the Economy Through the Labor market: the Myth of Rigidity", in N. Balkan and S. Savran (eds), *Ravages of Neoliberalism: Economy, Society, and Gender in Turkey*, New York: Nova Scientific.

Onaran, Ö. (2002b) 'Measuring Wage Flexibility: the Case of Turkey Before and After Structural Adjustment', *Applied Economics*, 34, pp. 767–81.

Onaran, Ö. (2006) 'Speculation-led Growth and Fragility in Turkey: Does EU Make a Difference or Can It Happen Again?', in E. Hein et al. (eds), *Macroeconomics and Macroeconomic Policies – Alternatives Approaches to European Policies*, Marburg: Metropolis.

Onaran, Ö. (2007a) 'Capital Flows, Turbulences, and Distribution: The Case of Turkey', *Intervention*, 4, pp. 353–74.

Onaran, Ö. (2007b) 'Life After Crisis for Labor and Capital', in E. Yeldan et al. (eds), *Neoliberal Globalization as New Imperialism: Case Studies on Reconstruction of the Periphery*, New York: Nova Scientific Publishers.

Onaran, Ö. (2008) 'Jobless Growth in the Central and Eastern European Countries: a Country Specific Panel Data Analysis for the Manufacturing Industry', *Eastern European Economics*, 46(4), pp. 90–115.

Onaran, Ö. (2009a) 'Labor after the Crisis in Turkey', in Z. Öniş and F. Şenses (eds), *Turkey and the Global Economy: Neo-Liberal Restructuring and Integration in the Post-Crisis Era*, New York: Routledge, pp. 243–61.

Onaran, Ö. (2009b) 'Wage Share, Globalization, and Crisis: the Case of Manufacturing Industry in Korea, Mexico, and Turkey', *International Review of Applied Economics*, 23(2), pp. 113–34.

Onaran, Ö. (2013) 'The Political Economy of Inequality, Redistribution, and the Protests in Turkey', II(6), pp. 20–4, Centre for Policy and Research on Turkey, London, Research Turkey. Available at http://researchturkey.org/?p=3717.

Onaran, Ö. and Aydıner, N. (2010) 'The Controversy Over Employment Policy: Low Labor Costs and Openness, or Demand Policy? A Sectoral Analysis for Turkey', *Developing Economies*, 48(2), pp. 203–31.

Onaran, Ö. and Galanis, G. (2014) 'Income Distribution and Aggregate Demand: National and Global Effects', *Environment and Planning A*, 46(10), pp. 2489–513.

Onaran, Ö. and Stockhammer, E. (2005) 'Two Different Export-oriented Growth Strategies: Accumulation and Distribution in Turkey and South Korea', *Emerging Markets Finance and Trade*, 41, pp. 65–89.

Onaran, Ö. and Yentürk, N. (2001) 'Do Low Wages Stimulate Investments? An Analysis of the Relationship Between Wages and Investments in Turkish Private Manufacturing Industry', *International Review of Applied Economics*, 15, pp. 359–74.

Onaran, Ö. and Yentürk, N. (2002) 'The Mark-up Rates in Turkish Private Manufacturing Industry During Trade Liberalization', *Journal of Income Distribution*, 11(3–4), pp. 21–41.
Oyvat, C. (2011) 'Askeri Rejim, Liberalleşme ve Sürecin Ardılları', Birikim Dergisi-Güncel. Retrieved from http://www.birikimdergisi.com/guncel/askeri-rejim-liberallesme-ve-surecin-ardillari.
Oyvat, C. (2014) 'Essays on the Evolution of Inequality' (Unpublished doctoral dissertation), University of Massachusetts, Amherst
Önis, Z. and Bakır, C. (2005) 'Turkey's Political Economy in the Age of Financial Globalization: the Significance of The EU Anchor', presented at a conference on 'Europeanization and Transformation: Turkey in the Post-Helsinki Era', Koc University, Istanbul, 2–3 December.
Önis, Z. and Senses, F. (2007) 'Global Dynamics, Domestic Coalitions and a Reactive State: Major Policy Shifts in Post-war Turkish Economic Development', *Middle East Technical University Studies in Development*, 34(2), pp. 251–86.
Öniş, Z. and Güven, A.B. (2011) 'Global Crisis, National Responses: the Political Economy of Turkish Exceptionalism', *New Political Economy*, 16(5), pp. 585–608.
Pollin, R., Burns, J. and Heintz, J. (2004) 'Global Apparel Production and Sweatshop Labour: Can Raising Retail Prices Finance Living Wages?', *Canadian Journal of Economics*, 28, pp. 153–71.
Porta, R.L. and Shleifer, A. (2014) 'Informality and Development', *Journal of Economic Perspectives*, 28(3), pp. 109–26.
Rauch, J.E. (1993) 'Economic Development, Urban Underemployment, and Income Inequality', *Canadian Journal of Economics*, 26(4), pp. 901–18.
Sabah (2008, 15 December) 'Küçülme Türkiye'yi teğet geçti'. Retrieved from http://arsiv.sabah.com.tr/2008/12/16/haber,32FE3B753D3D450F98D3BE33A5E5F5DE.html.
Sabah (2010, 27 November) 'Türkiye'yi teğet geçti...'. Retrieved from http://www.sabah.com.tr/ekonomi/2010/11/27/turkiyeyi_teget_gecti.
State Institute of Statistics (SIS) (1950–2001) *Survey of Employment, Payments, Production and Tendencies in Manufacturing Industry*, electronic data, Ankara.
Taymaz, E. and Ozler, S. (2005) 'Labour Market Policies and EU Accession: Problems and Prospects for Turkey', in Hoekman and S. Togan (eds), *Turkey: Economic Reform and Accession to the EU*, Washington, DC: World Bank and The World Bank and CEPR, pp. 223–60.
TCEA (1999) 'Flexibility in Working Life' (in Turkish), *TİSK İnceleme Yayınları*, no. 190, Ankara.
TCMB (2015) '"İktisadi Yönelim Anketi ve Reel Kesim Güven Endeksi'ne İlişkin Yöntemsel Açıklama'. Retrieved from http://www.tcmb.gov.tr/wps/wcm/connect/90b517db-1bf6-4b5d-a3c1-a71aa6017f9d/IYA-RKGE-YontemselAciklama.pdf?MOD=AJPERES&CACHEID=90b517db-1bf6-4b5d-a3c1-a71aa6017f9d.
Tellioglu, A. (2014) 'Turkey Seen Through the Prism of Occupational Diseases: Success Story or Hidden Disaster?', Global Labour Column, Number 178, July 2014, Global Labour University. Retrieved from http://www.global-labour university.org/fileadmin/GLU_Column/papers/no_178_Tellioglu.pdf.
Tekgüç, H. and Atalay, N. (2015) 'Sağlıkta Bireysel Sorumluluk ve Rekabet Toplam Maliyetleri Neden Düşürmez?', *Amme İdaresi Dergisi*, 48(1), pp. 141–71.
The Economist (2015) 'A Frenzy About Interest', 14 March.

Uygur, E. (2001) 'Turkey From Crisis to Crisis: 2000 November and 2001 February Crises' (in Turkish), Turkey Economy Institute, Working Paper, no. 2001/1.

Uygur, E. (2010) 'The Global Crisis and the Turkish Economy', Turkish Economic Association Discussion Paper, 2010/3.

Vasudevan, R. (2009) 'The Credit Crisis: Is the International Role of the Dollar at Stake?', *Monthly Review*, 60(11), pp. 24–35.

Yeldan, E. (2002) 'On the IMF-directed Disinflation Program in Turkey: a Program for Stabilization and Austerity or a Recipe for Impoverishment and Financial Chaos?', in N. Balkan and S. Savran (eds), *Ravages of Neoliberalism: Economy, Society, and Gender in Turkey*, New York: Nova Scientific.

Yeldan, E. (2013a) 'IMF Dönemi Bitti Aldatmacası', *Cumhuriyet*, 1 May.

Yeldan, E. (2013b) 'Talan Ekonomisi', *Cumhuriyet*, 5 June.

Yeldan, E., Taşçı, K., Voyvoda, E. and Özsan, M.W. (2012) 'Turkey On Her Way Out of Middle-income Growth Trap: Volume I: Which Turkey? Macro and Regional Analysis?', Turkish Enterprise and Business confederation, İstanbul.

Yeni Şafak (2010, 27 December) 'Kriz Teğet geçti, Üç Çocuk Şart'. Retrieved from http://www.yenisafak.com.tr/ekonomi/kriz-teget-gecti-uc-cocuk-sart-294647.

Yenturk, N. (1999) 'Short-Term Capital Inflows and Their Impact on Macroeconomic Order: Turkey in the 1990s', *Developing Economies*, 37, pp. 89–113.

Yükseker, Z. (2013) 'Tasarruf-Yatırım Dengesi: Türkiye Uygulaması ve Sorunlar'. Retrieved from http://www.researchgate.net/profile/Zafer_Yuekseler/publication/258808662_YATIRIM-TASARRUF_DENGES_TRKYE_UYGULAMASI/links/00463528f74aca5010000000.pdf.

Index

The manufacturer's authorised representative in the EU is Springer Nature Customer Service Centre GmbH, Europaplatz 3, 69115 Heidelberg, Germany. If you have any concerns regarding our products, please contact ProductSafety@springernature.com

Printed and bound by CPI Group (UK) Ltd, Croydon, CR0 4YY

13/10/2026

02232374-0018